A History of the Devil

A History
of the
DEVIL

Gerald Messadié

translated from the French by
Marc Romano

KODANSHA INTERNATIONAL
New York • Tokyo • London

Kodansha America, Inc.
114 Fifth Avenue, New York, New York 10011, U.S.A.

Kodansha International Ltd.
17-14 Otowa 1-chome, Bunkyo-ku, Tokyo 112, Japan

Published in 1996 by Kodansha America, Inc.
Originally published in France in slightly different form in 1993 as
Histoire Générale du Diable by Éditions Robert Laffont.

Library of Congress Cataloging-in-Publication Data
Messadié, Gerald.
[Histoire générale du diable. English]
A history of the devil / Gerald Messadié ; translated from the French
by Marc Romano.
p.   cm.
Includes bibliographical references and index.
ISBN 1-56836-081-9
1. Devil—History.   2. Demonology—History.   I. Title.
BL480.M4813   1996
291.2'16—dc20   95-4949

Book design by Margaret M. Wagner

Printed in the United States of America

96 97 98 99   Q/FF   10 9 8 7 6 5 4 3 2 1

Contents

v

A History of the Devil

Introduction

In the mid-eighties, the world saw an odd and symbolic case of geographical transference. The president of the United States, Ronald Reagan, called the USSR "the Evil Empire," while the de facto leader of Iran, the Ayatollah Khomeini, called the United States "the Great Satan." Both flights of rhetoric indicate that hell, the kingdom of the Devil, doesn't appear to be situated in the same place for everybody—and that the Devil is a politically useful figure.

In 1992, Ali Benhadi, the chief aide to the leader of the Islamic Front for Algerian Salvation, ascribed a political role to the Devil by declaring that "any party that strays from the precepts of God, the Koran, and the Sunnites is the Devil's party." Benhadi was relegating the near totality of the planet's political parties to hell. He then indirectly made a reference to the Devil's role: "As far as democracy goes, I maintain that in a Muslim nation supreme power lies nowhere but in the hands of God. We do not believe in the people's power over the people, but in God's power over the people."[1]

In other words, if God cannot exist in a democracy, then the Devil, the Creator's enemy, cannot either—and yet, a secular so-

3

ciety is a society that belongs to the Devil. Such pronouncements should elicit neither ready outcries nor easy jeers. Through its secular arms, Christianity has governed since its early triumph according to the principle of the Devil's existence and presence in all things that threaten the mutual will of pope and potentate. Tens of thousands of lives have been sacrificed to this theocratic conception of the state.

When one raises such an ambitious question as whether or not the Devil actually exists, modesty demands that one first explain a bit about oneself. As a Catholic, in my childhood I was subjected to various attempts to convince me that he does exist. I was thus threatened, I no longer remember why, with being spirited away by him in the night—a serious miscalculation, since I immediately realized that a figure of such theoretically tremendous importance would hardly deserve much respect if he stooped to pulling stunts like that on a mere child. Even worse, the people who threatened me with him also localized him: he apparently hung around toilets, which puzzled me—perhaps, I thought, he was dyspeptic. He was also said to loiter in cellars, which was hardly more respectable. When one is invested with the glory of being the adversary of God, one finds better places to live. It occurs to me again today that telling children nonsense always backfires—it was on the strength of such hokum that I began to doubt that the Devil existed at all.

Still, the attempts at convincing me continued. The Devil had tempted Jesus in the desert, I was told, but what he said seemed suspect to me. It was simpleminded to offer empires to the son of God, who presumably could have them anyway, if he wanted—and if the Devil were so stupid, why refer to him as "the Evil One"? Either Jesus was not the son of God, or else the Devil, who was supposedly able to read minds, didn't realize who He really was. The whole business, in short, seemed improbable.

In the course of my religious education under the Jesuits, he was referred to as "Satan," which is derived from the Arabic *shitan*, meaning, simply, "devil." It was asserted that he had once been an angel seated beside God, but that he had suddenly given in to the temptation of pride, rebelled against his master, and taken a few other evil spirits along with him in his Fall. Yet if he had been tempted, then temptation must have preexisted him, I argued, and therefore Evil did, too. How could that be, since he was meant to be its inventor? This line of argument annoyed one of my teachers, who in my trimester report accused me of having an evil mind. To this day, a half century later, the question still bothers me, and no theological tract has ever cleared it up.

Some called the Devil "Lucifer," a Latin name, or "Beelzebub," or any of twenty other names. He seemed to be everywhere—it is said that Luther saw him and threw an inkwell at his head. "Proven" cases of possession were cited for my edification, and these shed some light on the shadowy subject. Aldous Huxley, with whom one day I spoke on a terrace overlooking the Nile, and who had just completed *The Devils of Loudun*, explained to me that the hallucinogenic substance in the story of Urbain Grandier and the mad nuns of his entourage was probably rye ergot, a poison that causes symptoms closely resembling those of the Loudun nuns—it clouds the mind and causes visions. (Soon after that conversation, there was in fact a celebrated outbreak of hallucinations at Pont-Saint-Esprit in France's Gard region, where the villagers had eaten contaminated flour and experienced hellish visions.) We will never know whether or not Luther, too, hadn't been eating ergot-tainted bread.

Much later, a friend who was annoyed by my skepticism took me to visit a "possessed" woman. Oddly enough, there are many fewer cases of masculine possession than of feminine possession— no doubt because women are demonic creatures. The woman I saw spoke incoherently and often obscenely. It was assumed that she was possessed because she had been "cured" after being exorcised by a local priest, although the Devil subsequently came back. (He must have had quite a bit of time on his hands to keep returning to the body of that poor person.) It is impossible to tell today if the woman hadn't been hysterical or simply insane, if she didn't drink or overdo it with her prescriptions, or if she hadn't had a stroke. In the subway, after all, one often encounters obscenity-shouting drunks who in the old days would have been termed "possessed,"

and in psychiatry's Gilles de La Tourette syndrome, otherwise perfectly normal people suddenly emit a flood of scatological obscen-
ities (as was the case with Mozart).

Many other grounds for perplexity would come in time. For instance, images of the Devil: why is he so often, in the West, a
caricature of the ancient god Pan—human body, horns and feet of
a goat? And why is Evil—again, in the West—so often represented
in reptilian form, while the Egyptians and Aztecs deified snakes?
And above all, how did the Greeks and Romans, among others,
manage to do without the Devil altogether?

Given my skepticism about the Devil, the attempts to instruct
me theologically intensified over the years. God had to have a counterpart, otherwise all the woes of humanity would have to be ascribed to him—a fine piece of inductive reasoning. So then, I
asked, God *isn't* all-powerful? He is, I was told, but He gives human
will some leeway: it is up to us to resist temptation. Okay—then
what about children who fall ill and die? Ah, those are the Creator's
unfathomable designs. But if the Creator's designs are unfathomable
and also include Evil, then isn't He the cause of most of humanity's
troubles? "Blasphemy!" the priests reproached me. "Surrender to
the mysteries of faith." I would have liked to do that, but then why
did the Creator give me reason? Wasn't I meant to use it? The
Italian philosopher Giovanni Papini's argument only managed to
unsettle me: Since God is infinitely good, at the end of time He
will have to forgive His ancient enemy. This future magnanimity
seemed plausible to me, but its consequences were perverse: there
was little point in continuing to prosecute a defendant who would
ultimately be acquitted.

It is fair to say that the theology remains cloudy as far as the
Devil is concerned. The Church truly believes in him, but its ideas
about him seem contradictory. Oddly enough, the modern secular
world has a much more specific and powerful understanding of him,
yet it is confronted by a paradox: the Devil is no longer battled
with the same vigor as in the past—the trials, burnings, and other
devices of the Inquisition—yet he is to be seen everywhere, as
Reagan and Khomeini go to show.

Modernism holds that our era has rejected the superstitions of the past—we no longer, for instance, try "witches." What is most striking about Reagan and Khomeini's rhetoric is that both leaders succumbed to the common temptation to localize Evil in an attempt to define it. From the moment one defines Evil, when one names it, when one ascribes it a recognized representative, one gives in to the temptation of localizing it; once that has been done, the only remaining goal becomes to destroy it. Reagan called for the destruction of the USSR, and Khomeini for that of the Great Satan, even though their exhortations were both hypocritical—one at the time was openly negotiating with the USSR, the other covertly with the Great Satan to exchange arms for hostages. Either statement, however, could have aggravated tensions and led to actual war. The example goes to show the dangers in believing in Satan, Lucifer, or Beelzebub.

However, Reagan and Khomeini did not, in their excitement, succumb to other temptations; indeed, the greater part of contemporary humanity is always busy pinpointing, identifying, naming, classifying, describing, and localizing the agents of Evil and their master. Hardly a day goes by without someone, individually or collectively, proclaiming that Evil is so-and-so or such-and-such, the automobile, television, rock and roll, unemployment, AIDS, urban decay, drugs, pollution, sex, immigration, the Arabs, the Jews, Pol Pot, the Burmese regime, fascism, capitalism, noise pollution, cigarettes, cancer, nuclear power plants. We are all someone else's Devil.

Thus, we find ourselves waging an incessant and fanatical shadow war against Evil—and I do not use the word "fanatical" as a convenience. The very Manichaeism that claims this to be good and that to be bad predisposes us to ill will and mistrust, then to intolerance, and finally to murder. The foreign is always the enemy, and in this state of mind everything is ultimately foreign. We have surrounded ourselves with Evil, or difference, and we eliminate it at every moment in our lives.

The Devil's system—it is a system, above all—wields considerable political influence. Indeed, its existence is essentially political, and its most extraordinary effect is a distortion in moral and philosophical thought, something totally new in the history of ideas:

the belief in the "banalization of evil." The formula was coined three decades ago by Hannah Arendt. Little does it matter that she was linked with Martin Heidegger, one of the most debatable thinkers of the day; she sincerely believed that we had been so overwhelmed by the very image of Evil—that is, by Nazism—that we had become inured to it, that it had come to seem ordinary. The concept marked the dawn of postmodernism, represented by a good number of respectable thinkers who believed that history died at Auschwitz.

This is an excellent example of the dangers of believing in the Devil, and more important, of believing that we no longer have to be on our guard against him. In my youth, very few people believed that Stalin and Soviet communism were as bad as Nazism and equally deserved to be demonized. If one has to call upon such mathematics, the sixteen million dead in the USSR "count" at least as much as the six million dead in Nazi camps. On what basis could one prefer Stalin and the Communist Party of the Soviet Union (CPSU) to Hitler and the Third Reich? Because of the Nazis' anti-Semitism? Though Soviet anti-Semitism was less vocal, it existed, too, and the gulags easily rivaled the death camps. Yet under pain of being accused of "primary anti-Sovietism," no one wanted to think about this or believe it. When in 1949 Viktor Kravshenko told the truth about the gulags, he caused an uproar. He was called an American agent, a patsy, and even Jean-Paul Sartre's generosity didn't keep him from criticizing Kravshenko or from marshaling all the prestige he could to have others denounce his "montage."

The Devil, the common reasoning went, is Hitler and Nazi Germany—why deny it? How dare you put the martyrdom of Leningrad and the Nazi atrocities on two sides of an equation? Clearly, though, that was not the point: no one dreamed of making such a comparison. The fact of the matter is that the Devil had been localized and limited to a specific domain. He thus could not be anywhere else, and since Stalin had fought against Hitler, it was because he was good despite his "human faults."

Thus, practically until the coming of Mikhail Gorbachev, Europe—in particular elite, intellectual, refined, and scholarly

Europe—lived under the illusion that the CPSU was the beacon of the left. Picasso was a great painter because he was a communist, Franco a bastard because he had crushed Republican Spain. If one wasn't on the left, one was on the right and thus in league with the fascists.

This elementary theology would have been annihilated by the smallest knowledge of history, beginning with the Molotov-Ribbentrop Pact. The diabolical Stalin clearly made an agreement with the diabolical Hitler; it was not because he ended up being stung first that Stalin ceased being, from a strictly political point of view, a Devil in due and proper form. However, it would have taken a miracle for anyone to mention the Soviet-German pact during the fifties, sixties, or early seventies, even after the Khrushchev speech had begun to crumble the pleasant Soviet facade. If one did refer to it, the answering argument was that it was ancient history, and people would look at you suspiciously, like a synod at the cleric who asks awkward questions about the exact moment of the Host's transubstantiation.

Tangentially, I do not know what History (with a capital H, it goes without saying) is, and I am not sure that anyone ever has. From the first century on, there have been good reasons to have doubts about discourses on History; in his two books, *The Jewish Wars* and *The Jewish Antiquities*, Flavius Josephus, a scrupulous historian (though he believed in the Devil, too), barely mentions the event of the first magnitude that would fundamentally alter the following two millennia—namely, the ministry of Jesus and His death sentence. Josephus was certainly aware of it, since Herod Agrippa II, who provided him with much of his information, must have discussed the matter with him, but he doubtlessly deemed the episode as of little interest. A whole cohort of thinkers has subsequently assured us that History has a direction, toward socialism, but the events of the last decade seem to say otherwise. It is now forgotten that it was in this belief that some parishioners lauded, from the safety of their book-lined studies, Mao Zedong and then the fall of Cambodia's Lon Nol. Like those who love chocolate but not its results, they felt uncomfortable both during the Cultural Revolution and when the Khmer Rouge took Phnom Penh. I can't help thinking that History, like a dog with worms, often ends up chasing its own tail. I no more believe in History having a direction than I do in a postmodernism that preaches the banality of Evil.

I have often wondered what thoughts might have crossed the mind of a foot soldier in Xenophon's Ten Thousand in the fourth century before our era, under the terrible tribulations of the Anabasis, when hunger, thirst, cold, murderous heat, exhaustion, boils, dysentery, malaria, snakes, and mosquitoes plagued those mercenaries as they trekked through Kurdistan and Armenia toward the shores of the Hellespont. The soldiers had no intellectual recourse to any Devil, not even the *daimon* of Socrates. Believe it or not, they had none—they had monsters, yes, the miserable Gorgon, for example, but Perseus had decapitated her. Cerberus was a mere watchdog, and Hercules had taken care of the Stymphalian birds, the wild mares of Diomedes, and the Erymanthian boar. Centaurs and fauns could be befriended. There were no countergods, not even the Titans (the ancestors, perhaps, of the angels God cast from Heaven), who had been dispatched to the underworld and no longer challenged Zeus's power. The Greeks, including the soldiers of Xenophon, lived their lives knowing that dangers as well as opportunities depended on the gods and the offerings one made to them.

Our modern soldiers, who are often terrorists (which is to say, cowards), invoke Heaven when they murder (the Nation has fallen out of fashion), and if they are caught and put to death they proclaim themselves martyrs, since they have been fighting against the Demon and in the name of the Almighty. All I mean to say is that it is demonic to believe in the Devil, not the other way around, as the Jesuits tried to teach me when they said that the Devil's greatest trick is to make one believe that he doesn't exist.

Where did he come from, this bearer of all the ills of the world, since deities—and he is a deity—are always born somewhere at some particular time? Who were his ancestors, what was his history? Has he always existed? I first asked these questions as a child, and I hope I have answered them now.

It is not my intent to demonize belief in the Devil. The anxiety that is a part of every human being, even of every animal (and no one who has witnessed a cat's horror when it sees a dog for the first time—hackles raised, eyes wide, the embodiment of fear—can doubt that animals have their devils, too), needs to be exorcised, and the most effective of all exorcisms is to name the enemy, then describe it and, if possible, destroy it. It is hard to resist the revulsion and hatred inspired by an object of fear; and it is just as hard to resist the temptation of seeing in it if not the cause of all evils then at least a localization of Evil. Contrary to popular opinion, human beings are not rational; they rationalize, which is quite different. My hope in this book is to avoid justifying, a posteriori, the object of our fears and giving him a categorical habitation—which is to say, to avoid making the Devil into a mental object upon which we might graft the vicissitudes of our folly.

Given the magnitude of the subject, it is obvious that I have had to base myself on the work of others—the notes attest to that. It could not have been otherwise, since the Devil is knowable only through reports; never having met him, I cannot offer a firsthand account. I am thus obliged to pay tribute to the historians and ethnologists who took the trouble to gather the words of those who speak about him, and also to the anonymous scribes who recopied ancient texts. And to Annie Latour, archivist emeritus and historian, whose great insight has been invaluable to me in that she has often found what I didn't even know I was looking for.

It is with affection that I think of the ethnologists, whose labors were without a doubt the most difficult of all—working in the field, putting not only their minds but their emotions and their very lives to the test under very arduous climates and conditions, sometimes sinking into doubt and discouragement, like Bronislaw Malinowski, who came to loathe the Trobriand islanders, or like Michel Leiris, who, in his *Journal*, confesses to no longer having faith in either Africa or its inhabitants. I do not believe that either Malinowski or Leiris was ultimately disgusted; I think that their discouragement simply arises out of the immense, infinite task of translating one culture into another.

Even with finished books, clear, reasoned, printed black on white, and annotated, the same discouragement always threatens—

so many beliefs, so many fears, so much nonsense. Still, the people we are dealing with were individuals, worthy of both compassion and anger, of course, but they are unknowable today. Can we really talk about them at such a vast remove? Even less, can we judge them? Nevertheless, it must be attempted, even at the risk of being wrong, because there is no such thing as dispassionate knowledge any more than there is dispassionate thought. I should warn at the outset that my affections and enmities will be quite clear throughout.

There have already been histories of Heaven and of Hell, but I know of only one history of the Devil, which was written in the eighteenth century by none other than the father of Robinson Crusoe, Daniel Defoe. The topic was problematic at the time, and the book's author took good care not to sign it. To tell the truth, it is more a collection of anecdotes and musings than a history, and with two centuries' distance I can, I think, presume to borrow its title, though not without a grain of salt.

Histories are wholly made up of real events, but the Devil has never participated in any of them. He is scandalously absent from the great moments of this past century. Neither his tail nor his horns were sighted during the Russian Revolution. He wasn't seen at Hiroshima, or on the moon, no more than he was spotted in Pasteur's laboratory or Hitler's bunker. One would have expected him in Cambodia while it was being ravaged by Pol Pot or in Sarajevo, where women and children are being shot down by snipers. Yet in all these places, only the expression of human passions is to be found: freedom, dignity, intellectual discovery, and hatred, too— hatred that not even animals experience, because animals are never beasts. Only humans are that.

How then does one write a history of something that does not exist? This is a phenomenological history in the Hegelian sense of the word. I intend to present a decoding of the models by which humanity constructs the Devil for itself, as we do every day when we go to see horror movies about "things" or intergalactic monsters. My work has consisted of deciphering accounts ranging from the millennia when God was a woman, the Great Goddess, all the way to recent centuries, when attempts were made to describe crime as the product of undefined forces. These forces exist nowhere but in patterns stamped into the brain by society and its morality. They are inner, not outer.

In short, I beg the reader, who is perhaps not as hypocritical as Charles Baudelaire would have it, to seek from Greece the grace of examining before naming, of understanding before judging, of mastering anxieties—and of not fearing those things we call deities and demons. As Homer says, Odysseus was wily with the gods.

CHAPTER 1

The Ambiguous Demons of Oceania

For the Westerner, the Pacific is deeply confounding. When I flew out of Los Angeles in the sixties for a leisurely voyage through a part of the world made up of 95 percent water and 5 percent evanescent myths, all I had for traveling companions were Margaret Mead's *Coming of Age in Samoa*—which has subsequently been discredited—and Bronislaw Malinowski's studies on the Trobriand archipelago. A stopover in Hawaii was both incidental and charming; Honolulu seemed like an export version of Miami, not yet the Pacific.

A few days later, at dusk, I landed in Pago Pago, the capital of American Samoa. The only tolerable hotel in town was the Rainmaker, a huge barn of gray wood where, it is said, Somerset Maugham wrote *Rain*. In the hour before dinner, I decided to have a look around in a taxi. We drove along at walking pace, especially when, not far from the hotel, we entered a village. A crowd filled the road because it held a feast, and at its very center the village chief was holding court. A handsome man some fifty years old, squatting on a mat, his torso muscled and bare, he was presiding over a ceremony I had read many descriptions of before. He was being offered mats, and with a fleshy thumb and almond-shaped

eyes, he appraised them one by one, those of the highest quality
having the closest weave, the renowned "fine" mats mentioned by
anthropologists. They were expensive presents and symbolic ones,
too; the time that had gone into their making was a measure of the
esteem in which the chief was held.

Some ten hours by plane from Los Angeles and Hollywood, life
was going on as it had a century before—perhaps several centuries
before. In the time I was in Pago Pago, I think I only saw one
television, the hotel's, and the pictures it produced were so mangy
that I quickly gave up trying to make out a reflection of the world
in them. One of the many appeals of the Pacific is that if the world
ended you wouldn't hear about it until the next day.

Many Pacific archipelagos have, or at least once had, admirably
resisted the West. One immediately sensed that life here had hardly
changed in ages. Neither the modern gas stove that belonged to the
only pharmacist in Appia, Western Samoa, nor the woven plastic
baskets borne by the housewives of Nandi, Fiji, nor the transistor
radios the rich kids of Tonga were already sporting, nor the few
ancient cars in Port Moresby, nor even the "Mirabelle" bras of the
Marquesa Islands (imposed by the local bishop), had seemed to
make much of a difference. Not to give someone a cigarette in
Papua New Guinea was a legitimate cause for murder on grounds
of miserliness. Refusing a sexual encounter in Fiji was an insult
that only the fact of one's being a foreigner—that is, of simply not
knowing—could forgive. In Port Moresby, I always carried a few
packs of cigarettes around in my pockets.

It would be best to confess right now that this chapter is biased,
to say the least, and that I loved the Pacific. I loved, indiscriminately, the imposing dignity of the patroness, the nursemaid of the
last king, who presided over the eating hall at Appia's "Tusitala"
(a pidgin version of Robert Louis Stevenson's nickname, "the story-
teller"); the Rainmaker's all-woman staff, who danced one typhoon
night while serving me my perennial crayfish; the canny subterfuges
of the Papuan art dealer outside Port Moresby from whom I tried
to obtain a specimen of cargo cult art; the solemn grace of the young
boy in Tonga who informed me, on the beach where I was about to
dive into the water, that "religion" forbade swimming on Sundays,

and who by way of amends offered me a frangipani blossom; the smile, frightful in its ferocity, of the half-naked, feather-covered Papuan who grabbed my camera, only to remark that I would be better off using a zoom lens for the photo I was about to take; the gentlemanly courtesy of the young man in the Marquesas who saw me grunting my way up a steep path and dismounted from his horse to offer it to me instead; the sad smile of the taxi driver in Auckland, New Zealand, who when I asked why he was so sad replied that he was Maori, as if that explained everything; the houses in Samoa whose inhabitants drew up their palm-mat walls during daylight and then unceremoniously dressed and undressed in the open, because the honest have nothing to hide. An old-fashioned world in which not recognizing rites is a trespass only if it is deliberate, where the stranger is always welcomed with open, outstretched hands. The world of the Pacific is very ancient—a good place to track down the origins of Evil, and so of the Devil.

It is likely that the abstract notion of Evil has always existed. The tendency to arrange every sorrow, calamity, and accident under the aegis of one overarching value is hard to resist. That this value was a "spirit," or an entity against which the individual was powerless, seems equally likely. One is tempted to believe that, terrified by avalanches, thunder, earthquakes, the predation of wild animals, forest fires, and the deaths of relatives, human beings of thousands of years ago conceived the existence of a malefic deity who was to blame for all these catastrophes.

This theory, however, is only that—a theory. As far as religious beliefs at the dawn of humanity are concerned, we must admit that we know almost nothing at all. The existence of religious sentiments seems to be borne out by evidence of complex funerary rites. Certainly, too, the abundance of graphic symbols, notably those representing the sun, male and female genitalia, a god of strength and a goddess of fertility, point to a belief in the sacredness of life forces. Yet the reconstruction can hardly be taken much farther.

In the search for the Devil's genealogy, evidence from mid-paleolithic and neolithic cultures—a period that extends from 60,000 to 8,000 B.C.—and especially much more plentiful traces from the neolithic and Bronze ages, merits attention. Every indication is that religious sentiment was entirely directed toward the celebration of life, and in particular the sun. The hollower sort of divinity embodied by the Devil seems to be absent: fear or hatred of Evil is much less in evidence than is the worship of life.

All that can be reasonably inferred about the cultures that predate writing is that their religions had a social function. Since the works of Emile Durkheim, especially his magnum opus, *The Elementary Forms of the Religious Life*, one fact is clear: religion is the building block of culture. When it came to threatening forces that were unknowable and thus, to Neanderthal or Cro-Magnon logic, supernatural (such as the dawn, water, wind, the earth, wild animals, or, more abstractly, fertility, illness, or success in hunt or war), some sort of protocol—in other words, rituals—had to be established. These rituals necessarily created roles, since the individual, still a fragile notion at the time, could not be allowed to intercede alone or haphazardly with such forces. The act of intercession, which most probably involved sacrifice, obviously differed when one was dealing with, for instance, the god of dawn versus the god of water. Whether mundane or exceptional, the ritual also had to be accomplished at a predetermined time.[1]

Most important, the act of intercession had to be carried out by an authorized person, either someone who wielded power, such as the clan or tribe's chosen chieftain, or by someone endowed with magical powers, a "doctor" who knew the secrets of this or that flower, this or that substance, this or that configuration of circumstances.[2] In short, religion was what it would always be—a reflection of collective beliefs, of local experiences, a politics of reality. This politics has certainly varied over the millennia, with some rituals disappearing forever along with the peoples that celebrated them, and others springing into existence, like the cargo cult in Oceania.

All of this is why ancient religions—those that preceded the three great monotheisms, some by tens of thousands of years, some by mere thousands—cannot be analyzed according to what remains of them. Even if one accepts that so-called primitive societies might have, because of their isolation and rudimentary technology, remained outside History (a hypothesis raised here only for the sake of argument), they could have evolved over the course of time and events. The same historical framework cannot be imposed on, for example, the Papuan tribes as on continental populations, which are much larger and have been enriched by trade, invasions, and conquests; but nor can it be definitively claimed that the Papuans have remained the same since the Stone Age. The only thing that can be supposed is that these societies and their religions have changed much less rapidly than continental ones, and therefore there is a chance that they have retained significant traces of what they originally looked like. Nothing guarantees that the religions in Papua New Guinea today, which was first peopled some forty thousand years ago, or in Africa, where paleoanthropologists have for years claimed that the predecessor of our true ancestor, *Homo sapiens sapiens*, first appeared, have passed down in their original forms to the present. To study them is thus only to try to decipher our long-ago past. We will begin with Easter Island, one of the oldest and most famous of the Pacific isles.

Created a few tens of thousands of years ago by volcanic action, discovered in 1687 by Edward Davis, a buccaneer blown off course, afterward vaguely known to navigators as "Davis's Land," rediscovered in 1722 by the Dutchman Jacob Roggeveen, lost again, discovered again in 1770 by an expedition led by the viceroy of Peru, Rapa Nui (its official name) was first populated by at least the fourth century A.D. The island is a good example both of the dangers of accepting seductive conclusions too hastily and of the difficulty of reconstructing myths' family trees. For a long time the general opinion of anthropologists was that it received immigrants from two opposite directions.[3] One wave definitely came from Polynesia, as the Polynesian roots of the Rapa Nuian language show; the other is supposed to have come from the western coast of South America, perhaps from Peru, as certain anthropological traits, non-Polynesian words, and the celebrated statues seem to attest. Thor Heyerdahl claimed that the island's civilization came from Peru, even though neither ocean currents nor winds supported his theory—which nevertheless gained so much ground that by the early seventies it had practically become accepted.

In 1992, however, two anthropologists, Paul Bahn and John Flenley, tore Heyerdahl's theory to shreds. In the first place, the great majority of the island's flora is native to Southeast Asia and Polynesia. It had been claimed that one reed, at least, the totora, was native to South America; a study of ancient pollens, however, showed that the reed has been growing on the island for thirty thousand years, long before the Andean civilizations were even established.

Physical anthropology has made it clear that the Rapa Nuians' skull and tooth types are characteristically Polynesian, not Andean. Linguistically, again, Rapa Nuian is close to Polynesian language groups, not South American ones. The mysterious *rongo rongo* inscriptions also seem to be Polynesian both in conception and execution.

Lastly, the famous colossal statues—in which Thor Heyerdahl saw the influence of the megalithic Tiahuanaco civilization or another pre-Incan civilization—are most probably part of the tradition of monumental buildings and statues found in the Marquesas and on Tahiti and Tonga.[4] In 1774, Captain Cook recognized the Tahitian language as soon as the first Rapa Nuian he met uttered a word.

Easter Island has been primarily if not exclusively populated by Polynesians for more than a thousand years. In addition, it was Polynesian navigators who colonized the majority of Pacific islands scattered over an area of some twenty million square miles, one of the most spectacular maritime feats of all time. Isolated since it was first peopled, Easter Island therefore represents an ideal laboratory in which to study the possible formation of the idea of the Devil.

Alfred Métraux, who came to the island in 1934, long before it turned into an obligatory stop for lovers of exotica, wrote that the Easter Island religion counts one great god, Makemake, "the supreme *atua* and the Creator of the Universe." It was his name that the earliest Christian missionaries first heard, although his cult has fallen into obscurity since the massacre of the Rapa Nuian priesthood in 1862.[5]

Makemake was certainly not the only god, since the Easter Island pantheon also included Rongo, Ruanuku, Atua-metua (or "Father

God"), and a number of others who are similarly forgotten today. These gods enjoyed innumerable and unexpected couplings. Thus, the "god-of-the-terrible-aspect," by copulating with Roundness, produced the little berries called "*poporo*," while the god Grove coupled with Treetrunk to produce the marinkuru tree. Nevertheless, the existence of the supreme *atua* Makemake would lead one to imagine that he had a symmetrical enemy.

Yet this is not the case. Métraux also reports: "All supernatural beings are called indifferently *akuaku* or *tatane*—the latter expression being derived from our 'Satan.' In fact, however, the emaciated ghosts and the benevolent spirits that help mankind belong to different categories." There was no one *akuaku*—the roster of gods in Métraux's day numbered at least a hundred names, and that wasn't even a complete list. No one *akuaku*, then, and definitely no purely malevolent one, since akuakus are polymorphous: they can be pretty young girls or brave young men, each capable of leading perfectly normal lives, but they can as easily be half-decomposed, skeletal beings with protruding vertebrae and ribs. When such is the case, they are spirits of the dead. Evil and cunning, at night they find their way into houses to torment the living. Though generally malevolent, however, these minor deities do not represent Evil; though they have come back from the underworld, they are nevertheless not delegates of our Hell.

Rife with taboos and teeming with magicians, sorcerers, and other casters of spells, the Rapa Nuians' supernatural world was rich with benevolent or malefic entities, although it is in vain that one looks within it for a central representation of Evil that even remotely resembles our Devil. All forces conflict with one another on Easter Island. If one sorcerer casts a spell, it can be lifted by another, more powerful sorcerer. To kill someone by hexing him, take a rooster and bury it head-first in a hole; then dance around the spot where the animal's head is buried, intoning the name of the victim. Although the victim is doomed to die, another magician can lift the hex. In other words, there are no unequivocal representations of Good and Evil, which are no more than the products of antagonistic individual or collective forces.

No Devil, then, on Easter Island. We will have to look for him elsewhere.

The noted anthropologist Bronislaw Malinowski studied the peoples of the Pacific, among them the natives of the Trobriand Islands, for seventeen years. From 1914 to 1922, he devoted himself entirely to some thirty islands spread out over a hundred thousand square miles of ocean north of New Guinea. The record of his work "in the field," *Argonauts of the Western Pacific*, is one of anthropology's most celebrated works.[6] At that time the Trobrianders maintained a clear distinction between the world of myth, or *lili'u*, which existed at the dawn of time, and the real world.[7] Their myths abounded with flying canoes, people sprouting up from the ground (as, in Greek mythology, men were wont to do before the creation of Pandora, the first woman), people who can become younger at will or change themselves into animals and back, and so on; yet the Trobrianders knew very well that these things couldn't actually happen—or, more accurately, could no longer happen. When told by a missionary that the White Man had machines that could fly, the islanders asked Malinowski about it. When he showed them photographs of airplanes, they asked him if it were really true or just *lili'u*. Likewise, the Holy Scriptures of the missionaries were *lili'u*, and the islanders rejected them. The wonders of the past had been possible only because of magic, a faculty that had either disappeared or was so weakened that it was no longer capable of producing marvels. Sorcerers, on the other hand, did exist, and they served as mediators between the real world and the world of myth —in which spirits of Evil could indeed exist.

Evil, essentially illness, manifests itself mainly through the sorcerer or *bwaga'u*, but also through flying witches, the most fearsome of which are the *mulukwausi*, who are invisible, can fly, and steal people's "insides"—their lungs, heart, bowels, brain, and tongue. Then there are the *taura'u*, who are to blame for epidemics. Able to metamorphose into animals (when they do so, they can be recognized because they don't run away from humans and they have patches of brilliant color on their pelts), they strike down their victims with the blow of a stick or club, but one can get in their good graces by offering them precious gifts. The third group of harmful demons, the *tokway*, are types of sprites who cause only benign illness.

As in the three monotheisms, the spirits of Evil are localized: the spirits of the dead rush to the island of Tuma northwest of Boyowa, the *mulukwausi* live on the southern and eastern half of Boyowa as well as on the islands of Kitava, Iwa, Gava, and Murua, while the *taura'u* come from the north coast of the island of Normamby, in the district of Du'a'u, "and more especially," writes Malinowski, "from a place called Sewatupa."

If they can act quickly enough, sorcerers can hold the forces of Evil at bay. In this respect, Malinowski recounts a curious anecdote that was related to him by the daughter of a Greek merchant and a Kiriwinian woman from Oburaku. When the merchant's daughter was a little girl, a woman had come to offer to sell her parents a mat. The parents turned down the mat but offered its seller some food. A reputed witch, or *yoyova*, the woman expected better treatment and grew angry. The next day the little girl fell so seriously ill that her parents thought her at death's door. Her maternal grandfather appealed to another *yoyova*, who in the form of a *mulukwausi* went off to search for the stolen entrails. She found them, performed the necessary rites of compensation, and they returned to place. Malinowski notes that the account was told to him with conviction and no hint of skepticism.

I personally do not doubt the reality of the *yoyova's* action. Since magical rites are carried out with the help of plants and other substances, it is possible that the angry *yoyova* used poisons similar to those that Haitian witch doctors use to turn healthy individuals into zombies; the healing *yoyova* resorted to their antidotes.

The Trobrianders have a highly developed strategy with respect to the rites they use to protect themselves against spirits of Evil, and the strategy testifies to the wealth of their imagination. The *kayga'u* rite, for instance, produces a sort of mist in which *mulukwausi* get lost.

The structure of Trobriander beliefs about Evil would therefore strongly recall our own. Evil is caused by invisible and inherently malign creatures, but also by humans in contact with them, and the humans can counteract their spells through rites comparable to exorcism. The creatures are also geographically localized: Like our Devil in his distant realm, they live on remote islands; the *muluk-wausi* in particular live as far away as possible from the island of the spirits of the dead. The comparison, however, cannot be taken farther. In Oceanian animism, the spirits of Evil live "democratically" alongside those of Good; there is no larger structuring of the kind in the founding Indo-Aryan myths of the Devil.

The mythologies of New Guinea are very closely related.[8] Like the Trobriander myths, they do not contain a cosmogony of the sort found among some African tribes, such as the Dogons. Like the Trobriand myths, they maintain that in the very remote past there was a "dream time" when the myths had been real, but those days are over and will never return.

We should not assume, however, that those myths immediately vanished. Instead, up until very recently they structured the Papuan social life; they were strong, and celebrated with conviction. But the migration of Papua New Guinea's population to the cities, especially Port Moresby, has contributed to the gradual disappearance of rites. Cult objects from the Sepik and Maprik rivers, which in the seventies and early eighties I found to be abundant, are practically unavailable now. Much the same holds true for the Solomon and Fijian islands. Television, gradual dietary changes, and the constant incursions of industry—not to mention tourism—threaten to eliminate the religions of Oceania within the next two or three decades.

Nevertheless, in the seventies there were enough remnants of the religious beliefs to develop a fairly clear picture of them. "In what can be defined as the sketch of a cosmogony, in a large part of New Guinea and north-central Melanesia," writes Vittorio Maconi,

the mythology of the origins centers around an original pair of cultural heroes, often male and female and sometimes mutually antagonistic. The names of these great spirits vary from tribe to tribe; for instance they are called Siwa and Mafit among the Meibrats of Irian, Boli and Geru among the Kumas, and Kilibob and Manup among other New Guinean tribes. These spirits are considered the creators of everything on earth. The myths that refer to their labors to organize the world are collectively referred by a word that translates as "establishment."

These, then, are founding myths.

Malinowski has shown that this mythology is relatively fluid. In Western Irian, as Maconi also points out, the world's creation is credited to a whole legion of supernatural beings, the *dema*. Like the two great creative spirits, though, the *dema* (*vui* on the Banks island, *wuu* in the New Hebrides, *kibe* among the New Guinean Kumas, *banara* on Choiseul and in the Solomons) are antagonistic to one another.

Nothing is produced except by the will of one of the two great gods or one or more of the spirits in the two contending groups. Earthquake or illness, birth or rain—everything is the work of the founding spirits, either directly or through the agency of a witch doctor or magician. This is why the indigenous peoples view magic with suspicion: they always suspect that it is only used in a malevolent way.

The Melanesians therefore conceive the existence of two principal but antagonistic creators without necessarily implying that one is good and the other evil. Malevolence is not always specific to some founding spirits, nor is it always even their exclusive doing: to some tribes, the spirits of the ancestors, who belong to a distinct group of their own, are malicious or at least capricious when they belong to the recently dead (with time, however, they mellow into benevolence).

This same ambivalence—or, more accurately, this absence of the definite division among celestial or supernatural beings that, for us, is embodied by the separation of Devil and God—can be found among the Aborigines of Australia. Aborigine myths have been studied extensively since the beginning of this century; like Aborigine cosmogonies, they are very elaborate (these cosmogonies have one element in common—the world's creation in the Milky Way as the result of various couplings and conflicts among the deities) and vary from tribe to tribe.

In 1887, the anthropologist Andrew Lang caused a sensation when he claimed to have proved that the Australian religions were practically monotheisms. Some time later, it became clear that this assumption was completely incorrect, although it endured for years. In 1925, the British anthropologist Herbert Basedow wrote:

> Among the Arrundta the Supreme Being bears the name Altjerra. Altjerra the benevolent moves around ceaselessly in the sky, watching vigilantly over the deeds and gestures of the tribes on the ground below him. The natives are so firmly convinced of his omnipotence that the Arrundtas' favorite expression, for instance when they give their word of honor, is "*Altjerrim arrum*," which means approximately "May God hear me," a phrase that makes Altjerra a witness to what they have said.

Yet the Arrundtas' Altjerra is none other than the Altjira of other Aborigine tribes, who by no means answers to this blatantly monotheistic likeness—carbon copy, in fact—of the Christian God. More important, however, is that according to Geza Roheim, "the expression Basedow cites is used exclusively by natives in the missions, and it is a direct product of the missionary schools."[9] Thus, there is no such thing as Aborigine monotheism.

Less biased studies established that the Australian religions are the very antithesis both of monotheism and of what could be termed its moral centralism. To the Maras, the sky is indeed the abode of two spirits, the Minungara—but they are both good and bad at the same time. They are bad because every time someone falls ill they want nothing more than to descend to earth and finish him off (in this case, they are stymied by an antagonistic spirit, Mumpani, who lives in the woods); and they are good despite everything, since it is they who teach the witch doctors who heal the sick. This paradoxical state of affairs is encountered in a more or less similar fashion among many other tribes.

The contradiction arises from a worldview based on the dialectic complexity of roles: Nothing is "good" or "bad" in and of itself; rather, all things are sometimes one and sometimes the other. This is why, notes Roheim, "the demon and the healer are cut from the same cloth." The same great spirit in any tribe's religion can be described in one instance as good, in another as bad, or even alternately as one and the other. To the Arandta branch of the Iliinka group, Altjira is good or *mara*, while among the Tjoritja group he is "bad." Furthermore, Roheim notes, "*mara* doesn't mean 'good' in the Christian sense—it has no metaphysical implications and can apply to a demon as much as anything else. It simply refers to anything or anyone that lacks a legend of origin."

Semantic "revision" is a prerequisite to understanding Pacific religions. The term "demon" cannot be taken in the European sense, that is, as a servant of the Devil exclusively and inextricably bound to his brother demons. If the majority of demons in the Australian religions are in fact malevolent and eat human beings, there is also a demon, *mangukurata*, which Pindupi tribesmen believe consumes other demons. Not only does no comparable oddity exist in the monotheistic religions, but it would in fact be inconceivable to them: a demon that eats demons would in a way be an ally of God. Yet the Australian *mangukurata* is no less malevolent for the fact that he hunts and devours his fellow demons.

The idea of a supernatural being who inhabits Heaven irresistibly invites comparison with more familiar gods, indeed to God himself. As a matter of course, it seems to demand veneration. This does not hold true among the Australians. Altjira is, as Carl Strehlow writes, "the good deity of the Arandta. . . . He did not create humanity, and its well-being is a matter of indifference to him. . . . The natives are neither scared of him nor love him. Their only fear is that the sky will fall on their heads and kill them all."[10]

Though their conception of the divinities is more or less positive, many Oceanian peoples consider demons to be stupid and easily fooled. The Dayaks of Borneo's Ketungau River used to place wooden idols in front of their doors during epidemics, believing that the demons would carry *them* off instead of human beings. When an epidemic strikes the Dieri of central Australia, a witch doctor is dispatched to beat the ground with a stuffed kangaroo tail in order to flush out the demon responsible, Cootchie, and drive him away[11]—a practice that hardly expresses much respect for the demon's intelligence, courage, or prowess in battle.

Nowhere in Oceania or the Pacific is there even a hint of our great and solitary spirit of Evil, Satan, Beelzebub, or the Devil, the one whom the Lateran and Treat councils had accused of having voluntarily become bad and having driven Man to sin. If Evil, the catastrophic agent of illness, death, and natural disaster, is quite clearly recognized in the religions of Oceania, Polynesia, and Melanesia—or at least in what's left of them, which, unfortunately, is not much—it is considered to be the product of specific forces, not as something emanating from a central power antagonistic to God. "Primitive" peoples' interpretation of Evil is not reductivist. Their interactions with it take place through negotiating with a corpus of animist concepts, a dialogue comparable, in a certain sense, to the Christian practice of turning to patron saints. The native of Oceania, however, proceeds differently: he or she asks a sorcerer or witch doctor to deal with the demon who caused a particular woe. Though such comparisons are tricky, one could say that the monotheist convinced of the world's duality considers Heaven to be a centralized government, whereas the animist of Oceania sees it as more federalized.

The myths that constitute the mythologies of Oceania are the founding legends of the communities themselves, which is very different from the immanence of the monotheisms aiming at universality. These myths are like constitutions in democratic societies; they regulate the collective. That each island has its own mythology is therefore normal; it is as normal for the myths to postulate that Evil—which is in no way opposed to the Good that is equated with life itself as well as, above all, with social harmony—can be avoided through ritual dialogue with the spirits that cause it. In this sense, there is no immanent evil in Oceania.

To understand this difference, we can compare modern Christianity with the myths described by Malinowski. In Christianity, God exists, He created the world, and He is good. In the very distant past He often spoke to men in order to alter their behavior and influence their social relations; His last act of intercession was to send His son Jesus to earth. On the other side is Evil, which is controlled by the Devil. Both Good and Evil are immanent; they will outlive all societies. This is why there is a separation of Church and State in the modern world—Christianity's founding myths and those of the state no longer coincide. Because the idea of an immanent evil embodied by the Devil has survived, a chasm has sprung up between social good, such as it is understood by secular societies, and Church myths, which have long since been transformed into dogma. This is particularly evident in the realm of sexuality.

In Trobriand and Australian societies, or at least in the form they survived in until the middle of this century, there was not a whisper of an embodied sexual evil (except the incest taboo, understood in its larger sense of intercourse that violates the rules of kinship and tribe), and certainly no leering Devil. There, masturbation, male and female homosexuality, adultery, and contraception have social values only. In Papua New Guinea, for example, male homosexuality is codified; it is even obligatory for boys during a given time after puberty.[12] In a variation on a similar idea in ancient Greece —which was much less liberal than we often believe, for the codification was independent of the partners' desires, so that sex with other males, for example, was acceptable only if they were adolescents—the Papuans believe that daily sexual congress (duly codified) with adult males will, through "contagion," pass the powers of proven great warriors on to boys. The concept of adultery does not exist, either: until the very recent past, the traveler was offered the favors of this or that woman no matter whether or not she were married or whether or not any interest had been expressed. The practice of masturbation is equally unstigmatized.

There's no need to point out how such practices are looked upon in the monotheisms. However, it would be wrong to picture the Oceanians as debauchees, sexual or otherwise; the chief of the Kaitish tribe in central Australia, for instance, rigorously abstains from sexual contact with his wife during the whole time he is performing the magical ceremonies that ensure grass growth,[13] since he must consecrate all his energies to it. The Dieris of central Australia, like many other peoples, have a sacred aversion to menses, and they forbid menstruating women from bathing in running water for fear of killing the fish in it; on the island of Muralug in the Torres Strait, men forbid menstruating women from eating anything that comes from the sea—again, for fear of killing everything in it. On the other hand, on Leti, Sermata, and the other islands that lie between Papua New Guinea and northern Australia, the feast of the sun—Upu-Lera, the principal male deity and the fertilizer of the earth—is celebrated by a saturnalia in which sexual intercourse is very much encouraged as homage to the fertility principle.[14]

The notion of Evil and its causes is especially open to study in two little-known cultures, the Yami of Irala Island, which lies southeast of Taiwan, and the Naga, a Southeast Asian people who live in the Indian state of Assam, on the Burmese border.

The Yamis are Malayso-Polynesian, a part of the people that forms the juncture between Asia and Polynesia. They are of interest here for two reasons. First, they shed light on the transition between Asian mythologies and those of Austranesia. Given that they were isolated from Asia at a very early date, it will be interesting to see if their beliefs have evolved toward or away from a specific myth of the Devil. Second, the Yamis have had very little contact with Taiwan, the closest landmass, since at least the days of the Manchu Dynasty (1644–1912). The Japanese, who occupied the island from 1895 to 1945, declared it an ethnological museum and closed it off to outsiders.

Irala, a mountainous island inhabited by some two thousand people, would have been an ideal place for the anthropologist had it remained completely free of outside cultural influences. Though Christianity in its two most common Asian forms, Catholicism and Presbyterianism, was introduced in 1945, it happens to have been absorbed by the local culture and so has not supplanted traditional religion. Nevertheless, it is very difficult to establish the age of Yami beliefs, given that they still have no writing and that their tradition is exclusively oral.

The Yami ethical system begins with something as elemental as the consumption of fish: some of the 450 species the Yami know can be eaten by both sexes at any age, some by men only, some others by old men only, still others by both old men and old women. Some species can only be eaten by pregnant women, others only by women in post partum, while others are forbidden to the residents of certain villages. The list of what is and is not forbidden is quite complex: eighty-eight species are forbidden to everyone, sixty to men under specific circumstances (for instance, when their wives are pregnant), while sixty others are forbidden to women, though four of these are permitted pregnant women, and so forth.

This is a particularly "readable" model of the taboo system found all over Oceania. It is based not on ethics but, rather, on the classical worldview: to respect the taboos means to uphold the cosmic order. A Christian funeral can be denied to the Yami who dies in a state of taboo, even if he is Christian; yet, the Yami taboo system operates independent of any and all deities.

Despite Irala's small size, the Yamis have an elaborate cosmogony that involves genesis myths and a hierarchical pantheon, one striking feature of which is the presence of the primarily Eastern myth of the deluge (in this case, it is caused by a pregnant woman). At the summit of the pantheon is Simo-Rapao, who created the first human pair. Like the God of the Judaic Genesis, he is surrounded by a council of deities. At the base of the pantheon are the malevolent deities whose gluttony can deprive the Yamis of taro and yams and whose ire can bring about terrible infestations of grasshoppers or caterpillars. The Yami cosmology is complemented by a complex human genealogy that starts with the first Yami who appeared on the island.

Between the pantheon's two extremes are lesser deities and nondivine supernatural entities. Among the latter are two female ones, the Pina Langalangao, who preside over birth and life. The concept of gods does not seem to be the same as in other cultures—to the Yami, gods are celestial ancestors, *akey do to*, and "the people above," *tawo do to*.

Like others we have seen before, the Yami system is made up of a pantheon and a pandemonium: proof of this is that the Yamis make a sacrificial offering to all the gods once a year, in December. One odd element in their beliefs, however, is that in the realm of the supernatural the gods rank below the spirits. They believe that every person possesses a "principal spirit" as well as several secondary ones, which are located in the organs and limbs. Death releases these spirits, although a witch doctor or *makahaw* can magically harness them (the witch doctor is the only person who can actually see the spirits; he is even able to sniff out adulterers and to read adulterous thoughts).

When death occurs naturally, the principal spirit or *anito* goes to a mythical place called the White Island. If the spirit is unhappy, it can come back to torment the living, both human and animal. The Yamis live in perpetual, uncontrollable fear of *anitos*, and consequently their most powerful taboos surround funerals. No one in the deceased's family or circle of friends will shut his eyes during a wake, for fear of being attacked by the dead person's *anito*. The most horrifying act of black magic is to touch someone with sand from a grave, since the sand could contain an *anito*.

Two traits among these beliefs stand out. First, there is a clear distinction between spirits and demons from the lower level of the Yami pantheon; second, the ambivalent nature of the spirits—they are not necessarily bad but are capable of becoming so. The worst evil is the doing of the *anito*, a human emanation. There is quite obviously no Yami Devil.[15] Indeed, the basic philosophy is that the causes of Evil are not so much supernatural as they are human; they are due to the persistence of human ill will.

The Naga of Assam total a half million people divided into fifteen principal tribes, each with its own culture. Not much is known about their origins apart from the fact that physically they are predominantly Mongoloid, with sleek black hair and narrow dark eyes. Sometime after the great Mongoloid migration began thirty-five thousand years ago, extending all the way to the Americas, the Nagas apparently moved in and supplanted one or more now-vanished local populations. Some thirty tonal languages, all from the great Sino-Tibetan family, are spoken among the Naga tribes, who might thus have originated in China.[16] Until the last century, they were headhunters. In any case, they are an ancient people, if not a Stone Age one, as is their religion, which perhaps includes elements of their predecessors' ancient Southeast Asian beliefs.

The Nagas have been progressively Christianized since 1890 but still retain the memory of their primeval religion. Rituals and beliefs run from tribe to tribe, although there is no one unified mythology or religion. The Nagas recognize a creator deity—for some tribes, such as the Angami, this deity is a goddess, Kepenopfu, who is remote and hardly intervenes in human life at all, while for others, such as the Konyaks, it is a male god, Kawang, who intervenes heavily in earthly affairs. However, all tribes believe that two sorts of spirits exist—those of earth on the lower level, and those of Heaven on the upper. Among the former are the evil spirits as well as those of the hunt, fertility, and so on; the latter, the *potso*s of the Lhota tribe, for instance, are no "better" in an ethical sense because they too can cause bad things to happen. The Nagas ascribe the greater importance to the lesser spirits, including those of Evil, and they make propitiatory sacrifices to them.

For the Nagas there is no universal cause of Evil, which in any case they have no unified conception of. There are many varieties of evil, each of which has its own cause and its own remedy. The Konyaks, for instance, believe that earthquakes happen because the soul of a clan chieftain is trying to cut his way through thick liana vines. The remedy is a simple ritual: the village gathers together and shouts to him. An eclipse is caused by a tiger, frog, or dog trying to devour the moon, and the clan chieftain cries out, "Don't eat that, it's our sun!" It is possible for the Nagas to negotiate with the forces of evil, which are powers that require sacrifice like any other.

The object of primitive religions is to establish equilibrium among the various supernatural powers that surround the human being, and this is accomplished through ritual. Neither an irreversible split in the world nor original sin exist, and man is not in the thrall of supernatural forces. The goal of religion is to keep the to and fro of gods and demons from overly disrupting human activities; neither gods nor demons have an ethical value. They are ambivalent and somewhat troublesome strangers it is best to respect, but who do not dictate any theological system. In other words, primitive religion is really a process of exorcising the supernatural—the exact opposite of what the monotheisms claim. The difference might seem academic, but as I hope to prove, it isn't.

In the case of the Nagas, it appears once again that in the absence of a central government there is neither a centralized Evil nor the image of a unique Devil. The question that obviously arises here is why so-called primitive societies such as those of Oceania and the Yamis and Nagas haven't conceived of absolute Good and Evil. That is also one of the most important questions facing the anthropology of religions.

One partial answer is that societies as small and isolated as those of Oceania couldn't have anything but a relative notion of evil, since accidents, illness, famine, and death generally affect only a few individuals at the same time. The statistical index of misfortune is low; the disaster of a plague, which in other places would pile up bodies in mounds, is unknown. Cultural variation is also limited, or at least was until the very recent past. The populations of Oceania never encountered the great spread of literary information made possible by the theaters of Greece and Rome and, later, by the printing press. In Oceania, too, the very idea of Evil is ridiculous in comparison to the forces of life—the sun, the sea, vegetation, and the fertility of women, livestock, and the earth. In this respect, the myths of Oceania recall those of Greece: they are life myths, and ethical categories are relevant to them only in the loosest of senses.

Last, power in Oceania is limited by economic weakness; there are no great tyrannical tribulations of the sort endured by continental peoples. Above all, however, Oceanian social structures never left room for significant political systems. The great religious and the great political systems being inseparable, Oceania has never known centralized religions that at their very root associate social taboos with a resident genius of Evil.

The Devil has thus never had a place in Oceania. If the living are sometimes persecuted, the entities responsible have no ethical value. Perhaps this explains the enchantment felt by the first Western navigators, such as James Cook and Louis-Antoine de Bougainville, when they passed through: what our explorers perceived was that these peoples had no idea of Evil, or in any case not of our Evil—shadowy, poor, nasty, brutish, and cruel.

CHAPTER 2

India

Spared from Evil

With Asia, the investigation into the Devil becomes more difficult. After examining the Sri Lankan temple frescoes with their hunched up little demons, for instance, the traveler is tempted to say, yes, the Buddhists do recognize devils, if not *the* Devil—his children or his nephews or nieces, perhaps. Asia is difficult, first of all because there are so many aspects to it. Tibet or Siberia, Indonesia or Borneo, Malaysia or the Philippines, India or Pakistan, China or Japan—each of these countries is different from every other. From the Malay jungles—where life is so accelerated that barringtonias flower for no longer than an hour, leaving behind as solitary evidence of their passing a silvery rose corona on the ground—to the Gobi Desert, where Russian travelers of the last century reported that bodies had been found buried *from the inside* for all the sand they had swallowed, there is not a single ubiquitous living thing apart from the obstinate biped. How, then, could one imagine these countries having a religion in common, still less a shared devil?

Second, Asia is old. Europe, whose name was borrowed from a kidnapped virgin, was still in swaddling clothes, so to speak, when the Asians, a much more diverse collection of peoples than anthropology would once have had us think, headed northeast in search of who knows what, crossed the Bering Strait on dry (albeit freezing) foot, and populated the Americas down to Tierra del Fuego. That was some thirty-five thousand years ago, when our ancestors from Madrid to Moscow were still gearing up for the Stone Age.

Neither television nor cellular phones have changed anything very much; through time and space, Asia seems to resist all comers. The Siberian Yakut are a good example. Characterized by anthropologists as "northern Turks," the Yakut live on the rim of the Arctic Sea (an inhospitable land—a Soviet hydrological expedition sent in 1926 died of starvation there, where, at the time, a half kilo of salt sold for four grams of gold, a half kilo of meat for twenty). Near the end of the eighteenth century, some hardy Christian missionaries set out to convert them. A few decades later, this was the Yakut version of the missionaries' story:

Satan was the older brother of Jesus, but he was bad while Jesus was good. When God wanted to create the earth, he said to Satan: "You brag that you can do everything and that you're greater than me. Well then, see if you can bring back a bit of sand from the bottom of the ocean." So Satan dived down to the bottom of the sea, but when he came back up again he noticed that the water had torn the sand out of his grasp. He dived down twice more, always in vain, and on the fourth time he transformed himself into a swallow and managed to bring up a bit of ooze in his beak. Then Jesus blessed the ooze, which became the Earth. And the Earth was beautiful and flat and smooth. But, wanting to create a world of his own, Satan had kept a bit of mud hidden in his beak. Jesus saw through his trick and hit him in the neck. Then Satan spat out the mud, and when it fell it made the mountains.[1]

The story reveals that the figure of Satan has been absorbed by earlier myths. Despite the malice here transmuted into mischief, and despite his proverbial intelligence, he is outwitted by Jesus. He has lost all his cataclysmic and universal power and is now nothing more than a joker, a trickster (a decidedly un-Satanic but still universal figure that we will examine in chapter 7). Indeed, no

Asian society has ever believed in one God above and one Devil below.

Asian cultures, like those of Africa, Oceania, and the ancient Americas—if one is to judge from what remains of these—are deeply religious. The West believed Asia to be teeming with demons and marvels—in short, pagan, even idolatrous. Yet if today the continent seems divided among three religions only, Buddhism, Hinduism, and Islam (if Buddhism is considered a religion, not a philosophy), these religions' establishment and mutual influences are a much more complicated matter. Everything began in India, Asia's Greece, so that if one has the nerve to discuss Asia, one must begin with that, its spiritual mother.

Essentially, Asia's great religions derive from Vedism, which was introduced into the subcontinent around 1500 B.C. by Aryan (from the Sanskrit word *arya* or "noble") invasions from Iran. Vedism, which takes its name from the Vedas, the religion's sacred texts, supplanted one or more older, little-known religions.

We know that the Aryan invasion postdated the Harappa or Indus (after the great river along which it developed) civilization. This civilization did not have writing, was not very interested in the outside world except to trade livestock, never reached the sea, organized its defense around citadels, apparently knew neither horses nor chariots, and had no political structure to speak of; it was a primitive kingdom whose leader was at once its military commander and its high priest. The civilization's inhabitants, the Dravidians, were much darker than the Aryans and had flat noses, according to occasional descriptions by the invaders, who seemed to loathe and detest them.[2] This pre-Aryan civilization seems to have existed from the fifth millennium B.C. One can assume, based on the pattern of other very old civilizations, that its religion too was primitive, founded on basic cults such as those to the sun and to fertility.

We know almost nothing about these ten centuries of Asian Vedism; the Aryans built nothing out of stone and recorded nothing. The Vedas were passed down orally until they were written down in the third century B.C. In its version of the genesis myth—the Nasadiya, the Rig Veda's "Hymn of Creation" (X:129)—ancient Vedism postulates that in the beginning there was nothing, neither being nor nonbeing, neither air nor sky, neither death nor immortality, neither night nor day. There was only the One, who breathed without breath. According to the Nasadiya, the inner tension of the Original Being produced the first opposition between being and nonbeing, then between active energy and passive matter. The Purusha-Suleta, or "Hymn of Man," proposes a somewhat different version: the gods created the world by means of the sacrifice of an original being, or *purusha*, which is all that has ever existed and that will exist forever.[3]

Vedism was dualistic: the power of gods, or *daevas*—Varuna, Mithra, Indra, and the Nasataya twins—was balanced by that of the countergods, or *asuras*. The *asuras* are as multiform as the gods, representing, in mythical form, the Aryans' adversaries, probably the Pani, Dasa, and other members of the Harappa civilization. Indra's sobriquet is in fact *purandara*, or "destroyer of fortifications," clearly those of the Indus civilization.[4] This is an old story —the enemy demonized and represented as black (and the Dravidians, again, were dark-skinned).

This duality is also a symbolic opposition of being and nonbeing, of creation and chaos. It is the interpretation of a world based on necessary antagonisms. The cosmos is essentially benevolent toward humanity. This does not imply that evil does not exist, merely that it is normal, a function of the cosmic chaos, since there is never peace among heaven's opposing powers. If evil affects humanity, it does so because the human microcosm is part of the macrocosm. From this comes the importance of ritual exactitude, of domestic *grhya* and communal *srauta*: ritual is at the same time both an observance and a celebration of celestial laws, and thus a badly performed ritual can be a cause of disorder. The importance of ritual closely reflects the structures of Aryan India: a hierarchical and codified society in which religion was an instrument of spiritual and political cohesion. Since it exalted the power of priests, ritual was the underpinning of a society in which priests were the masters.

The equilibrium of the world was maintained through sacrifice and the ritual offering of *soma*, the juice of a plant that could well have been *Amanita muscaria* or *Amanita phalloida*—a hallucinogenic drink.[5] The meaning of that rite is worthy of reflection: The world exists only on condition that humans inebriate themselves on certain fixed dates and circumstances, thus partaking of the nature of gods.

This is the basic principle of the Greek mysteries, and it is also the basis of Judaism's reactive hatred of drunkenness—in this respect, the mythic story of Noah is most revealing. In any case, the Aryans hardly held intoxicants in contempt, since apart from *soma* they also drank a fermented beverage called *sura*, which had no religious significance at all.

Toward the fifth century B.C., Vedism in India began to decline into total confusion. No one any longer really knew the names, identities, or roles of the gods. Was Prajapati supreme? If so, why was he also called Hiranyagarbha, and sometimes even Brihaspati? Was he really the supreme One, the god of all things and phenomena, or merely the god of creatures? Was he greater than or equal to Surya, the sun-god, or to Agni, the god of fire? Were the gods separate entities or manifestations of one single entity? It was this last interpretation that was most widely accepted, as in the verses "The real is one, but the learned call it by different names" (X:129.2), and "with their words priests and poets multiply the hidden reality, which is one" (X:114).[6]

The Vedas are undated, but at least one of their verses reflects a definite historical event—the frustration of the faithful at the fluid, polysemous nature of the deities: "Who is this Indra? Has anyone ever seen him? To which god will we make our offerings?" ("The Unknown God, or The Golden Embryo," X:121).[7] This moment, again, came with the decline of Vedism in the fifth century B.C.

Yet it should be stressed that throughout its history Indian Vedism constantly voiced the fundamental doubt of the individual confronting the world; the end of the Vedic era saw the first known expression of agnosticism. According to the more recent Vedas— the Upanishads, or Vedantas—truth is unknowable and religion's purpose is to comfort the human mind. Although often considered unrelated to the agnosticism of the Vedas, this later agnosticism is nevertheless its product, since universal doubt was present in the Nasadiya from the start: "Who truly knows? Who will proclaim it here? . . . Where does creation come from? The gods came after

the creation of the universe. So who knows its birthplace?"
(X:129.6)

All Vedic teaching is informed by this "Who knows?" (*Ko
veda?*); the doubt in the Upanishads is merely more pronounced.
Because of this, the Vedic pantheon loses its preeminence; nothing
is explicable anymore. Matter, the elemental principle, does not
explain the phenomenon of life, and thus no entity is definable. The
mind cannot make sense of logical phenomena, and logic is powerless to make sense of the higher aspects of Being, which cannot
be reduced to the sum of its states—or, as Martin Heidegger (who
took a lively interest in Vedism) was to say much later, Being is
not Being-There. Being is an unchanging and permanent entity, the
Atman, which is identified with the essence of the universe, the
Brahman, the supreme bliss and the sole, total, ultimate explanation
of the universe. *Tat tvam asi*: "That is you." Given that the essence
of the universe is by definition unknowable, Being must be so, too.
There is no recourse; we will never know anything.

However—and this is the primary contribution of the
Upanishads—if the Brahman is the only and total reality, then
dualism has to be abandoned. Bliss, *ananda*, cannot accommodate
Evil. Thus, Evil does not and cannot exist, and so nor can either
demons or the Devil: both are illusions. This contribution would
show through in every religion that derived from Vedism—and
since India disseminated its culture over the whole continent, it can
be stated at the outset that the Devil is unknown in Asia. He is
considered nothing but a fiction. Thanks to the Upanishads' rejection of dualism, Vedism tore off its own mask and stripped the gods
of theirs; the gods were artificial, mere inventions that humanity
hung upon the face of the unknown.

When the Aryans first appeared in northern India in the fifteenth
century B.C., they were bands of warriors led by aristocracies that
in turn were headed by princes, or *rajas*, whose power was balanced
by tribal councils, the *sabhas* and the *samitis*. The Vedas give us
a brief but highly colorful picture of the Aryans: they were capable
warriors and competent farmers and cattle raisers, who enjoyed mu-
sic and dancing; they were fond of alcohol and feminine beauty.
They lived in villages (they are not known to have had a capital

city or even towns) centered among their fields and pastures, were constantly waging war, and spontaneously organized drunken festivities—a picture that also holds true for another Indo-European people, the Celts, whom we will encounter again.

The Aryans first settled in the Punjab, the "land of the five rivers," which today straddles the India-Pakistan border. Some of them ventured eastward as far as the legendary land of Sarasvati (probably in the area of what is today the Sarsuti River, which was destined to become deified as the goddess of eloquence, knowledge, and wisdom; it would later became sacred in Buddhism[8]). They lived according to tribal pattern.

In time, they developed empires. The Aryans entered the land of the Kurus, what is today Rajasthan, and founded their first known capital near Delhi. A true political and dynastic power had thus been established, and since there is no politics without religion, the overfluid Vedism therefore fell victim to its first waves of reform. When the Kuru empire collapsed, one group of Aryans pushed eastward down the Ganges River valley, establishing a succession of empires whose centers were Kosala, Videha, and Kasi; another group pushed down the western coast, reaching Ujjain and extending its power over the commercial seaports.

At once overly mutable and ossified, Vedism had to be reformed. The striking point is that the same thing occurred simultaneously in Iran and India; in Iran it was effected by Zoroaster from about 600 B.C. onward, while in India it was effected by Vardhamanna from about 570 B.C. onward and by Buddha from about 560 B.C. onward. In both places, the context was identical—a centralized political power was being established. In India, however, the reform of Vedism would produce something different from what it produced in Iran.

The change did not occur in the form of a "reincarnation" of the gods. In a stunning about-face, Vedism ridded itself of every trace of theism and instead stressed the religion's intellectualism. Three systems of thought, none of them essentially religious, came to flourish in the ensuing epic period.

The first was materialism, or *lokayata*: perception is the sole source of knowledge, and anything that can be known for sure is material. The intellect is imperfect, and the analogies and universal relations it thinks it can descry are nothing but contingencies. Consciousness is a function of matter; there is no afterlife, and the soul dies with the body. The world created itself; divinity is a myth we accept only because of our ignorance and helplessness. There is no ethics because vice and virtue are merely conventions.

The second system, Jainism, was developed by Vardhamanna, the inventor of philosophical relativism; this contemporary of Buddha's is surprisingly underrecognized in the West. Jainism can be encapsulated by the fable of the blind men trying to describe an elephant: the one who touches its ear concludes that the animal resembles a fan, the one who touches the leg concludes that it resembles a pillar, and so on.

The Jainist doctrine of points of view, or *nayas*, teaches that all knowledge is relative and that, given the complexity of everything, we can neither affirm nor deny anything. Jainism classifies the world according to basic categories—animate and inanimate objects, primary and subtle matter, objects moving and immobile, and so on. The universe is filled with subtle matter or *karma*, which contacts and permeates the soul. The nature of karma is such that all change is permanently inscribed upon it; in its individual projection, it determines individual fate.

One of Jainism's insights, remarkable in that it dates from the fifth century B.C., is that matter exists in two forms, either made up of atoms or aggregates of atoms (what we would call "molecules"), and that various combinations of atoms produce the different elements. Western physics did not incorporate this idea until after the eighteenth century.

There is no deity in Jainism, although souls can attain a state of divinity through ascetic living, which destroys one's karma and prevents its rebirth (and hence a new and painful transmigration of the soul). There is, then, no Devil in Jainism, even though ethics occupies an important place within the religion. The movement still exists today, albeit divided into five divergent sects.

The third system of thought that appeared in the epic period, Buddhism, is the product of the teachings of a great Vedic reformer whose influence matches, if not exceeds, that of Zoroaster, and who is perhaps one of the greatest religious figures in history—the person Schopenhauer called one of the three greatest philosophers ever.

The adventures of the Buddha—born a king's son around 563 B.C. in the kingdom of the Sakyas, on what is today the India-Nepal border—would seem to contradict the detachment of Rokayata materialism in particular and of Jainism in general, since at first glance they provide the clearest prefiguration of our Devil apart from the Egyptian Seth. After a six-month fast that made a skeleton of him and brought him to death's door, Gautama—still a novice, a *Bodhisattva*, "Buddha-to-be-born"—sat down under a ficus tree to await illumination. Mara the bad—also called Papimant, the Evil One, the personification of death—came to him at the head of a horde of malevolent spirits. The speech Mara made in order to tempt him does not seem all that evil. Mara points out Gautama's emaciation and says, "You are bound by earthly and heavenly binds. . . . O ascetic, you cannot free yourself."[9]

This is clearly a prefiguration of the speech Satan makes to Jesus in the desert. In order to understand it, however, we must place it in its own context, which is in no way Christian. Rather, it must be seen against the backdrop of the Buddha's quest for the elevated state in which there is neither perception nor nonperception, the realm of Nothingness or *akincanayatana*—in short, absolute truth or *nirvana*, the state in which a being is freed of the necessity of being reborn and suffering. This state is intrinsically the antithesis of the earthly existence Mara attempts to entice the Bodhisattva into by persuading him that detachment is impossible.

What seems to be reappearing here is the dualism rejected by Upanishad Vedism, the conviction that Evil really exists, and is not merely a projection of the human mind. It recalls (and in fact underlies) the Gnostic idea that everything earthly is evil. Mara, in fact, is not urging Buddha toward crime, voluptuousness, or theft; he is simply urging him toward life, and it is in this that he is "evil." Mara is not a devil, even less *the* Devil, at least not if comparisons with Christian concepts are not pushed too far. He is the god of death, since everything living must die, and from its very inception all life contains the germ of death. To live is to ready oneself to die.

However, drawing on the ten great virtues or *paramitas*, Gautama replies to Mara:

> Concupiscence is your first army, your second is repugnance for the higher life, your third is hunger and thirst, your fourth is desire, your fifth is sloth and laziness, your sixth is cowardice, your seventh is doubt, your eighth is hypocrisy and willfulness, your ninth is rewards, praise, honor, and false glory, and your tenth is adulation of oneself and hatred of others. These are your armies, Mara. A weak man cannot defeat them, and yet it is only by destroying them that one attains bliss.

And so it was on the night of a full moon in May, 528 B.C., that Mara had his greatest defeat inflicted upon him. In the middle of the third watch, between two and six in the morning, Gautama attained the Four Noble Truths; he became immune to the temptations of this world. Mara would persecute the Buddha several more times, the last of them successfully, because the Buddha did in fact end up dying.

After Etienne Lamotte's classic study on the pointlessness of efforts to reconstruct the historical Buddha,[10] the game isn't even worth the candle. Nor would it do much good, since even in the "great" Buddhism of the Mayahana strain—which after the fourth century established itself in China and Korea, then Japan, Sumatra, and all the way to Sri Lanka—the Buddha is considered to be multiform. To some, he is quintuple (Vairocana, Aksobhya, Ratnasambhava, Amitabha, and Amogasiddhi); others believe he has gone through twenty-four incarnations. So many forms of the Buddha exist, none of them ever having had to compete for dominance, that it could be said that there is a Buddhism for everyone. Only the teaching—compassion, and detachment from the world—remains constant.

The ferocious Naga of Uruvilva that confronts the Buddha after his duel with Mara isn't the Devil either but, rather, a legendary cobra, a relative of the dragons, that inhabits a house in Uruvilva; the Buddha will challenge and defeat it in its own lair. The Buddha goes into the house and sits with his torso straight and his legs crossed. As soon as the Naga sees him it belches smoke; the Buddha belches smoke too. Then the Naga spits fire; the Buddha spits fire too. The witnesses seeing smoke and fire coming out of the house are alarmed, but then they learn of the duel's outcome: thanks to his supernatural powers, the Buddha has reduced the Naga to submission and coiled him up in a bowl. This is a peaceable version of the myth of St. George, and in fact of every myth about heroes besting fabulous monsters—from Perseus killing the dragon Andromeda to Odysseus poking out the Cyclops's eye. It is a symbol of the spirit triumphing over matter.

In the cosmology of the Theravada, a school that disseminated ancient Buddhist teachings, no "Master Devil" exists, either; the inner sphere of the three universes, Desire, is populated by five or six kinds of creatures, including demigods, men, demons, and fierce, ravenous phantoms that are somewhat reminiscent of those on Easter Island. Nor does there exist a demon-in-chief such as our own. Indeed, and despite how important the Buddha's victory over Mara is to the various Buddhist traditions of India, Sri Lanka, China, and Japan, it is always held that, like the gods, demons exist only in the lowest sphere, Desire. Great contemplative minds can reject out of hand belief in any of them. Buddhism being, in essence, the teaching of a series of purifications that lead to nirvana, there can be no question of ascribing to the Devil, to devils, or to gods the transcendent and metaphysical status they enjoy in the monotheisms: they are real entities but wholly incidental. Even Brahma, a god borrowed from Hinduism and the equivalent of the monotheisms' God of Creation, isn't eternal; he is the first to appear and last to disappear at the beginning and end of each universal cycle. Infernal or heavenly, divinity itself is transitory.

The God/Devil antagonism does not exist in Buddhism and would not make sense if it did. One instructive example about theological avatars comes from Tibet, where it is believed that the old gods unseated by Buddhism in the eighth century became malefic demons that only sorcerers, or *bon*s, can restrain. This recalls the reorganizing of the pantheon carried out in the Zoroastrian reform of Vedism (see chapter 4), although in Tibet the process involves integration, not exclusion. The Tibetan Buddhists, like the ones in China, build little temples beside those of other religions in order to ward off the wrath of foreign gods. Asia was already a place of exceptional religious tolerance; when in the eighth century Buddhism began to compete with the Shinto religion in Japan (pleasantly enough, there was no conflict resembling a religious war; the Shintoists merely built chapels in Buddhist temples, and vice versa), the clergy began to question which was the "correct" religion. The emperor, Shomu, had a dream in which the goddess Amaterasu, the sun deity and the dynasty's founder, appeared to him. She told the emperor that, Japan being the land of the gods, all of them had to venerated and that the nature of Buddha Vairocana, the first of the Buddhist "quintet," was the same as that of their own gods.

Yet what about criminals? If there are indeed hells, the fruit of misled lives, they are not forever, since the cycles of reincarnation afford an escape from them. No crime, not even parricide, the most abominable of all, justifies eternal "damnation" (a term that also is inconceivable in Buddhism). The *Pettavathu*, or "Ghost Stories," a book in one of the three great "baskets" that hold the thirty-two canonical Pali texts, do in fact contain descriptions of the terrible places reserved for those who commit crimes. Yet these are not terminal hells as we understand them, but purgatories. In any case, it stands to reason that hells could not be eternal because Evil is not eternal either, since there is no original sin and man is not responsible for what evil really is, the product of celestial whim. There is obviously little room for the Devil in such a system, because the metaphysical underpinnings of Evil have been denied him. The gods know no Evil; rather, they produce evil only when they interact with humanity.

It would be wrong to assume from all this that Buddhists are agnostic in the Western sense. Since the universe was not created, and since it is nothing more than a chain of causes according to the elegant proposition of the Nyaya school's five syllogisms, and since causes are merely the effects of other causes, it follows that the Absolute is unknowable. There is no Buddhist metaphysics, and that has never been its goal; it is an ethics based not on dogma, which is alien to its teaching (no one is compelled to accept a religious proposition that defies reason) but on compassion. The virtues and vices discussed by the Buddha are a way of achieving the greatest harmony in one's relations with one's fellow creatures.

The first of the virtues or "sublime states" is compassion—*maitri* in Sanskrit, *mettra* in Pali—which enjoins the Buddhist against harming anyone, including himself. The others are love, sorrow at the sorrow of others, joy at the joys of others, and equanimity about one's own joys and sorrows. Vices or "ties" (to the world) number ten in all: the illusion that the ego exists, doubt, overzealous asceticism, sensuality, ill will, the desire to be reincarnated on Earth, the desire to reach heaven, pride, puritanism, and arrogance. Ascetic excess, the recourse of searchers for the Absolute overeager to transcend their earthly condition, is as wrong as ignoring the Buddha's precepts. Gautama himself commends the middle way.

The individual imbued with *maitri* will act compassionately without hoping for or counting upon a reward on Earth or elsewhere. If one were determined to Westernize this worldview, one would say that the Buddhist is guided by Heidegger's Being-There. Perhaps the comparison is not apt, though: one can only understand the Buddha's actions if one keeps in mind the context in which he taught. He was addressing himself to individuals who had rejected the two extremes of contemporary religion, the Brahmanism that preached the exaltation of the senses and the extreme asceticism of the Jainists, whose goal was to suspend not only physical processes but even mental ones.

Mythic though he may be, the Buddha as a historical figure deserves a glance. He was able to transcend the beliefs of his day, beliefs that postulated the endurance, even immortality of the soul, and to negate them. In Buddhism, there is no such thing as the "soul" in the Western sense. Everything that begins also ends, and since the soul begins with life it also ends with it. The pill was certainly bitter, so much so that Buddha's disciples softened it by falling back upon metempsychosis: the soul was immortal, they claimed, but provisionally—it reincarnates until it attains perfection, at which point it disappears into the great All. The Buddha can be accused of neither cynicism nor materialism: matter was transitory and he treated it as such. What the time demanded was a codification of Good and Evil; he reduced both to earthly illusions. In this drastic ethical reordering, all traces of the Devil were thrown out like a Mardi Gras carnival mask at dawn on Ash Wednesday. What the time wanted was a justification for well-earned pleasure —but that would be to justify desire, he argued, which would only muddy the waters in which the One is reflected. He counseled against desire because an enlightened soul shouldn't fall prey to it. He thus swam against the current of every religious aspiration of his day, and India deserves praise for having accepted his vision no matter how difficult and austere it was.

Alongside Buddhism and its three great systems, ancient Vedism meanwhile survived in the form of the body of beliefs called Hinduism, which was produced from the fusion of Upanishad Vedism, suppressed but not eradicated Harappa traditions, and probably more minor, often tribal traditions. All sources agree that "Hinduism" is more of a linguistic convenience than it is a description. If one were to attempt to distill a common body of beliefs out of the various Hinduisms, the differences among its numerous strains— Brahmanism, Vishnuism, Shivaism, Tantrism, Shaktism, popular Hinduism, and the many forms of Hindu mysticism—would be deep and numerous. In addition, Hinduism has changed and renewed itself over the centuries, absorbing countless foreign influences, endlessly producing new offshoots and reconfigurations. Otherwise, it is traditionally admitted that Hinduism has been largely forged by the teaching of three great masters, Shankara, Ramanuja, and Radhva.

The theology of Brahmanism, the form of Hinduism that is closest to original Vedism, postulates that in the beginning there was only Purusha, who was at once god and matter—an anticipation of the monotheisms. Of Purusha was born the goddess Viraj, who in turn again gave birth to him. Purusha had no enemy; the cosmos no longer witnessed the dramas that had rocked it in Vedism. However, Brahmanism evolved; in a striking prefiguration of Christianity, Purusha split into Narayana, the Son of Man, and into

Prajapati, the God of Beings and of all the other gods. He was thus both God and his incarnated human son. After having created life by differentiating himself into every form of it, he reintegrated himself and embodied himself in the rituals—in other words, the ritual itself was the deity whose perpetuation the accomplishment of the ritual ensured.

Evil as defined by the monotheisms—the desire to disturb the order of the world through wrongful conduct—does not exist in Brahmanism. Like absolute Good, absolute Evil is not the province of mortals; the absolutes come into play only as a consequence of celebrating rituals in a correct or incorrect way (whence the extreme formalism of this side of Hinduism). Illness or death, for example, is the consequence of ritual transgression, such as touching a corpse or even an error in the ritual protocol or the saying of a prayer. In these cases, normally benevolent gods such as Agni, the fire that devours evil things, or Varuna, the god of balance, are transformed into vengeful gods until a new sacrifice is made to propitiate them.

This point is important, since in Brahmanism as in Vedism only scrupulous attention to ritual can ward off the calamity of losing religious merits accrued over the course of successive reincarnations. This belief in reincarnation—a product of Brahmanism and the other Hinduisms—though already present in Vedism, had developed and diversified. According to one's merits or lack of them, one could end up reincarnated as a rat (a revered animal to Hindus) or as a cow or other human. The essential thing is not to lose the merits one has accumulated in this lifetime, which is possible only if one is aware of the cosmic connectedness embodied, once again, in ritual.

Vishnuism takes us even deeper into the complexities of Hinduism. Indeed, this cult of the god Vishnu and his ten incarnations is comprehensible to the Western mind only once it is realized that the Lord Creator of the Universe Isana (or Brahma) is in fact a trinity, the Trimurti, made up of Brahma, Vishnu, and Shiva. At this point, a certain amount of confusion arises for the Westerner, since in some of its variants Vishnuism raises the argument of Vishnu's divine oneness, a concept that in the twelfth century produced a monotheism markedly similar to the three great monotheisms, and to Christianity in particular. The Hindu obsession with reincarnation was transcended for the first time by Ramanuja, a Hindu philosopher and follower of the Vishnuist Srivaishnava branch of Hinduism (which predominated in southern India), who proposed that god, in this case Vishnu Vithoba, the eternal cause of all things in the universe, is the sole path to salvation. With this argument, Ramanuja rejected the impersonal theology of the eighth- and ninth-century monistic theologian Sankara; in his monastery, he set down his teachings and wrote his three great works of commentary, the first non-Christian vision of a personal God. At the same time, he proposed that Creation had never been accomplished absolutely, that Vishnu-God had never been incarnated, that Vishnu's nature is radically different from the nature of matter, and that in his perfection he constitutes the totality of the souls of all living creatures, of their minds and even of their "subtle" states.

In that it postulates God's immateriality and nonincarnation, Vishnuism's God/matter dualism is unlike the one that underlies Christianity; it is, instead, closer to the Jewish and Christian gnosticisms. In practice, it implies that nothing material can be divine, and thus matter is bad—although it doesn't say that God has an enemy of any sort. In its fidelity to Vedism, Vishnuism holds that God is a benevolent deity through whom the individual is capable of attaining perfection and rejecting what is erroneous. In other words, either the individual is deified by knowledge (which is attained either through asceticism or through a state of grace) or he doesn't exist at all. To simplify Ramanuja's teachings, God exists or there is nothing—which, we have to admit, brings us quite far from our conception of an omnipresent Evil reigning from Hell.

Ramanuja's teachings had a considerable impact on Vishnuism, although his gnostic vision was not taken up by all of its branches. Tradition accepted the idea of a God who at once constitutes the physical and psychic nature of all things, as well as the idea that ritual errors and faults entail risks; what it came up with on its own (apart from a taste for a highly erotic mysticism) was the notion that sin—jealousy, falsity, hypocrisy (as distinct from falsity), cruelty, and pride—can prevent one from participating in the essence of the god Vishnu.

It is Shivaism, the cult of Shiva—the god of destruction, the ancient Vedic Rudra, also known as Paravati, Prithivi, Uma, Ambika, Kali, and Durka, all of which attests to the Hindu pantheon's extreme polymorphousness—that is most likely to give the Westerner trouble. If the avatars of Vishnu (who goes as far as incarnating himself as a woman in his dealings with mortals) are already disturbingly multiple, then Shiva's fundamental amorphousness is cause for total confusion; yet it is here that Hinduism most closely touches upon Evil, the product of the Devil we have searched for, thus far, in vain. Shiva, "he who brings happiness," is at the same time, however, the source of all life and the god of destruction, the great avenger and the giver of gifts.

Shiva, bewilderingly enough, seems to have been a fickle god who symbolized the caprices of nature, and yet he was also only a minor deity. The god of livestock or Prasupati, but also the god of punishment or Aghora, at once a notorious cad and a model husband, sometimes mystical, sometimes abandoning himself to sexual frenzy after long periods of abstinence (his phallus assumes considerable theological proportions), he is bipolar and essentially contradictory. It was in the course of a later Hindu development that he assumed his characteristic traits—on the one hand, the elevated spirituality of a major deity, and on the other, the fury of a malevolent power. This capricious and violent side is not in and of itself condemned in Shivaism, which holds, as does Zen Buddhism, that enlightenment can be attained through a bolt of inspiration. However, along with his spiritual power, Shiva is surrounded by a cohort of demons that persecute unfortunate mortals.

In Shiva we might think we have found at last our spirit of Evil, a precursor of the Devil—but this is not so. No sooner do we isolate him here, bestial, grimacing horribly, covered with his victims' blood, than we find him there, benevolent and supremely genial, coiffed with the crescent moon forever glistening with the elixir of everlasting life.

Shiva became more fascinating as the centuries passed until, in

the fourth-century-B.C. Svetasvatara Upanishad, he reached his supreme rank and apotheosis into the Trimurti. The great Hindu philosophical school of Samkhia even claimed that his quintuple nature
corresponds to the twenty-five basic elements. In the twentieth century, the mystic and theologian Ramakrishna saw him (in the form
of the goddess-ogress Kali, since the gender of the Hindu gods often
alternates) as the supreme deity. In his dancing, which gives all
life its rhythm, and in his ritual drunkenness, he is strikingly akin
to Dionysus—although that Thracian god is never cruel nor bisex-
ual, like Shiva, who is sometimes male, sometimes female, and
sometimes both (as in his Ardhanarisvara avatar).

There are indeed demons in Shivaist theology, but they are secondary figures, a companion race to the phantoms. It would be
mistaken to consider them the siblings of "our" demons; the name
"genies" would suit them better. They are relatives of Socrates'
guiding *daimon*.

Under the aegis of such a protean god, the Shivaist ethical system
is obviously very elaborate. It does not conceive of a supreme spirit
of Evil, since the god Shiva himself incarnates evil according to
his whims, and the evil liable to affect humans in this ethics is a
product either of ignorance or impurity, both of which are apt to
arouse the anger of the gods.

The divine polymorphousness so evident in Shiva is also to be
found in Shaktism, a Hindu school often inseparably linked with
Tantrism. To define Shaktism in depth would take far more space
than is possible here, so numerous and interrelated are its branches
and strains. It can be described as the cult of the goddess Shakti,
the spouse of the god Brahman, whose energy she expresses. In
accordance with the involutions that abound in Hinduism, Shakti
is Shiva's mother while at the same time being identified, in the
Bengali Shakti cult, with one of his personifications, the ogress Kali,
who demands blood sacrifices. She is a capricious goddess as cruel
as she is creative; she takes back with one hand what she has given
with the other. Shaktism is so similar to Shivaism as to be almost
indistinguishable from it; however, in a vast departure from Vishnuism (in which asceticism is highly esteemed) and even from Shi-

vaism (in which it is still present, albeit in a more attenuated form), Shaktism excludes sexuality from its list of forbiddens. Quite to the contrary: on the condition that they are ritualized, sexual contact and sexual pleasure are exalted as ceremonies of union between body and soul, between the human and the divine. (Shaktism goes so far as telling men to seek out married women, since they are harder to seduce.)

It is pointless to continue rummaging around through Shaktism —or through Tantrism, a contemplative discipline whose aim is to drive away chaos by harmonizing the individual microcosm with the macrocosm—for demons malevolent, vicious, or lecherous. The supernatural entities that gave Saint Anthony so much trouble are inconceivable to Shaktism.

A stewpot of the various types of Hinduism described above, each geographically dominant in this or that region, popular Hinduism does not in and of itself make up an independent branch of the religion; demons abound in it, but the Devil is no more present in this than in any of the other constituent parts of Hinduism.

These descriptions are all necessarily schematic, since the various strains of Hinduism have over the centuries been altered and reshaped by mutual influences far too numerous to analyze in depth. What does emerge is that Hinduism considers Good and Evil to be complementary aspects of amorphous powers, and that it cultivates a metaphysics of balance, an intellectual tool to help the individual in the search for enlightenment. It is not Good or Evil that must mobilize the aspirations of the faithful but, rather, the seeking out of a fusion with the divinity.

This fact is all the more surprising given that the roots of the Indian religions lie in the same Vedism that gave birth to rigid notions of Good and Evil in Iran—although that, as we shall see, was a highly centralized empire, while India was not and still is not. No one has managed to homogenize the country, not the Maurya kings, nor the Andhra, nor the Satavahana, nor the Kalinga, nor, later, the Guptas or the Arabs who occupied it in the eighth century.

It was impossible to impose upon it the sort of rigid corpus of beliefs that, by drawing a distinction between Good and Evil, ended up generating a Devil. There was never a devil in Vedic, Hindu, Jainist, or Buddhist India—not our Devil, at any rate. India was spared that Zoroastrian invention.

CHAPTER 3

China and Japan

Exorcism through Writing

O son of noble family, listen very carefully. When the twelfth day comes, the blood-drinking emanation of the Karma family, who is called Karma-Heruka the Blessed, will rise out of the northern quadrant of your brain and appear before you clearly, united with his spouse; his body dark green, with three heads, six arms, and four legs spread apart; the right face is white, the left is red, and the middle a majestic deep green; his six hands are holding, the first to the right a sword, that in the middle-right a trident impaled with three human heads, the next to the left a bell, the next still a goblet fashioned out of a human skull, the last a plowshare; his spouse, Karma-Krodhisvari, is clasping his body with her right arm, her hand around his neck, and in her left she is holding a blood-filled skull to his lips. Do not be afraid of him, do not be terrified, do not be taken aback. Recognize in him the form of your own spirit. He is your *yidam* [a specific deity that represents the individual's enlightenment], so do not be afraid. He is really the Blessed Amogh-yasiddhi with his spouse, so feel deep devotion to him. Recognition and liberation are simultaneous.[1]

This is the admonition to the dying in the *Tibetan Book of the Dead*. In the moment of suspension that coincides with the final passage from life to death—the *bardo* or "leap"—the individual who sees the deity described here also sees light, and then attains the Body of Truth, the *dharmakaya*, the absolute essence of Buddha.

This is not the only vision that the being attaining *bardo* can have; untold others await the suspended spirit, including white Gauri brandishing a corpse in her right hand like a club and in her left holding a blood-filled skull, yellow Cauri firing an arrow from her bow, red Pramoha waving a banner depicting a sea monster, black Vetali holding a *vajra* (a ball studded with sharp points) in her right hand and a blood-filled skull in her left, orange Pukhasi holding entrails in her right hand and eating them with her left, and so forth.

For us, these would be hellish visions, but these terrible monsters are contemptible. The *Book of the Dead* counsels seeing them as "illusions of the mind," as "the individual's own projections."

Demons do not exist, as the prayer of the dead clearly states: "When I will have left my dear friends and gone on my own, and when the empty forms of my own projections appear, may the buddhas grant me the strength of their compassion so that the terrors of the *bardo* will not come. When the five lights of wisdom blaze, that I may recognize myself without fear . . ."[2] The only danger is believing in the creations of one's own imagination. Beyond the forty-nine day *bardo*, there is nothing. The passage is difficult only for those who are frightened of it.

If it is perilous for the Western mind to venture into Indian religions, the same holds true for the rest of Asia's religions— starting with Buddhism, which is transformed as soon as it crosses the Himalayas and produces different results, the way a European orange tree planted in Africa gives fruit of a different taste.

Northern Asia is indeed different. In the fifth millennium B.C., Chinese from the Barkol region (Shensi), which lies on the edge of the Gobi Desert, below the Altai foothills and south of present-day Mongolia, independently invented agriculture. They did so some two, perhaps even three thousand years later than the Indo-Europeans, but the fact that they invented it, along with other technologies,[3] proves that they had been living in the same place for a very long time. Their religion, too, developed independently of

Indo-European influences. For want of written records, we know absolutely nothing about it; the most one can say is that the northern Chinese probably believed in the immortality of the soul, since they placed foodstuffs and tools inside their sepulchers.[4] A fertility cult (as evidenced by representations of sexual organs), conceptions of a cosmic cycle informed by an awareness of seasonal cycles— nothing here is, as far as we know, exceptional, apart from the appearance of small ceramic pieces representing little houses, perhaps funerary urns or the "houses of ancestors." Some writers believe that the Chinese ancestor cult started before the second millennium B.C.

Every people produces myths according to its landscape, and the landscape that saw the birth of the first northern Chinese religion was not the same as that of the Hindus around the Ganges River —which is to say that when the first Buddhist missionaries arrived, the soil was neither virgin nor very similar to that of India.

By the second millennium B.C., Indo-Europeans had undoubtedly reached western Siberia. They probably founded permanent though far-flung centers, yet they do not seem to have disseminated their culture widely.[5] We are unaware of their relationship with local populations, and so it cannot be determined whether or not they communicated elements of their religion to the native Asians. The fact remains that by the time of the Shang Dynasty (ca. 1751–1028 B.C.), urban centers, a military aristocracy, a monarchy, and writing were already established. The religion's pantheon was quite different from that of the Indo-Europeans: it was ruled by a supreme god, Ti or Chang Ti ("Lord" or "Lord Up Above"), the sovereign of rain and fertility as well as the king of the gods and of the king's ancestors. The religion seems to derive from one that had already existed in the Neolithic era: beside animal skeletons in royal tombs were those of numerous human victims, as Mircea Eliade writes, "undoubtedly dispatched to accompany the ruler into the next world." Belief in the immortality of the soul has never inclined human beings toward respect for life or toward compassion—especially when immortality belongs exclusively to the aristocracy.

The ancestor cult seems touching in its filial piety, although the truth was, in René Grousset's words, that only the nobleman had any reason to concern himself with his ancestors, because only those of his class possessed souls capable of survival. They even had two souls, one of purely animal nature and destined, after death, to become a sort of remnant that lingered tenuously around the corpse, and another, spiritual one that after death rose up to the sky in the form of a spirit, but could only remain there insofar as its substance was nourished by the funerary offerings of its descendants.[6]

These offerings were primarily peasants: a serf was dispatched in order to maintain the aristocrat's soul in heaven. A peasant was not considered to have a soul at the time; that, apparently, was a luxury.

The last Shang king, Cheu-sin, was cruel and depraved; Wu-wang, a seminomadic tribal chieftain, cut his army to ribbons. After his defeat, Cheu-sin returned to his palace, went into the Courtyard of the Stag arrayed in his finest pearls and jade, and cast himself on a blazing pyre. Wu-wang beheaded the royal corpse with the Great Yellow Ax and then founded his own dynasty, the Chou. It is under the Chous, the longest dynasty in Chinese history (1028– 256 B.C.), that the conception ancient China had of religion, of Good and Evil, can first be determined for certain. Ti, who had become Ti'en (Heaven), was a personal, anthropomorphic god very similar to Yahweh-Allah-God. From his throne in the constellation of the Great Bear, he sees and hears everything. Not only is he the arbiter of cosmic order but he also lays down moral law for humans.

Here we encounter one of the most ancient manifestations of the heaven-imposed ethic, a pattern we shall run across again throughout history, notably in Iran. As soon as a totalitarian power is established in a centralized state, the sovereign deems himself the "servant of heaven" and claims the right to determine Good and Evil absolutely. Absolute Evil was, in effect, anything that contravened the law set down by the sovereign.

Little is known about ancient Chinese cosmogony, but it seems to have held that an original "ritual sin" caused a precipitate rupture between Earth and Heaven. "The Mountain that touched the sky was leveled."[7] This is the concept of paradise lost—the notion of Evil, and perhaps of the Devil, its progenitor, is nigh. Under the reign of the mythical Emperor Yao, "the Earth was not in order." His son, Yu, "worked the soil and drained the waters and chased dragons and serpents into the swamps."[8] Serpents and dragons violate order and so represent a precursor principle to Evil, which only the royal power can combat.

This ancient pattern, of the political power appropriating Good and Evil, is as old as the first centralized states. This archaic process can be reversed only by philosophies that encourage detachment (as in India) or politically, by democracy, as in Greece. The situation in China, which was comprised of large fiefdoms, does not at first glance seem very propitious for Buddhism, which as we have seen proposes that demons and evil are the product of earthly imagination and, further, preaches equality and tolerance among men. Indeed, Chinese Buddhism radically differs from Hindu Buddhism—it must, because it had to adapt to hostile terrain.

When Buddhism arrived in China in the third century B.C. (three hundred years after its birth in India), the landscape was no longer dominated by the primitive, bloody religion but, instead, by Taoism, an ideology native to China. Taoism appeared in the sixth century B.C., a period that was decidedly auspicious for the birth of great Eastern and Far Eastern religions. It is said to have been founded by Lao-Tzu, a scholar and government official who was later proclaimed the reincarnation of a god, even the incarnation of the primal soul of the universe.

The term "Taoism"—from the word *tao* or "way"—refers to a philosophy and to a faith at the same time. The philosophy has been closely studied in the West for more than a century; the faith has only begun to be studied since the sixties. The two have often been confused; practices that are magical, physiological (control of breathing, retention of semen during intercourse, and other sexual techniques), dietetic, and so forth have been called "Taoist" when in fact they derive from practices that predate Taoism, which merely absorbed, filtered, and refined them.

When Taoism appeared, the people were worshiping a vast collection of folkloric gods inherited from the old religion. The rites had much more to do with magic than with faith, or in any case than with the spiritual elevation discussed by Chinese scholars.

These rites were performed by shamans, sorcerers who claimed to have the power to communicate with supernatural entities and with gods and demons who could be made to tell the future or reveal the past; in other words, the rites were exorcisms or spells. Taoism held that this ancient pantheon was a grouping of spirits that in the best of cases were helpful to humans but for the most part were inimical to them, and that dealings with these spirits could lead to madness or damnation. To Taoism, the popular religion was irrelevant; the "way" could not be found through the ravings of peasants and uncultured barbarians.

One can easily picture the contempt the Taoists felt for the religious celebrations they encountered in villages and towns—gatherings of peasants hypnotized by aromatic smoke and drunk on alcoholic or alkaloid beverages,[9] accompanied by the dramatic gyrations of shamans and spontaneous but obscene ecstasies. They were called *yin-su*, "cults of excess," and condemnation by Taoists brought about their suppression by the authorities.

The Taoists replaced these celebrations with a worldview based on the balance of two antagonistic forces, the female Yin and the male Yang—which are opposed but complementary, like hot and cold, day and night, winter and summer, dry and moist. They also believed in a conception of the individual as a microcosm linked to the macrocosm and governed by symbolic numbers: the 360 joints in the body correspond to the 360 days of the ritual calendar, while the passions, like the five main bodily organs (heart, lungs, spleen, intestines, and genitals), correspond to the five directions, the five sacred mountains, the regions of heaven, and the elements. The human microcosm is inhabited by the same gods that inhabit the macrocosm. Evil in and of itself does not exist; only disorder does.

Taoism today is specifically a mysticism that preaches detachment: rejoining Buddhism by an independent road, it holds that all desires, including the desire for knowledge, disrupt the equilibrium and threaten to split apart the two essences, the vegetative and the spiritual, which could result in death. It preaches nonintervention, *wu wei*, and it enjoins the mystic ecstasy that alone can unite the inner mind with the oneness of the universe, the Absolute. One of its masters, Chuang-Tzu (late fourth to early third centuries B.C.), even condemned artisanship and commerce as leading to vice. The manufacture of even a pot disrupts the order of nature. Evil, Taoism maintains, is the product of misunderstanding. To Chuang-Tzu, the good and the bad, like the true and the false, were the result of not knowing or not understanding the All, the *tao*.

Of this radical, asocial, and ultraquietistic mysticism the people adopted only what could be called the secondary practices: secret societies, for example; the medical advances it produced; its breathing techniques aimed at "nourishing oneself with air" (whoever could hold their breath for a thousand beats was guaranteed immortality); gymnastics; divination; and, paradoxically, artisanship.

If "fundamentalist" Taoism was adoptable and adopted only by the educated elite, its influence was nevertheless vast, both at home and abroad. In the West, mystics such as the third-century Plotinus and the fifteenth-century Nicholas of Cusae echoed the Taoist principle of an absolute oneness in which all opposites come together; links have been identified between Taoism and such European mystics as Meister Eckehart in Germany, Saint Teresa of Avila in Spain, and the Hesychiasts of Mount Athos (who in the fifteenth century practiced breathing control and concentration on the bodily organs).

Like India, China was in effect too large a country for an ideological hegemony to be imposed upon it for very long.[10] The hegemony that gave rise to demons in China's ancient kingdoms was possible only because they were of limited size, the equivalent of one or two provinces, such as the city-states that proliferated in the wake of urbanization during the period called "Springs and Autumns." It wasn't until the end of the sixth century B.C. that the incessant warring of petty monarchies began to produce true states. The Qin kingdom, a small region of some six hundred square miles in the middle of the fourth century B.C., successively annexed the neighboring kingdoms; by the end of the third century B.C., its area extended over one hundred and fifty thousand square miles.

In addition to its vast size, another essential trait of imperial China was the isolation of its aristocratic world. From the very beginning, China's court functioned as a state within a state, a phenomenon embodied in Beijing's Forbidden City, which until the reign of the very last Chinese emperor was steeped in an atmosphere of rarefied culture, with a protocol so all-encompassing that it practically dictated the flight of butterflies. It was here that Lao-Tzu produced Taoism, and it was here that the aristocracy came to adopt it—to a degree that sometimes made no political sense, as under the reign of the Han emperor Hsiao Wu Ti (reigned 141–87 B.C.), when the imperial ministers, more familiar with esoterica than with statecraft, attempted to enact their doctrines about the ideal government.

In later centuries, the codification of Taoism did lead to a resurgence of demonism, since rules always tend to produce dichotomies. By then, though, it was much too late; a handful of imps did indeed infest the popular culture, but the Devil had lost his residence permit visa in China, or at least among its Taoist population.

Part of the reason for this was another school of thought, Confucianism, which was also profoundly to affect Asian culture, and also had its own ethics and worldview to impose. As with Taoism and Buddhism, opinions vary on the question of whether Confucianism is a religion at all. Westerners are so invested in the idea that religions must have a supernatural aspect that, to us, Confucianism seems to be little more than a philosophy (which it certainly is—Asians who call themselves Buddhist, Taoist, and even Christian continue to profess their Confucianism). A person can be both a Buddhist and a Confucian in the same way that in the West one can be (or rather, believe oneself to be) both a Christian and a Hegelian. Yet what philosophy, no matter how essentially irreligious, does not have religious undertones?

Confucius himself was religious in that he prayed, fasted, participated in religious ceremonies, made sacrifices, and swore oaths in the name of Heaven. This, however, did not prevent him from energetically assailing the religious practice of his day, the animism inherited from the Yin Dynasty and from the archaic cultures described earlier. Confucius's reaction was the same as Lao-Tzu's: rejection. (The *Chuang-Tzu* describes a conversation between Confucius and the older Lao-Tzu in which Confucius is depicted as thoroughly outclassed by the wisdom of the master. However, since the *Chuang-Tzu* was written by the famous and eponymous disciple of Lao-Tzu, we can suspect that the conversation—of which seven versions exist—proceeded somewhat differently.)

Born in 551 B.C., seven years before Buddha (again, the times were propitious), to a noble but impoverished family, K'ung-Fu-Tzu or Confucius certainly was a real person. It is known that he was orphaned very young, that his childhood was spent in poverty, and that as an adult he worked at state-owned parks and granaries. Though self-taught, he became the most learned person of his day —a claim that is perhaps not exaggerated.

The key to his character lies in his reaction to the misery caused by the era's feudal wars, famines, and the compulsory labor imposed by the nobility—a call for compassion. In an attempt to remedy the situation, Confucius undertook to educate young men, not by laying down authoritarian scholastic rules but, instead, by trying to develop each according to his nature, seeking nothing from them but sincerity. "Virtue is to love others; wisdom is to understand them," he declares in *The Analects*. And again: "Across the four seas, all men are brothers." Yet there is no hint of metaphysics in the master's teachings; he disdained that as much as he disdained logic, maintaining that reality cannot be apprehended through words.

If Confucianism clearly acknowledges Taoism, it accepts neither its esoteric nor its mystical aspect. Perhaps the master sensed the dangers they entail: "The master says: 'Imagine a man who can recite the three hundred poems. He is entrusted with a government, but he cannot manage it; he is sent on an embassy to the four corners of the world, but he cannot negotiate. What good has all his knowledge done him?'" And: "The master says: 'I have never had the good fortune to meet a saint. I would be happy enough to meet an honest man.'"[11]

Clearly, Chuang-Tzu caught the allusion and hastened to condemn the heroes and inventors elegized by Confucianism as well as the sages who made it their business to establish rites and regulations for society: "The Tao and its virtue were destroyed because men wanted to dictate goodwill and probity." There could be no more direct an attack on Confucianism and its claim to regulating society through imposed wisdom.

Nevertheless, Confucianism was elevated to the rank of official philosophy and has since then had a lasting history. The first of Confucius's two great disciples, Meng-Tzu (who lived from 371 to 289 B.C. and thus never met his master), Latinized as "Mencius," was faithful to his teaching and did not elaborate theories about forces either heavenly or infernal. "Heaven sees the way people do," he wrote. "Heaven hears the way people hear." In other words, Heaven knows no more than mortals; the higher powers are not omniscient. Much as Confucius was too busy furthering happiness on Earth by helping all men become as good as possible, Mencius couldn't care less about metaphysics. He did believe that a universal element existed, the *ch'i*, a vital force he maintained should be cultivated by all. When a person is filled with *ch'i*, his celestial and terrestrial natures become indistinguishable: "All the thousands of living things are within us"[12]—the Devil, had he existed, included.

Another Confucian, Hsun-Tzu, who lived in the third century A.D., wrote: "The nature of man is bad. His goodness is acquired." This could seem to echo Semitic ideas about original sin, but in whose eyes would the sin be a sin? Not in those of Heaven, for which Hsun-Tzu has little regard. Heaven isn't even a source of benediction; it cannot help him who helps himself. Nor is it the seat of an eternal god, still less an anthropomorphic one, a view that undoubtedly reflects Hsun-Tzu's disapproval of Christianity. Humanity can expect nothing of Heaven, a mechanical entity operating on behalf of nothing but itself. Nor do demons exist; Hsun-Tzu adamantly casts aside magic, augury, exorcism, and other superstitious practices. He similarly rules out the invocation of supernatural powers and thus rules out religion too. His goal is the Empire of the World: he exhorts his listeners incessantly to gain control over themselves in order to become better, which will make emperors redundant. "When each individual has found his proper place, when he has mastered himself and done his duty, the emperor will be as useless as a clod of earth."

Buddhism theoretically shouldn't have found much elbow room

in China—but it did. In the third century B.C., it was particularly adept at accommodating itself to Confucianism and Taoism. The Indian emperor Asoka (who ruled from 321 to 297 B.C.[13]) was the first ruler anywhere to send out missionaries, initially to Sri Lanka and then to Southeast Asia, where the Hmong were the first to be converted; from there his missionaries went to Burma, Cambodia, and Siam, and on to southern China. By the fifth century A.D., Buddhism had reached Java and Sumatra. How the teachings of Gautama reached Central Asia is still unknown, but they did, and in the roiling cauldron of languages, religions, cultures, and ethnicities that it the Tarim Basin, Buddhism transformed.

It would have been surprising had Buddhism not changed in Central Asia, where it was subjected to the influence of Iranian Mazdaism, Nestorian Christians (highly effective evangelists[14]), local religions, and, after the eighth century, Islam. Buddhism became very popular in China, especially under the Han Dynasty (one of whose emperors, Ming, interpreted a dream he had had about a golden flying deity as a revelation of Buddha), though in a corrupted form tainted by local Taoism and, above all, by popular magic practices.[15] The religion began a new life in China; it saw the creation, for example, of the Pure Land school, which taught that one could be reborn in Paradise (the Pure Land) merely by meditating on Amitabha ten times. Obviously a little too easy, this promise recalls the Christian device of indulgences.

That an imported religion could be so successful is surprising, considering the amount of baggage it had to sacrifice. Its popularity can be explained by an about-face: while Buddhism originally claimed that the soul does not exist, a radical idea that flew in the face of ancestor cults as much as did Taoism with its two-souls concepts, the new Buddhists declared that the soul was indestructible. Once the Void, Nirvana now became immortality.[16] While the Buddha had opted for a middle way that did not exclude the passions, it was now preached that these had to be suppressed—a rapprochement with the Taoists. Last, the virtues of charity and compassion were now being emphasized, which could not help but conciliate the Confucians. Another concession was that the Bodhisattva Avalokitesvara changed sexes and became a female deity identified with the Chinese mother-goddess Kuan-yin and her Tibetan homologue, Tara the White. This "Confucianized" rather than Indian Buddhism became pragmatic, even earthly: "Monasteries ran oil presses and general stores, maintained roads, and even engaged in commerce and moneylending."[17]

Of Evil little was said, however, and of the Devil even less. The T'ien-tai sect taught that the whole universe resided at every moment in every mote of dust. Did the Devil have to be looked for in every grain of rice?

When Buddhism became the state religion under the T'ang Dynasty and its monks found themselves compelled to turn to Confucian functionaries in government offices for their certificates of ordination (the Chinese mania for bureaucracy is not a recent development), even then no one conceived of the Devil. The state power, always ready to deem what is good and what is bad, always ready to see Evil as the product of a supernatural spirit, might have wished otherwise, but the wielders of power themselves had been trained by Taoists, Confucians, and Buddhists, and would have had a difficult time trying to believe in the existence of an Evil One. Granted, there still were, here and there, superstitious minds who thought that the vegetative souls of the resentful dead were bent on tormenting them; if they wanted to pay shamans the coin of the realm to make sacrifices and intone prayers that would drive those phantoms back to whence they had come, so be it—it was better to tolerate such practices than run the risk of disturbing the civic peace. The most important thing for the officials and governors was keeping things running smoothly, not provoking revolutions. Even in Japan, when the excesses of the Sudden Illumination sect (Ch'an, which became Zen) became intolerable, still no Devil loomed on the horizon.

Yet Zen did not lack the sort of full-blown fanaticism that would later lead Christians to believe that the Devil was roving about with his tail and his cloven hoofs. The sect derived from two bodies of teaching, that of the Boddhidharma, a buddha who came from India in 470 to settle in Canton (a half century later he headed farther north), and that of the monk Tao-sheng, who also lived in the fifth century. The school taught that the Awakening or Illumination—

wu in Chinese and *satori* in Japanese—had little to do with poring over texts: it came or it didn't, and that was it. It happened only if one knew how to empty oneself; at that moment, Truth flooded in.

Described in these terms, the original Zen seems like peaceful mysticism—although it was inclined toward rather colorful excesses. Boddhidharma, it is said, once fell so deeply into a trance that he remained in it for nine years; he didn't even notice when his legs fell off. Since the batting of his eyelids distracted him, he cut them off. As the master I Hsuan counseled, a Zen disciple should never let his meditating be disturbed at any cost: "Kill anything in your way. If you encounter Buddha, kill him. If you encounter the Master of Masters, if you encounter the *arhats* [sages who have attained Nirvana and, having spent their passions, are dispensed from reincarnation], kill them." It was a bloody program, but it eliminated the very basis for the Devil or demons, since there is nothing in the Void, neither God nor Devil. At the same time, writes René Sieffert, in Japan the sect's violence was adopted by members of the military class "who had come to understand how they could benefit from its mental techniques to obtain complete mastery over the body, sureness of reflexes, and contempt for death."[18] The martial arts were born.

Japan accepted Buddhism, which had arrived by way of Korea, after initially regarding it with suspicion. The country already had a religion of its own, Shinto, the "Way" (as in *tao*), or the "teachings" of the gods, known as *kami*. The acceptance, however, was not universal; the thirteenth-century monk Nichiren, the founder of a sect of his own, called Zen "demonic" and accused one of its branches, the Shingon (which had become nationalized and was even protected by the emperors), of "destroying the country"— although it is also true that Nichiren was fanatical and unstable.[19]

Above and beyond the complexities of the Japanese language, Shinto is difficult to grasp since it defies such major Western ideas as the very concept of religion itself. As the Japan specialist Jean Herbert writes, it "is not a religion like any other. Entirely devoid of dogmas, its only sacred writing being short texts that are very hard to interpret, and never having codified its moral tenets or established any ritual, Shinto is above all an awareness of the links that bind the Japanese to their fellow countrymen, to nature, and to the deity."[20]

The absence of an ethics means the absence of a definition of both what we call "Evil" and of a counterdeity to symbolize it. To say that there is no Devil in Shinto, however, might be too hasty. Shinto does in fact allow for the existence of celestial and terrestrial discord. In one of the many versions of the Shinto cosmogonic myths, conflict erupted when the two original spirits (there are myriad others), Izanagi and Izanami, engendered the mutually antagonistic universal masters, Amaterasu-o-mi-kami, the sun goddess, and her brother Susano-wo. One was associated with the sky, the other with the Earth (there was a third child, Isuki-yomi, the moon god). Susano-wo was unhappy with his domain—the Ocean of Plains, or in other words, dry land—and cried so much that he dried up all the rivers and seas. He wanted to rejoin his mother in the Lower Country, the underworld, a desire that earned him expulsion from Heaven at the hands of his father, Izanagi. Before the order for his expulsion was carried out, Susano-wo asked if he could see his sister Amaterasu for a moment, after which he promised he would leave forever. Amaterasu was alarmed at the arrival of her angry and impetuous brother, so along with her handmaidens she barricaded herself into the hall where she was weaving clothes for the celestial beings. This lack of sisterly love is explainable by the fact that the terrestrial *kami* couldn't have access to the celestial domain, since that would be against nature. Susano-wo nevertheless burst his way in, and Amaterasu's handmaidens, feeling themselves violated, thrust their weaving implements into their vaginas. Amaterasu resisted, then went off to hide in a boulder.[21] Vegetable life in the form of a tree, animal life in the form of a bird, the reproductive faculty as symbolized by a female *kami* exposing herself, a man displaying jewels (in other words, the human capacity for producing riches and beauty), and finally the perfect mirror (which points to the possibility of the human reflecting the divine) persuaded Amaterasu to leave her hiding place and return to Heaven. Susano-wo was permanently banished to the realm of the earthly.

There are several versions of this original antagonism, of which the foregoing is merely a synthesis. The symbolism is obvious: the opposition of irreconcilable celestial and terrestrial powers. Susano-wo, the terrestrial, manifests character faults—rashness, lack of decency, and excitability—that could be ascribed to Evil, or at the very least to the absence of wisdom. In one version of one of Shinto's principal sacred texts, the *Nihongi*, it is written: "This *kami* was one of a perverse nature and delighted in whining and being angry. . . . That is why his parents told him: 'Were you to reign on Earth, the result would certainly be the destruction of many lives.'" In another text, the *Bingo-fudoki*, it is written that Susano-wo destroyed the whole human race, sparing only his brother Somin (who had given him shelter one night) as well as Somin's wife and son. Like so many other Asian gods, though, he is ambivalent, since it is also he who teaches his host various agricultural techniques. He is not a demon but a contradictory spirit who embodies the Asian sense of the world's complexity. And he is not considered the Devil in Japan, where he is worshiped in some temples.

Shinto certainly recognizes the duality of the *kami*, who come in good forms and bad. There are indeed demons in Japan, but they are terrestrial *kami* as opposed to celestial ones. If they are volatile, it is because terrestrial life is too. This is not to say that Shinto considers Creation impure. "Shinto," Herbert writes, "envisions Creation as an event for which humanity must be profoundly grateful, and it makes no reference to its impending dissolution." The presence of evil in the world implies neither that the world is bad, nor that Evil is eternally distinct from Good, nor that it has a local habitation; evil, rather, is the product of the gods' ire.

Asia has certainly believed in bad gods, or in gods that are alternately bad and good. As J. M. Martin writes, "The Ainu of the Kurile Islands and Hokkaido . . . believe in the existence of bad gods, but these have no role in governing the world; only the good gods have jurisdiction over that."[22] The Tchuktche and the Koriak believe that both kinds of gods exist, although they seem to have a fairly low opinion of the bad ones, since all that is needed to chase them off is a drum, as if they were wolves or foxes (although the drum, as Martin adds, plays "a fundamental role in shamanic rites"). To the Koreans, "the gods are depicted as spirits scattered throughout nature; on the condition that no one has caused them displeasure, they are not to be feared."

The central point is that the higher one rises on the Asian social ladder, the less belief in demons one finds. To primitive rural peoples, demons are rude beings on a rank with animals; in the worldview of the literate population, they are interpretations of physical phenomena. Like everywhere else in the world, superstition prowls at the base of society. From this it could be deduced that in Asia it was the literate aristocracy that aborted the infernal egg; yet although to say so might not be incorrect, the argument remains uncorroborated, since the same does not seem to hold true in other countries and continents that possess a literate aristocracy.

It seems that much in Asia would have disposed religions to bringing the Devil into the world—notably, the superstition of local primitive peoples fueled by archaic religions and authoritarian state hegemony. However, two decisive elements intervened. The first was the size of the countries involved, along with their endlessly fluid frontiers—India is more than a country, it is a continent, and China's history is forty centuries of constantly redrawn borders. To paraphrase George Bernard Shaw's apothegm, a continent can be policed some of the time and a country can (relatively speaking) be policed all of the time, but a continent cannot be policed all of the time. Each new invasion, like each new expansion, produced cultural shocks that sounded the death knell for the dominant ideology.

Second, Asia's two great religions, Buddhism and Taoism (not counting Confucianism, its third great philosophy), were established by exceptional thinkers who, from the first, distinguished between ethics (which is a function of earthly society) and a supreme deity, whom they both refused to endow with human traits (and whom the Buddha went so far as to equate with the Void). In a place where prophets ought to have transcended preexisting beliefs in order to reinforce them (which was the case, at the very same time, with Zoroaster), each created a wholly new system of thought. The larval demons that ran rife through the countryside, terrifying peasants and the illiterate, did survive; at no point, however, did they reach the adult state of our own Devil.

The conclusion seems to be that the act of writing had exorcised Hell and its denizens—which are, as the Tibetan admonition to the dying points out, merely phantasms, hallucinations that a strong and true spirit should be able to sweep aside effortlessly.

It is with this farewell to demons—and to the Devil—that we shall leave Asia. The first Western travelers to the continent reported images of fire-spitting dragons (perhaps the enormous lizards of the Komodo Islands in Indonesia). What is certain is that Asia's dragons are nothing more than fantastic decorative motifs, or at most subterranean spirits whose self-pride must be respected.

When an edifice is constructed in Hong Kong, the builder must make sure he isn't disturbing a dragon. After the magnificent Bank of China skyscraper was erected, it turned out that this protocol had been overlooked. A sacrifice was made belatedly, but the over-all costs ended up being somewhat higher than anyone anticipated.

CHAPTER 4

Zoroaster, the First Ayatollahs, and the True Birth of the Devil

Some four millennia ago, hordes of horsemen from the south of present-day Russia—a vast region encompassing the Dnieper and Donetz basins, the low valley of the Volga, and the Kazakhstan steppes—descended through the passes of the Caucasus to settle on the fertile plains of Iran. They exchanged the shores of the Black and Azov seas for those of the Caspian and the Persian Gulf; some of their tribes headed for Greece and Anatolia, while others pushed toward southern Scandinavia and Finland and eventually, around 2000 B.C., reached the British Isles. They are easy to picture, dressed in close-fitting tunics and wearing caps like modern-day balaclavas, riding smallish horses, shouting out in their guttural language so as to be heard over the rumble of the carts laden with women, children, and baggage that followed in their wake.

Lying dormant among that baggage was one of the most volatile explosives ever imagined. It was nothing at first, a few beliefs symbolized in the form of little statues and amulets, but it bore the seeds of the Devil. These emigrants, a collection of warriors and shepherds today known as the Kurgan people (from the Russian word for "barrow"), were to found the first religion in the world that pitted a unique Devil against an equally unique God.[1]

These peoples have come to be called the Indo-Europeans, after the community of languages, all related to Sanskrit, that they spoke. The near totality of European languages, from High and Low German to Latin, Greek, and French, as well as Armenian, Norwegian, and Lithuanian, are thus all descended from Sanskrit; from Vladivostok to Los Angeles and Rio de Janeiro via Paris, Rome, and Athens, all the cultures that today we call "Western" arose out of the Indo-European invasion. Many of the systems we rely on to interpret the world, including our deities, would not exist had the Kurgan people not seized the Near and Middle East as well as almost the whole of Europe.

Despite their tribalism, when the Kurgan people arrived in the Middle East they possessed a structured social system as well as advanced technology and a religion. Politically, the power of the king was controlled by a council of aristocrats that prefigured the parliaments of truly modern states. Technologically, they had not only the wheel and the know-how to navigate rivers but also plows: they tilled the soil to produce the grains from which they ground flour. Philosophically, they believed in the immortality of the soul and a continued life in the hereafter, ruled over by a male god wielding an ax or a hammer. They worshiped a mother-goddess undoubtedly inherited from their predecessors, as well as the sun and sacred fire; they believed the horse, the snake, and the boar had magical attributes.

When the amalgamation with Indian religions began and how it occurred are unclear. Hindus were settled in the Near East by the last third of the second millennium B.C., as is proven by the list of gods recorded by King Matizawa of Mitanni in his treaty with the Hittite king Suppiluliumas in 1380 B.C., the same gods—the Mithra-Varuna-Indra trinity and the Nasatayas—as in the Hindu pantheon. For a long period, India and Iran shared the same gods, the deities featured in the sacred writings of the Vedas.

At least two and perhaps three millennia before the beginning of the Iron Age, the Indo-Europeans had established a true civilization, maybe the first worthy of the name. When they settled in Iran, they constructed fortified towns built on heights and girdled by semisubterranean villages. From there they spread eastward and out into the rest of the world—not only politically but intellectually as well.

The Indo-Europeans were probably the single most significant factor in the development of ancient religions, the greater number of Eastern and eastern Mediterranean ones having been influenced by both the geographical expansion that ensured the civilization's safety and by its advanced political organization. The Hellenic military resistance, which intensified with the Median wars, was not an obstacle; Indo-European influences can be found, for instance, in Greek Orphism. Postexilic Judaism, the various strains of Jewish and Christian Gnosticism, Christianity and Shiite Islam all bear its mark to some degree. It can be argued that much of the monotheistic theology that founded modern cultures was forged within the Iranian matrix; our Jewish, Christian, and Islamic angels and archangels, and consequently our Devil, were born there. It was from here that Islam borrowed its image of Paradise: as early as the *Avesta*, we find evidence of the belief that the elect soul is gathered up by a beautiful young girl who represents all the good works the deceased has performed. The Iranian religion thus warrants particular attention and, because of its immense influence, close analysis.

The Indo-European invaders did not arrive to find an unoccupied land; Iran's history, indeed, is exceptionally long. Unlike the rest of the world, Iran seems to have been continuously inhabited since the last two Ice Ages. There are incontestable traces of human habitation there dating from at least the Paleolithic era, or thirty-five thousand years ago, while finds uncovered in western Iran's Zagros Mountains in the thirties indicate that this time frame can be pushed back to the middle Paleolithic (Mousterian) era; the possibility of discovering similar evidence dating to the early Paleolithic era, one hundred and fifty thousand years ago, cannot be excluded. Iran has had a developed social sense for many millennia.

In addition, the communities the Indo-Europeans encountered were not scattered, as was the case in Asia, but concentrated on plateaus. Based around agriculture and the domestication of plants and animals, these were history's first permanent villages. As evidenced by the sites of Guran, Asiab, Ganj-e-Darah, and Ali Kosh in the west, and Karim Shahir and Zawi Semi Chanidar in the east (which today straddle the Iraqi border), Iran was one of the first places in the world, if not *the* first, where the neolithic revolution occurred. The foundations of a historical civilization had already been laid, and villages proliferated in the highlands and in lower Khuzistan.[2]

A religion was practiced in these villages, although there is little hope of ever knowing much about it. It can be supposed to have been polytheistic and to have varied from village to village. The Iranian plateaus that witnessed the first appearance of a social sense thus also displayed a religious awareness—although, properly speaking, it wasn't here that the Iranian religion began (the plateaus remained relatively underpopulated until the middle of the third millennium B.C.) but, rather, in the kingdom of Elam, which encompassed Khuzistan and a fringe of neighboring mountains. Elam counted four towns, including Suse, its capital.

The Elamese royalty was very ancient, dating back to 2700 B.C. Subject to strict dynastic rules, it was also under severe strategic pressure, since it had to keep the plateaus under control *and* repel the expansionist drives of the peoples to its east. Until the establishment of the Median kingdom in the middle of the ninth century B.C., the history of Elam was a succession of conquests of and invasions by Ur, Babylonia, and Assyria. Underscoring the etymology of the word (*religio* deriving from *ligare*, to bind), its religion thus performed a political function. When the Medes and then the Persians arrived, they found strong and long-standing political and religious structures among the Elamites—who remain unidentified to this day, but who were definitely not Indo-European.

Well before the Indo-European invasions, therefore, Iran was exceptionally well suited to the development of a centralized nation-state and a strong center of power. Potentates not only in Iran but in all ancient civilizations almost always invest themselves with what could be called "the signature of fate": even if popularly elected, they still are chosen by destiny—or, in other words, by the unapproachable deities whose earthly representative they are. The potentate is both the guarantor of the gods' cult and the enforcer of their will, which he himself expresses.

The divine cult thus came to apply not only to the deities but to the ruler himself, who consequently could not tolerate any excessive loss of control over the pantheon (although in Iran he eventually would be able to do so, as for instance under Cyrus and Darius, when royal power was unchallenged and at its peak). Too many nonhierarchized, overly diversified gods competing with one another would in effect place the king's own power up for grabs.

The political system required a religion that was strong and sufficiently rich in narrative and symbol to seize the collective imagination. What answered this need was Vedism, based on the sacred writings of the Rig-Veda (written between 1200 and 900 B.C.). By the time the Medes arrived, the whole Iranian people was Vedic.

But what does "the Iranian people" really mean? The description includes not only those of specifically Indo-European stock who came to occupy what is roughly present-day Iran, first in the third millennium B.C. and then again around 1700 B.C., but also Scythians and Sarmatians from either side of the Caspian as well as the Alains from the region between the Don and the Urals, who, like the Sarmatians, were nomads. It can be supposed that the city-states that helped to create the extremely structured character of the Iranian religion also extended its influence over neighboring peoples—mainly to the east (Sogdiana, Bactria or today's Afghanistan, Sachas, and Arachosia) and south (Carmania or today's Iranian Belushistan). However, their influence also extended over the Parthians (who lived between the Sarmatians and Iranians in a part of present-day Turkmenistan), as well as Assyria and Babylonia (which lay between the nearby Tigris and Euphrates rivers), and finally over the Kassite kingdom (which roughly covered what today is Iraq).

Vedism's hour of glory came with the Medes. Founded, according to Herodotus, by Deioces in 728 B.C. (though other evidence suggests a century earlier than that), the Mede kingdom, which some ten centuries after the last Indo-European invasion would become the nucleus of a new Iranian empire, was a warrior nation, and a successful one at that, except for a Scythian interregnum that lasted from the second half of the seventh century B.C. to the end of the sixth. From the middle of the sixth and in the fifth centuries, the

Achaemenid era, it was one of the greatest empires in history, stretching from Libya to India, from the Black and Caspian and Aral seas to Ethiopia, and covering the entire eastern coast of Arabia and the Persian Gulf. Called the Empire of the Seven Seas—Mediterranean, Red, Black, Caspian, Aral, and Arabian, as well as the Persian Gulf—it was one of the largest in history. Only Alexander, who conquered almost all of it, would bring it to its knees.

Other than the Rig-Veda there are few texts available on polytheistic, pre-Zoroastrian Iranian Vedism and its structure. It is known that the religion revolved around two main groups of supernatural entities, the *ahura*s or higher deities and the *daeva*s or lesser ones. These were ruled by two principal gods, Ahura Mazda and Mithra, who together governed the course of the sun, moon, and stars. There was no known countergod or demon comparable in importance to the Devil.

One fundamentally Vedic belief, however, that of salvation, an entirely new idea in the history of religions, suddenly came to assume great importance. (The Devil found as fertile a ground in this theme as a bacteria culture might in a petri dish—because if you say "salvation" you also say "damnation," and once you've said "damnation" you've already said "the Devil.") In Sarmatian and Alainic theology—the theology of the Scythians is little known—we for the first time witness the appearance of the irrevocable judgment over a dead person's soul. In the Ossetian funerary ceremony, the *bahfaldisyn*, a participant speaks out to recall that the soul of the deceased, which has left on horseback for the land of the heroes, the *Narts*, must cross a narrow bridge, the *Shinvat Peretu* or "Bridge of the Petitioner." If his soul is righteous, he will cross; if it is not, the bridge will collapse under him and his mount. In the Medean Zurvanite sect (named after Zurvan, the god of time and destiny), the bridge becomes as sharp as the edge of a sword when the guilty ride across it.

Where do the guilty go? If the judgment of Rashu, the god entrusted with deciding the soul's fate, is negative, the sinner will go to an infernal place of flames and terrible smells, *Hamestagan*. Yet this is only a temporary hell, since it will vanish with the universal resurrection at the Last Judgment, a concept that would become familiar to Christians. In short, it is closer to the Christian purgatory than to the Christian Hell. Nevertheless, it is obvious that the concept of salvation inherently entails that of sin.

This salvation theme appears even more clearly in the pre-Zoroastrian myth of Mithra, a savior who, like the Christian one, is announced by prophets and whose birth, recalling that of Jesus, takes place in a cave, with the miraculous child's arrival heralded by the appearance of an exceptional star. Mithra is the celestial intermediary between two antagonists, Ahura Mazda and Ahriman or Angra Manyu, the Good One and the Bad One, the governors of the universe, both of whom are engendered by unimportant demiurges whose identities vary from school to school. In the specifically Iranian school, for example, it is Ahura Mazda who conceives himself; according to the Zurvanite school, though, it is Zurrah, a hermaphroditic god, who engenders the twins Ahura Mazda and Ahriman, or Good and Evil. Later on, Mithra would supplant Vishnu, who in pre-Zoroastrian Vedism had been the world's savior: while gods and demons warred with one another, setting the world ablaze and even threatening to destroy space (an advanced metaphysical concept for the time), Vishnu had smothered the flames with his expandable body and thus allowed the world to be reborn.

The Iranian religion, which remained in existence until the third century A.D. and the Parthian conquest, did far more than any other religion to mold the Devil. The extent to which a deity can be imbued with a social role becomes clear when we look at Aryaman.

Aryaman, whose name means "friend," is often associated with Mithra and Varuna; along with Bhago, he is one of Mithra's principal "assistants." "He maintains the strength of the various bonds that united Arya society," writes Georges Dumézil. He also guaranteed hospitality obligations, freedom of travel (on earthly roads as well as in the hereafter), marriages, ritual, and gifts and loans. The main supernatural activity of this minister of internal affairs, so to speak, was to supervise the "Fathers," a term that Dumézil points out includes a number of ancestors as well as all the minor spirits. This aspect of the deity is significant in that it shows that the Aryas, the first true Aryans, had deliberately and directly fashioned their gods, or at least Aryaman, according to the workings of their society. To the Iranians, the gods existed to administer affairs on Earth.

Even after the Zoroastrian reforms, when Aryaman was stripped of his status as a deity only to resurface under the name Sraosa,[3] this "god of the Iranian fatherland" retained practically all his functions and was even given a new one, which made him the exact prefiguration of Christianity's guardian angel. Sraosa "protects against the demons that want to drag [the soul] to hell," Dumézil writes.

Iranian polytheism made up a centralized celestial government that, like earthly government, hinged upon a provisional balance between Good and Evil, and promised to disappear only after the ultimate victory of Good in an envisioned future. It was a government of conquest exactly like those of Iran, especially during the glorious Achaemenid era. Vedism reflected the royal and aristocratic political structure of the empire.

And then came Zoroaster (Zarathustra in ancient Persian, Zarthosht in modern Persian; what the name means is unclear), who was probably born around 628 B.C. and died around 551. Plato called him "the son of Oromazdes,"[4] certainly an image only, since Oromazdes is of course Ahura Mazda, one of the Vedic pantheon's major gods. In the first century A.D., Plutarch also ascribed to him a relationship with the gods,[5] while Pliny reported that he laughed on the day he was born.[6] To the Greeks, he was therefore legendary, the son of a god or a demigod himself. According to Saint John Chrysostom, Zoroaster had retired to a mountain that was soon after consumed by a fire; the prophet was unscathed, and only after that did he begin to speak to the people.

Zoroaster's personality warrants a closer look, since it is hard to imagine that a reformer's character isn't a determining factor in his will to effect reform, much as it's hard to imagine any reform not taking place at an opportune or appropriate historical moment. We would undoubtedly know a lot more about Zoroaster had not the thirteenth volume of the *Avesta*,[7] the *Spend Nask*, been lost—it contained his biography. The rest of the *Avesta*s do not provide much historical information about him. One, the *Yasht*, claims that all nature rejoiced at his birth, and that he was a poet and a sacrificial priest—an interesting point in that Zoroaster criticized those who sacrificed livestock. Yet the few personality traits that can be gleaned from the *Avesta*s are more revealing than they at first appear.

Anticipating the temptation of Jesus in the desert by more than six centuries, another *Avesta*, the *Vendidad*, reports that Satan tried to entice Zoroaster into abandoning his faith; the *Yasht* says that after a struggle with demons he triumphed and drove them away. The later books that speak of him—the *Dinkard*, the *Shah-Nama*, and the *Zardusht-Nama*—are hagiographies filled with tales of wonders and miraculous healings. By all accounts, both in his own day and over later centuries Zoroaster was considered not just a prophet but a supernatural being, which has led some Iran experts to call him a myth, much as some historians have called the existence of Jesus into doubt. It is the fate of many a prophet.

Zoroaster must have been born somewhere; while some historians claim it was in Bactria, others say it was in Medea or Persia. According to two *Avesta*s, the *Yasna* and the *Vendidad*, the house of his father, Purusaspa ("he of the spotted horse"), lay on the Dareja River in the province of Airan Vej; since another ancient text specifies that it was somewhere near Atropatene, one can deduce that it was in fact situated on the Arax River in the district of Aran, which is on the northwestern border of ancient Medea, close to the Armenian frontier and the shores of the Caspian Sea. He thus came from the land of the magi, and no doubt he was one. He was married, since we know the name of one of his children, his youngest daughter, Purucista. From the *Yasht*, we also know that he came from a clan of horse breeders, the Spitamas ("brilliant on the attack"). His full name would therefore have been Zarathustra Spitama.

Zoroaster made enemies easily. Not a wealthy man, as is quite clear from his imploration to Ahura Mazda ("I know, o Sage, why I am powerless; it is because I have little livestock and few men"), he somehow earned the enmity of a society of haughty and rich young warriors. We even know the names of the two of them, since Zoroaster cursed them in front of his disciples. One was called

Bandva; the other, "the princeling of Vaepya," had refused Zoroaster and his animals shelter one bitter winter night.

We now have enough to sketch out a portrait: a poor and temperamental poet, nonviolent, sensitive, perhaps a shaman, and someone who bore grudges. He attacked with particular virulence those who engaged in bloody sacrifices even though, as Mircea Eliade points out, such rites characterize men's cults. It is tempting to imagine that, as the son of a horse breeder, Zoroaster would have felt repelled by their sacrifice. It is even more tempting to picture Zoroaster's aversion to animal sacrifice as reinforced by the character of the sacrificers themselves, which was brutal and proud, as the *Gathas* show. Still, it would be rash to take this portrait too far twenty-six centuries after the fact. The only sure thing is that the prophet hated cruel aristocrats.

None of this, of course, is by any stretch intended to suggest that Mazdaism was solely the product of Zoroaster's personal rancor. What it does indicate is that Zoroaster's character, inasmuch as it can be understood from the few available details, seemed disposed toward rejecting an aristocratic, violent, and much too secular religion.[8] A religion of the powerful, Vedism as it then existed in Iran left the people with no real spiritual recourse. Yet Zoroaster himself was probably a magus—the situation could not have left him indifferent. The spiritual fervor of his *Gathas*, their torment and lyricism, is also enriched by compassion. Zoroaster is one in the long line of great prophets who are motivated by solicitude and tenderness for their people, and the time for him to act was ripe.

Zoroaster's appearance coincided with the establishment of the great Iranian empire under the reigns of Nebuchadrezzar II and Cyaxares, after the defeat of the Assyrians and the subjugation of all of Iran's neighboring countries. The empire was united against its enemies; it was centralized, and its capital, Persepolis, was magnificent. In Suse, Ecbatane, and other large towns, there were towering palaces and huge temples amid elaborate gardens, all the private domain of the upper classes. If Darius manifested the rudiments of a social conscience, as evidenced by his edict setting hourly wages for workers, the people remained excluded from the great cult ceremonies.

The need for a religion that matched the scale of the young nation began to be felt acutely. The size of the empire and the number of religions it encompassed threatened the clergy with decline. The magi were no more than one clerical caste among many others, some of which were corrupt; the Babylonian magi, for instance, were outright charlatans. The religion of the Median magi had to radically differentiate itself, through its rigor and simplicity, from the polytheisms of the day. It had to impose itself not by the magnificence of its rites, its sacrifices, or the power of its adherents but, rather, by its inner hold on the individual—and, to create that, it had to foster a feeling of urgency about what was at stake: the entering of or exclusion from Heaven, salvation or eternal disgrace.

A prototype of Jesus, as the legend of Zoroaster's birth goes to show, he was the founder of the first true monotheism, as his "evangelical" hymns, the *Gathas*, prove and as Pahlavi texts and Greek historians confirm.[9] The polytheistic façade of his teachings is only a vestige of the old religion, whose total destruction he had the wisdom not to call for.

Zoroastrianism was not created in one stroke, with the magi suddenly handed a religious system that was complete, immutable, and ready to go. On the contrary, the *Gathas* make clear that the process was gradual.[10] Fire was first identified with the Holy Spirit, then with the sun, the visible manifestation of the Lord, and finally with the highest of the gods, Ahura Mazda. The restructuring initially limited itself to condemning the orgiastic excesses that accompanied sacrifices and the ritual consumption of *haoma*.[11] The violent hallucinations it engendered were probably intensified by the sight of blood. In his youth, Zoroaster may have participated in the ecstatic hemp ceremonies of Scythian shamans; these would have seemed harmless compared to the Vedic celebrations.

Zoroaster's restructuring of Vedism indeed began as a reform; initially it seemed moderate and conciliating. It was only later, with the last of the *Gathas*, that it became an outright revolution, with monotheism well and truly established; as Dumézil points out, the ancient trinity of Varuna, Mithra, and Indra disappeared. The one and only god worthy of veneration became Ahura Mazda. The ancient god Indra was reduced to the rank of demon, as were the "secondary" deities, the Nasatya twins. According to the *Gathas*, Ahura Mazda is the creator of Heaven and Earth, of the spiritual and material worlds. He is the sovereign, lawmaker, supreme judge, master of day and night, the center of nature, and inventor of moral law. It would be hard to describe the God of the three later monotheisms any better. The relationship among Mazdaism, Judaism, Christianity, and Islam is obvious.

Ahura Mazda is clearly masculine, and he has no companion. The patriarchal system could not conceive of power being shared by a female or even that a female deity could be associated with it.

The later *Avestas* depict God as being surrounded by seven benevolent immortals, the *Amesha Spenta*. The first of these is the Holy Spirit (or, formerly, Fire); the other six are Justice, Rightness of Thought, Devotion, the Desired Realm, Abundance, and Immortality. These entities are creatures of God and must obey the same moral law as Ahura Mazda's human followers. The Desired Realm, or Kingdom to Come, is significant in that it bears the seeds of Judeo-Christian apocalyptic thought and eschatology.

The *Gathas* teach that, in the beginning, there were two spirits, and each made a choice. The first, Ahura Mazda, chose the good and became the "Wise God," a clear forerunner of our God; the second, Ahriman—Angra Manyu, the spirit of Evil—chose the bad and became the God of Evil, whose worshipers are "the followers of the lie," *dregvant*, who are led astray by untruth or *druj*. Iran thus witnessed the first appearance of the Devil.

Ahriman recruited the old gods, in particular the *daevas*: Indra (who became Indra-vayu, the god of death), the ancient Vedic Nasatya deity Saruva (demon of death and illness), Akoman (Evil Spirit), Tauru, Ashma (no doubt the biblical father of Asmodea, and demon of violence, anger, and criminality), Az (demon of lust), Mithrandruj (He Who Lies to Mithra, the demon of falsity), Jeh (the whore-demon created by Ahriman to corrupt the human race), and even—no tremendous surprise—Zairi, the god associated with the ritual consumption of *haoma* or *soma*. This was the final blow to Vedism's orgiastic practices and the affirmation of a religion of moderation and spirituality that anticipated the three monotheisms.

One vital point stands out: From now on there is a specific and unambiguous god of Evil. Ahriman is the peer of the god of Good, his twin brother Ahura Mazda, and the two are destined to battle mercilessly. In some lost *Avesta* apocalyptic texts, traces of which can be found in Pahlavi writings, it is foretold that a great war will come to pass during which Heaven will send down a great king, the reincarnated Mithra the Savior, who will destroy the forces of Evil by fire and sword. For the first time, the great prophetic tenets of the monotheisms appear: Good and Evil have become transcendent principles. The ambiguities associated with the pragmatic interpretation of existence have vanished.

Ahriman's malevolent servants included Azaziel, the demon of wild places who is incarnated as the Goat and as such transmitted wholesale to Judaism; Leviathan and Rahab, demons of chaos; and the pathetic Lilith, whose legend, also adopted into Judaism, holds that she was the barren first wife of Adam whose rejection at the hands of the First Man impels her to rage around at night, seeking revenge.[12] Whether Jewish, Christian, or Muslim, we are still living with this heritage; we still know these demons.

Apparently, but only apparently, Zoroaster had not come up with anything radically new. The opposition of Ahura Mazda and Ahriman was already present in Vedism, if only implicitly. Perhaps the reformer had merely restructured the pantheon—thrown out the lesser gods and banned sacrifices to Ahriman and Vedism's ancient secondary deities, the *daeva*s. In fact, though, the changes were radical: Zoroaster made the dualism of Good and Evil official. At the same time, he also invented demonology.[13]

One detail about Zoroaster's biography stands out: at the age of forty, or around 588 B.C., he converted a king named Vishtashpa, about whom little more is known than that he was supposed to be the father of Darius I, that he reigned over Chorasmia, a land south of the Aral Sea, and that he was Zoroaster's protector for the rest of his life. The significance of these facts will become apparent soon.

For now, the important thing is that Zoroaster invented a Good and Evil that were immanent and preexisting, and whose conflict was not to be resolved until the end of time. His theological conception of the world is so close to that of Christianity that one wonders if the church Fathers hadn't read the *Gathas* or even copied them[14]: life is only a passage in which each thought, word, and action determines the individual's fate in the hereafter, where the god of Good will punish the wicked and reward the virtuous. When the incarnated Mithra defeats Ahriman at the end of time, the dead will be resurrected; the Last Judgment will condemn the bad to Hell, while the good will live in Paradise for all eternity. The framework of the three monotheisms had been erected. The Devil's birth certificate was filled out by an Iranian prophet.

Historians formerly thought that Zoroaster's rejection of animal sacrifices led directly to the rejection of the deities to which they had been offered. It is hard, however, to picture Zoroaster as merely a party-pooper, since his goal was too obvious for that: more than repudiating orgiastic rituals and streamlining the pantheon, his reform was a top-to-bottom reformulation, with a complete ban on the ancient gods and the rites associated with them, as well as a radical reorganization of the divine hierarchy. On this point, however, historians are divided. Dumézil sees the reform as a "mere" substitution of gods[15] while Molé tends to portray it as the creation of a whole new theology.[16] Jean de Menasce believes that Zoroaster rejected the practice of sacrifices because it had become so uncontrollable.[17] The essence, however, is the unprecedented creation of a God-Devil pairing and of an equally unprecedented Good/Evil ethical dualism. The hypothesis that Zoroaster "reformed" the Iranian religion on the Protestant model is not entirely satisfactory.

Indeed, it's difficult to see why Zoroaster attempted his reforms when he did, against what seems to have been quite determined resistance (judging by the *Gathas*, which say that Zoroaster had to soften his stand and resign himself to tolerating some sacrifices and some of the ancient gods). It is even more difficult to see why the magi would have espoused Zoroastrianism and its Good-Evil dualism, and yet they did—because theology was not the only subject of reform.

As a priest and magus, Zoroaster was no doubt aware of the threat to his caste posed by the ambiguity of the gods and perhaps—though this is only a supposition—the danger of allowing religion too faithfully to reflect earthly society. Religion could never have power if it did not rest on unshakable pillars—that is, on a transcendent definition of Good and Evil whose arbiter on earth the clergy had to be. Only then could the priesthood consolidate its power.

More, Zoroaster strengthened the hand of the magus caste by arguing that the religion was of the people and worth anything only insofar as it retained the people's allegiance. This demagoguery initially had the advantage of rooting the clergy's power not only in the spiritual, in the definitions of Good and Evil, but also in the political, in the will of the people. Mazdaism created a parallel power that did not have to answer to kings, a reform unique in the history of civilization up to that point.

Although it was powerful, the magus caste felt threatened by a temporal power unrivaled in all of history. The strength of the priestly class paled against that of Cyrus and his generals, who were going from victory to victory and forging the first Persian empire. The Zoroastrian reforms at last gave the clergy a legitimacy independent of temporal power—which, however, it sometimes took too much to heart. In 522 B.C., while the Persian king Cambyses II was warring in Nubia (along with a phalanx of Jewish mercenaries), a rebellion broke out at home; an impostor claiming to be Cambyses' brother Bardiya had raised the provinces up against the absent king. The magi joined the rebels ("Bardiya" had promised to lower their taxes if they did), perhaps hoping that a king they helped to put on the throne would be more pliable. Their act was predicated on political ambition. In a stroke of bad luck for the empire, Cambyses meanwhile died. The impostor would have seized power but for a Chorasmian prince, later to be known as Darius I, who took the throne, consolidated his position, killed the impostor, and brought the magi to heel.

We shall take a closer look at this incident, since it is here that the key to the Devil's invention lies. The impostor, who was named Gaumata, was a magus. As with the present-day ayatollahs and the former shah, the magi plotted their coup d'état in the name of popular religion. With one of them on the throne, they hoped to establish the world's first theocracy, and they almost did. While he was briefly in power, Gaumata ordered, among other atrocities, that the temples reserved for the nobles be razed—in other words, he revoked the religious privileges of the nobility. That was a big mistake, since apart from a few satraps who sided with the impostor, the aristocracy was now determined to fight for its privileges, and with its help the royal power was restored.

Darius turned to the Achaemenid Dynasty; with the help of six of its princes, he skewered the false Bardiya on his own spear, cut off his head, and had it paraded in front of the populace. After his victory he had the nobility's temples rebuilt, even though he professed the cult of Ahura Mazda—although apparently not very enthusiastically, since the cult of the *daeva*s survived (his son Xerxes outlawed it throughout the empire). The victory, however, proved brief; Xerxes' successor, Ataxerxes II, reinstated a revised version of the ancient Vedic trilogy in which Mithra and Anahita were set beside the one god Ahura Mazda.

After his victory, Darius had the tale of his exploits engraved on the face of a cliff at Behistun in the Zagros Mountains, and he had it copied out in three languages—old Persian, Elamese, and Akkadian—so that no one would be unable to read it. In the text, Darius completely reclaims the role of legislator that the magi had tried to appropriate. The very fact that he did so is odd, however, since the monarch is by definition also the legislator. If Darius so vehemently insisted on retaining that right, it must be because it had been challenged.

That in fact was the case; the Zoroastrian priests had always tried to assume legislative power. The *Videvdat*, one of the five *Avesta*s written by Zoroaster himself, attempts to lay down not only religious but also civil law. Had their coup d'état worked, the magi would have granted the Devil, Ahriman, legal recognition. In the standard dream of every religious hierarchy, any breach of religious law would have been punished by the secular authorities; the Zoroastrian reform, which had begun with the naming of one sole God and one sole Devil, would have ended up with political power. It was politics that gave birth to the Devil, and the Devil is indeed a political invention.

The question arises as to whether the populist magi could be considered the forefathers of democracy. Although it might have seemed different in the eyes of Zoroaster himself, it is unlikely because it would imply the existence of very advanced political thought—and imply further that the magi were in a position to create a political party. This was not so: had they even tried, the monarchs, starting with Cyrus the Great, would have swept them away like so much straw. Second, no theocratic regime can be called a "democracy." No—if the magi turned to the people as the source of their power, it was for tactical purposes only.

The reason for the apparent "democracy" of Mazdaism lies elsewhere, in Zoroaster's brilliant intuition that religion could or should no longer address the empire's citizenry, but, instead, the individual himself. By preaching the salvation of the soul—that is, by moving the locus of happiness from this world to the next—Zoroaster stripped religion of the uncertainties of the ancient polytheism, in which the gift of Heaven could be bestowed by one god and taken away by another. If there was salvation, it now depended on one authority only. Zoroaster also wrested the individual from the grasp of the temporal powers, who had neither authority over Heaven nor the means to either grant or deny salvation.

From this point on, the clergy was invested with supreme power; it was capable of extending itself to the empire's frontiers and beyond, of placing itself over and above royal power. The only elements that were lacking for the religion's grip to become absolute were confession and sacraments, and in fact seven centuries later those complements to theocratic power would appear. Zoroaster's reform had sown hardy seeds, for the new Iranian religion would influence Judaism, which later sprouted Christianity.

Though severely checked by Darius, the magi survived insofar as they were the representatives of divine immanence (and, no doubt, thanks to popular support as well). They had partly won, especially once Zoroastrianism gained ground and Darius was compelled, on the surface at least, to pay homage to it. Some say that Darius was the son of Vishtashpa, the king whom Zoroaster had personally converted (this is not certain, for it has also been claimed that Darius was a relative of Cambyses). If it is true, however, then he would not have been able to reject the example set by his father—although it can be imagined that he was not thrilled at having to ordain the very priests who were challenging his power. Darius remained a Zoroastrian, but with reservations.

Most likely, Darius gave in to the Persian tradition of royal religious tolerance. Already under Cyrus, who ruled from around 550 to 539 B.C., all religions were permitted in Persia, even the Babylonian and Jewish. Zoroastrianism was practiced at court, but it was one religion among many others. Cyrus seems to have been a Zoroastrian, although it is not certain that his faith was as hard and fast as the priests would have liked. There are two reasons why this might be the case: first, had Cyrus been Zoroastrian, he would not have subscribed to the master's precept on exclusivity and forbidden sacrifices to any god other than Ahura Mazda; second, the religion itself had been forced to make various concessions[18] that rendered it less rigid.

Since the royal tolerance reduced their power and probably their income, it could not have pleased the Zoroastrian magi. By imposing the reformed cult of Ahura Mazda, Darius had nevertheless been forced to cross the magi's Rubicon, if such an anachronism be allowed. Despite the repression they had to endure, they had won an important battle by maintaining themselves as an independent religious power.

It is unclear who they were, these magi whose most illustrious member invented the Devil and who survived through to the New Testament, where they are present at the birth of Jesus. According to Herodotus, they were Medes. They were a caste of hereditary priests who augured on such occasions as the sacrifices that so galled Zoroaster. They apparently had arrived with the Mede invasion of the ninth century B.C.; no doubt because of their abilities at divining through astrology and their power as shamans, they apparently played an important role in the establishment of monarchy. They lasted through all the Iranian dynasties—Parthian, Seleucid, Achaemenid, and Sassanid—and their prestige only grew over the course of the centuries (but only theirs, since the Babylonian magi were generally deemed impostors).

This investigation could end here with the conclusion that Satan was born in Iran around the sixth century B.C., and that the magi held him over the baptismal font, as it were. His invention was politically motivated. The lesson is straightforward: Religious power is inimical to diversity and democracy, even in Heaven.

Overpopulated pantheons make for insubordinate mortals who are cynical about the immortals. The clergy in polytheisms also seems to be less cohesive: what right does a priest of Apollo have to tell a priest of Aphrodite or Hermes how to go about his business? It's everyone for himself and Zeus for all. Rivalries are bitter even in religions as centralized, in principle, as Christianity—Saul-Paul baptizing the uncircumcised, to the fury of the apostles who stayed behind in Jerusalem (Peter, James the Younger, Philemon, and John), or the bitter hatred between Antioch and Jerusalem or, later, between Antioch and Alexandria. If Zoroaster decided to reform the Iranian pantheon, it was because the religious power was too weak with respect to an ever-growing political power. Its cults were unorganized and its rites inchoate.

In a sense, the magi were the ancestors of today's ayatollahs. The product of a strong state, hardened by reaction and the Zoroastrian reforms, they couldn't help but cast an envious eye at the political power and attempt to forge a link between it and the religious power. However, it was here that the magi lost ground. They did indeed create the Devil, but they did not succeed in establishing him as a political opposition. Only the Christian church would carry off that feat.

CHAPTER 5

Mesopotamia

The Appearance of Sin

The history of Mesopotamia, which lay between the Tigris and the Euphrates in what is roughly present-day Iraq, is as swampy as much of the land itself. From Bani Lam in the northeast to An Nasiriyah in the west to the southernmost promontory, which is split in two by the Shatt-al-Arab that flows into the Persian Gulf, the whole region is one giant marsh. With a few exceptions, until the end of this century only the primitive *tarada*s and *balam*s, those slender, saber-prowed pirogues of the native swamp peoples could cut through it.

In the world's unconscious, Mesopotamia shares the fate of those places that ancient cartographers knew nothing about and defined with the three Latin words *Hic sunt leones*, "Here there are lions" —in other words, "Don't even bother." Venturing there today, amidst rush-dotted lakes that dusk transforms into seas of blood, the traveler would find it hard to believe that these flatlands saw the birth of such brilliant empires as Babylonia, Assyria, and Sumer. Still harder to believe is the fact that this was where the spiritual destiny of the West was forged.

Assur to the north and Babylon to the south, and within Babylonia itself the northern Akkad and the southern Sumer—in this flood-prone region, battling empires transformed first the fate of the East, then that of the West. The first loom appeared here around 6,300 B.C.; a few centuries later, the first wild cattle were domesticated and humanity learned to drink milk. Around 3,700 B.C., the first city-states sprang up in Sumer. Then, for the first time, the individual began to assert his uniqueness by using a signature; henceforth, a letter-sender could be identified by his seal. In 3,400 B.C. came the greatest invention of all time, the wheel. Around 3,100 B.C., writing was born in Sumer. The Bronze Age was still in full flower when the three thousand lines of the Gilgamesh epic were recorded on twelve tablets, which were later rediscovered in the royal libraries of Sennacherib and Assurbanipal at Nineveh. For the next four thousand years, all of humanity—actually, a few scholars tucked away in dusty libraries—knew that the Babylonian hero Gilgamesh rejected the advances of the goddess Ishtar, who was infatuated by his beauty; he, meanwhile, loved only his friend Enkiddu. When Enkiddu dies, the sorrow of Gilgamesh is uncontainable:

> Enkiddu, my friend, my little brother, desert panther,
> My friend who slew lions with me,
> My friend who faced hardship with me,
> His fate has found him;
> For six days and nights I have wept . . . .

The hero finally decides to confront Death itself on the banks of the Ocean of the Dead. The divine dancer, Siduri Sabitu, tries to reason with him and to show him the limits of human existence. In vain, though: Gilgamesh goes to the Beyond anyway, from where he will return with the knowledge of human frailty.[1] Utnapishtim, the lord of the Isle of Bliss on the other side of the Ocean of the Dead, teaches Gilgamesh that his heroic attributes are no more than a gift of the gods, that he has neither seized them for himself nor earned them as a reward. Divine injustice is encapsulated in a handful of verses: the powerful owe their strength to luck, the weak their weakness to misfortune.

This celebration of unconquerable virility is humanity's first great poem, and only the work of Homer compares to it in the expression of man's defiance against fate. If the presence of Evil within the *Gilgamesh* inspires its powerful depiction of despair, Mesopotamia had long known that it was the mere plaything of higher powers; it had experienced the Deluge, that unforgettable manifestation of the folly of the gods, whose tale Utnapishtim will relate to Gilgamesh.

The catastrophe of the Flood, which is recounted in cuneiform texts dating from around 2,000 B.C., did in fact take place, as is attested by archaeologists' discoveries of lime deposits in the upper strata of ancient sites—although no specific date for it has definitively been established. To the people of the day—as later to the Hebrews of the eighth and sixth centuries B.C., who reshaped the story for eschatological reasons—it must have seemed universal, since it struck almost all of Mesopotamia.

The Flood's (or floods') effect was to teach the Mesopotamians that the gods are not necessarily humanity's friends. To the Semites who immigrated to Mesopotamia at some remote and undetermined time,[2] the idea of divine enmity as the Mesopotamians conceived it was intolerable. The Hebrews reformulated it to include the theory of the Covenant, a more bearable theology—but one that did not completely eliminate the image of a jealous and vengeful God. In none of these regions was God a likeable fellow the way Zeus was in Greece.

Like Iran, Mesopotamia seems to have been inhabited since the dawn of time, although the precise identity of the inhabitants is unclear. At most, there is reason to believe the Sumerians came from east of the Euphrates, since their legends mention a lost city, Der in Ashunak, whose remains have been uncovered near present-day Asmar, some thirty miles northeast of Baghdad. Their language sheds little more light on them; it is not Indo-European, a fact that is still a thorn (or, more accurately, perhaps, a sword) in many a scholar's side.[3] This is vexing, since it would have been useful to trace the origins of Mesopotamian beliefs and technologies. Perhaps future discoveries will allow this.

From the kings of Ur to the Iranian conquest, which reduced Mesopotamia to the status of a province, came a succession of dynasties and a constant shifting of frontiers. The first Sumerian dynasty was followed by the Semitic one of Akkad, after whose destruction came the Guti dynasty, which in turn was followed by another Sumerian one, the Third Ur dynasty. When the Third Ur dynasty collapsed, the empire broke in two, with a series of Semitic kings ruling in Babylon and Assyrian kings ruling in Assur. King Hammurabi of Babylon unified the empire, but when his dynasty collapsed both Assur and Babylon once more became rival centers, rising and falling in power with respect to each other and enjoying a mutual hatred. The Assyrian dynasty at last seemed to be gaining the upper hand when the Medes invaded Assur. The ancient empire was then torn between the Medes and a Chaldean dynasty whose most illustrious representative was Nabu-kudurri-Usur II, better known under his Biblical name of Nebuchadrezzar. Babylon was now merely a province of Persia; when Alexander came in 330 B.C. he found that the great ziggurat Herodotus had described a century earlier was in a state of ruins. The curse of the Revelation of Saint John had come true, although four centuries before it was recorded: "Babylon the great, the mother of harlots and of the earth's abominations" (Rev. 17.5 [RSV]), the city that got drunk on the blood of God's people, vanished into the desert.

That the author of the Revelation to John, or the Apocalypse, so detested Babylon comes as something of a surprise, since it was there that Moses found, in the code of Hammurabi, the inspiration for the Ten Commandments. During the first century A.D., the period when John was penning his vengeful and visionary poem, Babylon was a phantom that seemed hardly worthy of such excoriation. Yet the Jews would never forget that in 598 B.C. Nebuchadrezzar had sacked Jerusalem, brought its king, Jehoiachim, back to Babylon in chains, and installed the puppet Zedechiah on the Jewish throne. When Zedechiah rose up in 587, the Babylonians returned and this time took a great many more Jewish prisoners back to their city. These successive captivities led to the destruction of the Kingdom of Judea—a bitter memory indeed.

It is also true, however, that it would be hard to find a more fitting object of Jewish execration than Babylon: it worshiped a number of gods, which the Jews considered an abomination. Who these gods were is a matter of some uncertainty. The principal ones, which governed the pantheon, were, first, Anu, the Lord of Heaven and father of the other deities, followed by Nintud, the celibate mother-goddess of the deities, the celestial virgin Innini, the god of the earth Enlil and his wife Ninlil, the god of water Ea (who in Sumerian is called Enkil) and his wife Damkina—three apparent pairs and a sort of female regent, each of whose names, attributes, cult sites, and even identities were variable. No less than forty-one names for Nintud have been catalogued.[4] These seven gods, or seven god-archetypes, endured throughout Mesopotamia's history.

"The number of gods lessened considerably with the passing of time," writes Jean Bottéro. "The Creation Epic, around 1200 B.C., mentions only six hundred." There was never a single Devil among the lot. Enki—the "Lord of Ki," the realm that extends from the earth's surface to the underworld—is not at all infernal in our sense of the word: he is the god of water, and the Mesopotamians believed that water sprang from the earth. Evil lies elsewhere.

As so often in ancient religions, the identities of the gods merged with or became superimposed upon one another. Nintud and Innini had similar attributes—when humanity sinned and the gods threatened to punish it, for instance, both goddesses interceded on its behalf. The very idea of sin implied that of forgiveness, which was the domain of female deities. In Mesopotamia our goddesses of intercession must have had their hands full, given that they were dealing with an eternally culpable humanity.

Which god did they intercede before? The answer seems to be Marduk—originally the Sumerian god Amar-Utuk or "Calf of the Sun-god," the Merodach of the Hebrews—who became the tutelary god of the city of Babylon and subsequently of the empire as a whole. He was later also the god of judgment and the "god of the light of spring," and his symbols were the "star" Jupiter and the dragon-serpent Mussussu. Again, in the wake of conquests and invasions the gods passed from one country to another and one religion to another, losing some attributes but gaining others in the process.[5]

The multiplicity of their gods and god names aside, the Mesopotamian religions also boasted a huge collection of myths filled with extravagant heroes. The epic scope of the Mesopotamian writ-

ing is so vast that in comparison the Genesis of the Old Testament
starts to look like something knocked off in a week. Even in later
versions, it is quite stunning: when Marduk is born—he is the
grandson of Anu, the supreme god of the universe, and a prototype
of the hero who must save the world, like Gilgamesh, Hercules, or
Jesus—Anu senses his own power slipping away and is outraged.
Using the four winds, he causes a sea dragon, the female Tiamât,
who is the mother of the river of hell and the creator of all life, to
rise up against the usurper:

> She made irresistible weapons, she bore giant serpents
> with sharp teeth and pitiless jaws;
> she filled their bodies with venom for blood,
> she clothed these furious dragons in dread,
> haloed them in splendor, and made them equal to the gods.
> Anyone who sees them would recoil in horror;
> let those in the front lines steel themselves not to retreat!
> She raised the hydra Bashma, the red dragon, and Lahumu,
> gigantic lions, foaming-mouthed dogs, and the scorpion-man,
> the evil demon of storms, the man-fish, the Kusarikku.

The Mesopotamian had a frightening image of his gods, perhaps
the most frightening in any religion. It would be wrong to take them
lightly, these deities so unfamiliar to the twentieth century, since
it is in Mesopotamia that the gods subjugated humans in a way that
never happened in Oceania or India or China or Egypt. Yet it is
hard to follow them through the convulsed history of the region; the
adoption of a deity by this or that state frequently involved changes
of name and sometimes of gender. Above and beyond the multiplicity of identities noted above, for instance, no one will ever know
why Ishtar—the future Astarte, then Aphrodite, who was originally
a male god, the Arabic Açtar, the deity of the planet Venus—
became female when she passed from Arabia to Mesopotamia. A
complicated series of congruences also has to be kept in mind, for
instance that Shamash, the Semitic sun-god, is also the Sumerian
Uta, otherwise known under the inoffensive name of Babar.[6] In
addition, the syncretism produced out of pollination among Sume-

rian, Semitic, Babylonian, and Assyrian religions means that keeping track of the region's four thousand or so original gods would demand a computer. The god of war Ninurta, for example, is the ancient Ninib, but he has also been fused with Nusku, the god of fire. Marduk of Babylon is identical to Nabu of Barsippus, although the antagonism of fire and water is breezily ignored, since the fire-god Gibil (another name for Nusku) is identical to the water god Enki. It is no understatement to say that Mesopotamia's theologians had their work cut out for them.

Two major myths nevertheless seemed to stand out from this mosaic in which, as the above-mentioned relationship of fire and water goes to show, every principle is wedded to its opposite. The first myth concerns the marriage between a god of the Above, Nergal, the lord of summer and heat, and a goddess of the Below, Ereshkigal, the mistress of the underworld and thus the queen of the dead and of the cold. The marriage is neither peaceful nor nobly conceived: after Nergal descends to the underworld at the gods' orders to apologize to Ereshkigal, whom he has somehow offended, he is seduced by the beauty of her body and gives in to the desire "to do what men and women do." He is apparently quite good at it, since after he has gone the seductress laments: "Nergal, lover of my delight! / I had not time to take enough pleasure with him!" (This madrigal tone, by the way, persists throughout the Poem of Nergal and Ereshkigal.)

Crazed with love, Ereshkigal sends a messenger, Namtar, to heaven; she wants him to trap Nergal and bring him back to the underworld, so she can have him in her arms again.

> Go, Namtar, speak to Anu, Ellil, and Ea!
> Stand at the door of Anu, Ellil, and Ea,
> to tell them that since I was a child
> I have never known the pleasure of other girls,
> I have never known the games of children.
> May he sleep with me again,
> the god you sent me, the god who made me pregnant.
> May he come back, that god,
> may he spend the night with me as a lover.

This declaration of amorous passion, something worthy of Richard Strauss's heroines of more than thirty centuries later, is made not by a weepy spinster but by a vengeful, threatening power. Namtar's message is to say that if Nergal does not return to Ereshkigal's bed, she will ". . . raise up the dead and they will devour the living, / I will make sure the dead on earth outnumber the living!"

In the Epic of Gilgamesh, a similar threat is made by Ishtar after the handsome Gilgamesh spurns her advances. Gilgamesh held out; Nergal, however, is compelled to submit to Ereshkigal's wrath. He goes down the staircase leading from heaven to the underworld, but he arrives in a very sour mood. One by one, he manhandles the guardians of the Seven Portals; when he reaches the throne room, he sees Ereshkigal, bursts into laughter, then grabs her by the hair, throws her down to the foot of the throne, and starts dragging her around while she cries and begs him to marry her:

> You will be my husband, and I your wife,
> I will grant you
> kingdom over the earth! I will place
> the tablets of wisdom in your hands.
> You will be master, and I will be mistress.[7]

Nergal at last calms down, embraces his dark lover, and agrees to share her throne with her. The symbolism of this violent, Wagnerian love story is not difficult to decipher: the world of the living is intimately bound to the world of the dead, and the power of the underworld is much greater than that of heaven; corruption lies at the heart of living matter; death and evil are represented by the femininity of Ereshkigal. This is the idea of original sin in an embryonic form; in the fundamental misogyny of the revealed religions, all of which derive from patriarchal systems, the vessel of sin is sexuality. Ereshkigal is the great seductress, the ancestor of Eve but also of Lilith, Adam's first wife. Indeed, the essence of the Mesopotamian religion is that it is based on sin and on the notion of Evil being inherent to existence.

The second significant myth is that of man's creation. Man is

born from the blood of an ancient god, Kingdu, who was fated to
become an archdemon and to be put to death at Marduk's command
for having brought disorder to the cosmos. Yet Kingdu is an un-
ambivalent demon. He is evil and only evil, like our Devil; nothing
else can be expected of him. The nature of man, the son of Kingdu,
is therefore essentially bad and demoniacal. Evil resides in his
flesh.[8]

Neither poetry nor comedy could ever manage to lighten this
negative view of the world and human nature, and yet both
abounded in the Mesopotamian cultures. Humor is present as early
as the tale of Creation (the text for which, ironically, was later to
be uncovered in the ruins of Assurbanipal's palace), in the reasons
why Marduk, demiurge as well as god of the sun and Babylon, has
to confront the female dragon Tiamât, the mother of all and the
deity of salt water. She is the wife of Apsu, the god of fresh water,
and together they engendered the gods. These offspring gods, however, were rambunctious in their youth. Apsu complains to his wife:
"Their behavior is intolerable. I can't rest by day or sleep at night.
I want to destroy them and put an end to this carrying on. Then at
last silence will reign and we'll be able to get some sleep."[9]

A bizarre discussion ensues. Like suburban parents worn out by
one too many loud Saturday nights, Tiamât and Apsu ponder the
wrathful Apsu's proposition of wholesale infanticide, but the gods
catch wind of it. Marduk, who has been delegated to defend the
celestial powers' cause against Tiamât, heads off on his chariot.
The harridan's eleven allies take to their heels when they see him
coming, although she stands fast. He captures her in a net of light,
unleashes a storm in her jaws, and riddles her with arrows. Once
she is dead, he splits her lengthwise and creates the vault of the
heavens by casting her speckled back half skyward. When he casts
her stomach half downward he creates the earth and the oceans. (It
is in the course of this titanic struggle that Kingdu, whom his
mother called upon for help, is killed by Marduk.)

This bloody cosmogony is based upon an act of matricide whose
virile heroism fails to mask its horror; symbolism-lovers will no
doubt want to decode the meaning of this other duel between male

and female principles, with the female once again being killed. Evil, it has been said, is Woman. In this context, the tenuousness of the "Oedipal complex" theory becomes obvious.[10]

The same sense of humor is even more markedly present in another creation myth, the one that explains why some individuals are deformed. In this myth, Enki is woken up by his mother, Nammu, the goddess of deep water, who complains to him about how backbreaking the gods' work is. Enki suggests that they create puppets to do their chores for them. What they need most of all, he says, is mud from the intermediate region between land and deep water (that is, from Nammu's body), which will serve as the puppets' hearts. Eight other gods contribute to the task, and so the human race is created.

To celebrate his deed, Enki organizes a feast, at which much beer is consumed. Ninmah, Enki's wife, becomes tipsy. Obviously not very impressed by Enki's work, she says: "What's so special about these humans you've created? I could come up with something better any day of the week."

"Go ahead, do your best," Enki replies with the combativeness of a drunk. "I promise to find a place for any human being you create."

Ninmah sets to work and produces a eunuch, a barren woman, and four cripples, and Enki assigns them all a role in society. The eunuch becomes a functionary, the barren woman a concubine; what becomes of the cripples isn't mentioned. Enki himself joins in the game and, according to one source,

> he challenged Ninmah to try it again, but this time with the rules reversed: he would come up with outlandish creatures, and Ninmah would have to find a place for them. When Ninmah accepted the challenge, Enki created "a man whose birth is far away"— that is, the first old person—and presented her with it. Ninmah offered it a piece of bread, but the old man had neither teeth to eat it nor even the strength to hold it. Ninmah was at a loss; she had no idea what to do with the unfortunate creature. Completely drunk now, Enki clinched his victory by creating five more men and women, each more deformed and disastrous than the last.

Ninmah couldn't find a place for a single one of them, and the
feast concluded noisily.[11]

The Mesopotamians seem no better than the Greeks or the Celts in
terms of the respect they accorded their gods, but the comparison
is not quite apt: what can be gleaned from this tale, in which Creation begun in earnest turns into a mean and drunken parlor game,
is a picture of the gods as cruel powers. All human beings are
either products of Evil or creatures the gods made to serve as domestic help. The Assyrian, indeed, was steeped in the conviction
of his own servitude—unless, of course, he was powerful, which
only princes could be.

There is little resonance here with Hellenic religion and culture,
in which freedom was taken to be the supreme good. The Sumerian
religion, on the other hand, never even conceived of individual
liberty; its liturgy thus prefigures not only the Jewish and Christian
ones, but also the darker manifestations of Eastern existential anxiety as they appear in the services of the Byzantine Church.

The Sumerian liturgy featured endless monodic hymns, the *ershemmas*, which were accompanied by the flute and peppered with
kishubs, or chants of prostration addressed to the gods, in particular
to Enlil. The clerics of the classical period—the great Sumerian
renewal under the last Ur dynasty and the kings of Larsa and
Isin—constructed complex celebrations in which the arrangement
of *ershemmas* and *kishubs* expressed the most penitential and somber theological themes. Each liturgy included a hymn to the "Words
of Wrath" of the gods to which it was addressed—the origins, undoubtedly, of the *Dies irae*. They were probably also the forerunner
of Catholic litanies, since Sumerian liturgies also featured long im-
plorations enumerating the gods and following every mention of
their names with extended funereal refrains. As though on a perpetual Catholic Good Friday, an imploration for penitence concluded every ceremony. In addition, there was, in the words of Jean
Bottéro, "a multitude of positive and above all negative injunctions.
. . . One could not make an oath without washing the hand that
was raised to do so, nor could one invoke the name of a divinity

while carrying a hoe, nor drink from a vessel of unbaked clay, nor cut saplings or break stems in a canebrake. . . ."[12]

Byzantium is near: the liturgical calendar is already traced out, complete and ready for action. Each month came with its ceremonies, its regular services to be sung by the priests or *galas*. Particular days demanded the celebration of several rites in a row. The liturgies were aimed at exorcising evil, and ritual specified where they were to be celebrated on this or that occasion. Ecumenicism was also at hand; for the first time in history, we witness the celebration of rites to ward off calamities that threaten all of humanity. However, they were not magical exorcisms whose dark tone could be explained by their occult character; rather, they were dry hymns to the gods, replete with pessimistic portraits of human suffering and the abject misery of life. Not without a tinge of recognition, we picture long trains of priests with black beards and gloomy eyes filing into gigantic temples to carry out, with scrupulous care, interminable services in the name of human suffering.

If the public ceremonies weren't enough, the Sumerian religion furnished a corpus of prayers of repentance that were to be recited in private—another innovation, also dating back to the religion's origins, that would leave a lasting imprint. These were penitential psalms, although another, later category also existed: psalms of praise, confession, and intercession that were to be sung in the company of a priest. Once again, we come across the ritual of confession. (When tablets with such texts on them were unearthed, archaeologists were surprised to learn that the liturgy was still recited in Sumerian long after that language had been supplanted, like Latin in the liturgy of the Roman Catholic Church.)

Again, the reasons behind the diatribe against Babylon by John, the author of the Apocalypse, are a puzzle: the "mother of harlots" was a place where, in comparison, modern Western services for the dead would look like pleasant light opera. Nothing was gloomier than the Sumerian religion—I would propose, in fact, that despair was born in the same place that gave birth to writing. More to the point, though, it is enlightening to consider the striking resemblance between the Sumerian religion and revealed religions, in particular Judaism and Christianity. One wonders what were the origins of this sense of sin, since it is here that we find, in even greater detail, the blueprint of the Devil already sketched out in Iran.

Theologically, the Sumerians and the Semites believed that most of their woes, and their essential sense of guilt, were the product of demons; thus demonology loomed large in their religion. While their neighbors in Iran had made the deity and counterdeity central, the Mesopotamians were still practicing a polytheism rife with demons. There were seven of these, half-human monsters with animal heads: lion, panther, dog, sheep, ram, bird, and snake. This imposing septet was crowned by two sinister inventions, the Assyrian Pazuzu, the personification of the southwest wind, a demon with four wings, a bat's head, and a scorpion's tail, as well as Lamashtu, an incarnation of the Sumerian Dimme, the she-devil of childbirth fever, a female nightmare generally depicted suckling a dog with one breast and a pig with the other.[13]

This is where we run across a great deal of ambiguity, much as was the case among Vedic gods. Even though Dimme was the daughter of Anu, the Lord of Heaven, she was in fact the sister of the terrible Indo-European Ahriman. In any case, she had a brother—Utukku Limnu, the chief demon and himself also the son of Anu—who was no less bad than she and about whom one would be hard pressed to say anything positive. (Divine couplings were hardly seen as felicitous by the Mesopotamians.) A third figure, Namtaru, the demon of fate, was the son of Enlil, Lord of the Earth; Namtaru was the messenger of Ereshkigal, whose task it was to visit death upon humans.[14] These horrifying offspring, collectively known as "the gods' bitter poison," were believed to have been conceived in the underworld, which increasingly came to take on the coloration of what, in the revealed religions, would become Hell. The underworld was the place where the almighty deities bred monstrosities.

The notion of sin is thus much older than the revealed religions. In Sumer, it was held to be the product of demonic curses; the demons won power over humans every time a human violated religious proscriptions or morals, or even touched taboo objects. Even the notion of original sin is foreshadowed; in the *Shurpu* and *Maqlu*

(Akkadian, hence Semitic, texts that catalogue ethical and ritual sins), we witness the appearance of transgression committed not by the petitioner himself, but by one of his ancestors.

The idea, then, has become concrete: demons attack sinners, so if someone is possessed it is because he has sinned. This idea would gain strength in later derivatives of the Assyrian and Babylonian religions, eventually making its way, through the vehicle of Judaism, into Christianity. The dating is crucial, since for the first time earthly ethics have come to hinge upon Heaven. Like the Vedic and Zoroastrian magi, Mesopotamian priests had laid claim to the authority of lawmakers, because law is a function of ethics.

Salvation thus came to depend upon the intervention of the clergy, the magicians or *ashipu*s, and here "salvation" is absolutely to be understood in the Christian sense—not as "healing," the sense in which it is taken in Oceanian, African, or Asian cultures, where the exorcisms performed by witch doctors, medicine men, or shamans have no eschatological significance. Only the Babylonian magus was capable of intoning the incantations likely to chase off the interloping demon—a long ceremony replete with magic rituals, descriptions of diabolical machinations, and the recitation of the demons' names (since the identity of the guilty party was unknown, it was only by enumerating them all that the magus could drive away the one responsible). Water, poultices, herbs, salt, and other substances were applied to the sick person's body; the magus's spells were aimed at luring the demon into these, which were subsequently destroyed. Colored ribbons were attached to the sick person's bed, then torn up to signify that the link with the demon was broken. This was the ceremony of repentance, or *kuppuru*, which was also making its first appearance in history; it, too, would be passed on to Judaism.

The ordeal was lengthy and sometimes effective in that it was often conducted in the presence of an *asu*, a sort of nonordained priest. In modern terms, the *asu* was a cross between pharmacist and physician, and although a good portion of his art was clearly based on superstition, the texts that have been found indicate that he did have some knowledge of the virtues of certain herbs and minerals. A decent emetic, antipyretic, disinfectant, or decongestant could bring the "devil" in question to its knees—and religion, of course, drew a windfall from the fact.

Humans are continually beset by demons, and thus arises the need to ascribe to everyone, from the moment of his birth, a protective deity whose powers transcend the mortal. The personal god inhabited the individual but left him if he sinned, and thus cleared the way for a demon to come in—much like the Christian notion of a guardian angel.

Most important, in Assyria and Sumer the individual was completely hemmed in by religion. One's only alternatives were faith or perdition. Life became a narrow and perilous path from which the least deviation earned the traveler eternal damnation. Since this scheme never reared its head in Asia, Africa, or anywhere else, one asks how this state of things came to pass.

The answer first depends on the smallness of the stage: ten Mesopotamias could fit inside Egypt, fifty into Bactria. A flood, a really serious one, could have washed it into the Persian Gulf altogether. The Scythians, the Sarmatians, the Getae, and the Massagetae who haunted Pontus and the Caspian occupied incomparably larger territories. After the successors of Alexander had incorporated Mesopotamia into the Seleucid Empire, the little oblong lump of dough that Mesopotamia was vanished into the immense Greek kneading trough. In such a small place, power had no trouble manifesting itself in a very radical fashion.

And power was concentrated. Sumer, Ur, Assur, Akkad, and Babylon were home to tireless potentates who built city-states that were incomparably larger than those of Hellenic Greece. Mesopotamia was also rich; from the third millennium B.C. onward, while Egypt was still teething and Greece was a hinterland, the region was trading with the whole world. Mesopotamian rulers of the fifth century B.C. were as fond of Greek art, for instance (they acquired pieces from colonies in Asia Minor), as was any later Roman or European.

The soil was fertile; once the floodwaters were tamed, the sediment they deposited yielded exceptional crops. Through royal corvées, by the end of the third millennium B.C. the kings of Ur began to build irrigation canals, and Mesopotamia's later monarchs would never forget that their wealth was owed to the harnessing of Apsu, the god of fresh water.¹⁵ Over the course of the centuries, these agricultural canals were improved into waterways; it was over these that Sennacherib had the gigantic stone bulls that would decorate his palace barged to Nineveh. Not until the arrival of the Arabs would the Mesopotamian waterways fall into neglect, then disrepair, then ruin. Once that happened, the two rivers reassumed their dominion over the land—a dominion they still enjoy today.

This wealth was controlled by the state until the third Ur dynasty, or 2030 B.C., when private capitalism took over. While the last Ur king, Ibbi-Sin, maintained a royal farm at Puzrish-Dagan and controlled all internal and external trade, everything changed with the coming of the Semites, when free enterprise predominated (the royal power did benefit in the form of greater tax revenue). The rest of Mesopotamian history was a parade of ever-more prestigious palaces, citadels adorned with frescoes, monumental bas-reliefs, statues, and edenic gardens that were guarded by archers and populated by courtesans and priests. After having been god-kings in the ancient days of Ur, the Mesopotamian monarchs became sun-kings.

The reconstruction of the palaces at Assur, Kar-Tukulti-Ninurta, Dur-Sharrukin (Sargon's palace), Til-Barslip, Arslam-Tash, and Nineveh (Sennacherib's palace) outlines the massive power available to the monarchs who built such prodigious edifices—24.7 acres and 209 rooms in Sargon's palace, to take but one example. Their overarching lust was for conquest, and from beginning to end Mesopotamian history is just that—a series of wars fought with an avidity that the centuries have veiled.

Born poor and, like Moses was later to be, consigned to a river in a chest by his mother, Sargon took the throne in the twenty-fourth century B.C. At the head of his armies he reached the Taurus mountains, crossed the Anatolian plateau, seized the entire kingdom of Ur, returned to "wash off his weapons" in the Persian Gulf, then built his formidable capital, Akkad. In the seventh century B.C., Esarhaddon boldly descended on Egypt, conquered it, and divided it into twenty-two districts under the governorship of Assyrian functionaries; when the country rebelled, Esarhaddon's son, Assurbanipal, reconquered it, took the pharaoh hostage, and razed Thebes, from which he brought two obelisks back to Nineveh as trophies.

From Sumer to Assur, all Mesopotamian regimes were tyrannies. A strict body of rituals and protocol regulated every activity in the empire, from the relations among members of the royal government to proper epistolary etiquette. In a letter to Sargon, one vassal introduces himself as "a slave born in my lord's house, a servant of the lord my king. I report everything I see and hear to my lord the king; I hide nothing from my lord." In this case, the writer was a provincial governor; others could be even more fawning. A short time after his accession, Assurbanipal received the following missive from Marduk-Shumur-Usur, a haruspex: "In a dream, Assur called my lord's grandfather a sage. . . . You have surpassed the wisdom of Apsu, of all learned men." Another opens his letter: "I, a dog who blesses the king my lord . . ."[16] Indeed, in the absolute theocracy of the Mesopotamian monarchies the individual was a derisory entity, an excrescence of the divine will, a blemish on the face of the earth. Only the king existed, and he claimed absolute rule not only over his functionaries and subjects but also over their offspring.

Above and beyond the power he wielded through the very extensive bureaucracy, perhaps the most highly developed in the ancient world, the monarch's authority over his subjects was increased in that he was the religious leader as well. "Reading the rituals," writes Jean-Marie Durand, "one has the impression that he was the most important figure in the Assyrian cult, either because all activity had to take place in his presence or, most probably, with him—not the person whose title we usually translate as 'high priest'—as its principal celebrant." Durand adds: "A number of kings also had themselves appointed priests of this god or that temple."[17]

From the Sumer dynasty onward, the Mesopotamian kingdoms produced, for specifically political reasons, religions that stressed subjection and abjectness even in the privacy of individual minds.

In no other civilization has the individual been so abased; the fundamental aim was to reduce the bulk of the population to the most humiliating secular and spiritual subjection.

The kingdoms of Mesopotamia invented a metaphysical Evil that was encapsulated in the notion of original sin. Yet the ways in which that sin was defined were determined by humans who were equal to the ones upon whom the concept was imposed: it was little more than the product of the political imagination of supercilious functionaries in a brutal theocracy, who happened to have anticipated Machiavelli's calculations by some thirty-five centuries.

Mesopotamia invented sin to abase the individual, and worse yet, so that the individual would justify his own abasement to himself. Iran, meanwhile, had invented the Devil to terrify him. The beds of our "demonized" monotheisms were made; all that was left now was for them to lie down.

CHAPTER 6

The Celts

Thirty-five Centuries
without the Devil

Little is known about the origins of the Celts—one of the most prominent peoples in the collective Western imagination, along with the Etruscans and the Greeks—apart from the fact that they belong to the vast collection of Indo-European populations. The very term "Celtic" has led to confusion, misinterpretation, speculation, and colorful fantasies about druids, menhirs, and supernatural knowledge. Since the word *keltoi* comes from the Greeks, the first to mention them, we should perhaps accept their description of the genuine article—a large, blond-haired, blue- or gray-eyed people that lived north of the Alps.

In the first century B.C., Diodorus of Rhodes (who, granted, was little more than a compiler of tales and hearsay) reported that the "Gauls"—the terms "Gaul" and "Celt" were synonymous—were terrifying in appearance, with deep, harsh voices; their vocabulary was limited, and they spoke in riddles, content with merely alluding to things and leaving much to be guessed; they exaggerated to make themselves look better and others worse; they were braggarts; but they were also intelligent and alert. Diodorus adds: "They also have lyric poets they call 'bards,' who sing both elegies and satires and accompany themselves on instruments similar to lyres. They also have philosophers and theologians whom they treat with special consideration and call 'druids'."

To Diodorus, the Celts were mean, mettlesome, and somewhat sentimental, but also given over to irony. At the beginning of the first century, Strabo found them touchy, courageous, and always spoiling for a fight, but otherwise straightforward and devoid of malice. They were ready to face danger at the drop of a hat, even if all they had to meet it with was their own strength and courage.

Also called the "Norse" or "Nordics," the Celts seem originally to have been split into three separate groups: the Scandinavians, who answer precisely to the Greek description, with aquiline noses, long (dolichocephalous) heads, and very blond hair; the Alpines, who were to be found in southeastern France, Savoie, Switzerland, the Po valley, the Tyrols, Auvergne, Brittany, Normandy, the Ardennes, and the Vosges, and whose traits differed from the Scandinavians' in that their heads were round, their noses large, their physiques stocky, their eyes hazel, and their hair brown; and the Mediterraneans, who were of medium height, thin, long-faced, dark-haired, and dark-eyed—a description that corresponds to the second wave of great invasions that populated the Old World.[1] The first invasion, from east to west, came from India, as far as anyone can tell, some five thousand years ago; the second, in the eighth century B.C., went from the west to the east and north, and came, most probably, from central Europe; and the third, concluding only in the Middle Ages with the settling of various Celtic ethnic groups in established kingdoms, began in the fifth century.

The theory that all three invasions involved the same stock of peoples is generally accepted. One can, in Duncan Norton-Taylor's words, "see the Celts as the descendants of the continent's original Indo-European invaders."[2] The best argument for this is the Celtic language, which came into existence some forty-five hundred years ago somewhere between the Carpathians and the Urals. The Celt is cousin to the Latin as well as to the Slav, to the Hindi as well as to the Greek. This is an important point, since it means that all the peoples who invaded Europe, including the Celts, originally shared the beliefs of the peoples who eventually gave rise to Vedism and Zoroastrianism. Yet the Celts did not create the same religions as the Indo-Aryans; the branches of the same tree yielded different fruit.

When the Celts burst forth, they did not find empty lands; their ancestors, the Urn-Field People and the proto-Celts, had preceded them. Yet despite a few scrupulously recorded genealogies, the Celts of the second and third waves seem to have been unaware of their own origins. This is hardly astonishing, since they had an oral tradition, not a written one, and all their literature—which was a late development in any case—indicates that if words were not poetry they were regarded as useless, and that the past was either a splendid tale or just plain boring. The legends that deal with the Celts' origins are very imaginative.

All that is really known about the Celts—to use the term in the specific sense of the second-wave invaders—is that they seem to have originated in central Europe, and that after the so-called La Tène period[3] of the fifth century B.C. they expanded at an astonishing rate, reaching the British Isles, Spain, Greece, and Russia. They lived in tribes and identified themselves with the territories they had chosen: some called themselves Irish, others Gauls, Danes, Norwegians, and so on. After these German and Bohemian nomads occupied Gaul, it took them only fifty years to cross the Pyrenees to reach Spain.[4] Alexander the Great was probably a Celt, as were Vercingetorix and the Vikings who, ten centuries later, discovered America.

The prejudice of Roman historians against the northerners is unjustified: the Celts had inherited the advanced metallurgy of the proto-Celts, who had also been using the wheel since the third millennium B.C. Whether or not they were barbarians depends on one's point of view; the Urn-Field People cooked their meat in bronze cauldrons, while their jewelry and clothes (roughly similar to those of Balkan peasants today) are a testament to their fine aesthetic sense. When the Vikings began to build ships, they created the drakker, a masterpiece of maritime genius that was capable of crossing the Atlantic some five centuries before Columbus's caravelles would do so again.

In 279 B.C., the Celts once more occupied Macedonia and invaded Greece by way of Thrace and Thessaly; after that, they were a permanent feature of the European landscape. Celtic mercenaries fought in the Hellenic wars of the third century B.C.; the elite guard of four hundred Gauls that Rome presented to the New Testament tetrarch Herod Antipas were Celts too. Some twenty thousand more occupied Asia Minor and settled in Galatia.

It is difficult to describe the Celts or to identify their legendary islands—the Isles of the Blessed, Lyonesse (lying between England and France, this was probably Jersey or Guernsey), or the Isle of Iti Brazil to the southwest of Ireland. Nor did they constitute a homogenous and distinct entity. The difference between Gauls and Vikings, for instance, is obvious. Over the centuries, their practices and beliefs had diverged.

Their beliefs all descended from a common stock, yet almost nothing is known about what these beliefs were in the Bronze and Iron ages. What little information is available comes from the work of an eighth-century Irish scholar, Snorri Sturluson, who collected Celtic legends into a compendium that provided the basis for all later studies: the prose Eddas, so called in order to distinguish them from the eponymous poems that were compiled at some undetermined time.[5] The few available odds and ends are not enough to support a reconstruction of the proto-Celtic religion, although their art and writings bear ample witness to the fact that the Celts did have a skull cult. The horrifying pillar at the temple of Roquepertuse, in France's Bouches-du-Rhône, which dates to the third or second century B.C., is one example among many; with an actual skull set into the stone, it has little to concede to the grimmest artifacts in Papua New Guinea. The Celts believed that they would benefit from the powers of any decapitated head they could lay their hands on—it would protect them against supernatural forces.[6] The obsession with the head was deep-seated, as Celtic legends go to show, in particular the exploits of the hooliganish adolescent hero Cuchulainn, who was incapable of having the slightest dealings with anyone without decapitating him. The huge leap it requires to reconstitute a religion from these scraps belongs to the realm of the poets.

Because the Celts believed that blue was sacred to the mother-goddess they worshipped, they often painted their bodies that color.

It is from this practice that the name "Picts" derives—the Scottish Celts, or proto-Celts, who gave the Roman armies so much trouble. To the Romans, members of the most highly civilized nation in the world, a people who threw themselves into battle in light chariots, their naked bodies smeared with paint, shouting war cries, must have seemed the last word in barbarism. When Tacitus recounts the spectacle that awaited the Romans on the shore of the Menai Strait, between Wales and Anglesey, it isn't difficult to picture the fear he is doing his best to convey (he did not witness the battle, for he was only a child when it was fought): black-swathed women bearing torches and throwing themselves at the Roman legions like Furies while a group of white-robed druids chanted spells. The Romans had never seen anything like it. On top of that, in Roman eyes the Celts' open lovemaking during their feasts was no great testament to their decency.

At least they had a pantheon, though. Theodor Mommsen delights in the "baroque and fantastic throng of terrestrial objects which fills this Celtic Olympus," although elsewhere he finds it to be "without beauty and without purity." Mommsen also declares that it would be "a waste of time to try to convey a precise picture of the druidic teachings, where speculation and fantasy strangely blend."[7] However, Mommsen was comparing the Celtic religion to that of the Greco-Romans, which undoubtedly he found more congenial—again, a very nineteenth-century point of view.

At least four hundred gods filled the Celtic pantheon,[8] including a Great Goddess, Dana, from whom Irish Celts claim to descend (they are *Tuatha de Danann*, "the Sons of Dana"). It is impossible to trace Dana's genealogy; so many ancient cultures worshiped the Great Goddess in one form or another that it is pointless to try to work out her family tree. Since the dawn of agriculture, most likely, the fertility of the soil and of livestock was deified, first as a guarantor of survival, later as the source of wealth, by every people that learned to sow wild grains and to tame wild cattle and sheep. Fertility and sexuality are practically a fixation in Celtic artifacts: from menhir-phalluses to depictions of goddesses spreading their labia with their fingers to giant chalk drawings of men with erections, the list is long. Dana was not the only mother-goddess; according to

Norton-Taylor, "The goddesses of the Celtic pantheon were generally mother-goddesses whose attributes were symbols of domestic life. They hold children, fruit, or loaves of bread in their arms."[9]

Even based on "recent" historical accounts—that is, from the second-wave Celtic invasions—it is possible to only partially reconstruct Celtic beliefs. The Celts believed in the fantastic, but clearly not all of them believed in the same thing at the same time. Still, many of their practices and rites are known to us. Their great feast, Samhain, which took place on the eve of November 1, celebrated the creation of the world, when chaos gave way to order— a frightening time when the dead came back to haunt the earth unless sacrifices were made to them (Christianity simply shifted this by one day to celebrate All Souls' Day on November 2). The Celts believed in the spirits of the dead, such as the agitated Draugr. These were invoked by druids, Strabo reports, who capped off their seances by sacrificing a human being. In his third-century epitome to Trogus's *Histories*, the Roman historian Justin writes that the Celts were expert augurs. The Celtic religion thus involved many superstitious elements.

The same genealogical difficulty that applies to the female Celtic gods holds true with the male ones. Lug, who gave his name to Lugdunum, the present-day Lyon, was a mixture of the Iranian and Greek pantheons: he was at once the god of war, magic, the sun, thunder, and the arts—Ares, Hermes, Helios, Zeus, and Apollo rolled into one.

However, no trace of a unique Devil can be found among the Celtic spirits. Cernunnos, whose name means "the Horned One," an ambiguous god often depicted with a head of horns (and, oddly enough, sometimes seated in the posture of the Buddha), was indeed associated with the underworld, but like the Greek goddess Persephone he was also the deity of fertility, luck, and the harvest.[10] If he was a devil, this "god of stags" to whom our Devil owes his horns was at times a benevolent one. Yet the significance of all gods blend in with one another. At the museum in Reims, one can find a representation of Cernunnos dating from the second century. He is seated, again in the posture of the Buddha, between Apollo and Mercury, both products of the Roman occupation. He looks somewhat like Pan and does not seem very threatening. But when one contemplates the Cernunnos in the Cluny Museum collection, also a Gallo-Roman piece, a certain uneasiness sets in: with his billygoat horns and his fixed stare, he begins to resemble the medieval Devil very closely—the last and worst avatar of a very ancient god, wall art representations of which in Val Canonica date back to the fourth and third centuries B.C.

Other images, however, are more ambiguous. The Monster of Noves, which was uncovered in the Bouches-du-Rhône town of the same name and dates from the third century B.C., has huge teeth and claws; he is holding a half-eaten human arm in his jaws, his hands are resting on two decapitated heads, and his phallus is erect. At first glance, he is one of the most perfect depictions of the Christian Devil that can be imagined; Roman and later Gothic artists certainly had a large enough body of images from which to cull the most characteristic features of the Evil One. And yet the Monster is the god Crom Cruach, "the hunchback of the hill," the supernatural figure present at the bloody rites during which the Celts sacrificed human victims and, as Julius Caesar believed, consumed them ritually.

Only stone images of Crom Cruach remain, although he was often fashioned out of gold, as an anonymous eleventh-century monk writes in the Book of Leinster:

> Flailing their hands, striking their bodies,
> Weeping before the monster that enchained them,
> Their tears falling like rain.
> Twelve stone idols were set up in a row,
> But that of Crom was in gold.[11]

That Crom was a major god is underscored by the legend in which the firstborn sons of all the vassal clan chieftains of the fabled sixteenth-century B.C. Scottish king Tiernmas are sacrificed to the deity on the Mag Slecht, the Plain of Adoration.

Looking more closely, however, this association of fertility and death reflects the ambiguity of supernatural powers who can be as benevolent as they are cruel—it is we, the inhabitants of a twen-

tieth century conditioned by two thousand years of Christian ico-
nography, who see a diabolical image in Crom. If he really were
the Devil, then we would have to ascribe to the Devil beneficial,
fertile powers that he does not possess.

A god who seems a more likely candidate for the title of the
Devil's Celtic ancestor is Loki. Georges Dumézil devotes an entire
study to him at whose very outset he writes that Loki is "one of the
most singular of all Scandinavian gods."[12] Loki is the canny trickster of the Norse, Scandinavian, and Germanic pantheons, the father and master of powers inimical to the gods—the wolf Fenrir,
the goddess of the netherworld Hel, and the serpent Midgard. He
is a protean god who can assume any shape he wishes; in Celtic
legends, he is also the father of the eight-legged horse Sleipnir.

Though a shape-shifter, Loki most often appears as a small-sized
man, almost a dwarf. If Loki isn't a devil, Dumézil nevertheless
doesn't want to restrict himself to seeing him only as a jokester, a
trickster, the mythic figure found in many religions who can be
equated with the court jester, the buffoon who can annoy the king
of the gods yet not be struck down. In all iconographies up to and
including the modern deck of cards, it should be noted, he comes
off as malign in the tame sense of the word—an operatic imp. The
most curious thing about this type of god is that it appears in religions that have absolutely nothing else in common; for instance,
in the pantheon of the Yoruba, a large ethnicity of Western Africa,
he is Eshu, the gods' messenger, the Yoruba answer to Hermes and
Mercury. Yet Dumézil is inclined to see Loki as a genuine spirit
of Evil.

Loki, however, is the servant of the god Odin, and he possesses
a trait that no other gods in the pantheon but Odin and Thor display:
sociability (he even gets along with giants and monsters).[13] Unfortunately, he wastes no opportunity to play nasty tricks on his master
and the other immortals, sometimes very nasty tricks: he causes the
death of the god Balder, and only by a hair does he miss destroying
the whole world.

In Germanic mythology Loki is the agent of the coming apocalypse, *Ragnarök*, the time of the Ax and Sword when men will fight
one another until the whole world is on fire. The gods will then gird

themselves for the final battle against the forces of Evil: the giants led by Ymir, the sons of Muspell led by Loki, and Surtur with his flames. The wolf Fenrir will swallow Odin, whose son Vidar will then slay Fenrir. Thor will defeat the serpent Midgard, but will succumb to his poisonous breath. Freya will be defeated by the fire-god Surtur, who will then set the world ablaze. According to one reference, "The sun darkens, the land is swallowed up by the sea, and the bright stars fall from the sky."[14] All apocalypses, it seems, are alike.[15]

Loki might have been a fire-god on the model of the Indo-Aryan Agni, although no cult in particular was dedicated to him. And yet to this day he is still alive in the peasant customs of Norway, Sweden, Denmark, the Faeroe Islands, and Iceland. "His name appears in a few proverbs and tales," writes Dumézil. "In Telemarken . . . one throws the skin of the milk into the fire and says that it's for Lokje" (who seems to be Loki), while "in many parts of Sweden, for instance among its ethnic Finns, a child who loses a tooth throws it into the fire and says, "Locke, give me a tooth of gold for a tooth of bone!"

Whether or not Loki is the god of fire, though, is uncertain. He is frequently associated with fire, which would argue in favor of his "hellish" nature, although some specialists have seen him as a god of water, of vegetation, of the infernal powers—as well, of course, as the joker who brings the world to an end. This last reading recalls the cynicism of a medieval play in which, after the history of humanity since Creation—including the most recent coronations, assassinations, wars, and royal marriages—has been depicted (with an actor wagging his buttocks while handing the apple to Eve), a grotesquely costumed dwarf comes out to drop the curtain and announce that the story had to end because it was too ridiculous.

History is indeed ridiculous, and if such is the opinion of Loki, and if Loki were the Devil, one would be tempted to subscribe to it. However, at root, what must be determined is Loki's nature: is he or is he not the Devil (or, more to the point, the nephew of the Persian Ahriman)? It is doubtful that he is—he is an Ase,[16] a member of the race of gods or Aesir, who inhabit Asgard, the Norse Olympus, along with other semi-immortals such as Odin, Thor, Tyr,

Balder (who will, again, die because of Loki), Herimdall, and the goddesses Freya, Nanna, and Sif. This fact alone weakens the argument that he is a devil, still less *the* Devil, since the infernal spirit and the heavenly have never been known to cohabit. We shall have to look elsewhere.

The theory that Loki is a god of vegetation can be discarded. One of his tricks is to cut off the hair (golden, of course) of the beautiful goddess Sif, the wife of Thor, who is the god of storms and fertility as well as the son of the great Odin. Writes Dumézil: "When [Thor] found out about it, he took hold of Loki and would have broken all of his bones had Loki not sworn to him that the Black Elves could spin Sif new hair made of gold that would grow like real hair."[17] Caught in the fearsome grasp of Sif's insulted husband, in short, Loki promised her a wig, and so saved his skin at the cost of a pittance. The episode is a farce. The Celts had little more respect for the anger of their gods than did the Greeks.

Yet Sif's golden hair is a poetic representation of wheat fields swaying in the breeze, which corresponds exactly to her function as the Norse Cybele, the goddess of harvests and vegetation. If the horrible Loki were the god of vegetation, first off, he would be redundant, given the existence of the august Thor; second, by shearing the unfortunate Sif, he would have been committing a crime against himself. Loki is something other than a harvest god.

The Sif episode, however, is not the only instance of Loki being malicious. On another occasion, he learned that the goddess Freya coveted a necklace fashioned by four dwarves, who agreed to give it to her if she spent one night with each of them, a salacious version of "Snow White." Loki revealed this to her husband, Odin, who ordered Loki to steal the necklace. Loki changed himself into a fly, entered Freya's room at night, stung her on the neck, and, while she was distracted by the pain, made off with the necklace. These vaudevillian goings-on seem, oddly enough, to echo the bawdier stories in Greek mythology, for instance the one in which Hephaestus surprises his wife in bed with Ares, traps the lovers in a net, and parades them in front of the other Olympians, who burst out laughing. These instances of humor in mythology are too rare to overlook; they seem to express a certain irony toward the supernatural powers, which in turn expresses the sense of freedom that was paramount to the Celts. Loki himself very much calls to mind Punchinello, the eternal enemy of policemen and braggarts.

Loki has been identified as a water-god, which also happens to be true of Agni, the Vedic fire-god, since in water "resides the soul of extinguished fire," in Dumézil's words. Dumézil also claims that Loki is the god of the subterranean powers; it would be unwise to draw hasty conclusions, but once again the same also is true for Agni who, tradition holds, was born in the bowels of the earth.[18]

Based on one observation made by Dumézil, however, Eliade became convinced that Loki is indeed the Devil. Though Dumézil did in fact point out that Loki is the homologue of a Satan-type character, Duryodhana, Eliade's feeling that he is an "incarnation par excellence of our day's demon"[19] is an overstatement. A resemblance exists, but in the Sanskrit epic the *Mahabharata* Duryodhana is not the Devil, much less the character responsible for the end of the world. Though a detestable sort, his worst transgression is to have won the fortune of the prince Dhritarashta during a game of dice; in the end, though, he didn't even try to steal the dead prince's soul when Dhritarashta arrived at the gates of heaven with his dog but refused to pass through (the celestial powers did not admit dogs).

It would be useless to persist in making Loki into a precursor of the Devil. In the final analysis, he is primarily a buffoon,[20] and secondarily a force who, like his Yoruba colleague Eshu, is vital to the ordering of the world.

As seen in the figure of Bricriu, "he of the poisoned tongue," the Celts had a particular genius for inventing Loki-like characters. Bricriu is not a god but, rather, the legendary chieftain of an Ulster tribe under the rule of the equally legendary king Conor Mac Nessa. Bricriu was vain, and he wanted all his guests to retain flattering memories of his hospitality; though a vulgar man, he had built himself a great castle that came to be copied everywhere. However, says the tale "The Champion's Share,"[21] he was a sower of discord. On one occasion, he invited all the Ulster chieftains to his castle and convinced every one of them separately that they would win the king's prize, the champion's share. On the day of the feast, the rivalries produced a disaster, with everyone claiming the coveted portion. Worse yet, Bricriu attempted to seduce all of the wives, once again telling each woman separately that she was the most beautiful of all. His greatest pleasure was to make trouble.

And yet Bricriu is not the Devil, either: he is wise, even prophetic,[22] and in late texts, as Dumézil notes, "he is often presented as an *ollam*, a sage." If he is malicious, it is because he cannot watch his mouth or keep a secret without a boil as large as a fist sprouting on his forehead.

Another example of the Celtic scoundrel is Evnissyen, who constantly pits people who should be on good terms against one another. He is sometimes an odious character; he horribly mutilated the horses given to the Irish king, who had just married Evnissyen's own half-sister, and so unleashes war. On another occasion, however, he uses his perspicacity to foil an Irish plot: they had planted warriors inside sacks throughout the banquet hall where peace was supposedly to be concluded.[23]

Dumézil also equates another mythic figure, Syrdon, with Loki and Bricriu. Syrdon appears in legends attributed to a vanished race, the Narts, and his tradition was maintained by a number of Caucasian tribes: the Ossetians, the last descendants of tribes Sarmatian, Alanic, and Scythian, as well as the Tatars, the eastern and western Circassians, the Chechens, and the Ingush.[24] He too has a taste for mischief, and his sobriquet is "the scourge of the Narts." He utterly lacks a conscience and is given to debauchery; he taunts the luckless and the dying, and he plays mean jokes. He also has a diabolical ancestry: in one version he is the son of a devil and a lovely Nart woman, while in another he is the child of a demoness made pregnant by a spell.

Superficially, at least, he thus seems to be another candidate for the Devil. Alas, the Narts often turned to him as an arbiter of their differences, since he is very intelligent and generally quite helpful—for instance, when he frees the Narts from the giants, who have trapped them by making them sit down on glue-covered seats (here Syrdon closely recalls Odysseus and the ruse he came up with to free his shipmates from Polyphemus). At other times, Syrdon provides game for the Narts to hunt—not a very diabolical thing to do. In the tale "The Nart Uryzmaeg and Uaerp and Aeldar,"[25] he wisely dissuades the illustrious Uryzmaeg from a love affair that would cloud his reputation. The same tale adds that "God had created [Syrdon] expressly so that the Narts could not live without him"—which hardly squares with the Devil and *his* relationship to God.

What is clear is that Syrdon, Evnissyen, Loki, Cuchulainn, and Bricriu are all figures who incarnate aspects of the Celtic temperament—they are brawlers and braggarts, devious and canny, but they are intelligent and, in the end, decent sorts who rally to their community when it needs them. They are relatives of the cunning clown whose jokes and exploits provide the evening's entertainment. We applaud the character when he hoodwinks the policeman, the representative of celestial power; but since he is also unbearable, we laugh when he is bested by the policeman. A direct reflection is to be found in the mischief of Hermes the cattle thief—and Hermes is by no means the Devil.

What remains to be seen is why the Celtic religion never reached the stage attained by the Iranian religion, which produced the Devil as a matter of course. Both peoples descended from the same stock; when the Celts arrived in Europe in the third millennium B.C. they no doubt had, among their luggage, a handful of the same clay the Iranians would use to construct Ahriman.

It seems unlikely that the Celts "lacked" the Devil because they lacked religious structures; the druids[26] seemed to have occupied a role in Celtic society similar to that of the magi in Iran. As we have seen, they were not a spineless clergy: they stood at the center of battles, rousing the martial ardor of their people. Curiously, the Greek scholars of Alexandria likened them to magi and Hindu Brahmans, and Julius Caesar esteemed their legal role even more than their religious one: "They act as judges in practically all disputes, whether between tribes or between individuals; when any crime is committed, or a murder takes place, or a dispute arises about an inheritance or a boundary. . . ." Their tribunals were held annually in the land of the Canutes, near Chartres: "Those who are involved in disputes assemble here from all parts, and accept the Druids' judgements and awards."[27] These judgments were no small matter in that they often affected "whole families, since according to Celtic law, as ancient Irish legal texts make clear, all the close relatives of the accused, not just the party himself, could be held accountable for his misdeeds. Thus a man who had allowed his livestock to trample his neighbor's fields could be ordered to put his own fields at his neighbor's disposal for a whole season."[28]

This blending of the priest's and the lawmaker's role is typical of a theocracy, in this case an even more radical theocracy than that of Iran—where, as we saw in the case of Darius, only the king was lawmaker. As Eliade writes, the Celts divided society into druids (the magi and lawmakers), warriors, and freemen (those who owned cattle). The druids sat at the top of the Celtic social pyramid, and their legal powers placed them on the same level as, if not above, chieftains. One wonders what phenomenon kept them from emulating the Iranian magi and undertaking a centralization (or rather centralizations, since there were a number of Celtic centers) of the pantheon that would have established a sole God and his counterpart, a sole Devil.

The answer lies in a number of factors. First, Celtic society was not as rigid as Eliade would have it. If its structures (that is, the economic structures that determined its social hierarchy) were quite well defined, with a royal government and a permanent body of druids, it was also characterized by great social mobility, since the warriors, wise men, and even artisans who made up the elite were "subject to the goodwill of the king according to their successes or reversals of fortune." In Celtic society, one had to stand out because of one's bravery, deeds, beauty, riches, or conquests, or by virtue of one's talents as orator or poet. It was a "meritocracy" in which the principal virtues were personal courage and individuality—the opposite of what one would imagine in a feudal society.

Even after they were converted to Christianity, the Celts' descendants retained the staggering ferocity in combat that their legends depict. In the *Saga of the Faeroes*,[29] a collection of stories about war and heroic quarrels that was compiled well after the Vikings had been instructed in Christian meekness, the ax and the sword still feature as the principal rhetorical tools for avenging fallen warriors and settling personal disputes: characters drop like flies, decapitated, amputated, skewered, and cloven asunder. The hero cult predominant among the Celts was incomparably stronger than it ever was in Iranian societies. Celtic gods were therefore gods of strength; since there aren't and never have been gods of weakness, a countergod representing that particular fault could not exist. As a theoretical power, the Devil could not be an enemy if he displayed courage, intelligence, and cunning.[30]

Second, the Celtic societies, being tribal, did not constitute a centralized state that demanded a unified religion overseen by an equally centralized clergy. There never were great Celtic states or cities. Each tribe had its own druids independent of those of neighboring tribes. Until the collapse of the Roman Empire, the Celts were a constantly moving and changing mosaic—the Jutes, Angles, and Saxons seized England, where they founded seven small states and imported their paganism, while the Franks, Vandals, Alemanni, Ostrogoths, Visigoths, and a host of others scoured the continent for lands they could settle upon with some modicum of security.[31] Even after the first European kingdoms were established, the Vikings continued to wander, pillage, and conquer, maintaining their hold on the Hebrides, the Orkneys, the Shetlands, the Isle of Man, and Dublin while occasionally raiding and sacking all the way to Paris and Hamburg; in 896, the Varangian Swedes pushed as far as Novgorod, while the still-pagan Vikings settled at the mouth of the Seine.[32] The conversion of the Vikings, it should be recalled, dates to around the year 1000. The first Viking state was Sweden, unified in 600 by the Uppsalan kings of the Yngling Dynasty, while the Vikings first renounced piracy as late as 911, in the Treaty of Saint-Clair-sur-Epte signed between the Seine Vikings and the Frankish king Charles the Simple.[33]

Last, and paradoxically, at no point was there ever a consciousness of nationality among the Celtic peoples: Celtic Jutes, Angles, and Saxons fought the Celtic Bretons and drove them out of Wales in 450, while other Celts, the Danish Vikings, battled Celtic Angles and Saxons to wrest Northumberland and East Anglia away from them in 862. Each Celtic tribe cast a jealous eye over the possessions of every other. Under such conditions, it was impossible to establish an organized religion.

When the Celts, now called the "Normans," settled down and founded states such as the kingdoms of England, Normandy, Apulia, and Sicily—or when they merely joined them, as in the Kievan empire, the duchy of Poland, and the kingdom of Hungary—they fell under the influence of a Christianity that had a firm hold on much of the continent. Their religion had never organized itself and so disappeared, passing merely a few of its rites and legends on to Christianity. Its cultural influence vanished until the fourteenth century, when it resurfaced as a primarily Anglo-Saxon literary nostalgia for the cults of individualism and heroism. The last of the great wanderers, the Vikings finally gave in to the pull of kingdoms founded by Celts in earlier days. If, as Régis Boyer writes, "all things considered, the Viking influence was not very significant in central and southern Europe," and if it was "very speedily reabsorbed in eastern Europe and overall not very enduring in western Europe,"[34] it was because it had hurled itself at stable and powerful political and religious regimes.

The end of the wandering and conflicts saw the coming of the Evil One; he had waited nearly thirty-five centuries to at last get the better of the intrepid Celts.

CHAPTER 7

Greece

The Devil Driven Out
by Democracy

To look for the Devil in Greece might seem absurd: we know very well that he never took up residence there, and we know this because belief in him gives individuals—those depicted in art, that is—a sorry look. The figures in Gothic and Byzantine art almost have a sickly air; they are scrawny and lined with wrinkles. The enigmatic "Smile of Rheims" is practically anemic, and the mournful countenance of Christ in his majesty at the Hagia Sophia in Istanbul is certainly not a convincing argument for the joys of divinity.

Until the first wave of the Renaissance, all Christian art rejected both the smile and bodily beauty. The first woman who smiles, the Mona Lisa—and she too might as well be in mourning—earned phenomenal fame for her daring; yet it isn't her smile that's so mysterious but the fact that she *is* smiling (or rather, that she rediscovered the sly and triumphant smile of the *kouroi* in archaic Greek art). Until it foundered into Hellenist pathos and the Eastern sensationalism of "Laocoön and His Sons" and the great altar at Pergamum, Greek art was always smiling, both in the harmony of its architecture and in the figures on its painted vases. The reason for this is simple: its gods never had enemies. With divinity triumphant, humanity was serene—or vice versa.

This investigation would be pointless if it could not answer this question: Why not Greece? How did it happen that Greece, which was so close in time and space to the Iranian Indo-Europeans who invented the Devil, was spared that particular scourge? What was so different about its gods, and hence its people, since a people makes its gods in its own image?

When we think of the Greek gods, we picture lightly clad heroes leading a contented life and remaining aloof of human affairs except in the case of disputes—a far cry from the monotheisms, in which the deity constantly and jealously watches over both the individual and the collective (sometimes, as in the story of Sodom and Gomorrah, weighing the one against the other), and in which each and every act must venerate the one God, as in the extreme cases of the Essenes and the Christian religious orders.

Compared to the God of the monotheistic religions, the Greek gods seem frivolous, if not silly. None of them occasions the outpouring of the self demanded by the monotheist gods that dominate today, Yahweh, God, and Allah, the transcendental fusion that sears away the slag of the individual, burning off his impurities so that he can bask in the light of faith. If we gave in to the inherent fault of the human mind that makes us believe every transition is progress, the mirror of an illusory "march of history," we might be tempted to conclude that the monotheistic deity is much vaster, deeper, more dynamic, and more mysterious than Zeus, the sovereign of Olympus.

Looking for the Devil or any of his prefigurations in the religions of Greece and Rome would therefore be pointless, since if there were some monster tucked away in a corner of Greek mythology who might conceivably be taken to feature in the genealogy of the Devil, it would be not be a compelling one (we get the enemies we deserve). Greece then would be no more than an odd episode in the history of the human mind, an archaic accident whose relics are fit only for museums and specialist books.

Yet, as we know, the truth is far different; history lacking Greece is inconceivable. Greece is much more than a mere historical accident: it is the place where the duel between individual liberty and the monotheisms' idea that "no Devil means no God" is fought. Only this mortal struggle is capable of destroying the notion that, without the Devil, humanity is doomed to impiety.

In essence, this struggle is the struggle of Theseus and the Minotaur, the only Greek monster remotely comparable to the Devil (who inherited his horns from him). In a strange, perhaps inevitable association between woman and terror, the Minotaur is symbolically the half-brother of Ariane. To study Greece is to enter the labyrinth in which the beast lurks, then to enter into a metaphysical bullfight at whose conclusion we are offered the freedom of the open sea, where the salt air dissipates the memory of the beast's breath and the foam washes away its blood, saliva, and sweat.

Greece managed to do without the Devil, and for that it deserves our admiration. But which Greece? The image most commonly visited upon us was based on eighteenth- and nineteenth-century theoretical constructs; in general, it was limited to the roughly half a century that in the humanities is known as the Age of Pericles. The Attic period, however, does not encapsulate the Greek spirit. Greece was not, as is still too often taught, a marble monolith carved by a single stroke of genius, appropriated by Rome, and then passed on to Europe; the Greek psychic pantheon is not just a well-painted piece of scenery.

Hellenic and Hellenistic Greece extended over the entire Mediterranean basin and reached the borders of Asia; the expatriate Greece of Alexandria was as much a part of it as were Athens and Corinth. From beginning to end, from the Mycenaean invasions of the second millennium B. C. to the rise of the Heraclian emperors of Byzantium in the seventh century A. D. , the Greek spirit endured for some thirty centuries, all the while experiencing metamorphoses on a scale unknown to any other empire on earth.

At first, during the Homeric period, Greece was merely a smattering of city-states ruled by minor kings and constantly waging, as Thucydides mentions at the opening of the *Peloponnesian Wars*, campaigns of rape and pillage. A religion existed by the Bronze

and Iron ages, but like the country itself it was free-form and composite, a collection of myths and legends that featured anthropomorphic heroes and ill-defined powers, such as the Winds.

The religion was more than just a body of folklore, yet it was not
very constraining, either; its cult of the gods did not involve elaborate rituals or demand the existence of a clergy. These traits would
remain until the last flicker of Hellenism died out: the individual
maintained direct contact with his gods, and the priests, whose
duties were limited to maintaining temples and celebrating certain
rites, never wielded as much power as they would have in other
civilizations, such as the Egyptian or Iranian. Over the centuries
the Greek pantheon became richer and more involved, but its character did not change—a society of heroes, all commanding admiration or fear, but none attaining the metaphysical dimensions of
absolute Good or Evil.

The singular thing about this resolution of one of humanity's
greatest problems is that in the beginning, there was nothing
"Greek" about Greece: it was a complete mosaic. Herodotus himself
said that its language derived from Phoenician, its religion came
from the East, its past lay in the brutality of the Aegean civilizations, and a good part of its greatness was due to a hero who was
anything but Greek—Alexander, a Macedonian and thus a member
of a barbarian people who didn't even speak the language. (To this
day, Greece lays claim to Macedonia the way Italy once claimed
Savoie or Nice, or Germany Alsace and Lorraine.)

Historically, and strictly speaking, the Greece of humanities
courses, the white Greece of "Prayer on the Acropolis" and the
"Young Fate," is a literary fabrication—as are the Greeces of Ra-
cine, Nicolas Poussin, Stefan Georg, and Friedrich Hölderlin, not
to mention that of eighteenth-century England. The Hellenes so
cherished by Western academia since the pedant Johann J. Winck-
elmann, Goethe's straight man, a people we would like to think had
dominated Greece since time immemorial, were in Homer's day no
more than a tiny Thessalian tribe.

The Mycenaean civilizations that laid the first stones of what
would become classical Greece were centered around Crete, from
which they spread to the Cyclades and other islands. Yet little is

less Greek than the Crete of four thousand years ago. The original Cretans were Anatolians or North Africans,[1] or even both, and they practiced the cult of the Great Goddess. Their contacts with Egypt were established and intensive; the palace at Knossos is very similar to Egypt's colossal temples, while the Cretans' stone vases were imitative of Egyptian ones. Not until the end of the second millennium B. C., during Egypt's Nineteenth Dynasty, did relations begin to cool; the Mycenaean empire had gained enough power and autonomy that king and pharaoh began to eye each other warily. It was, however, in this foreign land that Zeus was born, perhaps to counterbalance the power of the Great Goddess, who was later to become Cybele.

The Mycenaean civilization reached its zenith around 1200 B.C., when it occupied not only the Cyclades and the Sporades but also "our" Greece—Messenia, the Peloponnesus, Cephalonia, Attica, Euboea, and parts of Aetolia and Thessaly. Athens, Corinth, Thebes, and Delphi, illustrious sites in ancient tragedy and the modern imagination, were all in the hands of the conquerors from the east.

It was not the Mycenaeans, however, who founded Greece. For undetermined reasons, the peoples of Eurasia suddenly became expansionist; two proto-Celtic groups, the Illyrians and Dacians, penetrated the Balkans, while Thraco-Phrygians struck out in the opposite direction, toward Anatolia. At this point, the peoples who would later be called the "classical" Greeks—Dorians, Aeolians, and Ionians—attacked the Hellenic peninsula, drove out the Mycenaeans, and at last laid the nation's foundations. These invaders were foreign and barbarian tribes; the Dorians were from Crete while the Ionians were Asians,[2] like the later Phrygians and Aeolians (the latter were in fact Cnidians who colonized the Aeolian Islands, the modern-day Lipari). All these peoples had mixed foreign blood; the Ionians and Aeolians, for instance, had intermarried with Persians.[3] These groups were all more or less recent Indo-European immigrants, and they passed their many myths on to the Greeks. Homage should here be paid to the invaders, for it was, for instance, the Dorians, ancient Mycenaeans, who introduced Apollo and Heracles to Greece.

A unique culture was born of these endless invasions and the mongrelization they produced. Though we know the Greek pantheon by heart, it can be as paradoxical as the Hindu. In a violent fit of jealousy, for instance, Apollo—whom we associate with beauty, light, and divine splendor, and with all the virtues of magnanimity—flayed the satyr Marsyas alive just for being a better flautist than he. Though married to Hera, Zeus gallivanted endlessly, seducing, among others, Antiope, Alcmene, Leda, and Europa; hardly a sectarian when the chance cropped up, he kidnapped the pretty Ganymede (another less-often remembered handsome lad, Phaenos, also ended up in the sky). Poseidon, the god of the sea, enraged that Athens had preferred Athena to him, unleashed floods upon the city. Aphrodite, the wife of the ugly and clubfooted blacksmith god Hephaestus, cuckolded him with Ares, and for her pains and pleasures was caught with her lover, then produced before the other gods. Although Hermes was the god who guided souls to the netherworld (and was destined to become the patron of one of the largest Greek sects), he stole fifty head of cattle from Apollo's herd. There is no end to the list of the gods' all-too-human foibles, their misdeeds if not crimes.

Seducers, thieves, unfaithful and cruel murderers, rabblerousers, hypocrites. Why such unflattering portraits? First, it was necessary to remind the Olympic powers that they were, after all, creatures of the human mind, although this had to be done prudently: no one wanted to share the fate of Prometheus, who, claiming to be humanity's champion, stole the heavenly fire and brought it to earth—for this he was chained to a rock, with Zeus's eagle eternally devouring his liver. The gods were certainly powerful; they were, however, of dubious morality and often did terrible things. Greece, it should be remembered, was moral, but definitely not moralistic.

Yet the mortals did not let themselves be hectored by the gods. When Achilles is about to plunge his sword into Agamemnon, he turns around, having felt a hand in his hair; it is Athena. "What have you come to do here again," he exclaims, "have you come to see the insolence of Agamemnon, Atreus's son?"

The Greek gods were thus as unpredictable as their distant Indo-

Aryan ancestors—one could never be sure what would set them off next. In this respect, one wonders what possible religious sentiment could have been harbored toward them, and above all what the relationship between the ancient Greek religion and its gods really was—a question as old as the Greeks themselves. Here the word "religion" should not be understood in its monotheistic sense (as an individual practice carried out in solitude and leading to transcendence) but, rather, in its etymological one: the Greek religion was a linking-together of the faithful, or more accurately, of the city's each and every inhabitant. It is impossible, in short, to understand the ancient Greek religion without taking cognizance of the political role it played within the city—perhaps more so than in any other civilization, save the Mesopotamian.

Religion was the cement of the state; like all deities, the Greek gods were heroes who represented founding myths. Thus, the cults dedicated to them were not metaphysical, a ritualization of the individual drive to transcendence, so much as they were a celebration of a virtue identified with the very essence of the city (a virtue that was also liable at times to produce revolutions and wars). Greek democracy was intimately bound to the civic ideas personified by the gods; assimilated into the Roman pantheon, these gods would only decline when the tyrannical excesses of the emperors made a mockery of them. The Greeks toppled tyrants with the help of their gods; the Romans toppled the gods with their tyrants. The Greeks' true god was the *polis*.

The paradoxical genius of the Greeks was to come up with gods but to refuse them tyranny, since tyranny, the absolute power of one or a few, was incompatible with the Greek spirit. When a Theban messenger came to Athens and asked to see its king, Theseus replied: "Your speech, stranger, begins with an error; you are wrong to seek a king in this city, which no man rules. Athens is free. "[4] This is the reason the gods could be second-guessed, and why the myths were filled with enough vice, violence, misdeeds, and ribaldry to scandalize any good monotheist.

Greece represented a unique moment in intellectual history, when intelligence undermined the myths it itself had dreamed up, deflating them like a jellyfish left on hot sand. As early as the fifth century B.C., the Cynics began to ransack the stock of fables compiled by religion, poetry, drama, and tradition—an impressive display of the disrespect that is so elemental to freedom. Diogenes, the founder of the Cynics, suggested that "once Oedipus . . . realized that he had married his own mother and had children by her . . . he would probably have been better off not saying a word about it, or at least legalizing the union in the eyes of the Theban people. But he did entirely the opposite: he let everybody know about it, shouting at the top of his lungs that he was at once his children's father and brother and his wife's husband and son." His interlocutor then said, "Oh, come on, Diogenes, you make Oedipus out to be the dumbest man in the world. To the contrary, the Greeks believe that he was the wisest of men, even if he was unlucky." Diogenes burst out laughing and continued to portray Oedipus as an idiot, scoffing even about his encounter with the Sphinx, the symbol of stupidity.[5]

Diogenes was also reputed to have been famously insolent to Alexander the Great (when the hero asked Diogenes what he could do for him, Diogenes replied, "You could get out of my sunlight"); to have mocked Plato (he asked him why he had written *The Laws* after *The Republic*, since the republic presumably had laws already); to have debunked the exploits of Hercules; and, in short, to have reduced to ruins the collage that later centuries, especially the nineteenth and twentieth, have chosen to view with great solemnity.

Yet Diogenes and the other Cynics—Monimus, Onesicritus, then Demetrios, Demonax, and Heracleios—are as fitting representatives of Greece as Plato, Aristotle, Sophocles, Aeschylus, and Phidias. This "delirious Socrates" (as Plato called Diogenes) is startlingly akin to the sages of India, especially the gymnosophists, those who preached complete renunciation and resignation. This might be the result of another Indo-Aryan influence—the Greeks were aware of the Hindu gymnosophists—albeit duly transformed by Hellenic irony.

Given such a corrosive atmosphere, it is easy to see why the gods never enjoyed much prestige, and demons even less. Many years later, this would irritate the emperor Julian, who described the Cyn-

ics as impudent and found the plays attributed to Diogenes (they
have since been lost) vile and reprehensible, while those attributed
to Oenomaos were an "ignominy of ignominies," the "most extreme
of perversities."[6] This was, as we know, because gods and tyrannies
go hand in hand. When the existence of the Devil is denied even
today (as later chapters will show), the police become interested.
The distance from *polis* to police is short.

Nor did the Greeks, at least those of the classical period, always
believe in their own supposedly divine oracles. Theseus (once
again) scolded King Adrastes for having inopportunely given his
daughter's hand to a stranger on the recommendation of Apollo's
oracle at Phoibos.[7] Oracles, needless to say, were not viewed with
universal respect in Athens.

Nevertheless, thirteen centuries of Greek history should not be
imagined as populated by heroic mavericks utterly purged of religious sentiment, existential anxiety, and superstition or *deisidaimonia*
(which means not the superstitious fear of anything and everything
but, rather, an inordinate fear of the gods, the *daimons*). All the
talk on the part of later Christian theologians about the "demon"
that allegedly inspired Socrates arose out of misreading the word,
which simply means "god," or, secondarily, "spirit" or "genie," as
any good Greek dictionary will go to show. Beginning in the fifth
century B.C., the Greeks of Greece itself and then of Magna Graecia
and the Roman world enthusiastically subscribed to shadowy practices and the incantations of magi, sorcerers, thaumaturges, spell-
casters, *magoi, goetoi,* and *pharmakoi,*[8] the equivalent of our
run-of-the-mill witches. Though scorned, these charlatans featured
in the private lives of citizens with surprising frequency, and the
everyday life of all Greeks, especially of the Hellenistic period, was
filled with imprecations, spells, and witchcraft. The sulfurous Hecate, another manifestation of Artemis, was often invoked, as were
Hades, Persephone, Hermes, and so on—including, in later times,
a version of the Judaic god, rebaptized Iavoth, who was entrusted
with sowing discord in such-and-such a place or making sure that
a given individual, male or female, derived absolutely no pleasure
from sex—anterior or posterior, as the case might have been.

In addition to the exotic or imported deities, the official Greek gods could also be "worked with," for they were not always the figures of light that humanists once thought they were. Indeed, they did have a dark side; however, they weren't threatening enough, so the superstitious adept turned to other equally official but foreign gods such as Thoth and Anubis. They even turned to improbable deities such as Barovchambra, Barbaramcheloumbra, Abrathabrasax, Sesenbarphalages, and other Pakeptoh, made up of Phoenician or Asian gods transmogrified by the imagination of the sorcerers.

The sorcerers also worked with the malevolent dead, or with spirits eager to remain involved with the world they had just left (like many others, such as the Melanesians, the Greeks found it easy to believe that those who had met violent, painful, or unhappy ends remained angry at the living). Since they were eager to express their spite, one could always call upon them to carry out base designs. In other words, the Greeks were as superstitious as anyone else, if not more so, as is attested by their deep fear of the evil eye, the terrifying *phtonos*, a manifestation of the envy of the less fortunate toward the lucky ones.

Yet nowhere in all of this is a single reference to a central Devil. The main concerns of Hellenistic sorcery were carnal love and petty squabbles. The gods and the dead were most often evoked for lubricious ends, which all in all are not so shadowy, or to take revenge for a perceived injustice—in other words, to satisfy one's own *phtonos*. The recitation of convoluted names is not the same as a black mass, and the philters these frustrated lovers came up with probably made their contemporaries laugh. To the twentieth-century mind, it seems as though their only real effect was to intensify the coveter's desire for the coveted.

At first glance it seems unreasonable to place these superstitious practices on the level of religion, since their universe is so restricted and their aims so derisory that only petty minds or categorical theorists—both of which we shall soon meet—could confuse the two. At second glance, though, there is more to the matter. What it points to is the clandestine slide of pseudo-religious practices toward the negative, toward what would later become Evil. As in the Middle Ages, fear and foolishness wove themselves into a second-rate religion that in turn would produce a Devil who was never noble, always shameful, a wretched and spiteful creature of fear and ignorance.

If what motivated the superstitious were frustration and personal grudges, then not only had religion lost its primordial function of upholding the virtues of the *polis*, but it even undermined the city. The services of the evil spirits were not solicited in broad daylight, nor did the rituals involve what might be called the "great" gods, such as Zeus, Apollo, Dionysus, Athena, or Aphrodite; rather, they involved the secondary or subterranean gods, chthonian ones such as Pluto, or shadow-sides of the great gods, such as Hecate, the double of Artemis, or the spirits of the dead. Even more significant, again, is the fact that these gods were often foreign. A perennial feature of the monotheisms, as we will see, is that malefic forces are never considered native.

The harsh words the philosophers leveled at this counterreligion now become more understandable. To Plato, *magganeia* or magic was "deceit by witchcraft"[9] —the honest citizen has no reason to be too afraid of the gods. Socrates specified that the *goetes* was a charlatan.[10] By using the spirits of the dead for personal ends, these individuals menaced the city. Yet in order to have a better feel for this conflict between superstition and the official religion, it should be remembered that Socrates and Plato, master and pupil, were partisans of a quasi-totalitarian society, a fact that is often overlooked; their ideal city is a utopia whose description in *The Republic* chills the blood.[11]

It is not unreasonable, in this context, to wonder what Plato's religious sentiments were. Even when he distinguishes religion from sorcerers and the initiates and participants in the mysteries, his reasoning is suspect:

> As for those who like wild beasts are content neither to deny the existence of the gods nor to think them negligent or corrupt, who hate other men to the point of captivating the minds of a good number of the living by claiming they can raise the spirits of the dead and even seduce the gods with their sacrifices, prayers, and spells; who for the love of money alone try to destroy individuals, whole families, and cities; the tribunal will condemn anyone con-

victed of these crimes to incarceration in the central prison, and no free man shall visit them. . . . [12]

Now *this* is being categorical. Yet one must wonder what Plato is really after, since it is hard to imagine anyone both denying that the gods exist and making sacrifices to them—ruinous sacrifices, Plato makes clear, that it would cross no one's mind to perform lightly. The speech is at best contradictory. The allusion to "those who like wild beasts" implicitly but directly refers to celebrants of the Bacchanalia, who wore panther skins, the animal traditionally associated with Dionysus. He, then, is who Plato is talking about.

Plato, who surely knew his gods, was well aware that they are, in his words, both negligent and corruptible (as underscored by the determination with which they pursue beautiful mortals of either sex), as well as capricious, violent, and partisan. In truth, under the pretense of vilifying sorcerers, Plato is indirectly attacking not only the excesses of religious fervor but also the gods themselves. The same holds true in the *Eutyphron*,[13] when Plato has the eponymous theologian listen to Socrates holding forth on the subject of piety; Eutyphron is depicted as a mediocre thinker incapable of understanding Socrates. In the ideal republic, he would no doubt be a bureaucrat.

In reality, the *Eutyphron* and *Timaeus* both betray Plato as a Pythagorean, which is to say, a mystic much more in keeping with Zoroaster and Orphism than with the Attic spirit. The Pythagoreans believed in metempsychosis, an idea they directly derived from Hindu Vedism, and thus in the survival of the soul—a concept to be found in the *Phaedo* and especially in the *Symposium*, where Plato postulates the existence of intermediaries between men and gods, or in other words the *daimon*s, who are essentially good (it was from Plato, paradoxically, that later Christians borrowed the notion that demons are in the air around us). All of this would be adopted by Christian scholasticism.

In the first century, neo-Pythagorean teachings began to intermix with Platonic ones: in both philosophies, the world is inhabited by a supreme order, by the Idea. Jacqueline de Romilly's encapsulation of this is worth citing: "the Idea to which Plato wanted to subordinate the whole world takes on a luminous and ineffable nature; everything we believe to be real is in fact its blurred fac-simile."[14] Here we come across the conception that the real world is an illusion, an idea that Gnosticism would carry to the extreme by stating that anything material is evil.

What this means is that the Platonic religion is not Greek. No-where is this so clear as in *The Republic*, in which Plato delineates and glorifies the principle of absolute, perfect, knowable, and in-telligible Good, and in so doing he reveals, without circumlocutions, his aversion toward the Greek pantheon and the whole Hellenic religious tradition, something that in the other dialogues he either does not dare confess or hides behind doublespeak and rhetoric. This religious totalitarianism, with its brutal contrast to a Greek culture based on the dialectic between object and subject, finally removes Plato from the Hellenic landscape in which later teaching, much more than the facts themselves, assigned him a place. The absolute Good celebrated in *The Republic* also implies absolute Evil; it also implies the imminent evacuation of Olympus and the deportation of its deities. Plato came very close indeed to the Devil.

One of Plato's disciples, Xenocrates, formulated a true, system-atic demonology: in his mind, *daimon*s were free-floating souls (he differentiates among good ones and bad ones) who exist both before they have incarnated into bodies and after those bodies have died.

Aristotle himself believed that sorcerers were motivated by envy. Since envy could only disrupt the harmony of the city, which was the Greek world's absolute ideal, witchcraft could only be inimical to it; unlike religion, which was celebrated solemnly and publicly, witchcraft was practiced secretly, in murky little hideaways. As André Bernand has shown,[15] many Greek thinkers believed *phtonos* to be the cause of all strife. This made its instrument, witchcraft, anathema to religion, whose purpose is to uphold order. However, in condemning envy, Aristotle did not go so far as to suggest that it was a form of Evil; instead, he called it a "lack."

Influenced by the East and, no doubt, by Iran, Plutarch (ca. 50–125 A.D.) wrote two works that dealt with *daimon*s: *De Iside et Oriside* and *De defectu oraculorum*. Appropriating some of Xeno-crates' ideas, he described *daimon*s as intermediary souls that can either become gods or fall back into the ranks of men. He drew a difference between good ones and evil ones; and, in a fairly elaborate argument, he accused the evil ones of inciting gods and men to evil actions while the good ones inspired them to generosity. The mark of Gnosticism is overt: there are spirits of Evil as well as of Good. It is here that Christian apologias rear their head, since the existence of evil *daimons* means that the gods are not responsible for their evil actions—not a very Greek idea, in that it denies freedom by making men and gods the thralls of supernatural forces. We have clearly not yet reached the Devil, although he is not so far away, either, since dualism looms once the distinction between good and evil *daimons* is made: one can, in fact, begin to imagine angels and demons.

We have yet to find a unique picture of the deity of Good among the Greek philosophers, and we have some way to go before finding a unique picture of Evil power. Since Greek philosophy was a product of Greek civilization, it would be wrong to consider it purely intellectual and totally separate from either the Greeks' day-to-day reality or their beliefs, as Alexandre Kojève has pointed out.[16] In the Hellenistic period, the Stoics reformulated Aristotle's Platonic philosophy by claiming that the supreme deity is in a state of perpetual becoming, and that the cosmos in which the deity manifests itself moves in a circular and cyclical pattern. Here, once again, we encounter the critical skepticism that features in all Greek literature: if everything always returns to the same point, then no one principle can be victorious over another—which is to say that Greek philosophy rejected the concept of history in the modern Hegelian sense. It also rejected the Judaic notion of the apocalypse. Nothing moves forward and all movement is illusion, as Zeno's paradox expresses it. Hellenistic Greek philosophy itself illustrated this all-encompassing image by closing the circle opened by Heraclitus when he proposed the concept of eternal re-beginning. Thought no more moves forward than the cosmos does.

There is no room for absolute Good or Evil within this arrangement, as Kojève says,[17] and so no god of Good or god of Evil. With the later Stoic-influenced Hellenistic thinkers and rhetoricians, such as Apollonius of Tyana, Gnosticism itself would pick up this theme; to Apollonius, Creation was the work of a Demiurge above and beyond Good and Evil, while the Judeo-Christian God and Devil were no more than secondary and transitory deities.

If it is true that the "Greek philosopher" (a term that should be taken in the broadest sense, since there is a world of difference between, say, Heraclitus and the Cynics) was at something of a remove from Hellenic and Hellenistic practice, it is because he paid little attention to the anxiety inherent in all existence. The philosophers barely even addressed the sentiment of the sacred. Yet the Greek religious sensibility overwhelmed the state religion, and not only in the realm of superstition—the mysteries are proof of this. We must look elsewhere to find out how the Greek dealt with the monsters bred of existential anxiety.

One likely means is human sacrifice, which persisted until very late. The idea of such a thing occurring in Greece comes as a shock, yet it is confirmed by Plutarch. As chief magistrate in his native town, Chaeronea, he himself presided over the ritual called the "expulsion of hunger," which consisted of beating a slave with branches from the *Agnus castus* tree (which was believed to have magical powers) then running him out of the city while the citizens ritually shouted, "Out with hunger, and in with health and wealth!"[18] However, as Sir James Frazer notes, the sacrifice was not always symbolic. When Marseilles, one of the richest and most brilliant of Greek colonies, was beset by a plague, a man, generally from the poorer classes, would offer himself as victim; maintained for a year at the city's expense, he was then dressed in ceremonial garb, coiffed with holy branches, and paraded around town while all the citizens prayed for the city's woes to fall on his head. He was then driven from the city or stoned to death outside its walls.

During times of epidemics or other calamities, such as earthquakes, in Asia Minor, a specially selected ugly or deformed person was laden with all the community's ills, beaten on the genitals to the accompaniment of flutes, then burned on a pyre. This type of sacrifice was not limited to extraordinary occurrences; it could, in fact, be a regular event. In earlier centuries, Frazer also notes, a man and a woman were led out of the city and stoned to death during the harvest festival of Thargelia, which was held every May.

In Abderos (Thrace), the sacrificial victim was a citizen of high rank. In the Leucas islands, a man was thrown into the sea once a year as tribute to the sea god Poseidon.

While maintaining the beliefs that the gods were as vain and greedy as humans, and that their anger had to be placated through sacrifice, the Greeks also understood the practice as a purification of their cities. Since purification implies impurity, the Greeks must have had some concept of an immanent Evil that could be exorcised through the mediation of the gods. Yet this Evil wasn't the province of a specific deity; instead, it was the negative manifestation of the very god to whom the sacrifice was made. The young man thrown into the sea in the Leucas islands could have been consigned to Apollo as much as to Poseidon, or even to both.

Sacrifices were carried out ritually, of course; yet, as the mysteries go to show, they were not the only component in the Greek ritual system. There were three main mysteries in the Hellenic period—the Dionysian, the Eleusinian, and the Orphic. The first of these was devoted to the Thracian hero Dionysus, the god of the grapevine, according to the best-known version of the myth. (He was also the god of wheat, orchards, or flowers, depending on the region; in Attica and Achaea he was the god of flowers, in Athens of fruit, in Corinth of pine trees, and in Thrace of wheat.) The bastard son of Zeus and Semele, and as such hated by Zeus's lawful wife, Hera, this masculine fertility god, Demeter's counterpart, was, according to one Cretan myth, dismembered, boiled, and eaten by the Titans at Hera's behest. This act proved fatal to the Titans; in a fit of wrath, Zeus exterminated them. Dionysus's body was reconstituted by Apollo and then buried at either Delphi or Thebes. Eventually, he was resurrected or, in some versions, reengendered by Zeus; there are numerous variants of almost every Greek myth.

The first thing one could ask is whether the Titans were not merely another avatar of the mythic demons that kill off the eternal hero, who is then elevated to godly status. Like Lucifer and his legions cast out of Heaven, the Titans were thrown to the foot of Mount Olympus before they were dismembered. The phonetic leap from the theta of *theos* to the zeta of "Zeus" is easy to make, and this god-king who dispatches his evil servants "to the devil" closely recalls the Christian God. Yet the Titans' ghastly act of cannibalism was their final bow; they did not feature again in the mythology, which mentions that their ashes were used to create the human race. It is also possible, as Mircea Eliade claims, that the Dionysus myth recapitulates the stages of initiation, which indeed involve ritual passages through symbolic cooking and dismemberment.

Introduced around the seventh century B.C. from Thrace or Phrygia, where he was called Sabazios, Dionysus is mentioned in early Mycenaean texts; some writers claim that he was the object of cult worship in the pre-Minoan era (around the third millennium B.C.), and that he therefore appeared in the neolithic era. Others claim that he might be an avatar of the Egyptian Osiris, whose fate—as the god of rebirth, Osiris too was dismembered—closely recalls his own. (A number of gods of rebirth in other civilizations were similarly the subjects of murders and glorious resurrections; the Babylonian Tammuz, for example.)

The Dionysus depicted in Greek art is a charming god, plump and constantly smiling, whose only reproachable fault is the temper that drives him to have the maenads slaughter Orpheus. His own horrible death is owed to the *phtonos* of Hera—who, however, sits beside Zeus and in no way represents an infernal principle. The Greeks liked him enough to consecrate a major feast to him; the Dionysian rites took place annually in some regions and biennially in others, such as Crete, where the god's passion was savagely reenacted—a bull was dismembered and the celebrants ripped bloody chunks out of it with their teeth.

It has been suggested that in ancient times, perhaps around the seventh century B.C., the women who celebrated the mysteries—they were called maenads or "madwomen"—ripped apart human beings (*sparagmos*) and devoured them. This, at least, is what Aeschylus says in the *Bacchae*, and it is possible: since the Greeks were not wholly averse to human sacrifice, the Thracians or Phrygians who introduced Dionysus might well have had shared such savagery. By the fifth or fourth century B.C., however, this type of homicidal enthusiasm seemed to have disappeared, and for a good reason: the Dionysian rites, which involved an almost mystical communion with natural forces, were not expiatory. Rather than driving out Evil, they celebrated life—a metaphysical union with the dead, the living, and the generations yet to come. This is where one could say that religion largely surpassed the framework of the *polis*. It should be noted, however, that the transient "madness," the corybantism, of the Dionysian mysteries disturbed more than one observer. Herodotus and Demosthenes heaped scorn upon it; in their opinion, its excesses were unseemly. If they did not go as far as seeing the Devil's hand in the matter, the reason was that they didn't know he existed.

The second type of mysteries, the Eleusinian, were agricultural festivals held at Eleusis, which lies between Athens and Megara; under the double aegis of Demeter and her daughter Kore, they celebrated sowing, germination, and the harvest. The myth they are based on has it that Pluto, the god of the underworld, was looking for a wife and so kidnapped Kore. In her search for her daughter, Demeter came to Eleusis; though she was the goddess of fertility, she refused to make the sown wheat germinate. Pluto was ordered to release his captive, and so Kore was returned to earth, which made the wheat germinate. Yet Kore had eaten a pomegranate— the double symbol of death and birth—while in the underworld, so she could not remain on earth forever. A compromise was reached: for a third of the year she would stay with her husband, and the rest of the time she could be with her mother. Satisfied with this arrangement, Demeter then founded the Eleusinian mysteries. (Since Pluto represents transitory death as opposed to eternal death, it is pointless to identify him with the Devil or any of his precursors.)

As Sophocles wrote about the mysteries, "O, thrice blessed are those mortals who go to Hades after having contemplated the mysteries; they alone can live there; for the others, all will be suffering." In other words, participating in the union of nature's contrary forces transforms the individual into an initiate who is guaranteed a happy life in the beyond.

The third mysteries, the Orphic, very closely recall the Dionysian. Orpheus was torn apart by maenads at the instigation of Dionysus, according to some tellings. Such cruelty on the part of this otherwise likeable god is somewhat similar to Apollo's jealousy toward Marsyas; Dionysus had Orpheus killed because the hero-musician persisted in celebrating Apollo rather than him. Citing Diodorus Siculus,[19] Eliade writes that Orpheus might have been a reformer of the Dionysian mysteries, although "reformer" is perhaps too strong a word. The Orphic mysteries are similar to the Dionysian only in that they also involve a journey to the underworld and rescuing someone from the dead; in this case, the person was Eurydice, who had died of a snakebite.

It is easy to lose one's way among the tangled variants in Greek mythology, their disagreements and their respective sources. What should be noted is the decided antagonism between Orphism and the whole of Hellenic and Hellenistic culture, especially given the Eastern roots of the Orphic mysteries and their pre-Christian character: far from exalting carnality, the Orphic hymns prescribed an austere life of vegetarianism, sobriety, and sexual abstinence. Only through great discipline, they held, could one reach salvation in the Elysian Fields (an unprecedented idea in Hellenic civilization) and escape suffering in the netherworld—the fate of those who led a Dionysian existence. This preoccupation with the hereafter and with salvation was a very significant novelty.

Orphism was the first Greek movement to contain, not in germ, so to speak, but fully germinated, the principles of antagonism between Good and Evil and of original sin. According to Orphism, the fact that humans are made from the ashes of the Titans, who are malevolent spirits, clearly indicates that there is a good deal of evil in humans, too—and yet, since the Titans partook of a god's flesh before they were struck down by lightning, their ashes, and thus human beings, also contain elements of the divine. Each human, therefore, must recover his or her portion of divinity before being able to attain salvation—a foreshadowing of Christian eschatology. There is no Devil yet, of course, but the stage is set for him. All the Evil One need do is show up.

Orphism is so un-Greek in spirit that until 1962, when Orphic texts dating to the fifth century B.C. were discovered, it was suspected to be a much later fabrication; after 1962, there was no doubt that it was in fact an ancient mythological tradition, and that it had tried to take root in Greece early on but failed utterly to do

so. Called "the prophet of Dionysus" and "the founder of all initi-
ations" by Diodorus,[20] Orpheus was at least contemporaneous with
Dionysus and probably even predated him. This antiquity is astonishing given the fact that the unity and coherence of the Greeks'
casual attitude toward the gods—"those eaters of gifts," in Hesiod's
words—was established at a very early date. Hesiod, who can be
considered one of the founding fathers of Greek religion, lived at
the cusp of the eighth and seventh centuries B.C. The line of descent
from his *Theogony* to the very last of the Hellenistic thinkers is
functionally direct. To Hesiod, the world was chaos in the beginning, and Zeus managed to impose his sovereignty only after the
bitterest of struggles. To Orpheus, on the contrary, the Egg from
which the first god issued (Eros or the antichaos) had always existed. To the first, order was established when the vicissitudes of
chaos were overcome; to the second, order was eternal. It is hard
to imagine that the Orphics were unaware of Hesiod and the dominant current of Hellenic religious thought. It can only be supposed
that they lived in active opposition to or isolation from it.

One would be tempted to think that the Greeks tried to repress
Orphism and only barely tolerated its survival. Orphism could not
but arouse Greek suspicion, since it made the priest into the des-
ignated intermediary between humanity and the gods. Such an act
would have sounded the death knell for the democracy that constituted the essence of the city. From there, it would have been a
short step to a Holy Alliance founded on the tyranny of law; at the
very least, it would have ended up with a fusion of ruler and priest,
or even with a deification of the ruler, as was the case with Egypt
and imperial Rome.

One then understands why the exasperated Dionysus handed Orpheus over to the furious maenads one particular aspect of the
Orpheus myth undoubtedly postdates the establishment of Orphism,
and it is definitely a reflection of Greek distaste for this songster
hero. Where Orphism and Orpheus came from, however, is unknown. Archaeology is an incomplete book, and the flow of Indo-
European peoples in the third and second millennia B.C. is only
partially known. This abstinent, vegetarian, austere Thracian god
resembles neither his compatriot Dionysus nor any other god. He

is not Scythian or Phrygian; something in his character, on the other hand, brings Iran to mind. If that is where he was from, he must have appeared in the course of the great migrations that stirred up the peoples of central Asia and the near and middle East between the fifteenth and eighth centuries B.C. Perhaps one day a portrait will be found, maybe in Afghanistan or Iran, of a god with a lyre, and from that it might be possible to say that he was born in this particular place at this particular time. Until then, all that can be said is that he almost brought the Devil to Olympus. Though so near to the Indo-Europeans and the East, Greece managed to avoid the Evil One by a hair's breadth.

The fact remains that Hellenic and then Hellenistic democracy kept the Devil from penetrating the borders of Greece, since in the end the fallen angel is no more than the logical stratagem of a totalitarian power. Never was a Greek cleric to arrogate the supranational right of distinguishing Good from Evil. The Greeks never forgot that they had invented their gods, and that the gods reflected them; they were never slaves.

The paradox is too telling to go unnoticed: the civilization that invented tragedy, the story of slavery, triumphed through drama, the story of rebelling against one's own destiny.

CHAPTER 8

Rome

The Devil Banned

It is a paradox that the genius of Rome was of no great help to its historical image. Over the centuries, especially after the Renaissance, it is the rare potentate or ideologue who hasn't tried to don its robes—from Louis XIV and Napoleon, who commissioned "Roman"-style portraits of themselves, to Mussolini and Hitler, the list is long indeed. Versailles is an overgrown Roman villa, as are the official buildings of Wilhelmine Germany in Berlin, while Washington's White House and Capitol are merely copies of Rome's great edifices. England believed it was giving its youth a "Roman" education; later it even appropriated the classical Roman pedestal for the radiator grille of its most famous car.

Rome was originally a commercial nation that ruled on political principles alone. Some have found it vexing that it had no "soul" —at least not one that was Christian, Fascist, Nazi, and so on— and have assiduously tried to concoct one for it. Many a learned brow has been furrowed over the problem of the Roman religion's origins, and many have tried to prove that Roman religion was never, in effect, actually Roman but, rather, was awaiting the arrival of Christianity. Eminent specialists such as W. Ward Fowler refused to admit that the Romans might have worshiped "miserable depictions of the Greco-Roman gods and goddesses stretched out on their couches and eating their dinner like any average citizen."[1]

This was obviously intended to "sacralize" Rome, the supposed forebear of the British Empire as well as any number of other imperialisms; and it remained fashionable until the middle of the twentieth century. Rome, of course, had to be taught in school, but the problem lay in explaining away its polytheism, which everyone knew produced nothing but mental degenerates, barbarians, and pagans. Writers therefore went weak in the knees about Suetonius and Tacitus while vying with one another to criticize the emperors who had persecuted the Christians—a long line of twisted, vicious, and bloody imbeciles who certainly did not represent the "real" Rome of Virgil, Cicero, and Marcus Aurelius. Not until the twentieth century did it become clear that Tacitus was overspiteful, or that Nero did not watch Rome burn, since he was thirty-five miles away at the time, that he played neither fiddle nor lyre amid the ashes of the Eternal City, and that he was in fact very much concerned about a fire that consumed, among other things, the most lovely palace he possessed. This "hysterical clown" (he had in reality been tutored by Seneca) rebuilt the library of the Augustine Temple and was a considerable supporter of belles lettres and the fine arts.[2] Many other painful reappraisals were to follow.

Historians have made every effort to imbue the Roman gods with a mystical divinity akin to that found in Judeo-Christianity. The word often used to refer to this divinity is the Latin *numen*. Since no unanimously accepted definition exists, I propose "divine presence," which is plausible, since from its origins humanity has had a sense of the supernatural. We know that the Romans always had a highly developed sense of the practical, and that their gods had functional names (the deities were, in effect, stewards): the god of the first plowing was Vervactor, of the second Reparator, the god of the harrowing was Imporcitor, of the sowing Insitor, and so forth.

The question is where these utilitarian gods came from, and, therefore, who populated Italy and what their religion was. Italy was peopled long before Rome was founded, and the Romans themselves were descended from first-millennium Italians who seemed to enjoy a great heterogeneity of cultures. The two main peoples were those of the Pit Graves (*fossa*), who inhumed their dead, and of the Urn-Fields (we have met them before), who cremated their dead. The former includes the Villanovan, Adriatic, Apulian, and Siculean cultures; the latter includes the Golasecca, the Atestine, and the Latial. Little is known about their religions; all that can be inferred is that the two had different relationships to the dead.

When the Trojan Aeneas, fleeing the war, arrived at the mouth of the Tiber (after having lost his father in Sicily and given in to the charms of Dido, the queen of Carthage), he was welcomed by the king of Latium (whence "Latin"), who gave him the hand of his daughter Lavinia (whence the name of Lavinium, the city Aeneas founded). At least one civilization thus already existed in eighth-century B.C. Italy, the time Herodotus says Aeneas reached it. Latium had a religion of its own, and it is from this that the above-mentioned gods in part derived. I say "in part" because another Italic people, the Sabines, who were related to the Samnites, also had a role in the foundation of Rome; a few of their gods were also incorporated into Roman religion.

The Latin and Sabine religions seem, like their many languages, to have been Indo-European (or at least were so by the time Aeneas arrived), which is to say that they were polytheisms. There were gods for all the great forces and human activities the Latins and Sabines recognized—the sun, heaven, the stars, thunder, fertility, crops, war, the arts, commerce, love, and so on. Like many others, the Roman religion had a sky-god; initially the god of thunder, he was later transformed into the guarantor of the word of honor. This deity, Jupiter, ruled over the world without actively involving himself in it. His pantheon was later joined by Mars, Quirinus, Ceres, Hercules, Bacchus, Venus, and the rest.

One singularity about Italy should keep us from the temptation of identifying it too narrowly with the other Mediterranean peoples of Europe, either the Greeks specifically or the Indo-Europeans in general. When Rome was founded sometime between 753 and 749 B.C. by the legendary heroes Romulus and Remus, who the Greeks claimed were descendants of Aeneas,[3] the people called the Etruscans—who were, perhaps, *not* of the same Indo-European stock (their language wasn't)—were already in the area; they were the third of the three major peoples who founded the city.

The question, then, is where the Etruscans came from. Herodotus says that they were natives of Lydia, in eastern Anatolia, and migrated to Italy around the end of the second millennium B.C. or the beginning of the first.[4] That would make them Indo-Europeans of an early branch,[5] whose language would have evolved quite differently over the centuries. One intriguing hint is that Aeneas, a Trojan and thus a Phrygian (a people geographically close to the Lydians) is described as a "relative" of the Etruscans—which is to say that a good percentage of the primitive Romans had come from Turkey in the first millennium B.C.

What is of interest to this investigation into the origins of the Devil is that the Etruscans, like the other peoples who came to inhabit Italy, had emigrated from the Indo-European heartland well before the Zoroastrian reforms; in other words, they escaped the Vedic pantheon's polarization of God and Devil. Not even a hint of the Devil is to be found in either Etruscan or Roman religions. The chances of encountering him decrease even more from the sixth century B.C. onward, when Italy fell under the influence—the irradiation, if you will—of Greece, a fact that annoyed Cato greatly. There was no Devil in Greece, as we have seen, merely a few demons who nettled the superstitious and whose chief function was to avenge the petty foibles of thwarted lovers, cheated merchants, cuckolded husbands, and envious neighbors—barely enough to warrant more than the services of streetcorner sorcerers.

This said, I would like to add that Greece's influence on Rome was much less profound than is sometimes believed. To begin with, the association of Jupiter with Zeus is purely formal, formalist, and superficial; in Greece, for instance, Zeus never became the guarantor of one's word of honor. Whether or not Ceres is Libera, Ariane, Venus, or Semele is a question that has been and still is argued to death.[6] Rome is not a die-cast copy of Athens.

The Etruscan, Latin, and Sabine religions eventually merged into one Italian religion, and the question is whether or not it was lacking in religious spirit. Georges Dumézil perhaps humorously writes that "in the centuries of enlightenment the Romans did not have a mythology, and Dionysus of Halicarnassus lauds the sobriety of imagination that removed the need for sacrifices and allowed them to bind their rituals to pure, unadulterated theology."[7]

From the very beginning, the Roman gods were consuls, prefects, and functionaries—in a word, state employees. "The Roman pantheon reflected earthly Rome," notes Theodor Mommsen, and "it strove to reproduce everything down to the smallest detail. The state, the family, natural phenomena and those of the moral universe, men, places, things, even legal issues appear in Rome's system of divinities. . . ."[8] There was even a god for the thieves. Roman cults were celebrated by associations such as the brotherhoods of the Arvals or Twelve Brothers of the Fields and the Sodales Titii, who were responsible for maintaining the sacred flames of the thirty *curiae*, and by specially chosen families, such as the Potitii and the Pinarii, who were responsible for the cult of Hercules.[9]

Roman mythology may never have been very colorful; but the Romans should not be taken to task for having kept their feet on the ground and not having been too preoccupied with the supernatural, which represented the disorder they abhorred. Greece had made religion the aegis of democracy; the Romans made religion the guarantor of order and, ultimately, of the state, neither of which was tolerant of such eccentricities as saying that men were born of a stone or a bird with a lizard's tail or from some cosmic copulation of monsters. From very early on, it was a religion of the *gens*, of the clan, the household, the dead, and especially of the curia, the basic social group, as well as of professional groups or *collegia*. It could not conceive the excesses of the Eastern-influenced Greeks or, above all, of the spiritual torments of Eastern and Asian religions. This singularity would also come to brand Roman portraiture, in which there is no interpretation, no idealization, nothing but pure realism—which, it could be argued, was a Roman invention.

The key to the Roman religion is, paradoxically, a point often overlooked, or maybe even intentionally ignored, by a great number of otherwise rigorous analyses: the injunction against direct individual contact with the gods. Any transgression made the individual Roman guilty of *superstitio*, which roughly means "anarchic religiousness" (it is the often misunderstood root of both the word and the aberration it refers to). Though the individual was free before them, and constantly subject to their gaze, he was not allowed to establish a personal relationship with the gods.[10] The reading of omens by a haruspex was an activity controlled entirely by the collective. Even the emperor Vespasian, who while in Egypt became convinced that he had thaumaturgic powers, changed his tune when he returned to Rome, where any talk of supernatural abilities raised senatorial brows.

The prohibition of direct communication with the gods remained constant. Seneca, for instance, wrote an entire treatise on the subject, *De superstitio*, in which he criticized the Roman cults he considered excessive, especially the Eastern-influenced ones that were beginning to proliferate in the Eternal City. The ban explains, first, why the rites were the responsibility of groups, the *gens*, *curia*, *collegia*, and others mentioned above.

To the modern and Christian-informed eye, this might seem incomprehensible, but it becomes clearer once one understands that direct recourse to the deities created two dangers. The first was the illegal individual appropriation of the tutelary gods' powers—that is, of the spirit of the city itself. If one person invested himself with the divinity of the supreme powers, the way would be open to tyranny. For this reason, any citizen who witnessed anything supernatural or extraordinary was obliged to report the matter to his group's religious authority, which alone had the right to discuss it. The second danger was the circumvention of the laws of the city, which were predicated on the primacy of the collective. As soon as one individual claimed to be invested with godly powers, others could do the same, and that would mean the end of laws.

The same interdiction explains not merely the absence but the very impossibility of mysticism within the Roman religion that has puzzled later historians. Yet this rejection was a duty, since the person who spoke to or was spoken to by the gods was no longer a member of the community (in any case, everyone knew that it was easy to slip from mysticism into madness, depravity, or at best hysteria).

The interdiction, finally, is the reason for the absence of the

Devil. Any entity that wields power as extensive as that which Maz-daism or Judaism granted to Ahriman or Satan couldn't help but be a god itself; it would have been a threat to civic order to let the individual invoke such a deity for personal ends. This is why the few demons that appear in the Roman religion had extremely cir-cumscribed roles—for example, Robigo, the demon who caused wheat rust, or the secondary divinities that caused other worries, such as the fire demon Cacus or the "evil Jupiter" Vejonis—and were an obscure part of a pantheon so immense that it had a god or goddess for every moment of the day. Otherwise, the Roman deities were almost exclusively positive; it is not by chance that the Capitoline gods were the guarantors of the three cardinal Roman principles: Jupiter for oaths, Juno for marriage, and Minerva for the city of Rome itself.

In the realm of ethics, the Romans recognized evil, although absolutely not in the religious and metaphysical senses. The Ro-mans had gods of miasmas, fevers, and illnesses, but these had bit parts on the religious stage and do not even begin to form the outline of a central Devil. In the ultimate form of primitive taboo, evil arose from not paying attention to cults. As Seneca writes, it is also a form of ignorance: "What is good? Knowledge of reality. What is evil? Lack of knowledge."[11] If misfortune occurs, it is be-cause the gods are taking revenge. "But," comments Mommsen, the Roman religion "cannot arouse . . . the mysterious shiver the heart seeks out."[12] Yet either the Romans did not have hearts or they had another kind than the one imagined by Mommsen, since for centuries they seem to have been comfortable enough in the ab-sence of this mysterious shiver.

Were the Romans, then, an uncommonly unimaginative people? Was Rome boring? Mommsen continues: "The fundamental char-acteristics of Roman religion were pleasure satisfied by earthly things and, at a secondary level, a fear of natural phenomena when Nature unleashed its power. . . . In Italy oracles and prophets never had the prestige they enjoyed in Greece." This atrophied meta-physical sense would almost warrant terming the Romans "barbar-ians," and yet we are talking about a highly regulated civilization that, unlike Greece, never practiced religious human sacrifice.

Perhaps Mommsen, as befitted his century, is either divinizing Rome or ceding to the European habit of identifying with it; he tends, in short, to portray Romans as if they were living in Victorian England. Yet they were human beings, capable of both the sublime and of bestial ferocity. It is difficult not to recall the brutal murder of Cicero,[13] or the time when Fulvia, the shrewish widow of Claudius and wife of Antony, thrust her hairpin, in public, through the decapitated orator's tongue.[14] From the birth of the Republic (little is known about the monarchy, although the Romans remembered its last king, Tarquin, with bitterness) to the empire's collapse, Rome was a city of passions, intrigues, blood thirst, excess, unheard-of luxuries—and culture too, it should be remembered.

There is a good reason why so many countries have strived over the centuries to emulate the Roman model, its polytheism notwithstanding. It was, indeed, the most highly developed example of the nation-state, a configuration that Greece, preoccupied as it was by the *polis*, paid little heed to. In its primarily colonial but also civilizing genius, Rome absorbed the *polis* and expanded it into the much vaster state. There was a Pax Romana; there was never a Pax Graeca.

Roman religion presents a challenge to our era, steeped as it is in Manichaean diabolicism and existential torment. Like ivy growing over the bleached stone of an ancient temple, a large and determined body of scholars has attempted to enmesh Rome in a framework of speculation that ascribes to it the fears and terrors that paved the way to Judeo-Christianity. Since the beginning of this century, a number of historians,[15] vexed by the "inertness" of the religion, have tried to prove that in fact it was not the actual religion of Rome, and that we should not be fooled by contemporary texts and inscriptions (an attitude that would later be termed "revisionist").

Joining in the attempt to "pre-Christianize" Rome, Dumézil suggests that the Romans did at one point have a religious sensibility, but subsequently lost it;[16] he does not, however, define this sensibility or specify when and why it vanished. As early as 1939, Jerome Carcopino wrote about religion in the imperial era and passionately argued that it had declined:

The Roman pantheon still persisted, apparently immutable; and the ceremonies that had for centuries been performed on the dates prescribed by the pontiffs from their sacred calendars continued to be carried out in accordance with ancestral custom. Yet the spirits of men had fled from the old religion; it still commanded their service but no longer their hearts or their beliefs. With its indeterminate gods and its colorless myths, mere fables concocted from details suggested by Latin topography or pale reflections of the adventures that had overtaken the Olympians of Greek epic . . . Roman religion froze the impulses of faith by its coldness and its prosaic utilitarianism.[17]

This desire to ascribe to the Romans a somehow pre-Christian faith left utterly unsatisfied by the imperial religion is puzzling, since from the Republic to the Empire the Roman religion remained constant; it is hard to see how, as Carcopino claims, the people drifted away from it, or why under such conditions it could have endured for twelve centuries.

Carcopino's philippic could ironically be as effective in proving the complete opposite, that the Roman religion was as free of devils as it was of those mysterious gods everyone is hoping to graft onto it. The object of his criticism, it appears, is the fact of this double absence of both God and Devil.

That the Romans ever left off practicing their religion is nonsense, as Carcopino himself recognizes: "The populace, it is true, still showed lively enthusiasm for the festivals of the gods which were subsidized from public funds. . . . Among the celebrations most eagerly attended there were some that pleased the humbler people better because they were 'gayer, noisier, and seemed to belong more particularly to them' " (Carcopino is citing Marcus Aurelius). The fact that public funds were used is by no means abnormal since the religion was, again, the guarantor of the state. Many contemporary studies of the Roman religion bear the stamp of a similarly Christianizing bias.

The tenacious view that Roman religion was little more than a shell, a fiction from the first, ought to be rejected once and for all. True, the modern historians who attempt to decipher mystical signs from it are merely following a very ancient path; writers have long sought to prove both that the Romans had a frustrated religious sense and that they felt frustrated by this fact. The story of the "ineffable God" is a case in point.

In 181 A.D., a tomb was uncovered at the foot of the Janiculum hill; some inscriptions on it indicated that it belonged to Numa, the second king of Rome. Rumor had it that some mysterious writings were found at the same time, and that the Senate, led by the urban praetor Quintus Petilius, made haste to burn them. The writings were destroyed before anyone had a chance to read them, but they do seem to have existed; Plutarch refers to them in his life of Numa.[18] At the time, the suspicion was that the writings were burned because they posed too much of a threat to the ancestral religion.[19] Much later, it was said that they had been Pythagorean writings, and that in composing them Numa had been inspired by Pythagoras himself.[20] What they really were was an intellectual hoax of the highest order.

The Numa theory is, to start with, chronologically impossible. Rome was founded around the middle of the eighth century B.C. by Romulus; his successor, Numa, could not have ruled until the end of the eighth century or, at the latest, the beginning of the seventh; the traditionally accepted dates are 715–672 B.C. Pythagoras taught at Croton, a Doric colony in southern Italy, around 530 B.C. The century and a half of disparity needs no comment: there was no Pythagorean yet alive when Numa ruled. Nevertheless, the Roman religion required a mystical soul, and that soul had to have been proscribed by the Senate.

A twentieth-century historian, Armand Delatte, has produced an erudite and fascinating study of this topic in which he persuasively argues that the vanished texts were the work of an obscure second-century Roman writer, Fulvius Nobilior,[21] who was convinced that Numa had been a Pythagorean because of his knowledge of astronomy. Numa did in fact take an interest in the skies, and it was he who divided the Roman calendar into twelve months, but if what Plutarch wrote about him is to be believed,[22] the Romans hardly thought him a great astronomer. Nevertheless, Fulvius and a friend, Ennius, worked out their theory: at its center they placed a god of their own devising, Hercules Musagetus, or "Hercules Protector of the Muses" (an unusual juxtaposition, to say the least), as well as an "ineffable God," based on the misreading of a number of other texts, including Ovid's *Pythagoras*.[23] In short, what the Senate burned was total rubbish. Pythagorean thought did, in fact, profoundly influence a number of Roman thinkers, but it was extravagant to claim that Numa had believed in an "ineffable God," clearly a precursor of the Gnostic God, or that the Roman Senate snuffed out a nascent Roman monotheism in its infancy.

That hoax once disposed of, it must be stated that not only was religious practice alive and well in imperial Rome, but so was the religious sentiment that had informed the city's every action from the start; writing about the sale of goods, for instance, Tacitus said that "breaking one's word must be considered to be cheating Jupiter."[24] A nation of merchants as much as of soldiers, and thus very sensitive about promises and questions of honor, Rome worshiped a god much more likely to satisfy moralists than mythologists—the god of good faith, *Deus fidius*, who was manifestly the protector of trade but quite distinct from the god of commerce in general and thieves in particular (there is a certain amount of irony in the distinction). In Mommsen's words, "he was honored, says an ancient, in every town in Italy; his altars were everywhere, in city streets as all along the main roads."[25] This should be enough to do away with Carcopino's assertion that the Romans flocking to feasts was no more a reflection of their faith than today's flocking to Midnight Mass is a reflection of Catholicism's continued vigor.

It is hard to imagine that the Romans built so many expensive and beautiful temples to the gods for no reason at all. There were simply too many feasts for this to be possible: the Carmentalia, the Parentalia, the Regifugium, the Equirria, the Cerealia, the Vinalia, the Lemuria, the Vestalia, the Matralia, the Nones Caprotines, the Neptunalia, the Saturnalia, and so on—not to mention, of course, the Lupercalia that so scandalized generations of historians, since it involved young people dancing naked around the Palatine hill. Nor to mention the games, purification rites, and the immense sacerdotal system with its magisters, curia, flamens, pontiffs, vestals, and augurs. To think otherwise would be to denigrate the common sense that was one of Rome's greatest strengths. Impiety, after all, was a crime that carried the death penalty.

We owe the claim that the Romans didn't believe in their own religion to the skepticism later writers bore toward the myths, such as that of the underworld, that the monotheisms came to incorporate. "That there are such things as Manes and kingdoms below ground, and punt poles, and Stygian pools black with frogs, and all those thousands crossing over in a single bark—these things not even boys believe," writes Juvenal, whom Carcopino paradoxically cites as proof of how much religion had declined under the Empire.

How Juvenal's words are to be interpreted is the key here—in other words, the implication is that no one who doesn't believe in the underworld can be religious. Yet this is to misconstrue the Roman religion, which had no dogma: there was no Roman Vatican other than the physical hill, nor any mention of Hell or the Devil in any of the references to divinities. The underworld was a sort of poetic invention, and one was free to believe in it or not. Its inventor in Rome was Virgil, who was definitely no theologian.

"The myth of the *Aeneid*," Georges Minois has written, "enjoyed a considerable success. At once poetic, allegorical, and rational, it seduced generations of intellectuals and, through popular art, exerted a true fascination over the people."[26] It would be wrong to deduce from this that belief in the underworld was a vital part of the Roman religion; it was simply a fortuitous literary invention. With perfect justification Minois writes: "At no time does Cicero envisage the existence of hell; he believes that everything the poets have said about it is a tissue of fables. The alternative is between happiness with the gods or nothingness."[27] The problem with modern historians is that they judge all other religions according to the standards of Christianity, and are incapable of understanding them as they were or of conceiving of a *religio* that, not arbitrated by fear, limits itself to the role of social cement.

What the Romans thought about the underworld was, like almost everything else, influenced by the Greeks. Plato talks three times about the underworld, in the *Phaedo*, the *Gorgias*, and the *Republic*—in which Er, who descended into it and was then brought back to life, confirms the existence of a judgment that separates the just from the unjust, an undeniably pre-Christian idea. However, Plato did not have the force of theologian in Roman thought, whether republican or imperial. In addition, it remains to be determined why Plato's thinking, at least insofar as it has come down to us, is so clearly derived from the Academy's Pythagorean and Orphic affinities (that is, those that arose out of Iranian monotheism) with pre-Christian gnosticism—affinities that are quite evident in the *Phaedo*, with its quasi-Manichaean dualism between the essential world (which never manifests itself) and the perceptible world (which is never real).[28] This was pointed out by Friedrich Nietzsche, who in one often misunderstood passage—misunderstood, that is, as anti-Semitic, whereas Nietzsche had already voiced his objections to Wagner's anti-Semitism very clearly—wrote, "it has cost us dearly that this Athenian went and joined the Egyptian school, probably the Egyptian Jews."[29] The main point is that, for the Romans, there was no impiety in rejecting Plato's teachings; in a 1992 poll, by way of context, the majority of Christian Germans expressed the very same incredulity vis-à-vis the likely existence of Hell.[30]

There is no doubt that the Roman elite, those who could be called "intellectual," were skeptical about the Greek myths; the Olympians' arbitrary characters, as well as the Hellenic and especially the Hellenistic irreverence toward them, couldn't help but shock them. This can be seen as early as the Republic; as Mommsen writes, "the Roman national theology always strived to make the phenomenon and attributes of divinity as intelligible as possible."[31] Common sense and logic left little room for the notion of the supernatural that non-Roman peoples associated with divinity; to the Romans, divinity reinforced their intrinsic virtues and tradition, and as such was the tutelary genius of the collective rather than the individual. There was never a question of personal transcendence: Roman culture was functionally immune to mysticism.

It is a fact that the Roman intellectual elite was "irreligious" in the modern sense of the word—in other words, it was atheistic. But the Roman *religio*, again, had almost nothing in common, apart from etymology, with the modern Western idea of religion; *religio* was a body of moral principles whose function was to bind society together, an ethics and a social adhesive at the same time. This "spirit of law" has little more to do with divine immanence than it does with transcendence, and it definitely has nothing to do with revelation—notwithstanding the fact that Numa supposedly went into a grotto to seek counsel from the nymph Egeria. A word that often crops up in Roman texts, *pietas*, must be understood in this context: instead of the Christian piety, it actually means respect for the gods of the city. As Pierre Boyancé writes, "By [*pietas*] we do not mean the Christian 'faith' . . . rather, it is a mode of conduct that expresses [one's] permanent obligation . . . to responsibilities one has assumed."[32]

Pietas, then, is a form of honor; it is inseparable from *virtus*, which is not virtue so much as it is courage or manliness, as well as from *fides*, which in Polybius's formulation is the obligation that a Roman not help himself to public funds. *Fides*, as symbolized by the handshake, is the equivalent of the word of honor, of the agreement based on trust.[33] *Pietas*, *virtus*, *fides*: these are the terms that sum up the Roman feeling that one is the master of one's own destiny; they are an assertion of human liberty and dignity. The apparent aridity of the Roman religion was in actuality a guarantee of cultural cohesion.

According to Lucien Jerphagnon, the title "August" the emperors valued so highly "actually signifies the state of being endowed with *augus*, a greater strength."[34] A term originally applied to temples, the symbolic seats of the ancestral spirit, it implies that the emperors were both the embodiment and the protectors of the nation's might.

The Roman was, in essence, a philosopher, and his theology was therefore civic above all. When the Senate burned the writings ascribed to Numa, it was not only because they were "Pythagorean" but also because they raised the question of the gods once having been deified men. That was an aberration and a folly that the Senate could never tolerate, and there was good reason not to: the emperors were only too eager to have themselves deified. No reasonable mind could help but be inwardly shocked when Octavian, a Pythagorean in his youth and therefore more than ready to believe in secret correspondences among things, chose Apollo as his "patron saint" because the victory at Actium had taken place near one of his shrines.[35] To deduce from this that the Romans did not respect the gods, however, is to give in to the desire to find what one is looking for even when it does not exist.

Some historians[36] believe they have detected a secret sympathy for Judaism, and thus for Christianity, in writers such as Tacitus, and go so far as to presume that this sympathy reflected a disavowal of Roman religion. They ought to have read better. The only mention Tacitus makes of Jesus (he refers to him as "Christ" and seems to confuse Judaism with Christianity, probably because most Christians in Rome were converted Jews) is the following passage from the *Annals*:

> To suppress this rumour [that he was responsible for the burning of Rome], Nero fabricated scapegoats—and punished with every refinement the notoriously depraved Christians (as they were popularly called). Their originator, Christ, had been executed in Tiberius' reign by the governor of Judaea, Pontius Pilate. But in spite of this temporary setback the deadly superstition had broken out afresh, not only in Judaea (where the mischief started) but even in Rome. All degraded and shameful practices collect and flourish in the capital. . . . First, Nero had self-acknowledged Christians arrested. Then, on their information, large numbers of others were condemned—not so much for incendiarism as for their anti-social tendencies.[37]

"Notoriously depraved," "deadly superstition," "mischief," "degraded and shameful," "anti-social tendencies"—it is something of a reach to read these as signs of Tacitus's "unformulated approval" of Judeo-Christianity.

Two lessons emerge from the Roman religion at this juncture. The first is that civilizations can live long and well without the Devil. The second is that there is no such thing as "racial" or ethnic determinism; though the Romans, like the Iranians, were Indo-European and imperialist, the Romans no more than the Etruscans, Latins, or Sabines inherited any great taste for myths, nor any propensity to overstreamline their pantheon. In this respect, one might ask if there was not some sort of cause-and-effect pattern involved, if resident geniuses don't exist, and if, in the end, landscapes don't determine religions; it is hard to imagine an Aztec Virgil or a Venetian or Neapolitan Moses. From Apulia to Tuscany, the Italian terrain is too pleasant to harbor the Devil, at least if he is the hideous beast so complacently described. A native of the harsh Iranian plateaus, weaned on the bitter shores of the Dead Sea, the poor devil would have wasted away under the Roman smiling sky.

CHAPTER 9

Egypt

Unthinkable Damnation

The Egyptian religion stirs the imagination—most often, unfortunately, the literary imagination. Some half-baked theories propose that monotheism was born under the reign of the Eighteenth Dynasty pharaoh Amenhotep IV (or Amenophis IV by his dynastic name, or Akhenaten by the name he called himself), a favorite character in the twentieth-century popular intellectual mythology —or, more precisely, the mythology of intellectual romanticism. (By way of background information, the Eighteenth Dynasty was the most brilliant in the era of the New Empire, which began with Ahmose I; Akhenaten, its most mediagenic representative, ruled between 1375 and 1350 B.C. respectively.)

According to this modern mythology, Amenhotep IV, the son of Amenhotep III, had a flash of intuition when he came to power in 1375 B.C. and replaced the Egyptian pantheon with one single god, Aten or the Sun. A convenient herald of the universal and ultimate monotheism to which humanity would have always been destined, this famous and—why not?—*mysterious* pharaoh with the feminine body and foxlike head was the husband of the no less memorable Nefertiti, a pale beauty whose strangely morose death mask lends her the look of an anachronistic Greta Garbo. I say "strangely morose" because, in every other case the pharaohs and members of their families are portrayed smiling the smile of incarnated divinity. In its blissful serenity, the calm of the person who has contemplated everything but feels no sadness in his detachment, the Egyptian smile is reminiscent of that of Buddha. For a reason that escapes us, however, it does not grace Nefertiti.

Along with the luckless Tutankhamen, more famous for his tomb than for anything he actually did, Akhenaten is the pharaoh who has caused the most modern ink to be spilled. Of all the costumes he has been dressed up in at various times, the most incongruous are those of the mystical pacifist (he was a mystic, maybe, but also a totalitarian ruler who waged military campaigns) and of the almost-Christian monotheist. Sigmund Freud, rarely at a loss for theories, even proposed that Moses, an Egyptian "prince," might have cribbed the notion of the single god from Akhenaten and passed it on to the Hebrews. As we shall see, this hypothesis owes much to fancy.

The combination of this strange-visaged pharaoh, his prophetic monotheism, the beauty of his wife, and the purported transmission of his message to Moses has led a number of writers, not all of them necessarily silly, to construct a mythical triad. To support the speculation that Aten was the conceptual father of Jehovah, they cite the songs of love and adoration that Akhenaten addressed to the "new" deity he had created:

Your rays! They touch everyone . . . You fill the Double Kingdom with your love, and when you rise for them, men begin to live . . . You have separated the sky from the earth so that you can rise in it to contemplate your creation; you are the One, but there are millions of lives in you. . . .

Because Akhenaten did in fact replace the Egyptian pantheon with Aten, the revolution he brought about warrants attention—inventing a unique god, it seems, would logically entail the invention of a unique adversary. If this turns out to be the case, we will have found our Devil alive and well fourteen centuries before our era and eight centuries before his official birth in Iran. The truth, though, is quite different.

The idea, first, of expanding the cult of the sun god Ra or Re and, then, of unifying and simplifying the pantheon had appeared as early as the reign of Amenhotep III the Great. According to Adolf Erman and Ernst Ranke, for instance,

> In the New Empire, Amen of Thebes, Horus who reigned the horizon, Khnum of Elephantine, and Atum of Heliopolis are all identified with Re. . . . Taken to the extreme, this tendency would logically have resulted in the gradual suppression of polytheism, and indeed there were some attempts to do so. In the Hymns to the Sun [which antedate Akhenaten], the composite divinity Amen-Re-Horakhte-Atum is addressed as *one god.*"[1]

Amenhotep IV's "flash of intuition" thus exits; the trend toward monotheism predated our ambiguous monarch. Erman and Ranke continue: "In a very ancient era, the cult of Osiris, originally based in the Delta village of Dedu (later called Busiris, 'the house of Osiris'), took hold all over Egypt and incorporated other gods, such as Ptah and Sokar from Memphis and Khenti-Amentiu from Abydos, into him."[2] This movement toward unification, however, can be explained by the makeup of the Egyptian nation: "Insofar as the peasants in every Egyptian nome [province] were becoming aware that they belonged to one homogeneous people, and insofar as contacts among the various sections of the country were intensifying, the cult of the gods must have increased national cohesion."[3]

In other words, the country's unification, as well as the religion that accompanied it, was based on a national consciousness that itself was subject to political influences. If the Eighteenth Dynasty accelerated the unification of the pantheon, it was because that dynasty in particular contributed much to the ascendancy of Egypt. Its founder, Ahmose I, crushed the Hyksos in the northeastern Delta, first seizing their stronghold at Avaris and then driving them into Palestine, where after a three-year siege he sacked another of their strongholds, Sharuhen. Ahmose then wiped out the factions that were contesting his power in Nubia. His precedent was followed by the first Amenhotep, who waged wars in Libya and Nubia, extending Egypt's borders as far south as the third Nile cataract. Nubia and the lower Sudan were placed under a vice-royalty whose power extended southward to the fourth cataract; the Nile valley was thus controlled almost all of the way to the river's sources. Amenhotep's successor, Thutmose I, expanded the empire to the Euphrates. This pharaoh, who did so much for his country, was the first to be buried in the Valley of the Kings.

Egypt had become rich and powerful, but it had also been centralized. The Eighteenth Dynasty abolished the provincial seignories that had flourished under the Middle Empire. After the reigns of Thutmose II, Thutmose III (who came back from a campaign along the Orontes river with no fewer than seven captured kings), Amenhotep II, Thutmose IV, and Amenhotep III, Egypt enjoyed unrivaled power. Tribute poured in from every part of the known world, indirectly financing the massive projects that still can be admired today, the temples at Luxor and Thebes and the spectacular sights at Karnak.

In a way, each Eighteenth Dynasty pharaoh was not only a god-king, since divinity was synonymous with royalty, but in fact a sun-king. By lessening the relative brilliance of the other deities (though, as we shall see, not eliminating them), the state religion necessarily increased the pharaohs' divine status. Unification therefore proceeded in the standard way, with the other gods becoming identified with the sovereign Ra.

Our Akhenaten thus enjoyed a great inheritance, although not in the biological sense; with their large, hermaphroditic hips and abnormally elongated faces, his effigies strongly hint at genetic anomalies. It has been supposed that this fanatic[4] was a priest of Ra-Horakhte ("Ra-Horus of the Horizon") at Heliopolis. His cult to this deity was not traditional but, instead, based on an archaic reading of the name "Aten," which referred not to the deity but to the solar disk itself. As Erman and Ranke make clear, the word "was in no way hallowed by usage in the religious vocabulary."

Contrary to the legend, Akhenaten did not bring about what in modern terms we would call a "transubstantiation" of the solar deity Ra—very much the opposite, in fact. He did not establish a symbol of divinity that transcended the Egyptian pantheon or concretized the monotheist tendencies of the Egyptian religion; instead, he commanded that the sun be worshiped in its specifically material manifestation.

The monotheist interpretation is based on the fact that Akhenaten made the solar disk into "the god beyond whom none other exists." On the face of it, this was indeed a monotheist revolution, but it introduced the particularity of abolishing the whole symbolism of the Egyptian pantheon, which in any case already revolved around the cult of a single but multifarious divinity. Now, instead, that symbolism was radically impoverished. Akhenaten ordered the worship not of a deity that assumed the form of the sun but, rather, of the sungod pure and simple. The deity had once encompassed everything: birth, death, spirituality, sexuality, vegetation, sky, stars, moon. Now it was reduced to nothing more than the day star. Akhenaten replaced traditional religion with a reductivist idolatry.

The action was all the more strange in that royalty itself was contingent upon the Egyptian religion's apparent polytheism. To the Egyptians, the polymorphous nature of the universe was really the expression of a single, unique truth; from this it followed that the pharaoh's power, reflecting the divine reality, covered every aspect of life. Since the pharaoh was now only the god-sun, nothing more, Akhenaten effectively alienated himself from the manifestations of divinity and from the miracles of life. This point is vital, since the various Egyptian gods were expressions, indeed metaphors, of the divinity, which was ungraspable and unknowable and therefore omnipresent in its mystery. "The myth of Osiris," writes Claude Traunecker, "that god who dies and is reborn . . . was a way of expressing all cyclical phenomena, whether these be vegetation, the rising of the Nile, or even life and death."[5]

This is not to say that polytheism was superficial and unimportant, or that Akhenaten had exposed, brutally but perhaps usefully, a mythological and liturgical sham; to do so would be to oversimplify the Egyptian philosophy, in which, as Traunecker once more points out, "several objects can be the points of emergence of the same force."[6] Caught between the impossibility of apprehending the divinity and the necessity of paying it homage, the Egyptian dedicated his cults to the expressions of the divinity that he could know, fear, and worship.

Egypt's religion, like its civilization, is undeniably of African origin, and as elsewhere in Africa the sentiment of divinity is natural to it. The divinity is inherent in life, and life in all its forms is divinity. Given that the Egyptian word *neter* means both "god" and "renewal,"[7] the divinity is what renews itself continually—a concept essential to understanding ancient Egypt as well as the reason that the clergy and the people maintained so many altars.

Perhaps because it disconcerted Western Egyptologists, the original nature of the Egyptian gods was for many years the subject of debate: Were they totems, fetishes, or fully formed gods? The argument is obsolete today; S. Morenz has proposed that the very idea of gods—which remains to be defined—cannot appear until the individual has become conscious of his identity,[8] much along the lines of the child's process of distinguishing himself from his environment. It is possible, however, that the importance of writing has been overlooked: any concept that can be written down, fixed, becomes richer in meaning and power over time. The Egyptians had writing; that, no doubt, is how they were able to transform totems or fetishes into gods (before, in turn, the monotheisms transformed a few of these into demons, then into one Devil). The Egyptian gods seem to have appeared during the Thinite dynasties, or around 3150 B.C.; some with animal heads can be identified by that time, such as a falcon, the predecessor of Horus, a cow, the precursor of Hathor, and an elephant, which later fell out of the pantheon. All these bear witness to the "passage from nature to culture" posited by Claude Lévi-Strauss.

While these animal heads guaranteed their individuality, the Egyptian gods operated in a mutable field where the same deity could sometimes be masculine, sometimes feminine. The roles changed too: Amon was sometimes father, sometimes mother, while "the goddess Neith, the creator of the world, is a man acting as a woman, a woman acting as a man"[9]—bisexuality was merely an expression of the androgyny of the eternal ones. Sobek, the god-crocodile and deity of aquatic animals, could turn into Sobek-Re, who governed the course of the sun.

In a sense, polytheism was a lesson in human humility, a statement of the impossibility of a terrestrial being ever knowing the essential nature of the divinity. Akhenaten's revolution was an involution: in one sweep, it claimed to have unmasked the nature of divinity. The self-pride it betrays was not only intellectual but also personal and dynastic, since because the pharaoh was of divine essence, Akhenaten was identifying *himself* with the god-sun.

One could claim that Akhenaten had resolved the tension that Mircea Eliade identified between the pharaoh's twin paternities: according to the solar theology, he was in fact the son of Re, but since he also succeeded the previous, deceased sovereign as represented by Osiris, he was in equal measure Horus as well. Akhenaten supposedly was the exclusive incarnation of the sun. Yet this is doubtful because, on the one hand, the solar theology of the Old and Middle Empires had progressively become dominated, if not replaced, by the royal ideology of the Osiris filiation, while on the other, the pharaoh had always been the son of Re, never Re himself, who was by definition unknowable. One wonders where Akhenaten could have found his heretical idea. As Pascal Vernus and Jean Yoyotte claim, he seems to have been influenced by Heliopolitan thinkers who "held only the disk of the sun as evidence of the creator."[10] It is difficult to see how Moses borrowed his monotheism from this.[11] As we have seen, the Jews had many other sources of inspiration.

It would thus be wrong to see Akhenaten as the inventor of monotheism. As Vernus and Yoyotte note: "Some histories have portrayed him as an emancipator struggling against an obscurantist idolatry, a pacifist with ecumenical ideas, an anticlerical populist fighting against the oppression of Amen and his priests. All of these have either been contradicted by other sources or are anachronistic and speculative."[12] Akhenaten invented neither God nor the Devil.

What remains to be seen is whether or not the Devil existed in whole or in part in the Egyptian religion; but before we can do this, we must define the very vague term "Egyptian religion," which implies that it was a homogenous and stable set of beliefs. And that it was not: it lasted three thousand years, but since it was a worldview as opposed to a body of dogmas, it was subject to a great deal of change and transformation.

For many years, it was taught that Egypt had two principal gods—Horus, master of Upper Egypt, and Seth, master of Lower Egypt, both sons of Isis and Osiris—who vied with each other for power. Seth murdered his father Osiris and thus threatened Horus's patrimony. Horus challenged Seth to single combat, defeated him, and so came to rule over the unified Two Kingdoms. In the myth, which serves to illustrate the legitimate transfer of royal power, Horus is the good, while Seth is the bad. Seth comes off quite negatively in a number of other myths as well, and for that reason he could prefigure the spirit of Evil.

Yet, once again, the truth is much more complex. Two major points emerge. First, the cult of the sky-god Horus began in the Delta sometime in prehistory, and from there it spread all over Egypt. It has been proposed, erroneously, that the Horus cult revolved around an Upper Egyptian god, since the city that was dedicated to him, Hierakonpolis ("the town of the falcon"), at Kekhen, was then the capital of the Upper Kingdom. Seth, on the contrary, was indeed a god of Upper Egypt; he ruled in the city of Ombos. In very ancient times, both lived in peace and were considered protectors of the monarchy. Sometime before the Fifth Dynasty, one part of Egypt was assigned to each to justify their coexistence; in an inversion of their origins, Seth was given Lower Egypt, and Horus was given Upper Egypt.

Second, the opposition between the two gods was a relatively late development; toward the end of the Fifth Dynasty, or around 2245 B.C., the deceased king began to be represented by Osiris and his successor, the living king, by Horus. Only then did Horus become the son of Osiris and Isis. Since Seth couldn't share the kingship with him, under the circumstance he became Horus's rival and enemy. It was then, too, that the story of Seth's murder of Osiris was created.

In other words, the apparent Good-Evil/Horus-Seth conflict was the religious translation of dynastic problems. In Egyptian religion, there was never a Good or Evil in the Christian sense; only by extrapolation can these concepts even be used. "Evil," that which is baneful, was produced by the irruption of Chaos into Creation, which in its totality is "Good." "Evil" as described in the post–Fifth Dynasty religion was whatever the king considered to be a political enemy, a scenario that was subsequently to be repeated in the religions of all monarchic states. In other words, "Evil" as a manifestation of the Chaos that threatened Creation had an indirectly political role.

Yet Egyptian rituals were aimed at helping to maintain Creation. From the beginning of Egyptian history to the Roman occupation, the religion's myths changed continually, in the north as in the south, enriched by foreign imports as much as the religion itself enriched foreign pantheons—the Assyrians would adopt Seth, for instance, since they saw him as quite similar to their own Baal. The myths of Horus and Osiris are eloquent testimony to this variability; even their names would come to change. As the acme of metamorphosis, the Greeks were to identify Horus with Apollo, while the image of the Egyptian god killing the crocodile Setekh became an inspiration to the Christians, who transformed him into the Saint George who slew the dragon. The same held true of Osiris, the hero of innumerable myths.

This variability was not the product of incoherence; instead, it reflected the Egyptian conviction that it is impossible to apprehend the truth of divinity in a direct way. It is also a reflection of the religion's political and economic structure: the temples constituted economic powers and often possessed huge territories, and large sections of the populace were integrated into the priestly hierarchy and employed in the administration of the estates. The temples were an important part of the national economy. Each province and each high priest enjoyed the freedom of honoring such-and-such a god, as well as of interpreting the sacred writings after their own fashion. Egyptian religion had no central seat, no equivalent of pope or imam.

Moreover, the recognition accorded to Chaos never spilled over into the realm of ethics. Good or Evil could only exist down here, and so Chaos or "Evil" was contingent; the need for cosmic balance made sure it was checked. It was also respectable in that it represented a force that predated Creation. Until the time of the New Empire, there was no ethical system in ancient Egypt other than the one that governed society, whose basic principle was to maintain harmony and to make the use of force needless. It was only later that religion established a relationship between the moral sense and religiosity, arguing that the faithful were inspired to virtue by their fear of the gods.[13]

The human being could only probe the deities; he could not penetrate their inner essence. Until the Roman occupation, the Egyptian pantheon retained what could be termed its polysemy, its multiplicity of meanings, and the pervasive feeling was that all events and actions were relative. Though Seth many have been the enemy of royalty, the sower of discord, and the embodiment of aggression, he kept both his godly status and his potential usefulness. When a resurgence of the original Chaos appeared in the form of the serpent Apopis, which began to wreak havoc, causing famines, floods, and locust plagues, when it was said the Re's boat had run aground on "the sandbank of Apopis," it was Seth whom Re dispatched to deal with the monster and reestablish order. At times like this "Evil" became good.

One is tempted to look elsewhere for the Devil, for instance this serpent Apopis. Born from the spittle of the demiurge Neith, he rebelled, as would Satan. Yet since he arose out of the original Chaos, out of metaphysical Evil, he was the unknowable issue of a struggle between the created and the uncreated; Apopis no more embodied Evil than did any of the other divinities who represented the forces of destruction. His reptilian form should not fool us: to the Egyptians, "the snake is associated with chthonian divinities or the forces of growth" because it is always seen coming out of a hole.[14] The snake is the quintessential image of the creator-god Atum.[15] In the *Egyptian Book of the Dead*, Men, a god who in this case is identified with Horus avenging his father Osiris, dons a diadem crowned by two feathers or two vipers, "the two great vipers that are before the face of the god Atum."[16]

Rebel powers and sometime messengers of Chaos, serpents are not malefic as such but, instead, represent the forces that predate Creation and that one must be careful not to destroy, since they could prove useful. This is also the case with the *Nun*, an inert yet threatening liquid that envelops the created world (and from which all life issues) but also can manifest itself in a destructive way, for instance torrential rains or disastrous floods; after the revolt of Men, the Lord of All declares that "this earth will return to the state of *Nun*."[17] Even if it lends its form to the monster Apopis, the serpent is not the emblem of Evil: along with the hawk and the scarab beetle, it is one of the three animals sacred to the sun-god Re. More telling still, the cobra is the central ornament on the white crown of Upper Egypt. The Egyptian pantheon in general displays little fear of other dangerous animals: the goddess Selkis, the guardian of Osiris's body, has a scorpion's head, while Sobek, the god of fear and fertility, has a crocodile's head; Ermutis, the goddess of crops, has a serpent's head, as does Meresger, another form of Isis.

This is not to say that the Egyptians didn't have demons—they had legions of them. As in the Pacific religions, these secondary deities were held responsible for illnesses and misfortune, and as in the monotheist imagination they were odious and repugnant— thus "he-of-the-repulsive-face," "he-who-lives-on-worms," even "he-who-lives-on-excrement." In Traunecker's words, "they were especially dangerous at times of transition, like the five days of journeying before the deceased reached *duat*," the hereafter.

These demons were called the *akhu*, and, according to Trau-necker again, they "preferred the edges of the settled world"[18]— the desert, darkness, faraway places, and water. In this respect, they are undeniably the Devil's ancestors, since he tends to favor the same locales; they probably influenced the Judaic imagination, which passed them on to the two later religions. Yet these "sub-alterns of Chaos" nevertheless have little symbolic import.

In the Egyptian cosmogony, Creation is a fragile moment in the heart of Chaos, and in and of itself it does not contain any good or evil principle—ethics, again, being a feature of human and thus terrestrial society. The deepest proscriptions in Egyptian society were aimed not at enforcing a metaphysical principle of Good as we might be tempted to understand it but, instead, at guaranteeing the stability of Creation, the source of all life. Original sin did not exist, and purification rituals were reserved for funerary rites and the statues of the gods.

To the Egyptians, the whole world, including the deities, was transitory. "The death of gods, whoever they be, is often mentioned in religious texts," wrote Egyptologist Alexandre Moret at the beginning of this century. "The *Book of Knowing What Is in Hades* depicts the sepulchers of Ra, Tumu, the god of the living, as well as of Osiris or Socharis, the god of the dead. The author of *De Iside et Osiride* [that is, Plutarch] also mentions this tradition: 'The Egyptian priests say not only of this god [Osiris] but of all the gods (who are neither eternal nor incorruptible) that their bodies lie among them, buried and venerated, and that their souls are brilliant stars in the sky.' "[19]

The gods live thanks solely to the cults of mortals, and if the kings and priests neglect their sacred offices, they will wither, fall into decrepitude, and petrify.[20] This amounts to saying that divinity is the product of Creation and of human will; since there is no eternal divinity, nor is there absolute Good and Evil. Earthly good and evil are the reflections of the struggle between Chaos and the order of Creation, whose arbiter is the royal power, and the human transgressions punished by the temporal power are those that could create a breach through which Chaos might flood in. Until the end of all things, though, Creation is merely a series of re-beginnings: every night the setting sun is swallowed in the west by the celestial vault, the goddess Nut, from where it emerges again the next day, spreading her thighs to rise in the sky.

The Egyptians believed that the world would eventually end. Egyptian religion had an eschatology, its own rather unobtrusive vision of the final end. It is from the Egyptians that the Greeks borrowed the idea that there will be an end of time, and that afterward a golden age will dawn over a new and more stable world. It is from the Greeks that we in turn borrowed it.

Wisdom and serenity, we might think—the Egyptian lived without sadness, protected by his faith in countless smiling gods. However, in reality the Egyptian mythology is rife with tears, beginning with those of Isis, when her brother Osiris has fallen into Seth's trap. Envious of Osiris's glory, Seth brought a splendidly decorated sarcophagus to his palace one night when Osiris was holding a feast; he promised to give it to whichever guest could fit into it most perfectly. Osiris innocently accepted the challenge; when he got into it, seventy-two of Seth's accomplices leaped onto it and nailed it shut. They ballasted it with molten lead and threw it into the river, which bore it out to sea. But Isis cried and cut her hair as a sign of grief, then went off to search for the coffin, which the sea had carried to Byblos, in Phoenicia, where a miraculous tree had grown up around it. Once Isis had freed it, she put the sarcophagus on a boat and made for the sea. She opened it, placed her face against her brother's face, kissed him, and wept.[21]

These are eternal fears, and they prove that the Egypt of granite and glorious sunlight was also sensitive to sorrow, pain, and anxiety—that it wasn't just the country of hypostylic chambers, of stone giants, and of the Sphinx. The smiles on the statues should not let us ignore the suffering of mortals, which comes across more clearly in the papyri. The Egyptian also understood death.

Yet Osiris's death was not the shadowy and sordid downfall that is our legacy from the Middle Ages, with its vision of cadavers devoured by worms and demons; instead, it is an entry, as prudent as it is majestic, into the kingdom of the gods. The corruption of the flesh was as well known in Egypt as anywhere else, but they held that it could and should be exorcised by divine grace. One of many proofs lies in the "Hymn to Osiris" chapter of *The Book of the Dead*, also known as "The Chapter of the Body That Does Not Have To Die."

Homage to you, O my divine father Osiris. I have come to you so that you may embalm me, yes, embalm my limbs that are here, for I do not want to perish and be destroyed, but I want to be like my divine father Khepera, whose divine person never knew corruption. Come then, make it that I master my breaths, O you master of winds, who magnifies the divine beings who resemble you. Fortify me and make me strong, O lord of the funerary coffer. Allow me to enter the land of eternity, as that was allowed to you, to you and your father Tenu, O you whose

body has never known corruption. . . . When the worms see me
and recognize me, make them fall to their bellies, make their
fear of me terrify them, and do the same for every creature after
my death, animal, bird, fish, worm, or reptile. And make life be
born from my death.[22]

A marvelous and tender text, the hymn shows once again that the
Egyptian was no stranger to anxiety: his faith in the divinity transformed it into hope.

The notion of an eternal Devil to whom the damned would be
consigned at the Last Judgment was inconceivable. The idea of
salvation was as unheard of as was that of damnation. Convinced
of the ineluctability of death and of an ultimate return to the original
Chaos, Egyptian religion was no more than the mirror of human
society. It resembled the god Shu, or "space," who in his extended
arms holds up the arched body of the goddess Nut, the celestial
vault itself. Shu will die too, and the vault will collapse. Lacking
dogmas, resting only on rituals and myths, the religion imposed no
more ethical judgments on human actions than it did on human
nature, or indeed on Nature in general. All it demanded was rev-
erence for the divinity and its earthly representatives, the pharaohs.
Along with Greek religion, it is the last of the great religions that
sought for nothing more than to keep the human being and the
Creator in harmony with the antagonistic powers. It could not, therefore, dream up a Devil; in a civilization in which even the gods
died, eternal damnation was unthinkable.

CHAPTER 10

Africa

The Cradle of Religious Ecology

By 2500 B.C., when Egypt was already in its Second Dynasty (the mysterious one with its black pharaohs), and when in the north the Danubian peoples were beginning to invade western Europe, the Sahara started to dry out. Its populations flowed southward; the Kalahari Bushmen are probably the last vestiges of these migrations. Its monuments, where they still exist, remain a puzzle, like the relatively recent temple uncovered in Rhodesia (modern-day Zimbabwe) by Leo Frobenius in 1928. Not only is there no clue as to what deity the temple honored, but its very age is impossible to establish; the likely range is some five centuries, from the twelfth century to the seventeenth.

The Africa of historical times is barely less vague. When Pope Gregory III addressed a missive to the legendary Prester John in 1177, he didn't even know where to send it. The enduring legend of this potentate, who was presumed to be an ally of Christianity, did not acquire a geographical seat until the fifteenth century, when it was settled upon that he was the king of Abyssinia, the realm that succeeded the Axumite dynasty. Any Abyssinian king was in fact a Christian; by as early as the fourth century, eastern Africa had begun to be converted by Syrian monks such as Frumentius, the *abuna* or bishop of Abyssinia and the founder of the Coptic Church. And the Axumite kingdom—named after its capital, Axum, which lay at the elevation of some ten thousand feet in what today is the province of Tigré—was more ancient still: the Axumite *Book of Abyssinia* says that the kingdom had been founded several millennia before, in other words, well before the advent of Christianity.

The question, then, is who founded it. That the kingdom was ancient was not just a local boast: references to its inhabitants, the Aethiops, are to be found in Homer. As for who they were and where they came from, the few available Sabean, Greek, and Ge'ez monumental inscriptions offer only isolated fragments of Abyssinian history. All that is known for sure is that Axum was founded in the second millennium B.C., perhaps earlier, by Semites who came from Arabia via the Red Sea.[1] They were colonists in that they came to power after defeating the Ethiopians, the "dark-faced people," who were the original inhabitants of the land then called the Kingdom of Kush, or Punt. The impressive monoliths they hewed out of the rock, contemporaries of Baalbek, indicate that they worshiped the sun.

Many questions crop up at this point, namely what Ethiopian religion was before the arrival of the Semites and how the solar cult the Semites introduced later combined with a freshly imported Christianity. We still have only a very schematic idea of the warren of religions in ancient Ethiopia, which included African creeds as well as others that were Semitic, Christian, and Hellenistic Greek and Roman (the port of Adulis, the present-day Zula, was a great Mediterranean trading center[2])—not to mention vestiges of ancient Egyptian religion, in addition to Judaism and, perhaps even Asian religions. It is difficult to unravel the tangled skein around each individual belief or to determine how this or that people dealt with its particular conception of evil.

We have barely touched the issue of Asian influences on Africa, for instance on the Bantu through Malay-Polynesian mariners from Indonesia, who around the fifth century introduced new pottery and agricultural techniques. Whether or not the Bantu disseminated this knowledge beyond their own tribes is unknown, as are the reasons behind the staggering rise of the Benin culture during the era of the European Middle Ages. We know almost nothing about Judaic influences on eastern Africa, for example via the mysterious Jewish state in southern Arabia against which the Axumite king Caleb, or el-Esbana, launched an expeditionary force in the sixth century.

The West has always considered Africa a passive land; in reality, it was in Africa that a man named Abraham helped to forge the destiny of the world by helping Christianity's greatest rival. An Axumite king, Abraham generously offered asylum to Muhammad and his persecuted disciples. Had he refused them this hospitality, the prophet and his followers would undoubtedly have been destroyed. As the historian Edward Gibbon first pointed out, Abraham allowed the nascent Islam to rally its forces and then to conquer, first militarily and then spiritually, an empire that today stretches from Gibraltar to Indonesia. In more ways than one, Africa has shaped the world.

Among other factors that have molded Africa is Christianity. It is often assumed that Africa was almost free of Western influences before the arrival of the missionaries in the wake of the great nineteenth-century colonial empires—the British, French, and, as is sometimes overlooked, the German. Yet by the middle of the fifteenth century, the Portuguese were Christianizing west Africa from Elmina in present-day Ghana to the Congo basin, where they managed to convert the monarch, or *manikongo*, and a good number of his subjects. This evangelizing involved a few setbacks, as when the *manikongo* unexpectedly renounced his friendship with Portugal and temporarily put an end to its missionary activities. Other attempts nevertheless took place over the following centuries, and these in turn produced a handful of composite religions. Since the peoples of Africa were highly migratory, it is much more difficult to trace the origins of their own religions than it is to trace the syncretistic religions that arose out of contacts with Christianity. Because of almost constant tribal movement, the African religions were chronically mutable in a way that left them much more prone to influences than, say, were the religions of Asia.

Until 1927, for instance, the Bwiti of Gabon's equatorial forests practiced a syncretistic religion that they had been introduced to by another tribe, the Mizogo. In Europe, paradoxically, this religion was seen as an obstacle to the work of Christian missionaries. In the words of Gert Chesi, "Using Christian symbols such as tapers, rosaries, crosses, and altars, the Bwiti practiced a religion that was something other than Christianity; their sanguinary rites were used to exorcise illnesses and to lay curses on their enemies."[3]

At one time, Africa had been on the road to Christianity; now it is on its way to Islam—when, at least, the continent isn't falling apart (the starving peoples of the Sahel have little time for either God or the Devil). However, the worst of it is that the destruction of African religions has been accelerated by *both* of the imported religions and their previously unknown sectarianism. The Kirdi of northern Cameroon, for example, were repressed by the Islamic Foulbe tribe, which isolated them in a religious and cultural ghetto, and even sold them as slaves.

It is clearly impossible, at this point, to find any "pure" African religion; in the wake of the general admixture among African religions and between the African religions and the monotheisms, all African belief systems now draw from what is practically the same well.

Insofar as they have survived, more or less, through ethnological accounts, African mythologies seem to have been rich in myths and legends. The one constant all over the continent is that only two evils exist, aridity and death, which are really the same in that aridity *is* death. From the savannah to the jungle, from the plain to the mountain, there is no life without water. "If it weren't for *nommo* [water] . . . the earth could not have been created, because the earth was dead and it was only through water that it came to life," says Ogotemmeli, one of the repositors of the Dogon tribe's memory, in *The Gods of Water*, one of the most famous works in African ethnology.[4]

Since it is possible that Africa was, along with Asia, one of humanity's two birthplaces, African religions are among the oldest in the world. If the religious sentiment is innate, it can be supposed that the Africans were among the first to imagine gods. These will probably never be known, however, given that there was no other way of handing down the African religions than through oral tradition. The bulk of African art is made of wood, a perishable medium, and apart from the bronze artifacts of the Benin culture, the oldest surviving objects rarely date back more than two centuries. Only in an extremely fragmented way can we determine what influence any one mythology might have had on any other, or how a given religion might have derived from any other.

The salient feature of all African religions is that they are organized around two poles or values—life or nothing, one or zero, with no logical opposition between the two. The beauty of African religions lies not in the wealth of their myths so much as in their organic nature. The African of Ghana or the Sudan is inherently religious because he lives in a world where existence itself seems magical. Religion does not manifest itself only during fixed ceremonies—birth, burial, circumcision, marriage, harvest feasts—but, rather, saturates the entirety of individual and collective behavior. As one African intellectual has wryly noted, "Black Africa is hopelessly religious."[5]

As opposed to religions in which one does one's duty by merely showing up at a cult center on specific dates, the Kenyan or Sudanese farmer goes to market in contact with an Almighty who will determine his success or failure. His aim is to celebrate life in all its splendor; the Devil has no place in this scheme, since the only inverse of life is death. One need only have seen a twentieth-century African raising his arms in religious ecstasy at the coming of the first rains to understand that water falling out of the sky can be the gift of a benevolent Almighty as well as a sign of his wrath; whatever the case, it is the expression of a cosmic dynamism, not merely the bland effect of a warm weather meeting a cold one.

The idea of animism has long clouded outside views of African religions. To the Arab colonists as well as to the Europeans, to Islamic as well as Christian missionaries, the diversity of Africa's myths and legends and the wealth of its pantheons made the religions seem childlike if not childish; Africans, it was thought, were incapable of transcending their beliefs in the spirits of baobab trees, snakes, and rivers to encompass the higher notion of one great God, the Creator of the universe. This bias has been propagated ad nauseam by that most redoubtable of all cultures, the media. It is often claimed, for instance, that Africans are fetishists, which is a total misunderstanding; they have never adored idols (in any case, "adore" is something of an overstatement)—they revere the genies and spirits the idols represent, and to whom any given propitiatory or sacrificial rite is addressed.

The equation of animism with atheism is just as misguided. To begin with, animism, or the cult of spirits, is based on a perception of the soul's immortality that is related, if not identical, to the one shared by the monotheisms; the only appreciable difference is that animism broadens the concept to include the soul of entities other than humans. To the African, every one of God's creations contains a portion of his breath, and even the acutest of minds could never penetrate all of its secrets. The Dinka and Chilluk of the Sudan, for instance, believe that there is a portion of the divine in all things, and that the balance of the universe hinges upon this fact. When someone grows old or falls seriously ill, the decline in his or her divinity raises the possibility of a more widespread catastrophe. It is for this reason that the sick or dying are—or, rather, were at one time—often killed. Almost every African religion attests to this sense of the cosmic.

Second, the overwhelming majority of African religions grant the existence of a supreme being who created the universe. The West has long, and wrongly, prided itself on having invented monotheism, and it has rejected all other religions as being pagan or primitive; this is untrue at best, since in the first place monotheism was "invented" by Zoroaster in the sixth century B.C., and in the second place there is every indication that the African religions have long been monotheistic, albeit with polytheistic tendencies. Dinka mythology, for example, rests on the same premises as the Semitic myth of paradise: in a time immemorial, all humans had direct access to God, and suffering and death were unknown. It is quite possible that the paradise myth is universal because it is the nostalgic tale of childhood lost.

The fact that this deity is surrounded by vassals and supernatural forces does not mean that his power is in any way lessened; instead, it expresses the need to represent his secondary aspects within the framework of Creation, which, in the African religions as well as in Genesis, assumes the form of a story. The intervention of powers such as the lion-man or the jackal-man is a natural reflection of the cultures that produced the African religions, just as the depiction of the Creator in the Jewish and Christian monotheisms—as an old man with a white beard who is jealous and unpredictable—reflects the patriarchy that shaped Hebrew society.

To the Westerner, God either exists and is mysteriously unjust, and thus cannot be credited with the privilege of being Good, or He doesn't exist and the world is absurd. To the African, on the other hand, this contradiction is a dilemma in appearance only, and it arises from the human inability to understand the world in its totality. "The Yoruba's belief in the simultaneous existence of these aspects of time [that is, "real" time and the timelessness of the gods] in the midst of his daily life has long been recognized, but it has also been misunderstood," writes the Nigerian writer Wole Soyinka.[6] "It isn't an abstraction. Unlike the European, the Yoruba is not interested in the purely conceptual aspects of time, which are too concretely manifest in his own life, religion, and sensibility to be mere conventions explaining the metaphysical nature of his world." Unlike some European assertions whose subtext is patently racist, the Yoruba, Soyinka continues, clearly distinguishes "between himself and the deities, between himself and the ancestors, between the apparent and the real."

Moreover, it should be underscored that African religions are in many ways extremely "modern," and that along with a few other soon-to-be-extinct religions, such as those of the North American Indians, they speak directly to the global consciousness that has sprung up in the late twentieth century. They are religions of unity with nature. As René Bureau writes, "The African is not the absolute master of nature, which is peopled by beings that control fertility, health, and natural phenomena in general." The deity, "the supreme ancestor, a sort of hypostasis of God, sometimes in the company of a double or two as well as a multitude of beings invisible to man . . . directs and dominates life, the fundamental reality of the universe. . . . Man is part of the cosmos; he is included in it; he enjoys the use of it, but he doesn't own it."[7] The best way to put it is that the African religions are creeds of the kind the West is rediscovering today after having plundered its air, water, and lands—in other words, after having for too long considered itself their owner.

This respect for nature means that in Africa "the simple organization of inhabited space (the arrangement of the village) perfectly reflects the concern for orderedness upon which the relationship between the individual and the environment is based," note A. Ba Hampate and Germaine Dieterlen.[8] "Though only the tiniest part of the cosmos," the house, writes I. Sow, "is at the same time an infrastructure entirely subject to the human's organization and control *and* a superstructure that to the highest degree expresses the concept of the universe."[9]

It would be impossible as well as useless to try to understand the African religions without grasping that their basic principle was to preserve the natural order. This conception of the world, which is far from being specifically African, naturally leads to seeing the world as it actually is in order to determine how its original purity can be maintained and the admixtures that would spoil it avoided.[10] The consequences of this idea can produce the oddest of behaviors. According to Jean Cazeneuve, "among the Kikuyu [of Kenya], a man can become impure by the mere fact of having witnessed a frog, an aquatic animal, leap into a fire. This is a sin and he must confess it."[11] Cazeneuve continues: "Among the Ba-Ila, who call anything alien or unusual *tonda* (a term closely analogous to 'taboo'), one woman refused to eat bananas when they were first introduced into the country because she said they were *tonda*."[12]

This is why many African tribes practice an ancestor worship similar to that of China (although there it is done for entirely different reasons): the dead are the vanished witnesses to a world that has remained the same from the very beginning, and as such they are invested with supreme spiritual authority. Among the Tallensi and Lo Dagaa of northern Ghana, for example, it is the dead who lay down moral and legal rules for the living.

The Devil—who plays such a large role in our own mythology, since he is part of the world as it has always been and could for that reason be called "natural"—has no place within African religions, despite every Christian and Islamic effort to make one for him. Were he really the Enemy, impurity would have had to have existed for all time; but this idea contradicts the philosophy of African religions, which recognize error but never original sin. All evil proceeds from the inability of individuals to fit in with or respect the cosmic order. This is the reason behind the abundance of rituals in African societies, which always seems to amaze Westerners, conditioned by the idea of laity, of the general insignificance of their own actions and the events in their everyday lives.

Not only is the Devil a complete stranger to the African sense of the cosmos but he is also excluded from the continent's religions: the very idea of the Devil presupposes that of free will, a notion incompatible with the philosophies of the African religions. The conscious choice of Evil makes no sense to Africans, except of course for those who have been Westernized. In fact, the vision that informs the mythologies underlying these religions is a tragic one: death rules over everything. This is particularly clear in the legend about the young man and death, as told by the Basumbwa tribe of Victoria's Nyanza district. A young man sees his deceased father tending Death's herds. The ghost leads the young man into a gully, which descends into the earth, toward a place where a crowd has gathered. When they reach the crowd, the father leaves the son. The Great Chief of Death appears; half his body is magnificent, but the other is rotted and crawling with worms. The faithful pluck out the worms and wash the sores, and when they have finished Death proclaims that whoever is born that day will be cheated if he goes into commerce, that the woman who conceives that day will die in childbirth, that whoever works his field will lose his crops, and that whoever ventures into the jungle will be eaten by a lion. Then Death vanishes, only to reappear again the next day. The faithful wash and perfume the magnificent side of his body. When they finish, Death declares that whoever is born that day will be rich, that the woman who conceives will produce a child who will enjoy long life, that whoever does anything that day will have good luck, and that whoever ventures into the jungle will find a lot of game and perhaps even an elephant or two. "Had you arrived today," the dead father tells his son, who of course had appeared on the bad day, "you would have been lucky, but what you got was poverty. Tomorrow you must leave."[13]

Destiny is preordained and ineluctible. The very thought of rebellion against the supreme will is inconceivable, since revolt would only upset the cosmic order, and this would be the ultimate crime. Whatever variations there may be among the African religions, they are all centered around the deity; none propose that there is a symmetrical empire of Evil. In *The Gods of Water*, Ogotemmeli says that no straying into an empire of Evil is possible; the tribe's proscriptions are established according to natural law, and their violation is an error, not a crime.[14]

Evil spirits, who are a manifestation of the "ill will" that opposes the cosmic order and whose neutralization is the main task of witch doctors, should not be seen as "secondary" devils but, instead, as the emanation of past errors or jealousies, the anger of the dead, and the residue of violated taboos. The object is to bring the defiant one back into the ordered fold, not to exclude him from it.

One of the more significant results of this worldview is the way that "insanity" is treated in Africa. Up until the eighteenth century in the West it was believed to be a curse, even a Satanic visitation, and treated as such. In Africa it is accepted by the community, which allows it to be resolved in a noninvasive way: 90 percent of the mentally ill are rapidly cured.[15]

Because there is no Devil in Africa, there is no struggle between one god and another rending the world in two—even if there are conflicts among the mythic powers. In Marcel Griaule's retelling, when the Jackal, "the deceived and deceiving son of God," desired the Word, the great female organizing principle, he laid hands on her clothes—in other words, he made an incestuous overture— even though she was his mother. The Word resisted and ran away, turning into an ant in an anthill. "But the Jackal followed her; there was no other woman in the world to desire." She capitulated, and "the incest had great consequences: first it gave the Jackal the power of speech, which for all eternity would allow him to forewarn seers about the designs of God."[16] In other words, the violated proscription was transformed back into order.

Such cases are common, it should be mentioned, since incest occupies a prime place in many mythologies. Vladimir Grigorieff identifies three main types.[17] Auto-incest or inner incest, "which is necessary so that the One can emerge out of its equal or other," is illustrated in Greek mythology by Gaea, the earth, who, after having freed herself from the original chaos, conceived her son Uranos in the absence of a masculine agent. Next comes primordial mother-son incest, the son uniting with the Earth Mother—also the case with Gaea, who couples with Uranos to produce the Titans and Titanids. Last comes incest between twins, which is a prerequisite for the birth of the generative principle; this was observed by the Egyptian royalty, where the pharaoh's legitimacy was assured only if he had married his sister beforehand.

However, incest, which theoretically is the bearer of disorder or, in the African religions, of impurity, has shades of meaning that are often quite different from those with which it is imbued in the contemporary West. According to Cazeneuve, "what is remarkable is that very often it is not the sexual act that is forbidden, only the marriage of relatives or individuals from the same clan."[18] Sexuality only has a value in that it is a social act, whereas as an act in private it is insignificant. The proscriptive systems the West has built up around it do not apply. The Devil as inducer of mastur-bation and adultery wouldn't make any sense in Africa. Colin Turn-bull reports having witnessed sexual acts between boys of the same clan, which raised no eyebrows at all,[19] while other observers have devoted lengthy studies to the ritualization of one sexual behavior, homosexuality, that at first glance would seem particularly threat-ening to cosmic order.[20] Among the Banda of Guinea, for instance, the miming of openly homosexual acts takes place in public.[21] Among the Masai of the Sudan and Kenya in eastern Africa, a tribe with egalitarian traditions, the practice of taking many wives, or polygamy, means that men of the same age lend one another their spouses without batting an eye.

By Western norms, again, homosexuality is one of the activities that by all rights should compromise the cosmic order. Yet this is not the case in Africa, and there are two reasons why. First, African mythologies accept the coexistence of the two sexes within one individual. "The *nommo* . . . gives each child two souls, each of a different sex," says Ogotemmeli. When asked if circumcision ridded a boy of his female soul by doing away with his "lizard" (foreskin),

Ogotemmeli replies, "No—he still keeps his shadow, which is a diminished female soul."[22]

Next, African cultures do not have the same "organic" or biological conception of sexuality that Western cultures do. The Azande of the upper Congo, writes Lucien Lévy-Bruhl,[23] "believe that the components of the fetus are not deposited all at once, but in the course of several successive fertilizations of the ovary extending over a number of days."

The representation of homosexuality as "contrary to nature" or of adultery as a violation of divine rules has no place in African religions, at least those which have yet to be tainted by Christianity or Islam; these representations are not associated with any Devil. The ritualization of both behaviors therefore arises out of a typically African desire to avoid a conflict that could threaten the social and cosmic order, as well as to integrate manifestations of sexuality that are minor though real (and generally limited to adolescence, in the case of homosexuality) yet socially inconsequential.

The Western system of dichotomies in which one thing cannot logically be something else has made it difficult for us to understand African ways of thinking, in which one thing is certainly not something else although the two cannot be differentiated. Among the Bambara, a people from the upper reaches of the Senegal and Niger rivers for whom water is of primordial importance, the following cosmogony is related. After the Void of Sound, or Glan, who was also the Sound of the Void, divided himself into two and produced Dya, their union produced vibrations in which the signs of all things yet to be created were suspended. Then Glan-Dya produced their will or "thought-action," the Yo; the Yo gave a structure to all creation, and "thinking-acting" man was indistinguishable from it. Pemba, the earth, who was in fact a masculine deity (another instance of "natural" hermaphrodism), received the fertilizing water from the sky, Faro, and came to life.[24]

In one version of this cosmogony, Pemba conceived the "woman-femaleness," Muso Koroni, who in turn became his wife and gave birth to plants and animals. In order to gain even greater power, Pemba wanted to couple with every human woman, and since the strength imparted to him by all women was still not enough, he began to desire not just their blood but that of the men as well. He violated all of humanity and gave it fire in exchange. The humans began to wither, but Faro saved them by giving them the tomato, a "sanguinary and bigeminal fruit," as Grigorieff calls it. Then a struggle broke out between Pemba and Faro, which resulted in Pemba's defeat, and with it came a retaliation against humanity: people became mortal. However, Faro imposed an order upon the world and delegated the spirits to maintain it.

This struggle between the antagonistic powers of earth and sky, however, has no ethical consequences apart from the condemnation of Pemba's sexual intemperance. This theme of self-control features prominently in many African religions: for example, one Yoruba myth relates that Sango, the god of thunder but also the tyrant ruler of the city of Oyo, abused the power he wielded, and for that reason was forced to commit suicide by his adversaries. In this context, it is difficult not to think of the Greek goddess Nemesis, the deity responsible for punishing excesses.

Another version of this myth, also reported by Grigorieff, recalls that of Osiris. The primordial egg in the heavens produced two pairs of twins, and the male halves were Pemba and Faro, again respectively the earth and the sky. Born first and early, Pemba tried to appropriate all of creation. He took a piece of the primordial placenta, which became the earth, but it was waterless and barren. He tried to climb back into the heavens to take the rest of the placenta, and then to couple with his twin sister. God foiled Pemba's plan by placing the sister in the care of the other set of twins and transforming the remainder of the placenta into the sun. Nevertheless, Pemba managed to steal eight male seeds from the sky, and he implanted them in the earth-mother—an act of incest, since the earth was, like him, produced by the primordial placenta. Though barren, the earth produced *fonio*, a type of millet. Meanwhile, Faro was castrated, and the trees grew up out of his severed organs. God resurrected Faro, transformed him into a human, and then lowered him down from the sky in an ark.

This version is as conflict-ridden as the others, but again the resolution of the Pemba-Faro struggle ends up producing order, a version of the universal religious concept of the reestablishment of order through sacrifice (in this case, Faro's). Pemba resembles Seth and Faro Osiris, another figure who is dismembered and drawn up into the sky. In Bambara mythology, however, Pemba is no more the embodiment of malevolence than is Seth in Egyptian mythology. If no Devil is to be found in the African religions, it is because all their conflicts play out into equilibrium.

That there is no Devil is also due to the fact that no African religion divides the world into irreconciliable opposites: the Yoruba god of smallpox, Shopona, who is also called Obaluaiye, sits beside the river goddesses Oshun and Oya along with Ifa, the god of divination (who also appears across the Atlantic, in the Brazilian rituals of Candomble). After the god of the Bushmen had created the earth-woman, then the sky-man, then the stars (the sky-man's eyes), and then the moon-woman and the animals, he completed his labors by creating the lion-man, humanity's ancestor; once Creation was done, no room was left inside it for a counterpower like the Devil.

The same holds true in the creation myth of Kenya's Wahungwe Makoni tribe.[25] The first man, Mwuetsi, got bored living on the bottom of his lake and wanted to live on land. He went there, but he grew bored again, and yet he could not go back to his lake. God warned him that he had become mortal and gave him a female companion, Massassi, the morning star. Mwuetsi and Massassi made love, giving birth to the grasses, bushes, and trees, and lived together happily. This bliss, however, came to an end with Massassi's death. Mwuetsi once again complained of boredom to the Creator, who, helpful as ever, sent him Morongo, the evening star. The new pair made love; on the first night they produced chickens, sheep, and goats, on the second antelopes and cattle, and on the third boys and girls. Creation was complete, although Mwuetsi didn't agree and, contrary to divine will, once again made love with Morongo. This time his wife gave birth to leopards, lions, snakes, and scorpions, not to mention the last one, an enormous black mamba. Not having learned his lesson from this experience, Mwuetsi expressed the desire to once more sleep with Morongo; this time, however, the mamba, Morongo's son and husband, burst out from under the bed and bit Mwuetsi on the thigh. The seriously ill Mwuetsi—by this time, he was king of the people he had incestuously conceived with his own daughters—was put to death by his subjects. In this instance, the mamba was the symbolic guardian of equilibrium.

African cultures consider rebellion a threat to cosmic harmony, although this is not to say that it doesn't exist. Among the Bantu of Zambezi, rebellion is treated humorously in the myth about how the first man and woman were born:

In the beginning God made two holes in the earth. A man emerged from one, a woman from the other. God commanded them to work the earth and sow it with millet as well as to build a house they could cook the millet in. But the man and woman did not obey God; as soon as they reaped the millet they ate it raw, and instead of building the house they lived in the forest. Then God gave the same instructions to a male and female monkey, who followed them to the letter. This greatly satisfied God, who cut off their tails and said: "You are human beings!" Then he attached their tails to the man and woman, and said: "You are monkeys!"[26]

Still to be determined is how and why no African political power modified these religions to transform them into ethical doctrines, as happened in Iran. The answer is not irrelevant in contemporary Africa, where Christian and Muslim clerics have already begun to take on political roles. However, there are several reasons this never happened in ancient Africa.

First, although it is certain that African religions were the mirror of African cultures, recent histories of such ancient kingdoms as Ghana, Songhai, and Zimbabwe do not say whether or not Africa ever had organized clergies on the model of those in Iran and Mesopotamia. It seems unlikely that there would have been, since Africa never experienced the nation-state, an imported colonial entity (though it has survived the decolonization process). Again, too, the Africans were great migrators, and migration tends to hamper the formation of nation-states.

The nation-state is not only foreign but even contrary to the essence of Africa, which in precolonial times was comprised of ethnicities defined by the very religions they possessed; if the ethnicities were in practice kingdoms, then the king had no need for a state, and so in turn there was no reason for the clergy to constitute itself into a statelike body. Seers, witch doctors, medicine men, and other priests never enjoyed the conditions vital to the establishment of ecclesiastical authority.

Last, the very idea of a clergy arises from a distinction between the material and the spiritual, which is impossible to draw in Africa; the Cartesian categories the West inherited from the Greeks do not apply. When the whole world, from buffalo horn to ant to acacia, is charged with divine power, tangible objects become as spiritual as the invisible spirits themselves.

> Listen oftener
> to things than beings,
> for the voice of Fire is heard,
> Listen to the voice of the Water,
> Listen in the wind
> to the crying bush,
> it's the breath of ancestors.

Thus writes the poet Birago Diop in one of the most beautiful peoms of his continent, one of the proofs of the spirituality of a culture so often accused of "prelogical infantilism."

If the functions of the diviner and the witch doctor are clearly defined (to perform great collective rituals as well as smaller, private ones for therapeutic purposes) within this system, if the king himself must consult the diviner on significant occasions, then the king is never anything more than an intermediary who lacks ideological power. Neither he nor the witch doctor can create either church or dogma. In the words of Emmanuel Terray, "within a limitless geographical and social space, no one person can assume exclusive authority, and no spirit—nor, consequently, any priest—can have a monopoly over efficacy; what one of them forbids another can always allow."[27] There is no absolute religious power in Africa (its non-Christian and non-Islamic parts, of course) that would sanction the proclaiming of either absolute Good or absolute

Evil. In addition, African religions are based exclusively on the celebration of life, which leaves little for any Devil, however horned or hairy.

With his place in the cosmos determined, the human being in Africa is thus part of the One as well as of the All. No chasm cuts him, no stain marks him. In his relations with the gods, he can only commit errors, never sins original or individual, since the very concepts are alien. He has no salvation to earn, since his salvation is that of the gods of his universe. In this respect, the African is brother to the Greek, neither angelic nor demonic. As a mortal, he is part of the divinity; as divine, he is related to the antelopes, lions, and snakes. His final sleep is filled with perfumes, fruit, and the nocturnal roar of his land.

CHAPTER 11

The North American Indians

Land and Fatherland

Important aspects of the Native American way of thinking can be gleaned from myths, including the following. A young boy named Nulque was walking around a lake with his sister, Manona. He decided to swing from a wild vine hanging out over the water. "Why don't you do it too? It's fun," he said to her. Manona did—but the vine broke, and she fell into the water. A water spirit called the Man of the Lake happened to be right there; he took her away and seduced her. When Manona married the spirit, Nulque was inconsolable; every day afterward, he sat by the edge of the water and cried. Manona came to him and told him to stop grieving for her, since from then on she was the Man of the Lake's wife and could never again return to land.

But Nulque remained as distraught as ever. He fasted and prayed that his sister be freed, and eventually he was so purified by his ordeal that he could no longer stand the smell of humans. One night a manitou appeared and asked him why he was so sad.[1] When Nulque told him, the manitou admitted that he could do nothing to help. Nulque kept on fasting and praying. After sixteen days he had a dream about a warrior, who he knew was the god of thunder. The warrior agreed to help him. He advised the boy to go to the lake, chop down a magnificent elm tree, and carve himself a canoe; the canoe would take him to a place where a tall tepee stood between two trees. This tepee belonged to Deer Man, who directed him on to Crane Man, who in turn told him to go see Beaver Man.

These spirits all decided to help him, even the thunder god, who unleashed a violent storm. Lightning bolts buffeted the Man of the Lake in his underwater home; the lake itself roiled. The Man of the Lake begged Manona to help him, which she did, and so Nulque's magical plot failed, since it could not be carried off without her help. When the boy began to grieve more piteously than ever, his supernatural allies took pity; they turned Manona into a lake and Nulque himself into a small island at its center so that the two would never again be separated.[2]

The myth has everything: the alliance between human being and nature spirits (thunder, deer, crane, beaver), the goodwill these spirits display toward a person in distress, the limits of their powers (they can grant wishes only if humans help out), initiatory rites (the manitou can be contacted only after arduous fasting and repeated purifying baths), and the partial presence of Evil, as well as of love and faith. It would have been easy for Europeans to find a rapport with the Native Americans; the poetry of their myths easily rivals that of the Middle Ages and the age of Romanticism. Yet these half-naked people who lived in harmony with their seemingly oversized territories were an inconvenience to the Westerners who claimed their lands in the name of progress.

Native Americans have always exasperated Westerners; they were seen as a threat to the founding values of Christianity. Since they did not recognize a spirit of Evil, they were considered amoral. In the seventeenth century, for instance, the Jesuit Savinien forced himself to concede that the tenderness Indian women displayed toward their children "is certainly no less than that of civilized women"—a comparison telling in the degree of its astonishment.

The odd position that Native Americans occupy in Western eyes has been reinforced by films that, initially, justified the seizure of Indian lands by portraying the aborigines as "savages" who wished for little more than scalps.[3] This picture has more recently given way to depictions of the Native American as possessors of an archaic and moving, albeit more or less useless, "ancestral" knowledge. Both, in any case, dispense with the reality.

There are as many American Indian cultures and cultural identities as there are—or were—tribes: 147 in North America alone. All Native Americans, not only those of North America, share the same Asiatic roots; ethnically speaking, they are Mongoloid. Some thirty-five thousand years ago (not the twelve thousand years accepted until 1985[4]) they crossed the Bering Strait on foot; they then diverged from one another, and in fact are not homogenous, ethnically speaking. It is an established fact that the first immigrants were dolichocephalic, that is, with a long skull, whereas the later ones were brachycephalic, that is, with a round skull. America's first inhabitants therefore had more than enough time to establish radically diverse cultures, each with its own myths and religion.

For lack of contact with other cultures, and since their territories were large enough to sustain them completely, they came up with self-contained systems of thought that never had to be modified. The land was vast and verdant, and the inhabitants were relatively few in number. In *The Primitive Mind*, Lucien Lévy-Bruhl cites the following passage from the *Proceedings of the Jesuits* (published in the seventeenth century), concerning the first contacts between that order and the Indians of eastern North America:

It must be supposed that the Iroquois are incapable of reasoning, unlike the Chinese or other civilized peoples, who can be instructed in matters of faith and in the truth of one God. . . . The Iroquois is in no way guided by reason; his first impression of something remains his only way of apprehending it. The reason that theology relies upon to convince those with the brightest minds is simply not listened to here, and our greatest truths are called lies. Nothing is believed except what can be seen.[5]

This passage is representative of the overall Western attitude toward Native Americans, and yet to the contrary, as Sir James Frazer was later to write:

The Hidatsa Indians of North America believe that every natural object has its spirit, or to speak more properly, its shade. To these shades some respect or consideration is due, but not equally to all. For example, the shade of the cottonwood, the greatest tree in the valley of the Upper Missouri, is supposed to possess an intelligence which, if properly approached, may help the Indians in certain undertakings; but the shades of shrubs and grasses are of little account.[6]

The Jesuit missionaries were no doubt ill-equipped as ethnologists, all the more so for being evangelists and since ethnology had not yet been born. Their yardstick in judging a people's intellectual capacity was willingness to believe the Catholic dogma. Lévy-Bruhl also mentions, however, that after having classified the Greenlanders as incapable of reason, the order did concede that "they can be credited with a simplicity that is not necessarily idiotic and with common sense even in the absence of reason." (One wonders what is meant by "common sense even in the absence of reason.") The crux of the matter is the inescapable paradox that since the Native Americans didn't grasp the concept of God, the most impossible of all concepts to grasp through reason, this was proof that they could not reason.

In truth, the American Indians believed in something much more specific than spirits or "shades"—they believed in actual deities, although they definitely did not believe in the famous "Great Spirit," which is a missionary fabrication. The Hopi of Arizona, for instance, had Muyingwu, the god of vegetation, as well as the goddess Tupawong-tumsi, who was his sister (she made the leaves fall), and Masa'u, the god of the underbrush, fire, and death[7]; if the Ahone worshiped by the Indians of Virginia was so lofty a deity that humanity had no contact with him at all,[8] the Coyote of the Apaches and Navajos can clearly be identified with the heroic trickster—it is he, for instance, who ridded the universe of the offspring of Tieholdtsodi, the sea monster, so that the world as we know it could emerge.

As in other civilizations, the roles of the deities varied from tribe to tribe. The Coyote, who is a hero to the Apaches and Navajos, turns out to be the antagonist (though not the enemy) of the gods in the mythology of central California's Maidu Indians. Though the Indians did not have one unified religion, some did share belief in certain deities, such as the Great Hairy Serpent (an avatar of Mexico's Plumed Serpent) of New Mexico's Paiute, Mono, Pima, and Yuma tribes. A denizen of the underworld and lord of animals, plants, and in general everything that lives on earth, the Great Hairy Serpent was capable of making one rich at a stroke, although his friendship was sometimes dangerous.[9]

Spirits responsible for a given number of misfortunes, the kind of spirits that abound in almost every religion in the world, are certainly to be found in the Native American ones: essentially believing neither in his own freedom nor in his complete subjection to chance, man projects the inexplicable or unexplained onto a demon. One example is Iya in Sioux mythology, who devours or maims people and animals; Iya sometimes assumes the form of a hurricane, and his pestilential breath spreads disease.[10]

Yet this type of demon is by no means exclusively a Native American invention; many other peoples have conceived of it under other forms and other names. It is the equivalent of what the Tamils of India call the Peys, hirsute demons who suck the blood of the dead at night, or the Serbs' Psezpolnica, the "Woman of Midday," who as her name might indicate appears at noon during the harvest season and either makes people go mad or lops off their heads and limbs (she can also manifest herself in the form of a tornado). The list of similar creatures worldwide is long.

The world has always been haunted by spirits evil as well as good; the fact that the good can sometimes be evil and the evil ones good is due to the mysteriousness inherent in supernatural powers. When the Hopi wish to call forth rains, they gather rattlesnakes from their pits, collect them in a great earthenware vase, and chant incantations over them, since the snakes are the messengers of the gods who produce rain. The rain dance begins with chanting and drumming; led by priests covered with symbolic paintings, the dancers perform serpentlike undulations. Then, according to René Thévenin and Paul Coze, "the witch doctors reach into the sacred vase, pick the snakes up with professional dexterity, and carry them around in their teeth without ever being bitten themselves."[11]

Though a symbol of Evil in Western civilization, to the Native American the snake represents the powers of the earth, chthonian forces with which humanity can very well live in peace. This is strikingly borne out by the description of part of the snake-antelope ceremony in *The Book of the Hopi* by Frank Waters:

> All members of the society seated themselves in a circle around it, each sitting cross-legged and touching the next man's knee. Then one of the men opened the buckskin tops of the jars and let all the snakes loose on the sand. At the same time the singing began, soft and low. . . . There were all kinds of snakes: rattlesnakes, big bull snakes, racers, sidewinders, gopher snakes— about sixty all tangled on the floor. The singing stirred them. They moved in one direction, then another, looking over all the men in the circle. The men never moved. . . . Then a big yellow rattler moved slowly toward an old man singing with his eyes closed, climbed up his crossed leg, coiled in front of his breechcloth and went to sleep.

Waters adds:

> Contrary to popular belief the fangs of the snakes are not extracted nor are their sacs of venom emptied. . . . One precaution is taken, however. A concoction named *chu'knga* [snake medicine] is given to all Snake members, who drink a little and rub their hands with it before going out on the snake hunt.[12]

The Native American walks upon the sacred earth of his ancestors imbued with the feeling that he is part of a universal brotherhood. This brotherhood can assume a magical form, the kind that in Melanesia is referred to as *mana*; the Iroquois call it *orenda*. As Marcel Mauss writes, *orenda* is "power, mystical power. Nothing in nature, and more specifically, nothing animate, does not possess its own *orenda*. The gods, the spirits, and human beings all have it. Natural phenomena such as storms are produced by the *orenda* of those phenomena."[13] This is the basis of the universal sympathetic spirit. "The grasshopper," Mauss continues, "is called 'the ripener of corn' since it sings on hot days because its *orenda* brings on the heat that makes the plant mature."[14]

Both this fraternity and the *orenda* from which it arises extend to animals as well; when the Gros Ventre butchers a bison, he is careful not to break its bones since he is convinced that the integrity of the skeleton will permit the animal to come to life again *in this world*, not in the hereafter. This is the reason behind the careful arrangements of skulls seen on the Great Plains at the beginning of this century;[15] the Native American sowed intact bones the way a farmer would sow seeds.

The whole world was thus a natural reservoir of life in which the natural and the supernatural were closely interwoven—as, for example, in the Ojibwa myth about the origins of maize that Henry Wadsworth Longfellow used as an inspiration for his famous poem, "The Song of Hiawatha." A youth goes through the ritual initiatory fast, in the midst of which he is visited by his manitou. On the third day, he sees a beautiful young man resplendently dressed in clothes of green and yellow descend from the sky. The celestial creature challenges the boy to a wrestling match, and though the boy is weak he accepts, preferring to die than to forfeit the contest. The celestial creature reappears the next day and challenges him again, as he does over the following days, and each time the boy forces himself to fight. One day, however, the supernatural emissary announces that the boy's courage has won him the favor of the divine powers. He says to the boy, "Tomorrow I will wrestle you for the last time. As soon as you've won, undress me, throw me onto the ground, hoe the earth, make it soft, and bury me. After that leave my body, but come back from time to time to tend my grave and clear it of weeds. Throw fresh soil over me once every month." In Joseph Campbell's telling, "The adolescent does so. One night at the end of summer he sees a tall and graceful plant with golden hair and lush leaves growing out of the grave—it is maize, the friend of mankind."[16] The essence of the supernatural passed into the vegetative world; the *orenda* of the handsome celestial youth combined with the boy's *orenda* to produce corn.

The idea of a magical power that can be harnessed to seduce, threaten, or enslave is exclusive neither to the Iroquois nor to Native America in general. The Sioux call it *makopa*, the Omaha *nube*, the Dakota *waban*, the Shoshone *pokunt*. For our purposes, we shall continue to refer to it as *orenda*. The totality of the aboriginal American peoples believed in the omnipresence of this unnamed spirit, whose operation and essence it was vital to respect.

Surrounded on all sides by the natural *orenda*s that weaved the fabric of universal brotherhood, the Native American did not and could not conceive of the world as arbited by the antagonism between a unique God and unique Devil. Such anthropocentrism was completely alien to Native American thought; if the American Indian was aware of his human singularity, it was in the context of a general kinship among all natural entities, including vegetation.

However, the West persisted in considering the Native American "inferior" because he believed neither in God nor—and for much better reasons—in the Devil. Over the course of the centuries, a pseudo-ethnology evolved that came to see the aborigines as "savage pagans" barely worth the effort of converting. In 1922, Marcel Mauss wrote: "The rareness of references to magical forces or places should not lead us to doubt that they were universal. We are ill-informed about this topic; after having known the Iroquois for three centuries, our attention has only now, in the past year, been drawn to *orenda*."[17] Some seventy years later, neither our knowledge about nor the fate of native North Americans have substantially improved. To Western eyes, the Native Americans had the supposed virtue of believing in a Great Spirit, an idea that was held to be a foreshadowing, if a "primitive" one, of religion's natural progress toward a God/Devil duality—but again, the Great Spirit was a fabrication. Since it had been so determined, though, Native Americans were "animists."

Yet the apparent "animism" (in Christian theological terms, it would seem much closer to theism) of the native North Americans was, paradoxically, in no way hostile to monotheism. The most puzzling and yet at the same time the least known feature about Native America was that it was incapable of conceiving of a unique Devil but perfectly capable of envisioning a unique God. The Sioux sun-god Wi, symbolized by the bison, was the supreme god and the omniscient protector of brave and faithful humans; one striking point about this deity is that his daughter Whope once descended to earth to bring the peace pipe to the Sioux. Elsewhere, Wi is depicted as one of the four manifestations of an even more elevated god, Wakan Tanka, the god of the gods.[18]

This inclination toward monotheism, however, must be examined in context. There is good cause to wonder whether or not the North American Indians were visited by Europeans prior to the arrival of Columbus—the Vikings, for instance, reached Vinland—and if these visitors hadn't introduced a version of Christianity later reproduced in indigenous beliefs.

One factor that might support this idea is the myth of Pahana, the vanished white brother of the Hopi Indians, a figure akin to Kukulkan, the bearded white god of the Maya, and to the Quetzalcoatl of the Aztecs and Toltecs. When the conquistador Francisco Vazquez de Coronado's soldiers reached the Hopi lands of Arizona in 1540, they found that their arrival had been expected for some time; the Hopi were awaiting the return of Pahana. Writes Frank Waters:

> Every year in Oraibi, on the last day of Soyal, a line was drawn across the six-foot-long stick kept in the custody of the Bear Clan to mark the time for his arrival. The Hopis knew where to meet him: at the bottom of Third Mesa if he was on time, or along the trail at Sikya'wa [Yellow Rock], Chokuwa [Pointed Rock], Nahoyungvasa [Cross Fields], or Tawtoma just below Oraibi, if he was five, ten, fifteen, or twenty years late. Now the stick was filled with markings; Pahana was twenty years late. But he came in the person of the Spaniard Pedro de Tovar, the first white man to be seen by the Hopis.[19]

Even if the tendency toward monotheism, and the belief in the soul's performance in some indigenous cultures, were foreign in origin and later diffused through the religions of Native America, this does not support the conclusion that what we are dealing with is an incipient Christian monotheism. What is lacking is a basic component of Christianity, the idea of original sin, which is so vital to the concept of the Devil. In the cosmogonies that can be gleaned from Native American mythologies, the conflicts among supernatural powers which produced life on earth do not entail any consequences for humanity, which is innocent. In short, humanity cannot be the vessel of Evil. For instance, the demigod Kitshikawano, the protective deity of warriors who came to earth at the beginning of time to battle the forces of evil, is not an incarnation of good; he is a symbol of courage, and he does not share the austere characteristics that incarnations of good are so often imbued with. Instead, he is a happy-go-lucky figure whose distinguishing feature is his hearty laugh.[20]

In the beginning, runs the Apache creation myth, there were nothing but shadows, water, and tornadoes. Human beings did not exist; the only entities that did were the Hactcin, the masked gods. The universe was a desert devoid of creatures. Yet the Hactcin possessed the material from which everything was to be created. First they made the earth, then the netherworld, then the sky. They created the earth in the form of a woman and called it "Mother"; they created the sky in the form of a man and called it "Father" (this is why it crouches over the earth). The Black Hactcin shaped an animal out of clay and said, "Let's see you walk on these four paws." All other animals descended from that original one. In those days, all beasts could talk; they spoke the Jicarilla dialect of Apache. The Black Hactcin stretched out his hand, and rain fell from it, which he blended with soil and mud to make a bird; he threw it into the air with a left-to-right spin. The bird got dizzy from its wild spiraling and hallucinated countless other birds, eagles, hawks, owls, and sparrows. When it came back to its senses, the other birds were really there.

However, the animals grew bored and asked the Black Hactcin to create man; when that was done, they asked the Hactcin to create a companion for him, and so woman came into existence.

All of this happened in the netherworld; at the time there was neither sun nor moon. The Black Hactcin and the White Hactcin pulled a tiny sun and moon out of their satchels, made them bigger, and tossed them into the sky. The sight of these astral bodies roused the men, among whom there were many shamans; these claimed that they had created the sun and the moon, and they even started arguing about which one of them deserved the most credit. The Hactcin grew annoyed and made the celestial bodies disappear. They said to the shamans, "Let's see you put the sun and the moon back in the sky."

The shamans tried all sorts of tricks, vanishing into thin air and leaving nothing behind but their eyes or swallowing arrows and trees whole, but they were unable to bring the two objects back. Only after many other ordeals did the Hactcin agree to restore them.[21]

Clearly, there is no trace of a spirit of Evil in this cosmogony, unless of course it lies in the boasting of the shamans. Nor is there a hint of original sin. If there are evil spirits in Native American mythology, they are freeloaders, not essential components of the universe—like the tricksters, the often-cruel practical jokers who are akin to the Loki of Celtic myth.

The Great Hare, Master Rabbit, Bluejay, Old Man, Crow, and of course Coyote—European missionaries and ethnologists found it hard to resist seeing one or the other of these wily figures as relatives of the medieval Reynard the Fox, the Devil's precursor. In the first place, however, the trickster is not a god so much as a super-shaman of sorts, as described by Joseph Campbell:

We may imagine this trickster-hero in his character as Coyote, standing one evening on the top of a mountain, looking south. And far away he thought he saw a light. Not knowing, at first, what it was, by a process of divination he learned that he was seeing fire; and so, making up his mind to procure this wonder for humanity, he gathered a company of companions: Fox, Wolf, Antelope—all the good runners went along. And after traveling a very great way, they all reached the house of the Fire People, to whom they said: "We have come to visit you, to dance, to play, and to gamble." And so, in their honor, preparations were made for a dance, to be held that night.

Coyote prepared a headdress for himself, made of pitchy yellow-pine shavings, with long fringes of cedar bark, reaching to the ground. The Fire People danced first, and the fire was very low. Then Coyote and his people began to dance around the flame, and they complained that they could not see. The Fire People made a larger fire, and Coyote complained four times, until finally they let it blaze up high. Coyote's people then pretended to be very hot and went out to cool themselves: they took up positions for running and only Coyote was left inside. He capered about wildly until his headdress caught fire, and then, pretending to be afraid, he asked the Fire People to put it out. They warned him not to dance so close to the blaze. But when he came near the door, he swung the long fringes of his headdress across the fire and ran out. The Fire People pursued him and he gave his headdress to Antelope, who ran and passed it on to the next runner; and so it went in relay. One by one, the Fire People caught up with the animals and killed them, until the only one left was Coyote; and they nearly caught him too, but he ran behind a tree and gave the fire to the tree. Since then, men have been able to draw fire with fire-sticks from the wood of trees.[22]

Campbell points out that roughly similar tales are to be found among many tribes. In the Georgia Creek version, Master Rabbit plays the Coyote role; in the Kaska version, Bear jealously treasures a Fire Stone or flint, which in the end a little bird steals from him.[23] The trickster is closely identified with fire, which Christian mythology associates with the Devil. The trickster, however, is the Thief of Fire, a figure long believed to be exclusively Indo-European, who works on behalf of humanity. If he really were the Devil, we would have to reidentify Prometheus as the Devil and to start believing that all rebellion is diabolical (which, incidentally, is what many in fact thought the French and American revolutions were). How the same myth arose among peoples separated by some six thousand miles, and when it did so, are unknown, but the coincidence is really no coincidence at all: like the Greek, the Celt, and the Oceanian, the Native American was free.

The Native American gods and myths—it cannot be stressed strongly enough that all deities are reflections of their inventors—

could not help but be cast in the image of the American Indian, and that image was about liberty. There was no cause to dream up the abjectness of sin or to invent a Great Liar or Great Enemy. The irony of fate was that it was the white invader who personified the Great Liar, violating both the land and treaty after treaty. Helen Maria Hunt dared to say this in 1881, and the title of her book expresses it best—*A Century of Dishonor*. But by then it was far too late to redress matters.

The waves of immigrants who flooded in during the nineteenth century through the Indian territories of Colorado, Montana, Idaho, Nevada, and Oregon were destined to alienate the Native Americans. To these Europeans, the Native American made poor use of his land.

This piratical mentality alone, however, is not enough to explain the terrible cruelty the invaders displayed toward the Native American. The histories written of the final defeat of Doll Knife, the Cheyenne chief, and of the Apache war of 1879 are astonishing; were trials for genocide and crimes against humanity to be held across the historical board, what would come in for infamy is the cream of the U.S. Army, which systematically and methodically exterminated a large part of the Native American nation. In the 1870s there were some twenty thousand Apaches in Arizona and New Mexico; as Thévenin and Coze write, "in 1875 there were seven thousand at most, and only a few hundred in the census of 1890."[24] The hatred the colonist bore toward the Native American was cultural and religious; to the Westerner, the person who lacks the Devil *is* the Devil. But there is no doubt as to who his true incarnation really was.

CHAPTER 12

The Enigma of Quetzalcoatl, the Feathered Serpent, and the God-Who-Weeps

In the spring of 1519, recounts the Franciscan monk Fray Bernardino de Sahagún, the Spanish mercenary and adventurer Hernán Cortés landed on the northern coast of the Yucatán Peninsula with eleven or twelve warships under his command. Skiffs filled with Indians headed out over the translucent water to bring these superhuman beings—who to the Indians seemed oddly pale, as they later told Sahagún—armfuls of flowers, fabrics decorated with colored feathers, and jewels. The Indians were expecting gods; what they didn't know is that their gifts fell into the hands of barbarians who were bringing them the Devil and who were looking for nothing but slaves and gold.

Cortés's expedition, which was soon to be bloodied by the senseless massacre of three thousand Indians at Cholula, would continue all the way to the capital of the Aztec empire at Tenochtitlan, where His Catholic Majesty's representative would meet the emperor Moctezuma. The Spaniards found the place splendid: an immense and flourishing city set in the middle of Lake Texcoco, cross-hatched by canals and linked to the lakeshore by floating walkways, Tenochtitlan was by Cortés's own admission more beautiful than any city in Europe. The marketplace alone was twice as large as the whole town of Salamanca. An aqueduct carried water from hillside springs into the very center of the city. This Venice of the West Indies was peopled by jewel-studded, loinclothed, and light-gaited individuals. According to Sahagún, it was "a vision of enchantment." It was here that Cortés and his men met Moctezuma and his court, two hundred barefoot lords with brilliant headdresses and fresh-smelling skin; despite the abundance of water, the Spanish neither washed nor changed their clothes and slept in their armor and cuirasses, while the citizens of Tenochtitlan followed their emperor's example and bathed every night. The encounter was apocalyptic: all those paradisiacal flowers and luxuries were already promised to the Devil whom the assassins were importing.

This tragic meeting of two cultures was on my mind at the outset of my second visit to Mexico in 1975, when, surfeited by book-knowledge and curiosity, I decided to go to Xochimilco, which lies just outside Mexico City; I wanted to take a look at the rather limited subway system that had just been built in the city. The moment I got out at the last station, which had a sort of pasteurized luxury to it—it was painted, I think, in blue and white—I had to transfer to a streetcar and return to the reality of the surface world. Over what seemed like an interminable stretch of time, the streetcar passed through a succession of shantytowns; with every stop, the passengers getting on and off, their bare feet covered in mud and their faces lost in joyless contemplation, my dejection grew.

Yet it was at that moment that I really began to take an interest in Mexico. Eventually, I rallied enough stoicism to make it through a terrible night in Palenque, with its calf-deep mud and waterless inn, only to slog through the desolation of Campeche, then to endure another hungry night, this time in Puebla, with nothing to eat but a bag of nuts. What, I wondered, was the reason behind the air of dejection in the Mexicans one met in villages and on the highways and streets where tourists never go?

The Indian civilizations of Central and South America were once Eurocentrically called "pre-Columbian" and then "Latin"; historians and ethnologists now call them "Amerindian" (I will use all these terms interchangeably). They begin at the southern border of the United States and extend down to Tierra del Fuego. Tourism, museum exhibitions, and the media have broadened our knowledge of Maya, Aztec, and Inca art. Those who appreciate this art love its exquisiteness, the rigorous grammar of form that is sometimes leavened with touching realism, its inventiveness, but most of all, I believe, its exoticism. More often than not, however, it is appreciated the way the French and British once loved *chinoiserie*, which has about as much to do with the real China as the motel does with the medieval roadside inn.

These civilizations are admittedly difficult to come to grips with. The traveler who arrives at the temple city of Teotihuacan outside Mexico City, or at the ruins of Machu Picchu in Peru after an exhausting trip along the edge of precipices at nearly fifteen thousand feet of altitude, feels a certain malaise above and beyond vertigo and the obligatory "wonder." Despite the guidebooks, the traveler finds it hard to comprehend what led to the construction of the arid temples to the sun and moon at Teotihuacan (both admirably reconstructed by the archaeologist Leopoldo Batres) or the undecipherable Wall of Beauty at Machu Picchu, a collection of massive granite blocks so precisely positioned that one could think them a mosaic built by Titans. The usual notions of "beauty" do not apply; another coin of cultural exchange is needed. The question is which one.

Until the eighties, it had been commonly assumed that the Americas had been peopled some 12,000 years B.C. Then, in 1986, the discoveries of prehistoric caves dating back to 33,000 B.C., or even 35,000 B.C., shook archaeology. Found by the French Nième Guidon and Georgette Delibrias, these caves raised an impressive question: Who indeed had peopled the Americas?

That question had first seemed to have found its answer: it seemed clear that it was Asiatics, and Asiatics only. The Indians of America, everyone agreed, were Mongoloids, and indeed for the most part they were. However, then the possibility—and only the possibility—had to be considered that Oceanians of obviously a different stock might have reached the South American coast. After pondering some of the monumental heads from Mexico's Olmec period, notably at La Venta and Tres Zapotes, it is also hard to resist the impression that they look African. It's possible that long before the ninth century, when the Vikings established colonies on the New Land—Vinland or "Land of the Vines" (the Vikings might have mistaken red currants for grapes)—the Americas, or at any rate South America, might have been visited and perhaps influenced by arrivals from at least two other parts of the world.

In 1976, a trove of several hundred Roman coins, the most recent of them dating from the fourth century, was discovered in Venezuela; similarly, a Roman bust of Venus was found in a tomb in the Mexican state of Veracruz in 1967, as was a collection of Chinese copper coins believed to date from the twelfth century B.C., in British Columbia. These discoveries have obviously not gone unchallenged, yet one of them seems indisputable: a Roman head from the third century in a Mexican tomb dating from the twelfth.[1]

If true this would mean that Mediterranean navigators knew the eastern coast of South America, where they might have brought traces of an as-yet-unidentified Mediterranean culture, perhaps Roman but also, perhaps, Asian. To this day, no one has satisfactorily explained some close and incongruous links between Greek and Nahuatl, the Aztec language: the Nahuatl stem *teo*, or "god" (as in Teotihuacan, "the place of the gods") is functionally identical to the Greek *theos*, while the structure of the name "Atlas," the Greek deity who held up the sky, is similar to that of "Aztlan," "sky," from where the Aztecs believed they had come. This also raises speculation about the name "Atlantis": is it related to the name of the mythical land Aztlan, or does it come from the name of the Atlas Mountains that extend all the way to the Atlantic?

None of these facts and questions have had much of an impact on even specialist knowledge today. It is a given fact that America was discovered before Columbus by the Vikings, and possibly by the Irish Brendan, but this is as far as anyone can say. Almost nothing is known about the first Mesoamerican civilization of which significant traces remain, the Olmecs, who appeared in the region of Mexico's Veracruz around 1,250 B.C.; they were great astronomers, they had the first recorded calendar in the Americas, and then they disappeared around 600 B.C.

So the Americas have been inhabited for thirty-five millennia, perhaps twice as long, and we have only the slightest information about even the last three thousand years of this whole period. What is taught about the civilizations of Central and South America could at almost any time be completely altered by new archaeological finds. The mystery is all the more perplexing in that Central and South America were undoubtedly populated, at least to some extent, by Mongoloid Asiatics who came from the north. While the Navajo or Ojibwa seem "clear" to us, the Olmec, Toltec, Aztec, and Maya remain opaque. Huge segments of their histories are undetermined or subject to ongoing debate. Not until the eighties, for instance, was it established that the Toltecs, who had at one time been thought restricted entirely to northwestern Mexico, in fact conquered the Yucatán Peninsula in the tenth and eleventh centuries; as late as the seventies, Americanists would have considered this idea farfetched. In short, we have a much better picture of the Egypt or Mesopotamia of three thousand years ago than we do of the so-called Latin American Indians of a thousand years ago.

Our perplexity is due not only to the insufficiency of archaeological data, but also to the fact that the Indians of South and Central America left, in absolute contrast to the Indians of North America, solid physical traces: temples, pyramids, sculptures in stone and clay, bas reliefs, frescoes, everyday and cult objects, and texts. A culture does not reach this level of production until it has amassed both material wealth and a history, a memory based simultaneously on a sense of self-awareness and a sedentary pattern of living—in short, once the culture has become complex. This is to expand on the observation made by the historian V. Gordon Childe, that writing appears as soon as the extent and wealth of a population have reached a given critical mass. At this point, accounts must be kept and thus a numbering system formulated. After numbers comes writing; once that is established, ideas mature. All of this is in fact the case with the Indians of South and Central America.

Yet how the American cultures formed, and how they were influenced by preceding populations, is still to be determined. All that can be theorized is that the Olmecs, the oldest of the known Mexican cultures, appeared around the middle of the second millennium B.C.,[2] and that the Maya civilization reached its zenith around the third century and collapsed soon after the middle of the sixteenth. As Jacques Soustelle noted, Maya civilization began at the time of Diocletian and ended during the lifetime of Philip II of Spain.

While most of their North American "cousins" were hunting bison and living seminomadically, those in the south had mastered architecture, agriculture, irrigation, and astronomy; they were technologically advanced enough to observe solar eclipses indirectly using mirrors of polished obsidian. They also had a political system, a hereditary nobility, a military caste, and, like all organized states, territorial ambitions. While to the layperson the North American tribes seem a fairly homogeneous mosaic, Mesoamerican and South American cultures were in fact radically different from one another, including in matters of religion.

What is not known, or only very sketchily known, is what these beliefs were. At first glance seemingly "primitive," the religions were based on cosmogonies that divided the universe into two separate realms, that of humans as represented by the surface of the earth and that of the supernatural powers, some of which lived in the sky, others in the subterranean world that we would refer to, by extension, as the underworld. The Olmecs conceived of the terrestrial world as made up of earth and water, a representation symbolized by the crocodile or cayman floating on the primeval sea; in the course of time, the crocodile became a fertility god. Water was symbolized by a fish, probably a shark; the discovery of actual shark teeth among archaeological relics seems to indicate that this deity was associated with ritual sacrifice. The third animal in the small and zoologically limited Olmec pantheon was the snake, the symbol of the ruling class.

The Olmecs have been depicted as having bloody rites.[3] They also had a rather blunt philosophy about the transitory nature of life: when a king died, his subjects ritually mutilated the statues associated with his rule and recarved his throne into the kind of monumental heads found at La Venta, San Lorenzo, and Tres Zapotes.[4] Of their probable demons there is little information; at best, their sacrifices can be imagined as intended to ward off the anger of the gods, who would therefore have been ambiguous and capable of both good and evil.

The Olmecs suddenly disappeared sometime around the sixth century B.C. and were succeeded by the so-called Teotihuacan civilization, a powerful city-state whose influence extended over all Central America and its neighboring peoples, the Totonacs of Veracruz and Zapotecs of Oaxaca. Although Teotihuacan was the cradle of Mexican culture, facts about it are sparse and not a shred of its writing has survived. Their artworks, on the other hand, give some clue as to their worldview. In the "Earthly Paradise" fresco found in the Tetitla section of Teotihuacan, spiritlike creatures dance with butterflies in an idyllic vision of the beyond, which hints that death did not hold many terrors for them. The corollary of this vision, however, is that they did not feel much esteem for life itself. Human sacrifice was ritualized; the heart was extracted from the victim's body and probably offered to a god of fertility or a rain god. Another deity, symbolized by the morning star and apparently a precursor to Quetzalcoatl, apparently rejected violent sacrifice and would accept only flowers and fruit. This pacific side of the deity, however, was hardly the norm; among the Pipils of Guatemala, the same god was presented with the hearts of sacrificial victims.

It would be tempting to picture the Teotihuacan religion as polarized between Good and Evil, with a benevolent God and antagonistic Devil. Political power was monopolized by a military theocracy that seems to reflect the pattern of Georges Dumézil's warrior-priest-agriculturalist triad. C. A. Burland notes, "The gods of Teotihuacan were agricultural deities, but they bore arms and sometimes were depicted as warriors. . . . The ecclesiastical hierarchy was in fact a military hierarchy."[5] Yet this pattern seems to be based on the facts that the gods were ambivalent, and that humans could influence them only through sacrificial offerings. The same god could be good or bad depending on whether or not it was content—the same thing we have seen in many other religions.

Like the Olmec civilization, the Teotihuacan collapsed for no established cause; it had declined since the middle of the sixth century, and after the fall of the city of Teotihuacan itself, in 700, it was gone; again, there is no real clue as to why. One hypothesis is that a rebellion of vassal tribes such as the Pipils or Totonacs could have cut Teotihuacan's trade routes—but this is only a hypothesis. The history of the pre-Columbian civilizations is as incompletely understood as is the nature of their religions.

The Maya civilization appeared with the same suddenness as its predecessors. What Jacques Soustelle wrote about the rise of its classical period seems to apply to its beginnings as well: its birth was sudden, "so sudden that one could believe in a sort of spontaneous generation, a creation ex nihilo."[6] Soustelle nevertheless pointed out that this is an illusion; there is actually far more information available on the Maya than on the Olmecs and the Teotihuacan culture. There was a pre-Maya population in the territory controlled by the Olmecs, and when the invasion took place this population split in two, with the southernmost half forming the basis of what would become the Maya people. They evidently did not drop down out of the sky.

Because of its large pool of Mayan monuments, sculpture, frescoes, art, and manuscripts,[7] the Mayan religion is also more open to study than the religions of earlier cultures are. Yet most of the information is to be reaped from works recorded after the Spanish conquest, the books of the *Chilam Balam* ("Jaguar Prophet"), the *Ritual of the Bacabs* (the Bacabs were secondary deities who, with the help of four trees, held up the celestial vault), and above all the *Popol Vuh*, which Soustelle called "one of the great achievements of world religious literature." However, "more open to study" does not necessarily mean that it is possible to trace a coherent history of the Maya religion. In the first place, the documents date from the Maya culture's decline and say nothing about what the preceding centuries must have been like; in the second, no one knows how much the texts, recorded in Latin script, were altered by European influences; and in the third, there are definite signs of non-Maya influences from Mexican invasions such as the Toltec one, which either introduced alien gods or changed the names of the existing Mayan ones (the rain-god Chac, for instance, is doubled by the god Metzaboc). Whether or not the Mayan religion was profoundly affected by the religion of the Toltec invaders is a matter of conjecture, and in any case the available information refers only to the Maya culture of the Yucatán, a late stage in the overall Maya history.

What we do know about the Maya makes it clear that they had the richest and most advanced of any pre-Columbian civilization, although it is a pity that this was not understood until four centuries after Christian Europe had devastated the civilization and permitted the jungle to engulf its "barbaric" monuments and works of art. The civilization was not truly discovered until the nineteenth century, when an American lawyer named John L. Stephens published an illustrated record of his discoveries in Mexico and Guatemala. The astonishing wealth of the American imagination before the European arrival is evident everywhere, from the stela in a Palenque crypt—on which a young man with a delicate profile is eternally contemplating, in an almost premonitory way, a cross surmounted by the bird of life, the symbol of the god Quetzalcoatl—to the exuberant and ornate sculpted scenes at Copan. The cross, obviously, is food for thought—and not without cause, as we shall see below. In the meantime, though, a vast quantity of data was lost forever.

As in the agrarian civilizations of the past, the three gods who dominated the pantheon all represented aspects of fertility: the sun, whose god was Kin-ix Ahau, rain, whose god was Chac, and corn. Next came the nine gods of the shadows and the underworld, since there were that number of subterranean realms, and the thirteen gods of the day, since there were that many heavens over the earth. The nine shadow gods were led by the god of death, Cizin, who was accountable for earthquakes and epidemics; the thirteen day gods were led by the "Great God" Itzamma, the "House of the Iguana," who was associated with the sun and was held to be the creator of the universe, even if he was "a wrinkled and toothless old man."[8] The Yucatan Mayas were later to give Itzamma—the husband of Ix Shemel Yax, the patron of weavers—the name Hunab Ku, "One God," which would perhaps have hinted at a drift toward monotheism were it not for the fact that he coexisted with the other gods. The gods were at the same time single and quadruple (that is, one manifestation for each of the four directions), and they were both benevolent and malevolent. In principle, this last point should eliminate any attempt at reading Cizin as being kin to the Devil. Depicted as an emaciated and skeletal figure, the god of death was accompanied by or associated with an equally malevolent homologue, Yum Cimil or "Lord Death," a distant relative of the Baron Saturday of Voodoo; Yum Cimil roves around, seeking out those tortured by illness. This myth, it might be mentioned in passing, is startlingly similar to the one shared by the Trobriand Islanders.

Most of all, what should be kept in mind is that evil was, to the Maya, the product not only of the wrathful and ambivalent gods, as is the case in other world religions such as Vedism, but also of the wrath of such decidedly malevolent gods as Yum Cimil. Cizin is certainly neither a devil nor the Devil, since he is in fact a god— ill-disposed toward human beings, granted, yet not the antagonist of Itzamma, the creator god. In the context of Maya religion, however, he foreshadowed, in a way, the Devil: though a god, he lived underground, like the Christian Devil, and he was without question very bad. All he lacks in order to be the brother of the Christian Devil is the spirit of rebellion that characterizes Satan. In essence, he is a distant cousin of the Zoroastrian Ahriman and the Mesopotamian demons, although he never attained their exalted status. In any case, he was certainly not out of his element in the dictatorship of the Maya kingdoms of the Yucatán. Isolated by two oceans and lacking any real cultural exchange, the Maya priests didn't manage to conceptualize the Devil—although they came close.

The structure of Maya society was, like those of ancient Iran and Mesopotamia, aristocratic. It was also theocratic in that it was dominated by priests and priest-kings, a fact that around the year 1500 would precipitate the collapse of Maya society in the wake of peasant revolts. The ossified clergy was incapable of mounting a defense against the jacqueries that devastated the Maya empire; the so-called Classical era, the civilization's most illustrious period, came to a close, and the majestic sites of Uxmal and Chichen-Itza were abandoned. The peasants did not, however, win their freedom; the Itzas, a foreign tribe, imposed upon the Mayas both a new militaristic tyranny and the practice of human sacrifice.

The omnipresence of tyrannies dominated by military and religious castes explains one of the more sinister aspects (in addition to human sacrifice) of the Mesoamerican religions—the perpetual and suffocating state of guilt in which the Amerindians lived. The extent and importance of the Maya penitential rites are remarkable. Soustelle described a sculpted scene in which a woman, seen kneeling down in front of a priest who is holding a banner made of feathers, is piercing her tongue with a needle-studded cord. The people slashed not only their tongues, but also their ears and calves. These mortification rites, aimed at exorcising a "demon," were very much like those prescribed by the Mesopotamian religion.

If human sacrifice seems rarer among the Maya than, for example, the Olmec, it was nevertheless far from absent. Many bas-reliefs and sculptures, notably the ones in the Temple of Jaguars and the Temple of Warriors, depict men being stretched out on altars, their feet and hands held down by officiants, while a priest is brandishing the knife with which he is about to open their chests and remove their hearts It was impossible for any individual to escape either self-mutilation or sacrifice.

One wonders about the state of mind of a people so regularly and frequently confronted by the spectacle of blood and flesh and bodies cut up like so many sides of beef. The fact is that Maya culture—which taught that suicides, who had their own protective goddess, would enjoy bliss everlasting—felt contemptuous toward life. If death is nothing, neither is its opposite.

As in Mesopotamia, in the Maya culture there was no hope of escaping from religious terror. Maya society was a rigid hierarchy, and life at the top as well as the bottom of the social ladder was strictly dictated by ritual. The general responsible for military affairs was surrounded, in Soustelle's words, "by an oppressive framework of taboos: in the three-year term to which he was elected, he could not have sexual relations with a woman, and he could neither eat meat nor get drunk. Apart from corn, he could only eat fish or iguana. The utensils he used were kept separate from all others in the house."⁹ For all intents and purposes he was a priest; the actual clergy, which judging by the sheer number of temples and rituals was a very large caste, was hereditary. Maya society was highly authoritarian, and as in all such societies (especially when they are militaristic), myths of Evil and the necessity of holding it at bay become supreme. It is easy to understand how these peoples absorbed Christianity with relative ease, identifying Jesus with the sun-god Quetzalcoatl or Kukulcan, and the Virgin Mary with the moon, as well as transforming the cross itself into a symbol of the beneficial rains. The population already knew both sin and repentance.

There was also the enigmatic figure of Quetzalcoatl; before moving on to an analysis of this deity himself, we shall examine the context in which he appeared.

Trudging on in the footsteps of Columbus, the Spanish discovered not only Maya religion, but also the religions of civilizations predating the Maya. At some indeterminate time, the Mexican landscape witnessed the appearance of two major populations and cultures, the Toltecs and the Aztecs, whose origins are unknown. The Toltecs appeared sometime around the eighth century; they left no other traces, and thus no clue as to where their religion came from. They might have been nomads before establishing their kingdom, but this theory by no means satisfies all Mesoamerica specialists.

There is a Toltec creation myth in which the god Quetzalcoatl, the Feathered Serpent and the "vegetarian" god of the Olmecs, appeared on earth to found the dynasty of the Toltec kings (it is a universal mania among kings to claim divine origins). Quetzalcoatl was a beautiful young man, the king of Tollan, and a benevolent god who banned the practice of human sacrifice. He fell in love with a princess who was also a deity; he had an enormous penis, and, drunk on either pulque or peyote, he hurt her when they lay together. Once he sobered up, he realized what had happened and repented. He took to the sea on a raft made of snakeskin, but the sun set it on fire and Quetzalcoatl's heart ascended into the sky, where it became Venus. In another version of this myth, Quetzalcoatl came back to shore, built a pyre, and immolated himself. In both versions, these events take place at the time of a solar eclipse.[10]

The English observatory of Hurstmonceaux established that a very rare congruence of a solar eclipse with the rising of Venus happened on July 16, 790.[11] The Toltec dynasty was established on that day, when the Morning Star, the Breath of Life, or the God of the Winds manifested itself on earth. The Aztecs were to inherit this deity, who had a sworn enemy named Tezcatlipoca, from the Toltecs.

The stories of Tezcatlipoca and Quetzalcoatl have many elements in common. Tezcatlipoca was a beautiful young man (though he was missing a foot, which was eaten by an alligator, and in its place was an obsidian mirror); like Quetzalcoatl, he had an impressively sized penis. He showed up stark naked at the Tollan marketplace (disguised, the legend paradoxically states, as a Huaxtec merchant), where the princess of the city, the Toltec capital, fell in love with him at the sight of his manhood. Sick with desire, she convinced her father to let her marry the young man. In another version, Tezcatlipoca got the king drunk on pulque, then seduced the princess. In any case, she conceived a son, who was born on the magic Day of the Nine Winds. Once he had fathered a prince of Tollan, Tezcatlipoca sowed such chaos in the Toltec kingdom that Quetzalcoatl renounced and abandoned the city. Tezcatlipoca reinstated human sacrifice, and it was in his honor that on his feast day a beautiful young man was selected and killed.

By all indications, Tezcatlipoca was the inverted mirror of Quetzalcoatl: both were young and handsome and had large penises, and both seduced princesses. One was against sacrifices, the other for them. One was benevolent, the other malevolent. Tezcatlipoca was thus, in one sense, the "Devil" counterpart of the god Quetzalcoatl.

In reality, this division reflected an entirely different symbolism than religious antagonism between Good and Evil. At least in his "vegetarian" form, Quetzalcoatl was the unchallenged deity of the Teotihuacan civilization,[12] whose religion seems to have centered around agricultural gods. These deities seem to have been no more disposed than was Quetzalcoatl toward human sacrifice. Then, in the sixth century—or shortly before Quetzalcoatl founded the royal Toltec line—the power of Teotihuacan waned. Its religion declined as well, and a foreign god to whom sacrifices were made, Xipe Totec, appeared on the scene. Quetzalcoatl had not vanished from the pantheon, but he was challenged by a new rival. In the ninth century, the Toltecs invaded, founded the new capital of Tollan, and imported Tezcatlipoca, the God of the Starry Night. For the whole next century, the Toltec religion was torn by the battling influences of Quetzalcoatl and Tezcatlipoca; at its conclusion, Quetzalcoatl lost his preeminence and quit Tollan.[13] One could not find a better example of religious myth as a reflection of actual historical events. There is no ethical content: Quetzalcoatl is not Good and Tezcatlipoca is not Evil. The two deities are, rather, emblems of antagonistic myths produced by different cultures.

Like all pre-Columbian societies, the Toltecs and the Aztecs who came after them were warlike. Battle was the sine qua non of survival, and the gods who ensured military victory demanded blood, and so the triumph of Quetzalcoatl would have meant the defeat of Xipe Totec and then of Tezcatlipoca, which was unthinkable. Only blood sacrifices guaranteed the respect of rival and neighboring tribes. When there was no war to satisfy the demand for sacrificial victims, the Toltecs celebrated a "Flower War," which was something of a misnomer in that these tournaments concluded with the execution of the defeated, a tradition the Aztec emperor Moctezuma revived. From all of this it becomes clear that there was something strange about Quetzalcoatl denouncing the sacrifices that were essential to war.

Again, in the victory of Tezcatlipoca we see that religious custom masked social and political considerations, especially in the south. Central America, the duodenum that connects North and South America, is divided by modern politics into a mass of states— Guatemala, Honduras, Belize, Nicaragua, and Panama—that are as artificially distinct as they are united in a visceral reaction to the meddling of northerners. Central America's ancient history seems to defy all description. Since the first millennium B.C., it has been characterized by a Brownian movement of populations, some going north, some going south, all meeting one another along the way, sometimes mixing their gene pools through rape or peaceable intermarriage, calling truces and then waging war again all the way until the arrival of the Europeans. Corn, manioc, quinoa, gold, trade, and war—this is about all that archaeology can make out. The only certain thing is that a tribe called the Chichas, who came from the region in and around Colombia, attempted to establish a hegemony over the area but failed.

Of the religions from south of Mexico, including that of the Incas, all that remains are the artistic representations: gods with the heads of jaguars, alligators, or monkeys, primitive deities to whom human sacrifices were sometimes made. When they didn't slaughter their victims outright, the Chichas let them die of hunger and thirst under the naked sun. Their deities seem to have been ambivalent; like the Olmecs, the Maya, and the Aztecs, the Incas believed their gods would produce good if they were sated and evil if they were not. The unfortunates who were left to die under the sun were no more than dogs.[14] In this respect, the Incas, a northern people who conquered the Mochicas and Chimus sometime around 1200, were not unusual.

The Devil therefore did not need to be incarnated in one specific figure: he was present in all the gods, which means that he was omnipresent. This is not to say, through syllogism, that he was nowhere; rather, he could surge up anywhere, as is the case in so many primitive religions. "We do not believe, we fear," an Aztec saying holds—a Kierkegaardian sentiment that could apply to all of pre-Columbian America. Like other Amerindian civilizations, the Incas paid homage to the jaguar god not because he was sacred, or *buaca*, but because he was frightening.

The breakdown of this theologically and socially closed system occurred in Inca-ruled Peru. Making the Fifth Catastrophe prophesied by the Inca religion itself come true in November 1532, Francisco Pizarro and a column of 160 men marched into the central square in the provincial capital of Cajamarca and up to the dais where the emperor Atahualpa sat amid his army of eighty thousand. The Dominican friar Vincente de Valverde presented a breviary to the Inca king, who admired its texture but then, because the Incas had no writing,[15] tossed it to the ground. At that point the Dominican cried out, "Onward, Christians! Attack these enemy curs who spurn the things of God!" A cannon was fired, and Atahualpa's army was cowed into paralysis. The massacre began. In two hours, six or seven thousand disarmed Incas were killed and Atahualpa captured. On July 26 of the following year, he was strangled according to the then-common Spanish practice of garroting people after forcibly converting them. Pizarro had solemnly sworn that Atahualpa would be freed once his ransom was paid—which it was. Like any good Christian, though, Pizarro probably felt that promises made to infidels did not need to be honored.

It was only then that the Devil as a distinct entity made his processional entry into Peru. The great god Pachacamac of the Chimus and the Mochicas, who had become the Inca Viracocha but remained the creator of the world and of the first man and woman (though by then he had also become the incarnation of the sun) disappeared from human memory. The Inca empire crumbled, and the Europeans took its gold.

The Incas had suspected that evil was multiform and omnipresent, since they encountered the wrath of the gods everywhere; the change was that Christians defined Evil as localized, though they too suspected that it was omnipresent. This convergence deserves special attention, since in this case it is situated under the sign of the mysterious Quetzalcoatl.

Inca religion, however, would not have horrified the invaders had they taken even the least interest in it. Had they displayed any "Christian" charity or open-mindedness toward what was so foreign to them, the conquerors could only have been struck by the fact that the Incas, like their Mochica and Chimu predecessors, believed that everyone had a guardian angel, a *hauqui*, a shadow or "soul" that functioned as friend and advisor.[16] They might have been interested in the fact that the vanquished savages believed, as they did, in a supreme god, the creator of the world and of humanity; and they might have wondered why this god was, like theirs, a weeping figure, as can be seen in the spectacular and mysterious relief that adorns the Portal of the Sun, which today still towers over the monumental ruins of the Mochica holy city of Tiahuanaco on the banks of Lake Titicaca.[17] This weeping god is unparalleled in any other Amerindian religion.

The sheer weight of these similarities, incidentally, was destined to pose a problem for the true Christianization of the Peruvian peoples; even today, some six to seven million descendants of the Incas still believe that God is the sun, and when they pray to the Virgin Mary they undoubtedly do not identify her with the moon, as converted Mayas do, but with the goddess of the earth. They still believe Saint James, or "Santiago," to be Apu Illapu, the god of thunder and rain, and the Christian feast days have ended up coinciding with Inca feast days, just as elsewhere the winter solstice, the day on which the rebirth of the gods of vegetation was celebrated, was transformed into the day on which Jesus was born. The Virgins of the Moon once commanded the same respect afforded Christian nuns; one Father Calancha wrote that "they are like our own religious sisters,"[18] which however did not keep the men under the command of one of Pizarro's lieutenants, Hernando de Soto, from raping five hundred of them in 1532.[19]

The many similarities between Christianity and Inca paganism intrigued the first European inhabitants of Peru as well as the *cholos*, the mixed-raced children born out of their intermarriage with Inca women. Even if they were not very well versed in Amerindian religions, the Christians who accompanied or were born after the Spanish conquest must have been particularly fascinated by the cult of the God-Who-Weeps. The *cholo* Felipe Guaman Poma de Ayala, who was born in 1534, felt this figure important enough to address a letter to the Spanish king about him; the missive, which was no fewer than twelve hundred pages long and included four hundred of Poma's own drawings, described the Inca civilization and its beliefs in great detail.[20] In 1609, another renowned *cholo*, Garcilaso de la Vega, compiled a history of Peru told from the Inca point of view.[21] Neither of these men knew much more about the subject than they heard tell of, which perhaps was inaccurate. Some other sixteenth-century writers theorized that the Incas were the lost descendants of Noah. If that were the case, the Christians finally had an opportunity to convert those errant Jews.[22]

Another Spanish writer of the day, Pedro Cieza de Leon, pointed out something very strange indeed. After a visit to the town of Huari in the Pacayccasa Valley near Ayacucho, he wrote that

[its name] is Vinaque. It contains large and very ancient edifices that, judging from their dilapidated state, have been in existence for an extremely long time. When I asked the Indians in the area about who had built this relic, they replied that other white men who also had beards had come and settled here long before the reign of the Incas. These ancient buildings and others in the realm are not, it seems to me, of the sort the Incas would have built. Their building construction is square, while that of the Incas is long and narrow.[23]

Since the Incas arrived in Peru around 1200, it must be supposed that Huari was built by predecessors of theirs from the Tiahuanaco period. The two peoples who predated the Incas were the Mochicas, who flourished between the third century B.C. and the tenth century A.D., and the Chimus, who flourished between the fifth and tenth centuries A.D. Neither people, however, was white or bearded. In addition, neither the Mochicas nor the Chimus controlled the regions the Incas held—another indication that the white men mentioned to Cieza by his Indians could not have been in Huari at the time of its construction (that is, between the year 1000 and the beginning of the thirteenth century, when the Incas appeared).

The idea that white people were on the high Andes plateaus some three centuries before Columbus seems outlandish, yet the strange tale is echoed by another, and when two strange tales converge they become a problem. Describing his visit to Tiahuanaco, which is located much farther south than Huari, some thirteen miles away from the southern edge of Lake Titicaca and not far from La Paz, Bolivia, Cieza reports:

I asked the natives on the *encomienda* of Juan Varagas, in his presence, if these buildings had been built in the time of the Incas. They burst out laughing and said that they had been erected long before the Inca reign, although they could not tell me who had made them. They had, however, heard from their ancestors that everything there had appeared in one night. For this reason, and because they also said that bearded men had been seen on Titicaca Island and that those men had built the edifice in Vinaque, I would say that before the Incas there had been a people here who came from no one knows where and built these things. Having been much fewer in number than the natives, they might have been killed off in the course of wars.[24]

The tale of Tiahuanaco's construction can obviously be disregarded. We are left, however, with the persistent story of bearded white men who built the temple called Vinaque in the town of Huari and were seen, at some undetermined time, on Titicaca Island; we are also left with Cieza's hypothesis. The two traits that the Indians mentioned to Cieza make it clear that the men must have been European or Mediterranean. The question is intriguing, since it suggests that visitors from the Old World might have had a role in inspiring the edifices of the Tiahuanaco period—which is to say, they might have imported into the New World the figure of the God-Who-Weeps who characterized the Tiahuanaco civilization.[25]

To reach South America's western shores, these navigators would in all probability have to have crossed the Atlantic and the Caribbean, then reached the Pacific coast of, say, modern Panama,[26] and from there descended on foot to Peru. They could also have crossed the Atlantic, followed the eastern shores of South America, rounded Cape Horn, then headed north along the Pacific coast until they reached Chile or Peru. Last, they could have crossed the Pacific, although this seems impossible; sailors coming from Europe or the Mediterranean would almost certainly have stopped at one of that ocean's numerous archipelagos. The passage around Cape Horn is notoriously dangerous, but it isn't impossible that a few drakkars could have pulled off the feat.[27] The most likely landing place seems to be Central America. It should be made clear that though the idea of transatlantic crossings predating Columbus was rejected some forty years ago as unfounded speculation, it has progressively gained currency, especially after the voyages of Thor Heyerdahl. Not only does every encyclopedia mention the discovery of America by the Vikings as historical fact, but many even admit the plausibility of the

Atlantic having been crossed by the Irish monk Brendan (also called Brandan or Brendon—his real name seems to have been Brenaind) in the sixth century. It is no longer shocking to think that the Phoenicians might have circumnavigated Africa by as early as 1500 B.C. Etymological similarities should always be viewed with a certain amount of suspicion, but it doesn't take much to be surprised by the apparent closeness of Kukulcan to Cu Chulainn or Cuchulain (there are variant spellings), the Irish hero, half-Achilles, half-Hercules, who according to legend died at twenty-seven after having been betrayed in a duel. The resemblance is not merely phonetic. The Mexican Kukulcan-Quetzalcoatl who became the Incan Viracocha is, like Cuchulain, a hero who died young after having attempted to bring peace to the world. One wonders what arguments Brendan would have used, and whether or not he would have found it easier to convince the natives and fire their imaginations by combining the figures of Cuchulain and Jesus into one. There are undeniable traces of the Jesus legend in the myth of Kukulcan (who descends into the underworld with his dog-headed friend Xolotl to gather up the remains of the dead and bring them back to life).

According to Amerindian tales—and in any case judging from the time that images of the God-Who-Weeps first appear during the Tiahuanaco period—these "missionaries" would have landed sometime between 600 and 1200. Earlier we examined the reasons for situating the visit of white men, possibly Irish, in the eighth century, which seems a reasonable date. In the time between 600 and 1200, the West had become entirely dominated by Christianity.

Given the current consensus on Andean archaeology, the theory that Huari is the oldest of all cities is untenable. Tiahuanaco was built first, and its influence spread along the whole western flank of the Andes sierra from Bolivia to perhaps even Chile; Huari bears marks of its influence.[28] The hypothesis that a group of foreigners (white and bearded or not) had inspired or ordered the construction of buildings on the scale of those at Tiahuanaco (in one night or a thousand) verges on utter fantasy.

Three facts are certain: only in the Tiahuanaco civilization does the God-Who-Weeps appear; this civilization originally expanded because of religious reasons; and the Amerindian stories collected by Cieza associate this god with the Tiahuanaco civilization. The Westerners whose memory the Indians passed on from generation to generation must have been Christians, and the God-Who-Weeps responsible for Tihuanaco's expansion[29] would thus have been an Amerindian version of Jesus—or of a white man, Christian and bearded (and possessing a large penis), who would have presented himself as a hero Celtic, Christian, or both.

The idea that there was a partial, pre-Columbian Christianization of the Americas is supported by the possibility of identifying Quetzalcoatl, the Feathered Serpent (who himself is associated with the Maya Kukulcan and, more interestingly as far as we are concerned, with the Inca Viracocha), with a Christian cleric. We know that in Mexico a wise monarch existed who was hostile to human sacrifice but who was subsequently routed by Tezcatlipoca, forced from the city of Tollan, and driven out to sea. In addition, some ancient texts describe him as pale-skinned and bearded, which are typically European traits, as well as wearing a long robe, which is very much an incongruous garb for Amerindian civilizations. In several instances, he is also conclusively associated with the symbol of the cross.[30]

What must be kept in mind, if one wants to accept this hypothesis, is that the Christianization would have been only partial and reabsorbed into the body of the Andean religions—which several centuries later would again be the case. The Quetzalcoatl-Kukulcan-Viracocha-Jesus syncretism did not manage to produce a home for the Devil in South America, despite the incorporation into Tiahuanaco mythology of the foreign image of the God-Who-Weeps. The penitential spirit was intrinsic to the Incas, just as it had also reigned among the Mayas and then the Aztecs; for unclear reasons, however, the notion of the Devil was rejected.

As it was presented to the pre-Columbian Amerindians, and of course over and above the language barrier, Christianity perhaps seemed dangerous to the Andean kings and high priests. Indeed, its principle of individual salvation threatened to wrest the people from their grasp, and that in turn threatened their power. The same political grouping that in the Middle East created the Evil One was, in this instance, to resist it until the arrival, in massive strength, of the Christian West. It was only then that children would be sacrificed to him.

CHAPTER 13

Israel

Demons as the
Heavenly Servants of
the Modern Devil

The official history of the West begins with a loss. This parochial tale, initially addressed to no more than a few tens of thousands, has in twenty-five centuries disseminated itself all over the world. True, hundreds of other civilizations have produced an equivalent number of creation myths; the human being's greatest concern is to retell the story of his origins, and if he does not know it he invents one, since no human in any century has known innately how to be what he actually is.

Human memory is short, at least in the absence of books, which is why they have been burned in auto-da-fés from the destruction of the library at Alexandria through the Inquisition and the Third Reich. Until the fifties, there was—from Brazzaville to Dublin, from Brest to Brest-Litovsk, from Goa to Los Angeles—no other tale of creation apart from the one in Genesis, which was written for the handful of Hebrews who survived the enmity of a tyrant called Nebuchadrezzar II. It is from that story that we know—or believe we know—that we are the Devil's prey.

Our ancestors Adam and Eve, as we learned in Sunday school, lived in the Earthly Paradise, a place of banal delights, a paradox somehow both Orientalist and Rousseauian at the same time—a place where, in the imagination of the elder Pieter Brueghel, lions lay down next to lambs (which means they were not the sort of lions around today). The East has always had a penchant for such fables, and Eden in fact is no Hebrew invention; the word, which is Sumerian and dates from the third or second millennium B.C., comes from the Akkadian *edenu*, or "paradise."[1] Archaeologists believe that the four rivers flowing out of one larger one that watered the Genesis Eden—the Pison, the Gihon, the Hiddekel, and the Perat—flowed into the Persian Gulf,[2] and in fact might have been the Tigris, the Euphrates, and two of their tributaries. In sum, Paradise once lay in Iraq.

According to Holy Scripture, Adam and Eve were originally innocent, but then the Devil tempted Eve, who succumbed and in turn tempted Adam, who followed suit, perhaps out of boredom. Forever afterward, we have borne the burden of sin incurred by people who had no idea what Evil was, since they had not experienced it before they tasted the infamous forbidden fruit. Their sin was juridically not sin, of course, because sin is committed in the knowledge of cause, and if cause is absent then it is merely error.

Yet we must wonder if it was really our Devil who in the guise of the "subtle serpent" of Genesis told Eve that she and Adam would never die if they ate the fruit from "the tree in the midst of the garden." The fable is as obvious as it is enigmatic, since the tree was that of the knowledge of Good and Evil, and one must ponder the soundness of a divine injunction against knowing the difference between the two—doesn't the fear of God demand precisely that distinction? Why would God have forbidden us from learning what they were? The snake told Eve that she and her spouse, who were already immortal, would be as gods if they ate of the fruit, the well-known *et eritis sicut Dei*, but they only learned about death *after* they left Paradise. For such a shrewd creature, the snake was engaged in some curiously illogical reasoning.

The truth is simpler, and most children end up realizing it fairly quickly: the sin lies in the fact that Adam and Eve made love. One can puzzle endlessly about the sense of creating two complementary organisms, leaving them naked in a garden with a pleasant climate, only to brandish a flaming sword at them when they commit the inevitable. I have never figured out why the talking snake features in the picture at all; he is made irrelevant by biological complementarity.

Granted, this tree of Good and Evil is a symbol, and, like all symbols, it is ambiguous—but the question is whether the snake is a symbol, too. It is tempting to doubt it, since Elohim or God talks to him in his specific capacity as snake: "Because you have done this, cursed are you above all cattle, and above all wild animals; upon your belly you shall go, and dust you shall eat all the days of your life." Further on: "I will put enmity between you and the woman, and between your seed and her seed."[3] One wonders if matters had ever been different, if even in the Garden of Eden there hadn't always been a distance between the seed of snakes and that of humans. The anathema arouses both bewilderment and skepticism, since the divine malediction against the snake seems to have been limited to the Middle East (the Egyptians, Hindus, Mexicans, and many others in fact deified snakes).

If it really is the Devil disguised as the snake, one also wonders what he was doing in Paradise—had God created Evil as well and given it a residence in Eden? If this is so, Adam and Eve cannot be faulted for having accepted an invitation from a legitimate tenant. Myths are indeed thorny things.

One of the many versions of the Bible tells us that "the serpent was more subtle than any creature that the Lord God had made."[4] Yet Genesis does not say what the point was of the stratagem by which Eve was persuaded to break the Creator's rule, nor what advantage lay in it for the snake. It is made clear that the serpent is a creature of the Lord; but the Bible never explains why He doesn't punish the snake, or what happens to this troublemaker later on.

The expulsion from Paradise does not seem to have adversely affected the original couple's descendants, whose longevity, a sign of physical and mental health, was prodigious: Adam lived for 930 years, Seth 500, Enoch 905, Cainan and Mahalalel 840, Jared 962, and Methuselah, who holds the record, 969. What is most odd is that the Creator seemed displeased by the proliferation of humans on earth; He "saw that the wickedness of man was great in the earth, and that every imagination of the thoughts of his heart was only evil continually." If there is any doubt about the Creator's malevolence toward his creatures, the next verse dispels it: God repents "that he had made man on the earth, and it grieved him at his heart."[5] He decided to "blot out man whom I have created from the face of the ground," and not only man but the rest of Creation as well: "man and beast and creeping things, and birds of the air; for I am sorry that I have made them."[6] All of Creation earned God's disappointment or resentment; according to Genesis, for centuries afterward all humanity—not to mention sheep, birds, fish, flowers, and ferns—would pay the price for it as well as for sin, and that price was the Flood.

If all of that was the consequence of the underhanded trick the serpent had played, or of the crime of Cain, jealous at the sight of his brother amassing more riches than he, then it is hard to see why the birds of the air also had any responsibility to bear. The Creator was acting like a feckless despot. The first book of the Book thus portrays God as an angry tyrant, wrathful and unjust, a stranger to the idea of forgiveness who, in his ire, decides to drown the whole world. Noah finds grace in the eyes of the Eternal, but that is not enough to soothe the divine temper. Indeed, "I have determined to make an end of all flesh; for the earth is filled with violence through them; behold, I will destroy them with the earth."[7] From Judaism's earliest beginnings, Evil is therefore ambiguous. ("Judaism" in this case means Judaism after the invention of the Hebrew script, since the Bible postdates the people that Mesopotamia specialists refer to as the "Habiru," the Hebrews, who were very much more ancient.[8])

The Bible itself is a late text; since the publication of the now-celebrated analyses of Karl Graf and Julius Wellhausen in the nineteenth century, which later came to be referred to collectively as the Graf-Wellhausen theory, it has become accepted that Genesis is a composite text written after Exodus, or in other words after Nebuchadrezzar took and razed Jerusalem in 587 B.C. and the subsequent captivity of the Jews in Babylon, which lasted until 538 B.C.[9] Genesis must therefore have been written after the return to Jerusalem at the beginning of the fifth century B.C.

It is hard not to be struck by the similarity between the Creator's disappointment in Genesis and that of Apsu, the bilious Babylonian creator god who was annoyed by the racket being made by his children and decided to exterminate them. There is also some similarity to the story of humanity's creation by the god Enki and his wife Ninmah, who in their drunkenness produced a collection of misfits and abominations. In all three cases, an arbitrary creator bungles the first attempt at Creation, which the deity then almost destroys.

The possibilty that the authors of Genesis brought their version of Creation back from Mesopotamia is supported by the close affinities between the Mesopotamian and Genesis versions.[10] Since there are other similarities as well, it seems likely that an appreciable fraction of the Old Testament was the product of contacts with the religion of the Mesopotamian oppressor.

The story of Noah exists in a Babylonian version that is much older than Genesis. In 1965, the British Museum discovered in its collections two tablets referring to the Flood; they had been engraved in the Babylonian city of Sipar during the reign of King Ammisaduqua (1646–1626 B.C.). The tablets say that the Creator regretted his work and decided to destroy it by drowning; however, Enki, the god of waters, betrayed the planned catastrophe to a priest-king named Ziusudra, who built an ark and survived. This character did in fact exist; he was the king of the southern Babylonian city of Shuruppak sometime around 2900 B.C.[11] Unless there were two arks, Ziusudra and Noah seem to have been the same person.

It is still unclear where the Hebrews drew their version of Satan from, because even if the snake of Paradise is not called Satan by name, it is at least a prefiguration of him. In the Babylonian Epic of Gilgamesh, there is a seduction episode whose terms definitely recall those of Adam and Eve in Genesis. Once he has succumbed to the charms of Ishtar, Enkiddu finds himself endowed with "wisdom and a higher knowledge." The words Ishtar speaks to her lover are an even more remarkable echo of the serpent's "You will be like God": "You are wise, Enkiddu, you are as a god." In the Babylonian religion, though, Ishtar is far from identified with a spirit of Evil: she is a goddess and a temptress, and though she is wild and at times cruel, she does not represent Evil.

The innovation of Genesis is the snake that foreshadows Satan. The fact that Satan had existed since the dawn of time seems to be underscored by God's admonition to Cain when the latter offered him the fruit of his first sowing, a sacrifice that for some unexplained reason God did not look upon favorably: "If you do well, will you not be accepted? and if you do not do well, sin is couching at the door; its desire is for you, but you must master it."[12]

This, however, is the sort of simple, unidentified demon that abounds in every world religion, especially those of the Middle East; it is not our Satan. Proof comes from the book of Job:

> Now there was a day when the sons of God came to present themselves before the Lord, and Satan came also among them. The Lord said to Satan, "Whence have you come?" Satan answered the Lord, "From going to and fro on the earth, and from walking up and down on it." And the Lord said to Satan, "Have you considered my servant Job, that there is none like him in the earth, a blameless and upright man. . . ."[13]

Satan is explicitly a member of the heavenly council; he is even on familiar terms with God. This Satan is an inferior god, but a god nonetheless, who recalls similar figures in the religions that derive from Vedism, for instance the trickster Loki. With God's consent, Satan will test the unfortunate Job by tormenting him, although all will turn out well in the end. Satan is thus the instrument of the deity, who paradoxically would like to know if Job really is as virtuous as he seems.

At this point, Satan is far from being the fallen angel, the rebel and sworn enemy of God. The same impression is conveyed in the words the prophet Micaiah speaks to the king of Israel, Ahab, who is planning a war against the Arameans. The king consults his prophets ("about four hundred men," which is a fair number), and then Micaiah appears. He advises against war, which mightily annoys Ahab, who calls him a prophet of doom. But Micaiah insists that he has had a vision:

I saw the Lord sitting on his throne, and all the host of heaven standing beside him on his right hand and on his left; and the Lord said, "Who will entice Ahab, that he may go up and fall at Ramoth-gilead?" And one said one thing, and another said another. Then a spirit came forward and stood before the Lord, saying, "I will entice him."

And the Lord said to him, "By what means?" And he said, "I will go forth, and I will be a lying spirit in the mouth of all these your prophets."[14]

Micaiah's temerity comes to naught; his face is slapped by the chief prophet, Zedekiah, and then the king, who will die that very night, throws him in prison. God has fulfilled his intention to destroy Ahab through this mysterious lying spirit. This is an extraordinary episode, since the only spirit capable of dividing its voice to whisper in the ears of four hundred prophets would be the Devil we know so well. Once again, we find him in the heavenly council and carrying out the designs of God. He is not hard to recognize as the brother of spirits Babylonian and Egyptian.

Practically the same story appears in an earlier Egyptian version. Osiris, who is anxious to send one particular general into battle, dispatches spirits to him: "The two demons penetrated into him, and at the same time his heart forgot the feast. 'By life, my friends, I feel like going to war!' "[15] The Hebrew God was undoubtedly inspired by Osiris's subterfuge.

However, as we have seen, divine ruses, like myths, circulate among religions, and neither Judaism nor the Old Testament is immune to borrowings. The demonic spirit is encountered allied with God once more in the book of Isaiah. The oracle that expresses the divine curse against Egypt announces that God has visited the Egyptian chiefs with a "spirit of confusion" that has caused Egypt to "stagger in all her doing," and it will fall "as a drunken man staggers in his vomit."[16]

The book of Isaiah, which was written between the eighth and sixth centuries B.C., yet again confirms that, for Judaism, neither Satan nor the demons were enemies of God, but in fact his servants. It is not unusual for Yahweh's vengeance to be exacted by demonic agents; when they aren't busy with their own meddling and black-guard doings, they turn into celestial factotums. In other words, Satan is both an ally and servant of God.

In I Chronicles, however, matters are otherwise. Satan reappears, this time to inspire David to carry out a census, which will have unfortunate consequences of bringing down a plague on the population: "Satan stood up against Israel and incited David to number Israel."[17]

Chronicles dates from the beginning of the Hellenistic era, or the third century B.C. In the space of some two centuries Satan has undergone a transformation; he no longer acts in concert with God but, instead, independently. After two more centuries, the status of the ex-member of the council of God has radically changed: he has been doomed to disappear. This is evident in the Book of Jubilees, an intertestamentary text written by the Essenes of Qumran (and so dating no farther back than the second half of the second century B.C.), which tells that at the end of time—that is, after forty-nine jubilees have elapsed—neither Satan nor Evil will exist anymore, and the nation of Israel will be purified forever.[18]

Hebrew ideas about the Devil must therefore have changed in the time between the writing of Genesis, around the sixth century B.C., and the first century B.C. It has been pointed out that devils infected Judaism between 150 B.C. and 300 A.D.[19] They were relatively few in the Old Testament: Mevet, the demon of death, Lilith, the thief of children, Reshev, the demon of the plague, Dever, demon of illness in general, Belial, lieutenant of the demons, Azazel, demon of the deserts (and probably the one who tempted Jesus), and Satan, although as we have seen his role is ambiguous. The list is short compared to that of Babylon, where a large portion of the Jewish people suffered long captivity; Babylon's considerably more elaborate pandemonium makes up a detailed hierarchy. Perhaps these devils seemed too disturbing after the Hebrews returned home, or perhaps the Hebrews thought that granting them all a separate identity would risk making them too important, and so they retained only a few of them.

There was, in fact, no Jewish version of Hell; the place the dead went to, Sheol, was not the Christian Hell but, instead, a "land of silence and forgetting," a place "made up of nonsubstance and emptiness; it is characterized by darkness and dust."[20] It was the "land of no return," an expression also borrowed from the Mesopotamians, just as its description was modeled after the Assyro-Babylonian Arallu. According to the Book of Job,[21] Sheol was "the house appointed for all the living," good or bad, king or slave. There was neither Heaven nor Hell, and certainly no purgatory.

The notion of the soul's survival as it is understood today does not exist in the Old Testament, or if it does it is undefined. It would not appear until much later, during the second century B.C., in a Hebrew book that mentioned the resurrection of the dead for the very first time.

One episode in the Old Testament that has as much to say as the Book of Job about the calm if not indifferent Jewish attitude toward the Devil is Saul's visit to the medium of Endor. The description of this consultation (I Samuel, 28:1–25) is expressed with extraordinary poetry and symbolism. It begins with the Philistines massing their troops on the border at Shunem, preparing to mount an offensive against Israel. Saul has gathered his men at Gilboa, but he is anxious: "When Saul inquired of the Lord, the Lord did not answer him, either by dreams, or by Urim, or by prophets." Saul is also tormented by his conflict with David, whom he had tried to kill the way he had killed Samuel. The scene is Shakespearian in its intensity (although perhaps it would be more correct to say that Shakespeare's finest scenes have an intensity that evokes the story in the first Book of Samuel).

Samuel is dead, and Saul, the story goes, has by way of precaution "put the mediums and the wizards out of the land." Their banishment is not due to any interdiction against dealing with necromancers and spirits, something mentioned nowhere else in the Old Testament; obviously it is because Saul is frightened that Samuel's ghost will reappear. Nevertheless, he commands his servants to "seek out for me a woman who is a medium, that I may go to her, and inquire of her." Despite the banishment of mediums that he himself has ordered, he is searching for a seer who can inform him about what the Lord intends for him. He is compelled to call forth the spirit of the man he fears so much—a startlingly vivid portrait of this complex and tormented person, the man who was in love with David and yet attempted to run him through with a spear, the man who is steeling himself to confront the ghost of Samuel, the thing he most fears. His servants tell him that there is such a woman at Endor, and so, disguised and in the company of only a few of his men, the king goes to consult her.

He comes at night, and when the medium receives him he asks her to summon a spirit. She apparently does not know who she is dealing with, since she objects by citing Saul's injunction against mediums. He promises her immunity in the name of the Lord. She then does as she has been asked, and Samuel's ghost appears. It tells him that the war against the Philistines is already lost, and that three of Saul's sons will be killed in the course of it. Saul collapses, and the ensuing events bear out the ghost's predictions.

Yet at no point is the work of the seer associated with the diabolical; on the contrary, it is indirectly God who is speaking through the voice of Samuel as relayed by the medium. The medium of Endor is the equivalent of the sibyls of pagan antiquity: she is the mouthpiece of God.

If any doubt remains about the Jewish attitude in the Old Testament (one is tempted to say the old "Old Testament" as opposed to the later books, whose ideology is totally different), it is resolved by verses that occur earlier in I Samuel: "Now the Spirit of the Lord departed from Saul, and an evil spirit from the Lord tormented him" (16:14). No ambiguity is possible: it is "an evil spirit from the Lord." But what does "evil spirit" mean? No doubt a demon, and so demons are part of God's design, just as Satan was an instrument of divine will in the Book of Job. This is no error of transcription, since the expression is repeated twice in the following verses, when Saul's servants tell him: "Behold now, an evil spirit from God is tormenting you. Let our lord now command your servants, who are before you, to seek out a man who is skillful in playing the lyre; and when the evil spirit from God is upon you, he will play it, and you will be well" (16:15–16). The musician is David, the story goes on to say, who will from then on soothe the king whenever the evil spirit from God is upon him.

In the Old Testament, God is thus at once good and evil; the

Devil is his servant, no more, and there is no hint of the conflict that so strongly colors the New Testament, in which the Devil is always God's enemy, the "prince of this world" who stands against the King of Heaven. In its submission to the supreme will, the theology of the Old Testament allows for only one pole in the universe, and the Devil never does anything that is out of harmony with the Creator. Satan is not the Devil: he is the suffering desired by the will of God. Nowhere in the Old Testament are there the demonological episodes such as one finds in the New Testament.

Similarly, Satan's name—har-Shatan, "the Adversary," which the Greeks translated with the equivalent term *diabolos* and from which our "Satan" derives—has absolutely no negative connotations. If he is God's adversary, he is also, as we have seen, His servant; he couldn't wish for God's destruction, since that would mean the end of Creation and of Satan himself. The God of Good, who is also the God of this world, constructed the world on the principle of equilibrium, and the Adversary is one of its two terms. With this laudable lesson in wisdom, one of the most profound in ancient Judaism, the authors of the Old Testament had by the seventh or sixth century B.C. resolved the theological problem posed by a God of Good, the master of the world, who also tolerates Evil—a dilemma that the Gnostics were later to find themselves caught in, from which they would extricate themselves only through the artificial formulation of the Demiurge, the true Creator who is above Good and Evil, the former being exclusively spiritual, the latter exclusively material. In the Gnostic conception, the "God of Good" is only a secondary deity on a par with Evil or the Devil. However, in the Old Testament, the omnipotence of the Creator is as incontestable as his goodness; it is the Devil, and the Devil only, who is secondary.

Another and equally significant alliance between God and the Devil in the Old Testament is to be found in the third book of the Pentateuch, Leviticus, whose importance lies in the fact that it contains nearly half of all the biblical commandments. Here one reads that after the death of the two sons of Moses's brother Aaron (they were killed for having made an unfit sacrifice to God), the Lord appears to Moses and tells him that Aaron must take two kid goats and a ram and present himself at the holy place, where God will appear to him above the veiled Ark of the Covenant (16:1ff.). Aaron must come only at the specified time, however, or he will die. A divine sign will mark which of the kid goats the Lord will accept as a sacrifice; the other kid goat is to be offered to Azazel, who is, if not the Devil himself, at least one of his lieutenants. That kid, the now-familiar scapegoat, is to be cast, alive, off a cliff.

Often ignored or smothered under complex and confusing explanations, this episode—though difficult—is related with utter clarity in Leviticus: in the sacrifice He is demanding, God makes an explicit allowance for the Devil.

The few demons who drift about on Earth cannot formally be identified as servants of the Satan who sits on the heavenly council. In addition, these demons imported from the Middle East were themselves ambiguous until a relatively late stage in the game. According to one Old Testament apocrypha, the Book of Enoch, which was probably written between the third and second centuries B.C., demons are angels that did not rebel against God but, rather, fell in love with mortal women and came down to earth to couple with them[22]—the inverse of the story of Sodom and Gomorrah, in which it is mortals who become enamored of angels, although in those two cities they become enamored with angels of their own sex.

The union of lubricious angels and mortals supposedly produced giants "three hundred cubits tall" as well as demons. The angelic nature of the fathers scarcely explains why the children are evil, but the lesson the text seems to convey is that Evil is the product of sex. Nevertheless, one of the angels, Azazel (or Azaziel—the spellings vary) of the book of Leviticus,

> showed man how to make swords, knives, shields, cuirasses, and mirrors; he taught them to make bracelets and jewelry, how to use pigments, how to paint their eyebrows, and the use of precious stones and every sort of dye, and in such a way the world was corrupted. . . . Barkayal taught how to read the stars. Akibel

taught how to interpret signs. Tamiel taught astronomy. And Asaradel taught about the motion of the moon.

Reading further, we discover why Azazel is treated with such opprobrium: "He revealed all that happens in Heaven to the world." This crime was indeed unpardonable, and God supposedly punished Azazel by ordering the archangel Raphael to bind him up, stone him, and cast him into the shadows before destroying him with fire. For unascertainable reasons, however, Azazel seems to have survived the ordeal.

The most astonishing feature about the Enoch is that he seems to have completely ignored not only Leviticus but also the Old Testament in general. Since God can hardly be pictured offering a goat to a character he had consigned to destruction, one wonders if the writer had ever even read Leviticus. If the Book of Enoch is indeed the earlier text, as seems to be the case, it seems unlikely that Azazel could have flouted God's will. In any case, the episode openly contradicts every other reference to the Devil in the Old Testament; it marks a complete break between the theology of the Old Testament and that of the intertestamentary corpus to which the Book of Enoch belongs.

Enoch's conclusions are not the ones we would draw today: his demons, in truth, scarcely seem malevolent. Apart from the mirrors and dyes, which for some unfathomable reason struck the book's editors as containing the germ of Evil, writing (without which Enoch would have gotten nowhere) and astronomy are certainly not diabolical inventions. Were astronomy a cause of Evil, it is difficult to understand why the angel Uriel would have provided a complete course on it in chapter seventy-one of the same book.

As in the whole body of intertestamentary writing, in the Book of Enoch we witness the unleashing of sudden wrath against anything that the authors deemed foreign. Above and beyond his unconvincing pastiche of veterotestamentary prophesy, Enoch's overarching motivation is a mind of singular austerity whose like is not found anywhere else in the Old Testament. It is the work not of an inspired prophet but, rather, of a disturbed fanatic who tries to pass off fables and terrifying, outlandish stories as revealed truth. Its most interesting feature is the substitution of the Devil himself for the scapegoat: it is the Devil who henceforth will bear the blame for anything that goes wrong in the world—and it is here, perhaps, that the Devil assumes his familiar goatish form.

The essential thing is that until the third or second century B.C., the image of Satan as God's declared enemy is absent from Judaism. Satan and the demons—who do not seem to have a master-servant relationship, the former being nowhere referred to as the chief of the latter—are the servants of God. As troubling as this might seem, the texts are there to prove it.

Yet the Devil came to exist in the Jewish tradition: the whole New Testament is characterized by his malevolence and that of his demons. The exorcisms performed by Jesus are almost beyond counting, and in all of them possession is explicitly referred to as the cause of malady. Before that, as we saw in the story of Saul, the "evil spirits" had been sent by the Lord himself. By all evidence, the Evangelists seemed to have a very poor knowledge of the Old Testament, and every one of them, especially John, was clearly influenced by the fundamentalist Jewish cult of Essenism. Satan's role changed, and we must find out why.

The forecurrents of transformation predated Christianity; one of the first texts in which demons appear as completely malevolent enemies both of the God whose vassals they had once been and of humanity in general is the Book of Enoch, which as we know was a relatively late work. Sometimes attributed to the Essenes, it probably is in part due to them, given its composite nature[23] and its numerous Gnostic themes. Above all, it is essential to address the political context, beginning with the role and trial of Jesus, behind the apparition of the Devil, since without doing so there is little hope of understanding anything.

The period when Jewish texts first assumed a resolutely hostile attitude toward Satan coincided with the full bloom of Hellenistic Judaism; as we will see below, at the time Judaism was in the process of being co-opted by Hellenism. The last Jewish prophet, Malachi, had long since fallen silent. The messianic hope—that a successor to David would take up his scepter and restore Israel to glory—was frustrated and seemingly destined to remain so. Despair set in.

The Jews had only just shaken off the threatening shadow of the Babylonian empire when they fell to Alexander in 332 B.C. After that hero vanished into the sands of history, awaiting his rebirth as legend, Palestine was annexed into the Hellenistic empire of Ptolemaic Egypt, then into that of the Seleucid kings of Syria. Independence seemed out of the question for a long time to come, if ever. From then until the creation of the Jewish Palestinian homeland in 1949—and even then for a few years more—Jews in the country would live under the sword of powers far too strong to defy.

The yoke of the Ptolemies and of the later Seleucids was uncommonly light, and the Jews enjoyed a freedom unprecedented since their first deportation into Babylonia. One of the advantages of living in the shadow of empires is that it is difficult to imagine a foreign tyrant ever sending one into captivity. The Mediterranean breezes blew gently for the first time in centuries. Nevertheless, Judaism was in crisis; not only had the dialogue with God, which thanks to the prophets had been continuous since the time of Moses, given way to weighty silence, but from the second century B.C. onward the nation's essentially theocratic structure showed signs of cracking.

The rifts became irreparable after 175 B.C., by which time the high priest Jason had wholly Hellenized Jerusalem; abomination of abominations, the city was renamed Antioch-at-Jerusalem. All the institutions were Hellenistic and the Jews themselves profoundly Hellenized, largely in proportion to their wealth. One of Judaism's basic rites, circumcision, was no longer the norm and struck many as archaic.[24] Jason was supplanted by someone even more Hellenizing than he, a high priest named Menelaus, and civil war broke out between the aristocratic partisans of Menelaus and the populist partisans of Jason. The ensuing bloodbath, which was caused by the obviously absurd rivalry between Hellenizers and "hyper-Hellenizers," exasperated Antiochus IV Epiphanes, the Seleucid king of Syria and suzerain of Palestine. The monarch decreed that Judaic practices be banned, a decree he enforced with vigor, even cruelty. The elderly Mattathias remained faithful to ancient Judaism, and he and his sons rebelled ferociously; the six men assassinated, in public and by stabbing, an apostate Jew who sacrificed to pagan gods, and then a person named Apelles, an official who served Antiochus, as well as the soldiers who were protecting him.[25]

Thus began the open war between the Jews and the pagan occupiers, which would end only with the sack of Jerusalem by Titus in A.D. 70; sixty-five years later, when Hadrian razed Jerusalem and nearly liquidated the Jewish nation, Judaism itself almost disappeared. It was a religious war, and a political one as well, since the two are inseparable in theocracies and theocratic religions. The Maccabees fought out of personal ambition as much as they did to restore the Torah.

Yet the Maccabees' triumph devolved into compromise. Their heir, Jonathan, also ended up ceding to the charms of Hellenism, and he signed a friendship treaty with Sparta; his successor Aristobul termed himself Philhellenus ("Lover of Hellenism"), and his successor in turn, Alexander IV Janneus, was a Hebrew king who heretically coined money stamped with Greek figures. The penultimate in the line, John Hyrcanus II, persecuted the anti-Hellenic Essenes. All of them come to the attention of twentieth-century exegesis because one of their number made the whole dynasty notorious by cruelly putting to death (perhaps by crucifixion, although this is still the subject of argument) the famous and mysterious personage known only as the "Master of Justice," who was the leader of the Essenes and the precursor of Jesus. Which of the Hasmonaeans actually had the deed done remains uncertain to this day.[26]

What is most important is that, by giving in to the seductions of Hellenism, the originally anti-Hellenist Maccabees in fact revived the spirit of revolt out of which they themselves arose. The Jews no longer recognized them, rejecting them as collaborators with the pagans. The reaction wasted little time settling in: toward the middle of the second century B.C., a group of pious traditionalists, the Essenes, expressed its contemptuous horror for a regime it considered faithless to the Torah by retreating into the desert.[27] Their opposition was obviously too vociferous; anathemas flew back and forth, and conflict became inevitable. It was at this point that the

unnamed high priest executed the Master of Justice, the most revered of the Essenes and the interpreter of divine gnosis. By the
beginning of the first century (A.D. 6–7), the Jewish revolt had
become much more than contemplative; armed bands began to attack Roman troops in Galilee, since they were the symbol of Hellenism as well as, of course, pagan foreigners themselves.

It was in the context of this protracted religious hardening of the
line—comparable to what today we would call fundamentalism—
that the break with the Old Testament occurred and Satan lost the
status as member of the heavenly council he had enjoyed in the
Book of Job. The Jewish faith became apocalyptic, a feature it
would retain even in its Pauline avatar, when Saul-Paul removed
"Christism" from its Jewish matrix to create Roman Christianity,
an action the original apostles bitterly objected to. Indeed, the early
Christians so feverishly awaited the return of Jesus and the end of
the world, the millennium, that they lapsed into a terrified inaction
that Saul-Paul found himself compelled to deal with.

Not once—or, to be more accurate, never again—was the name
Satan or its synonym, Belial, the Babylonian Baal,[28] to be found in
the Dead Sea Scrolls or in the corpus of intertestamentary writings[29]
without being identified as an evil irreconcilable with the deity. To
survey all the instances would require a separate work entirely,[30]
but references to the Prince of Evil are categorical in any number
of writings—the Scroll of Psalms, the Order of the Community, the
Document on the New Covenant in the Land of Damascus (also
called the Damascus Document), and in the War Scroll. Belial is
damned, condemned to extinction with the coming of the Prince of
Light; the Angel of Darkness, sometimes called the Prince of Deceit, he is always the Enemy and always divorced from God. Among
the inscriptions prepared to adorn banners and trumpets (since the
Essenes thoroughly prepared for war), one proclaimed, "The wrath
of God descend mercilessly upon Belial and all those with him."

There are no less than twenty-six references to Satan and seventy
to his eponyms Belial or Beliar in the collected intertestamentary
writings, not including the other names for the Prince of Darkness,
such as Baal (four citations) or Mastema (eight). Whether there was
one Satan or a number of Satans is not clear; there does not seem

to be any Essene dogma on this point. While relating his visions, Enoch exclaims, "I heard the fourth voice [among the mysterious voices he hears singing the praises of the Lord] drive away the Satans and forbid them from approaching the Lord of the Spirits. . . ."[31] Once more, we are very far away from the Satan of the heavenly council.

The about-face, however, is more complex still. Apparently having forgotten the Old Testament, which had established a covenant between Noah's descendants and a God who still commanded Satan, the author of the Book of Jubilees writes: "In the third week of this jubilee, the corrupt demons undertook to seduce the children of the sons of Noah, to lead them astray to their destruction." So the presumptive victims ask their grandfather to intercede with the Lord so that no evil spirit can hold them in thrall. Strangely, though, "Mastema, the prince of the spirits"—in other words, Satan again, that master of shifting identities—is no longer Enoch's "Lord of the Spirits"; stranger still, this Satan proposes a compromise with God; and, the height of strangeness, God accepts. He grants what Satan had asked for: "Lord creator, leave a few [of these spirits] before me, that they do as I command them. For if I am left with none, I will not be able to exert the power of my will over men."[32] It might be hard for us to accept an agreement between absolute Good and absolute Evil, and yet that is what this is. A partial return to the Old Testament seems to have come about, with God and the Devil on generally good terms. Yet it is also obvious that from the second century B.C. onward, opinions about the Devil and God's politics are, to say the least, at odds.

The Damascus Document holds that God protects those within the covenant from the Devil: "They were saved at the time of the First Coming, but those who slipped backward were delivered unto the sword. And such will be the fate of all those who have entered into the Covenant but do not obey its precepts, whom He will judge for extermination at the hands of Belial."[33] Yet there seems to be little reason to unleash the Devil against Noah's grandchildren. This latest Devil has once again turned into a mercurial evildoer.

The intertestamentary and Qumran texts' views on the Devil's eschatological role are incoherent; if the authors agree that he is the Enemy of God, each nevertheless offers a different picture of him. Another Essene text, this one describing the seven heavens, notes that "in the third are the soldiers of the camps built on Judgment Day to exact vengeance upon wayward spirits and Beliar."[34] One is almost tempted to feel compassion for this Beliar, who one moment helps carry out the designs of God and the next is consigned to the fury of the heavenly warriors.

One newer subtlety, which seems to harken back to Genesis, is that woman is now the Devil's ally. The fundamental misogyny of the Essenes often shows through, and the texts are quick to accuse woman of being the Devil's servant: "Women are evil, my children, and since they have no power or authority over men, they use tricks to draw them in . . . woman cannot openly defeat man, but with the wiles of a prostitute she lures him. . . ." These words, which come from the Testament of Ruben, are spoken by the Angel of God, who has also just finished pointing out that "if your mind is not corrupted by luxury, nor will Beliar be able to corrupt you."[35] This recurrent theme also crops up in another intertestamentary text, the Testament of Simeon: "So gird yourself against luxury, for luxury is the mother of all evils, and it draws one away from God and closer to Beliar."[36]

The Essenes were hostile to marriage—and, in addition, they only took on recruits after satisfying themselves that they were physically beautiful.[37] Yet another intertestamentary text, the Greek Life of Adam and Eve, recounts that Eve went to Paradise with her son Seth (she has a total of thirty sons in this particular version of Genesis), where he was bitten by an animal. She admonishes the animal and begs it to let Seth go, but the animal retorts: "Why did your mouth open to eat of the tree from which God had forbidden you to eat? That is why our nature changed as well."[38] All the evils in the world after the exile from Paradise are thus woman's fault.

And so it was during what could be called the great crisis of Judaism that the Devil came to be defined as God's sworn and eternal Enemy. While the two had collaborated in the period immediately after the Babylonian exile, by the time the Christian era was approaching they were doomed to execrate each other forever. This evolution directly mirrored the current—one could even say the tide—flowing forth from the depths of Essene Judaism: Gnosticism, the theology of absolute dualism. With Gnosticism, all Evil is material, all virtue spiritual. The division of the world between God and Devil was achieved.

Though it came to prominence in Judaism, this dualism was not a Jewish invention; it had already been formulated by Mazdaism in the sixth century B.C. To pre-Zoroastrian Iranians, the universe was organized around the two mutually exclusive and mutually abhorrent poles of God–Ahura Mazda and Devil-Ahriman. Judaism might, in a roundabout way, have been influenced by Mazdaism, and the evidence seems to confirm that this was so: despite the great humiliation of captivity, the Jews retained a positive memory of the Iranians after Cyrus, whom they considered "anointed" and a "messiah."[39] They were prisoners in Babylon when Persian and Medean troops conquered the city and freed them from the yoke of its polytheistic, pagan rulers. Darius was better still: he had the famous golden idol of the god Marduk melted down and the Babylonian priests massacred. Darius's successor, Ataxerxes, continued in his turn to treat the Jews with special benevolence; it was under his reign, for instance, that the temple and walls of Jerusalem were rebuilt (445 B.C.), and it was thanks to him that Ezra was proclaimed chief of both Jerusalem and Judea. To the Jews, the Persians were always benefactors.

The good feeling the Jews had for the Persians (and their allies, the Medeans) also had excellent political motivations: the Persians had made Babylon a subject state. It is sometimes overlooked that when at last Cyrus allowed the Jews to return home to Palestine, many of them—perhaps the majority—preferred to remain in Babylon, according to Paul Johnson.[40]

The Jews thus had plenty of time to become acquainted with Mazdaism; it is, for instance, to the Talmud of Babylon that we owe what little we know about Mazdaism in its early stages.[41] The debt Judaism owes to Mazdaism has been recognized by more than one writer; in the words of Romain Ghirshman, "the Persians made the ancient Semitic belief in the survival of the soul into a belief in its immortality; this in turn made its way into Jewish doctrine, a channel through which Zoroastrianism penetrated even Christian theology."[42] Like many other religions, Judaism tapped into the wellsprings of Vedism.

Four centuries later, the Jewish-Persian affinities were still strong. When in 53 B.C. the Parthians inflicted a crushing defeat on the Romans at Carrhae, in Ghirshman's words again "those western Semites who were hostile to the Romans, such as the Palestinian Jews, the Nabataeans of Damascus, the desert Arabs, and the Palmyrans, all turned a hopeful eye toward Persia."[43]

The Jewish sympathy with the Persians was wholly justified: the Jews' own convictions could only help to inspire them to be particularly open to the Persian religion, which after the Zoroastrian reforms was the only other monotheism in the world. They studied it closely, and it was from Persia that they borrowed the celestial creatures called angels.[44] In addition, write Maurice Meuleau and Luce Pietri, "as did Jewish thought, postreform Mazdaism established a close relationship between devotion and the individual moral life."[45]

The name of the Essene leader, the Master of Justice, seems to echo that of Ahura Mazda, "Truth-Justice," deepening the temptation of viewing Essenism as a Judaic avatar of Mazdaism.[46] The Jews borrowed the pattern of their Genesis; they could as easily have borrowed their God/Devil dualism. Yet the fundamental difference between Mazdaism and Essene Judaism is the latter's apocalyptic tenor. To the Mazdaists, the universe was nestled in an immanent divinity, Cosmic Time or Zurvan, which was eternal and immutable and reconciled the opposites of God—Ahura Mazda and the Devil-Ahriman. To the Essenes, on the other hand, time was destined to end. This is obvious from the events of 31 B.C., when a powerful earthquake rocked Judea, killing thirty thousand as well as severely damaging the buildings in Qumran and causing a massive fire to break out in the city: convinced that Judgment was nigh, the Essenes fled into the desert.[47] They awaited the end of the world with ever-increasing anxiety and conviction; the Persians never even thought about it.

That the notion of the Devil as God's Enemy was borrowed is certain, since the very idea was alien to ancient Judaism. Yet it began to manifest itself the moment the identity of the Jewish people was threatened—initially by military domination, then later by cultural pressure. The process took place in a period of stagnation, when the Jews despaired of ever recovering their national autonomy, and when the Essenes believed themselves the last lawful spokesmen for their people and the only guardians of the Torah and Jewish virtue. The borrowing of the Devil, therefore, was at root politically motivated: at that moment, the enemy had to be clearly identified and stigmatized. The enemy was a foe of the Jews, and so of the Chosen People, and so of God. The Essenes turned to the Devil of the Mazdaists; paradoxically, though, they called him not Ahriman but, rather, Belial, which comes from the Ugaritic Bel or Baal. The reason for this is not difficult to understand, since this god had a temple at Jerusalem so large that when Jehu convened the faithful inside it, "there was not a man left that came not."[48] Given all that anxiety, the ancient Babylonian creator deity, the god of procreation, fertility, thunder, and warriors thus became execrated by the hermits at Qumran:

> Cursed be Belial
> for his hostile scheming,
> for his shameful offices.
> Cursed be the spirits of his ilk for their impious scheming,
> for their tainted, impure offices,
> since they come from the darkness.[49]

Though liberated from the Babylonians by Cyrus, and as much as they detested them, the Jews did not escape their persecutors' religious influence. The Devil of the Iranian Zoroaster could not have settled so easily on the banks of the Dead Sea had the ground there not been prepared for him—as it had been, by the Mesopotamians in general and the Babylonians in particular. It was not only the scheme of Genesis and the Ten Commandments, to name just two, that Judaism borrowed from Mesopotamia; it was also the notion of sin inextricably associated with penitence, as well as the association of woman with the Devil.

No one has ever believed in the fact of his own abjectness, and so, to explain it, he accuses others. As captives of Babylon, the

Jews found themselves reduced to indignity. This community of misery created brotherhood, even among people of different faiths. The shame of the Mesopotamians dated back to Creation itself; the Jews had an external cause, the exile. For both peoples, however, the root of the matter was sin. If the Jews had lost their freedom, it had to be, as the prophets said, because they had disappointed the Almighty and broken the Covenant. They were victims, and if anyone was to blame it was the Devil. Since the Iranians liberated them from Babylon, they couldn't help but think that the Iranian gods were the relatives of their own, or at least were favorable to their own solitary God—because the plural form *Elohim* is a linguistic impossibility,[50] since the Jews claimed to have only a single god.

The Iranians had given their own one God, Ahura Mazda, a son whose name was so closely related to Jewish hopes—Mithra, or "contract"—that they must no doubt have conceived of the Covenant at the same time as the Jews, if not before. This god named "contract," a promise of peace for centuries to come, was practically the Messiah, the herald of a new covenant. How could the Jews then not have also borrowed the Iranian Devil, Ahriman, the common cause of all woes, and thus of Evil?

The Mesopotamian influence was, on the other hand, a function of hatred, as can be seen in the symbolic role late Judaism attributed to women. In Mesopotamian mythology, woman, even when a goddess vested with the illustrious name of Ishtar, is never less than a harridan—a pudendum equipped with that most fearsome of weapons, a brain, and incessantly harrying the purest, noblest, and most handsome of men beginning with Gilgamesh himself. There is a parallel development in the Old Testament, especially after the Babylonian captivity: woman falls from grace until she practically disappears in intertestamentary literature, where for all intents and purposes she is reduced to the status of a freak of nature.[51] The adoption of Mesopotamian misogyny was all the easier in that Mithraism exalted fraternity and loyalty among men but excluded women. All that remained to be done was to pen Genesis and lay sin at Eve's door.

With such imports as sin, penitence, misogyny, and the Devil,

Judaism came back from the East well stocked, and it was in this state that the disciples of Jesus and their Essene predecessors were to find it. The Devil was henceforth assured a long life—if, that is, one considers two thousand years a long time in the context of human history.

CHAPTER 14

The Devil in the Early Church

The Confusion of Cause and Effect

Then Jesus was led up by the Spirit into the wilderness, to be tempted by the Devil. And he fasted for forty days and forty nights, and afterward he was hungry. And the tempter came and said to him, "If you are the Son of God, command these stones to become loaves of bread."

But he answered, "It is written, 'Man shall not live on bread alone, but by every word that proceeds from the mouth of God.'" Then the Devil took him to the holy city, and set him on the pinnacle of the temple, and he said to him, "If you are the Son of God, throw yourself down; for it is written, 'He will give his angels charge of you,' and 'On their hands they will bear you up, lest you strike your foot against a stone.'"

Jesus said to him, "Again it is written, 'You shall not tempt the Lord your God.'" Again, the Devil took him to a very high mountain, and showed him all the kingdoms of the world and the glory of them; and he said to him, "All these I will give you, if you will fall down and worship me." Then Jesus said to him, "Begone, Satan! for it is written, 'You shall worship the Lord your God and him only shall you serve.'" — Matthew 4:1–10

This celebrated confrontation with our very own and at last fully realized Devil is improbable from the outset. It occurs immediately after the deeply paradoxical celebration of Jesus's baptism, a specifically Essene rite—and not at all a Jewish one. This means that Jesus has been identified as an Essene, although the sect is never mentioned in the New Testament. In addition, the Essenes believed that baptism was a redemption from original sin, so to perform the rite upon Jesus—who was conceived by the Holy Spirit upon a woman who herself, according to modern theology, was immaculately conceived—seems at best pointless and at worst blasphemous.

The point of this episode in the desert is unclear; the Synoptic Gospels reach no common agreement about it. According to Matthew, the temptation occurs at the end of the fast; according to Mark and Luke, it takes place during it. John does not mention it at all. Only Matthew and Luke mention the three parts of the temptation; Mark omits them.

Yet the tale immediately raises three problems. The first is the fact of the test itself, which from all appearances is conducted by the Holy Spirit—the same spirit who in Mark's abbreviated version (1:1–12) assumes the form of a dove at the moment Jesus is baptized, then sends him off into the desert. The confrontation is very similar to the trial that Job was forced to undergo, and so it seems that God is using the Holy Spirit to put Jesus through precisely the kind of test that Jesus himself mentions is forbidden to subject the deity to. It begins to look like God is uncertain about the divinity of His Son, or that He is not sure that divinity will protect him against temptation.

The second problem is Satan's ignorance. As his every word makes clear, he knows that Jesus is the Son of God, just as he knows that Jesus knows he is, and yet he stupidly persists in trying to tempt him. The Enemy comes off as a moron.

Third, Jesus's disciples are convinced of his divinity because of the miracles he has performed; the Devil knows Jesus is divine, and yet Jesus refuses to perform the kind of simple miracle that would rid him of his tempter once and for all. This refusal is all the more incomprehensible in that on other occasions Jesus didn't hesitate for a moment before using his miraculous powers against Satan.

One is inclined to conclude that the narrative is a ham-handed and sloppy attempt merely to introduce Satan in his new guise as the Enemy of God. Modern theologians, indeed, deny its authenticity. Rudolf Bultmann notes that three-part arguments of this type, when in each instance the answer is provided in the form of scriptural citation, are to be found in a number of rabbinical texts. In the end, Bultmann concludes, it is impossible to determine whether or not the story of the duel with Satan is "a nature myth analogous to Marduk's battle against the Dragon"—that is, if the episode is borrowed from Mesopotamian mythology.[1]

Until the Dead Sea Scrolls, it seemed a foregone conclusion that Christianity was born with Jesus. After the scrolls became available, however, that conviction was progressively undermined by the obvious relationship between the teachings of Jesus and those of the Essenes as underscored by the role of John the Baptist, an active partisan of the sect. The rite of baptism itself sealed the issue.

Although the events have yet to be confirmed, it seems that Jesus was at one point a disciple of the ascetics at Qumran and then more or less broke with them. As we saw in the last chapter, the Essenes superimposed Mesopotamian mythology onto late Judaism; one of their subsects, the Elcesites, was in fact based in Mesopotamia, and it is they who were the forebears of the Christians of John the Baptist, a group we shall encounter again. It is the Essene Devil, not the Satan of the Old Testament, that Jesus would pass on to Christianity. Not only the four canonical ones but *all* the Gospels were, without exception, to incorporate the basic Essene idea that only by struggling with the Devil could the coming of the Kingdom of God, the end of time or Apocalypse, be hastened.

The whole of Jesus' public ministry in fact revolved around foiling Satan, Beelzebub, Azaziel, or whatever other name the Devil went by. He was continually ridding people of "demons," the servants of Satan,[2] and he taught the practice to his disciples: "On that day, many will say to me, 'Lord, Lord, did we not prophesy in your name, and cast out demons in your name . . .?' "[3] The Gospels are rife with tales of his exorcisms, so much so that one ends up wondering how Palestine could have contained so many possessed souls. "That evening they brought to him many who were possessed with demons; and he cast out the demons with a word. . . ."[4]

A new phenomenon unknown in the Old Testament now appeared: violent possession. The demon who possessed the man from Capernaum[5] began to scream when he saw Jesus, and before leaving him by Jesus' order, the demon hurled the man to the ground. The son of the man from Cesarea of Philippi had also been tormented since his youth by a demon; the demon caused him to foam at the mouth and thrash on the ground.[6] The story is somewhat embellished in Mark: the man from Capernaum had a habit of visiting graveyards, where others in vain tried to capture him; the poor man was also the victim of a self-mutilation syndrome — he wounded himself with rocks.[7] When he saw Jesus, he ran to him and cast himself at his feet, screaming, "What do you want from me, son of God Most High?" Mark takes these words to be a sign of anxiousness on the part of the Devil, although they are hard to square with Satan's character.

For the first time, the Devil is associated with illness, which the Gospels qualify as an "unclean spirit." The leper from "a certain town" who demands to be healed by Jesus says to him, "Lord, if you will, you can make me clean."[8] The blindness of Bartimeus is healed by faith,[9] as are a whole range of other maladies, from paralysis to arthrosis. "Man, your sins are forgiven you," Jesus tells the paralytic, who stands up and walks.[10] The same holds for the hunchbacked rheumatic woman of Galilee: "And there was a woman who had had a spirit of infirmity for eighteen years; she was bent over and could not fully straighten herself."[11] The disease is the image of the demon that is causing it, as in the story of the man who cannot speak because the demon inhabiting him is mute.[12] The identification of deformity and ugliness with demons is another innovation that would persist until the twentieth century—and it is also a regression toward the Mesopotamian superstition that every ailment has its own specific demon.

The regression to Mesopotamian beliefs appears again, in the words Matthew attributes to Jesus: "When the unclean spirit has gone out of a man, he passeth through waterless places, seeking rest, but he finds none. Then he says, 'I will return to my house from which I came.' And when he comes he finds it empty, swept, and put in order. Then he goes and brings with him seven other spirits more evil than himself, and they enter and dwell there; and the last state of that man becomes worse than the first."[13]

The third innovation is that the Devil's actions have become erratic and pointless; he possesses the little daughter of the Phoenician woman from Syria[14] for no better reason than he had for tormenting the man from Cesarea of Philippi or the graveyard madman. In the Old Testament, Satan's acts have a purpose; in the New Testament, he behaves like the demons of Oceania and Australia, doing everything willy-nilly. Everyone had come to believe himself threatened by a Devil who was as uncontrollable as a rabid dog.

The fourth innovation is that the demoniacal assumes a fantastic nature missing in the Old Testament. When Jesus exorcises the cemetery lunatic, a whole legion of demons emerge. They ask Jesus permission to inhabit a herd of pigs that happens to be wandering around on a nearby hill. (Since the Jews did not keep pigs, though, the herd must be symbolic.) Even more extraordinary is the claim that Jesus allows them to, upon which the unfortunate pigs cast themselves like lemmings over a cliff to drown in the lake below. The story makes little sense, since in his wisdom and goodness Jesus has little cause to inflict such torments on creatures of the Lord—creatures that, in the bargain, Jesus's followers will gladly come to eat in the centuries to follow. The story is also characteristically Jewish,[15] because at the time they were the only people who believed that the flesh of swine was unclean.

We will probably never know what Jesus truly said, since the early Christian community transcribed his words the way it wanted them to be understood. Yet in the Garden of Olives, just before his arrest, Jesus abandons all references to "impure spirits" as well as to other Mesopotamian images; for the first time in all his discourse he returns to a Devil who corresponds to the one in the Old Testament: "Simon, Simon, behold, Satan demanded to have you, that he may sift you like wheat. . . ."[16] This is a direct reference to the Devil of what could be called the "old" Old Testament, especially the Book of Job. The statement implies that Satan has been entrusted with a mission—and this could be at no one's instigation but God's. The Devil is therefore no longer merely the chief of a legion of impure and unpredictable demons; he is, rather, the acolyte of God, who in His supreme wisdom has decided to put humanity to the test. The Devil, in other words, is a faithful servant of the divine will. This vision of Satan, the only one of its kind to be found in the canonical Gospels, is, however, fundamentally opposed to that of the Essenes. Two things can be deduced to have happened: that Jesus renounced the Essene idea of the Devil as the Enemy of God and humanity; and, more likely, that Luke, an educated and perceptive Greek who must have been aware of the difference between the Devil of the Old Testament and the Essene version, put words in Jesus' mouth that distanced him from the Essene position.

After Jesus' mysterious disappearance,[17] the Devil enters, as it were, a period of interregnum. In the episode of the sale of Ananias's land, Peter evokes him in a manner that leads one to think he is indeed the spirit of Evil and lacks any fealty to God. Ananias had reserved for himself a portion of the proceeds from his land, and Peter asks him: "Ananias, why has Satan filled your heart to lie to the Holy Spirit, and to keep back part of the proceeds of the land?" Upon hearing these words, Ananias falls down dead.[18] Yet Peter's accusation is wholly unfounded, since Ananias had not lied to anyone, the Holy Spirit had never ordered the collectivization of the community's property, and Satan had nothing in the least to do with anything.

Still, Luke or Paul, torn as they were between the apostolic Council of Jerusalem—which considered Paul an impostor and heretic—and a universalist, Roman vision of Jesus' teachings, had other things on their minds. Neither was concerned with a new reading of Satan; Luke was merely a compiler and at times a propagandist, and Paul had enough on his hands trying to tailor the Old Testament and what little he knew of Jesus' teachings to the Hellenized peoples of the eastern Mediterranean; he didn't have the energy to devote to the perilous venture of creating a new cosmogony. He only very rarely referred to Satan, as for instance when he delivers the man to Satan on charges of fornication,[19] or when in a fit of platitude he says that we should forgive others "lest Satan should get an advantage on us."[20] One can never tell if Paul's Satan is

God's Enemy or is entrusted by Him with the task of testing humanity.

This is where matters remained until the time of the Church Fathers, a term that includes the first Christian disciples who went on to instruct others as well as, eventually, the bishops—especially, after the fourth century, the bishops who convened at the Council of Nicea.[21]

The fathers were compelled to address the problem of Evil, which desperately needed a genealogy of its own. They started by affirming that Satan was the chief of the powers of darkness, or in the words of François Bonifas, "a creature who emerged pure from the hands of its creator, an angel holding one of the highest ranks in the heavenly hierarchy."[22] This Eastern, specifically Iranian, idea is reflected in the Book of Job's celestial council. According to the Church Fathers, this angel rebelled against God, the upshot of which was the creation of an inverse angelic hierarchy. Since the fathers clearly modeled this on the hierarchy conceived of by Paul, who, as a way of increasing the intermediary steps between God and matter, envisioned three descending orders of angels—the archangels, the seraphim, and the cherubim—governed by one supreme angel.

The first problem, never to be resolved, was the exact cause of the angels' fall. If it was Evil, then Evil must have preexisted Satan, and therefore Satan could not be held responsible. This was a real dilemma, since Satan was the only candidate for the position of Evil's inventor. Sensing a trap, one Church Father, Tatian, dissented from the opinion of his peers and situated Satan's fall after that of man, which merely shifted the problem instead of resolving it—as Bonifas puts it, "because how could the Devil have caused man to fall if he were not already morally fallen himself?"[23] Tatian's casuistry was to create unforeseen entanglements, to the point that Irenaeus tried to place Satan's fall between man's creation and the Fall.[24]

This does not do much to solve the problem, since the origins of the Evil that brought about Satan's fall remain unclear as well. In the fourth century, Lactantius, an adviser to Emperor Constantine, tried to sidestep the issue by attributing Satan's fall to his jealousy not of man but of the Son, the Logos. The Son was the firstborn, second in power only to God Himself; Satan came in at a lower rank. "He was envious of the Son's superiority," Bonifas writes, "and it was to distance himself from him that he rebelled against God, who then drove him from Heaven."[25] Lactantius is not very far from the Gnostic division of the world into light and darkness, and in fact he argued that "the creative will of God desired two antagonistic spirits, one as the principle of Good, the other as the principle of Evil."[26] Thus, God is no longer just the God of Good but also the demiurge who is above Good and Evil—a quintessentially Gnostic concept. Lactantius goes "farther," if one can say that, than the pseudo-Barnabas, who proposes "two paths: one is taken by the angels of God, the bearers of light, the other by the angels of Satan."[27] Barnabas held that God and Satan were rivals, while Lactantius considered them both vassals of one Great God.

The question nevertheless remains as obscure as ever, since if Satan had existed for all time, if he was as old as Creation, there was no need for the story of his fall. Were that true, the opening of the Book of Job would contradict the rest of the Old Testament: did the council perhaps include representatives of both Good and Evil? In that case, the question becomes which God was asking Satan about his recent activities—the demiurge who reigns over both Good and Evil, or the God of Good alone. The Book of Job is unambiguous about the fact that it is the God of Good, yet it is impossible to imagine the God of Good having some sort of arrangement with Satan unless the two were on equal footing.

The Church Fathers proposed other solutions. The evil angels had fallen, for instance, because they had succumbed to carnal lust—an explanation hardly more plausible than the preceding ones, since, like pride and jealousy, licentiousness emanates, theologically speaking, from the spirit of Evil—and once again the question becomes *when* Evil first appeared. Some argued that angels didn't begin to covet human women until after their fall, while others argued to the contrary that lust came first and was the cause of their fall.

In the third century, Origen wrote that demons have a knowledge of both sidereal and human events, which at once justifies and condemns astrology: since a relationship between celestial and earthly events exists, astrologers must be inspired by demons. Origen seemed to be implying that the Devil and the damned would be saved at the end of time[28]—a dangerous thesis, for its corollary is that there is thus really no need to struggle against Satan. Origen, Clement of Alexandria, Justinian, and Irenaeus all believed that the demons would be converted in the end, which was wholly contrary to what Barnabas argued: "The path of the Black One . . . is the path of eternal death and punishment."[29]

Curiously enough, in the first three centuries the apostolic fathers seemed to distinguish between Satan and demons, the Devil and his angels. According to one theological dictionary, the fathers "say almost nothing about the nature of demons"—all except Ignatius, who holds them to be "incorporeal."[30] It is unclear whether the fathers assigned them different abodes or not, but the amorphousness of their ideas is reflected again in Justinian, who declares that the serpent is "the prince of evil demons." If there are good demons, he does not say.

The most troubling idea was advanced in the fourth century by Saint Gregory of Nyssa, the brother of Basil the Great: in effect, God pulled the wool over Satan's eyes. By virtue of original sin, Satan had acquired certain rights over humans. Then, writes Bonifas, "a sort of bargain was made by which God offered Jesus Christ in exchange for man, which Satan quickly accepted, since he felt that the possession of so pure and saintly a being as Christ was more precious than the possession of all of humanity."[31] The death of Jesus revealed his divinity, however, and Satan recoiled from him in horror; the Devil had been made the victim of a divine confidence game.

The strange and shocking theory of God's deceit gained currency at the time; the argument was taken up by Ambrose, Leo the Great, and Gregory the Great, who all described Satan as a fish caught in a net. It was, however, to be rejected in the fourth century by Gregory of Nazianzus, who found it unthinkable that the Son of God, who is in fact God Himself, could be ransomed to Satan. Yet Gregory had no more pronouncements to make than did any of his predecessors about the origins of the Devil or Redemption.

And so the fathers were caught in a logical dilemma: Is the Devil the cause of Evil or its effect? The passing centuries did not produce a satisfying answer, which is perhaps to be expected, given that the debate was about unverifiable concepts. By the fourth century, the discussion had begun to focus on Satan's role rather than his essence. On this point, there had been no progress since the second century, when the Assyrian-born, Greek-educated Tatian had been content with merely claiming that some angels had become evil,[32] though without explaining why or detailing the nature of their sin. In fact, over time the debate increasingly tended to shift to the role of God, skirting the Devil's ontology altogether.

This new development, on the other hand, only created a new problem—whether God would allow humanity to become Satan's prey, or if in His infinite goodness He would take pity on it and rescind the sentence. The latter theory was supported, also in the fourth century, by Athanasius, an Alexandrine Hellenist who happened to be in Constantine's black book for two reasons: he had been accused (unjustly) of having Bishop Arsenius assassinated, and was also accused of having attempted to cut off the supply of Egyptian wheat to Rome.[33] Because of Athanasius, for the first time in the history of the early Church, God and humanity were left face to face, with Satan relegated to the sidelines. The diabolical machinery encapsulated by the imaginary figure of Satan—a machinery, in operation since the appearance of the Essene doctrines, that had endlessly complicated the relationship between humanity and its Creator—seemed at last to have been cast out of theology. In the manner of a true Hellenist convinced by the idea of human liberty, Athanasius looked as though he had given the Devil his walking papers.

Yet to believe that the Devil's elimination was definitive would be to overlook the dynamics of popular beliefs and rival religions at the time, and, more important still, the conflicting strains that were developing inside the early Church. After all, there were as yet neither dogmas nor doctrines, merely a nucleus of beliefs derived from the teachings of Saul-Paul over which priests, bishops, and Church Fathers were striving to establish a modicum of coherence, even if some were pulling in one direction and others in another.

Caution, not to mention finesse, was the order of the day. Most of the civilized Western world was still part of the Roman Empire. Until Constantine the Great's rejection of paganism in 312, which for the first time put a Christian at the empire's head, the disciples of Jesus had little room to work in; they were constantly threatened by persecution, even after Constantine's conversion (his rival and co-regent Caesar Licinius reintroduced anti-Christian laws in 321).[34] The bishops could not openly challenge other religions and sects—for example, by calling the gods of other religions demons —without the risk of offending the emperor's friends or communities that were useful to imperial policymakers. Once Christianity was declared the state religion, official imperial protection still did not eliminate all the difficulties facing the bishops, since Constantine retained the right to intervene in theological affairs—for instance, by banishing Athanasius.

If the tensions between Christians and non-Christians had lessened somewhat since the days of Saul-Paul (the unconverted sections of the population had in the meantime become familiar with Christian ideas, and the Christian communities themselves had matured), the infidels were nevertheless not pounding at church doors in order to convert. Until Constantine's triumph, Christians were foreigners in the empire, and their preachers were often harassed, assaulted, and even murdered by crowds.

Under these conditions, the nascent Christianity's foremost rival was Judaism, which was very active and toward which Saul-Paul, as the founder of the Roman Church, was overtly hostile. Flavius Josephus wrote that "there is not one Greek city nor a single barbarian people" that did not count a Jewish colony. Mediterranean Judaism had not been significantly penetrated by Eastern Essenism, and it remained faithful to the Old Testament. The Devil was not a prominent feature of this Judaism, for the good reason that the Jews had never put much stock in the idea of redemption. Christianity, on the other hand, is nothing without its doctrine of Redemption, which as we have seen alters Satan's role considerably.

Thus, it was imperative for the Church Fathers to distance themselves from Judaism, even if only by redefining Satan. The task was
all the more pressing in that Jewish proselytism was effective—as
effective, in fact, at converting infidels as Christianity was. In the
words of Marcel Simon, some Gentiles went "as far as complete
conversion, including the seal of circumcision,"[35] even though the
practice was a crime according to imperial law.

Christianity's second rival until the accession of Constantine was
the Greco-Roman religion, the official state religion that had been
intimately familiar to Mediterranean peoples for centuries. Neither
of its two rivals entailed notions anything like redemption; and, as
we have seen, the idea of the Devil was completely alien to both.
Moreover, the two religions offered their adherents a moral and
intellectual comfort that Christianity could not match: they did not
rely on the sense of individual subjection implicit in original sin,
nor on the existential anxiety that arises out of it. The virtues they
prized had only a philosophical basis.

The Church Fathers such as the second-century Clement of Alexandria (an Athenian by birth and a late convert to Christianity)
were perfectly conscious of all these facts.[36] Clement undertook the
extraordinary rhetorical exercise of representing Greek philosophy
as "a road leading to Jesus." A Hellenist despite himself, for Clement "sin is that which is opposed to the common sense that the
Word or Logos has instilled in man"[37]—a breathtaking claim that
one became a Christian through logic, and that faith was of little
account. The Devil, the cause of sin, was now equated with
nonsense.

Notwithstanding, Clement was the first to anathematize the gods
of other religions. "The verdict of the prophets," he says of the
Sibylline oracles, "is that the gods of all the nations are images of
demons."[38] This is sleight of hand; unable to come to an agreement
about Satan among themselves, the Church Fathers were content to
give him many identities—Zeus, Jupiter, Baal, Ahura Mazda, and
so forth. The trick is even more devious in that, over the first centuries, the fathers tolerated the identification of various Greco-
Roman deities with Jesus—Apollo, Hercules, even Dionysus.

Dionysus was particularly useful to Christian rhetoric; like Her-

cules, he was a sacrificed demigod, but beyond that he was a symbol of life too, and his dismemberment by the Maenads was the
prelude to his eternal rebirth. Little did it matter that the Dionysian
mysteries, like the Eleusinian mysteries, were celebrations of life,
of the mystical marriage with nature, or that they recognized neither
Evil nor the Devil; they were transformed into a prolegomena to the
coming of Christ the Savior. Orpheus was, of course, an authentic
precursor to Christ, right down to the voyage into the underworld
that mirrors Jesus' own—which is not so surprising, since Orpheus
derives from the same Asiatic sources that so influenced both the
Old Testament and Essene Judaism and contributed to the formation of the Christ myth. The Christians thus found excellent opportunities in the Greco-Roman religions.

By the opening of the second century, the success of Christian
proselytism was so great that the passion of its enemies was rekin-
dled, and the persecutions began again, an unrelenting succession
until Constantine came to power. Some were savage, such as the
Roman edict of 259, which compelled the priesthood all over the
empire to sacrifice to Roman gods alone, under pain of exile, and
banned the Christian cult under pain of death.

By drawing on Greco-Roman religious and philosophical themes
in their sermons and rhetoric, the early Christian proselytizers, like
Clement of Alexandria, were only falling back on the tradition of
the *interpretatio graeca*, which instead of imposing new gods on
indigenous peoples allowed them to worship their gods under new
names and in new forms. This exchange of gods, as well as the
interchangeable nature of the gods predating Christianity, are essential to an understanding of why Christianity was so successful
in the Roman provinces. An often-overlooked feature of ancient
religions is that peoples in the centuries preceding and following
the start of the Christian era were steeped in the beliefs that all
gods are universal, and that only names and secondary characteristics differentiate them from one another. They were adopted with
the same ease that Rome, for example, adopted the cult of the
goddess Isis, unarguably the city's most popular foreign deity. As
mother and wife, she was associated with Demeter, Aphrodite, Artemis, and Persephone, as well as Athena for the Athenians, Cybele

for the Phrygians, and Artemis Dyctinna for the Cretans.[39] Jesus was therefore identified not only with Dionysus but also with Apollo and Hercules as well. One of the best examples of this syncretism is the third-century statue in the Vatican that depicts a beardless Jesus in the guise of the Good Shepherd Apollo, complete with a ewe on his shoulders.

Under the banner of the *interpretatio graeca*, Christianity represented itself as the continuation and perfection of Greek philosophy and religion, and it was readily acceptable to Hellenistic audiences. Yet this also meant that the evangelists' work was cut out for them, since the Hellenistic diaspora had preceded them wherever they preached, from the Pillars of Hercules to the Hellespont—and, as we know, Hellenistic thought rebelled at the idea of the Devil.

From this arose the difficulty of producing not just a coherent theory of the Devil but a theory that was universally acceptable—and the problem became more extreme the farther afield Christian missionaries went. By the end of the third century, all of Asia Minor was converted, as were many other provinces, such as Armenia, Bithynia, Phrygia, Pisidia, and the territories of the former Carthage. There were Christians throughout Greece and most of Italy. The Aquitaine basin was being converted, as was all but a small part of Hispania. There were Christians in Germany, Belgium, as well as London, Canterbury, and York in England.

The missionaries thus had to preach to Celtic peoples who also had no knowledge of a Devil. As long as it was a question of spreading the teachings of Jesus, the work was arduous and often dangerous; yet it was also glorious, because the dynamic of Christ was irresistible. Matters were much different when it came to the Devil.

Especially in the East, it was also necessary to confront Mithraism, which had been solidly implanted since the sixth century B.C. This raised a paradoxical difficulty of its own: its one God, its one Devil, and its savior, Mithra, who came from God, all meant that it was liable to be mistaken for a pre-Christianity. This danger struck at the very heart of the nascent religion, in that Mithraic dualism had given rise to a current of thought that already had solid roots among the Jews, especially the Essenes, and threatened to sprout them among Christians as well—Gnosticism.

It was not Mithraism itself, at least not in its Greco-Roman form, that presented the greatest peril;[40] the cult was not very significant in the Roman East, and it was limited to men and to soldiers in particular (although soldiers were stationed throughout the empire). The biggest danger was that Gnosticism was so close to yet so dissimilar from Christianity. In the highly complex Gnostic doctrine, Evil was considered to reside in everything living and in everything material: Evil, and thus Satan, had existed for all time.

This view of Evil and of Satan could in no way square with Christianity, for two reasons. The first, obviously, was that it gave the God of Good only a secondary role. The second flowed directly from the first: by claiming that the material world was the world of Satan, Gnosticism denied the importance of the Son of God having been incarnated in the form of Jesus.[41] By his very incarnation, Jesus entered the realm of Evil—or if he did not enter it, then he was never incarnated. Neither of these two alternatives was acceptable. Worse still, since we are all creatures of Evil, Satan is perforce victorious.

Though some apologist fathers, such as Tatian, were much influenced by Gnosticism, they were only committing individual errors; worse was the fact that some Gospels (there were many more than four at the time, since the Gelasian edict had yet to be promulgated) incorporated specifically Gnostic tenets—in John, for instance, Jesus says, "I will no longer talk much with you, for the ruler of this world is coming."[42] Jesus grants Satan dominion over the world, and so what the Gnostics were saying was true. (The Gospel of John only barely missed being proscribed by the censors of Pope Gelasius.) To Saul-Paul's disciples Gnosticism was a much more dangerous foe than was "paganism," since after all it shared the same matrix as Christianity.

The danger was more acute in that Saul-Paul had left his own flanks open to Gnostic attacks: he had committed the supreme blunder of admitting that God had sent us Jesus in a form similar to that of our own sinful one,[43] which is to say that Jesus was tainted by sin, that he too was Satan's prey. The Savior's immaculate conception was impossible, his divine essence denied—it is easy to understand why Clement of Alexander cried out in indignation when Basilidius reiterated that idea. Yet Saul-Paul's writings left many other openings to Gnostic subtleties as well: it was he, for instance, who consigned the flesh to eternal damnation when he declared that "flesh and blood cannot inherit the kingdom of God."[44]

Gnosticism had the Church Fathers on the defensive until around the fifth century. Had it become accepted, its Devil would have been an incurable sickness, and the ideas of sin and redemption wouldn't have been worth a copper coin. The disturbing abundance of messiahs—with Simon Magus (whom Jesus met in Samaria) in the lead, they included Dositheus, Menander, Apollonius of Tyana, every last one of them Gnostics—forced the Church to mobilize its greatest powers, especially considering the fact that potential allies (such as Bar-Kokhba in second-century Palestine, an implacable enemy of Rome whom one would have thought might look favorably upon the Christians) persecuted the Church with a hatred that grew more bitter the more it claimed Jesus to be the true messiah. In addition, the Sabians, the followers of the John the Baptist who had announced the coming of Christ, turned out to be deadly enemies. Simon's disciples were still flourishing in the third century, and John the Baptist's survived through the beginning of the twentieth.

Virulent eradication thus became commonplace, and many of the day's writers and writings have only survived thanks to men like Irenaeus or Hippolytus or Epiphanus, whom the other Church Fathers tried to wipe out through anathemas and to whose teaching Christians were forbidden from lending either ear or eye. In Laodicea as in Alexandria, in Ephesus as in Dyrrachium, furious amounts were written and copious treasures of rhetoric and argument were expended to hold the Gnostic plague in check. The process of expurgation, which went on for five centuries, was effective; Gnosticism at last gave up the ghost. It came very near to disappearing forever, and would have, had not an entire Gnostic library been found by chance in Egypt in 1945—some sixty treatises that somehow escaped the censors. Their importance rivals that of the Dead Sea scrolls in understanding the sources of Christianity.

"Had Gnosticism prevailed," Marcel Simon writes, "it would have meant the end of Christianity, which would have dissolved into the general syncretism."[45] The worst thing for the early Church was that the Gnostics were in an advantageous position: since their religion was very close to those of the empire, they were never persecuted. By virtue of this preferred treatment, they were likely to outlast Christianity.

The Gnostic plague, however, was not the Church's only problem; schisms and heresies proliferated everywhere. The first major schism was effected by an Alexandrian priest of the Antioch school, Arius, who at the beginning of the fourth century clashed with his bishop over the nature of Christ. After he was expelled from Alexandria, Arius disseminated ideas that imperiled the self-defined orthodox Christianity all over the eastern Mediterranean basin. Given that, according to the Old Testament, there was a time when Christ had not existed, Arius argued, He therefore postdated the Father; if Christ were God, He was only so secondarily. In addition, the Son is the Father's only creature, and all the rest of Creation is the work of the Son through the will of the Father. In this view, all the theology that had been so painstakingly built up by heterodox Christianity now had to be reconstructed. Among other consequences, the Devil faded into practical insignificance, since he, like the rest of the celestial creatures, was created by Jesus.

Constantine himself led the reaction by convening the Council of Nicea in 325. The Christians of the West, it should be mentioned, only displayed lukewarm interest in participating, since they were irked by the byzantine squabbles, as it were, of the East.

Other heresies included Monarchian Adoptionism, an idea advanced in Rome by Theodotus of Byzantium; this held that Christ was only a human being who had been adopted as the Son of God because of his merits.[46] It was only after the adoption that Jesus began to perform miracles, Theodotus maintained. Gospel references seemed to support the theory, notably in Matthew ("And whosoever says a word against the Son of man will be forgiven; but whosoever speaks against the Holy Spirit will not be forgiven . . ."

[12:32]) and John ("but now you seek to kill me, a man who has told you the truth . . ." [8:40]). This was a tenacious heresy; under the leadership of a disciple of Theodotus's—also called Theodotus and also from Byzantium, though styled "the Banker"—it lasted until the middle of the fourth century. The consequences were obvious, as far as Satan was concerned: if redemption was even viable anymore, it was very much weakened, and mankind was once more in Satan's clutches.

The Ebionites, too, had little regard for the Pauline concept of Redemption. The Ebionite heresy, which shared points with Adoptionism, obviously rejected the teachings of Saul-Paul: Jesus had been a man, nothing more.[47]

A number of first-century movements also weathered all attacks and anathemas, foremost among them being the disciples of Simon Magus, Jesus' bitter rival for early Christendom. A disciple of the Essene Dositheus, Simon called himself, and was accepted as, the incarnation of "the absolute power of God"; his followers argued that the Passion of Christ was an illusion, and that the coming of Simon made the words of the prophets irrelevant, since they had been inspired by angels who were unaware of God's true designs and only wanted to enslave humanity.[48] Because of all the holes in the confused doctrine about him, the Devil as a concept held no water—there had never been a redemption, and a triumphant God whose designs no Devil could ever foil manifested Himself through the figure of Simon.

Another heretical group, the Sabians, were a semi-Christian yet anti-Christian Babylonian sect descended from the Elcesites[49]—or, in other words, from a Mandean and thus Essene offshoot (the name "Mandean" coming from *mandaje*, or "Gnostic"). This strange sect came into being in the heartland of the Semitic religions, Mesopotamia and Iranian Khuzistan, and its theology was Essenism gone back to its Mazdaist roots: the Sabians were little more than dualist Essenes who practiced baptism and believed implicitly that the world was irrevocably split between Good and Evil, with the world of light inhabited by divine beings and the world of darkness by the feminine spirit of malevolence.

This heresy would never have been of much concern to the

Church, which had much else to contend with, had not the Sabians (who were also called "Christians of Saint John the Baptist") been followers of the person who had baptized Jesus—that arch-blasphemer who sent emissaries to Christ to ask him, "Are you really the one we are waiting for, or will there be another?" The Sabians believed that Jesus had not been the Messiah, that he was not the Son of God, and that Adonai, the Hebrew God, was malevolent—and the Gospels were there by way of proof. If Adonai himself was an evil God, one wonders what the Sabian Devil was like. And what to make of this female Satan?

The Eastern Christians were also fascinated by Manichaeism, the doctrine of Mani, son of a Parthian prince and a Judeo-Christian woman—and yet another religion that derived from Mazdaism. Manichaeism was yet one more syncretism, this time of Zoroastrian Vedism and Judeo-Christianity. Mani himself wanted to unite Buddha, Zoroaster, and Jesus within the same system. At first glance, Manichaeism seems to be little more than a reformulation of the ancient Zoroastrian idea of the world's division into lightness and darkness, to which Mani merely added a magnificent and poetic epic, the revolt of Light against the powers of Dark.

If the whole world had refused in its heart to accept that it was actually the Son of God who had been condemned to die, tortured and naked, on the gallows of shame, we might all be Manichaeans. The very possibility of that happening could have been glorious—it would at last have wedded the three great Eastern religions into one. (Saint Augustine himself was a Manichaean.) In the real world, though, pyres were already burning on the horizon. Mani was martyred, and his much-later disciples—the Albigensians, the Cathars, the Bogomils—were to follow him into the flames. It was intolerable that Satan might be, as Jesus had said he was and as the Manichaeans professed, the prince of this world.

Young churches have a horror of sharing, and the Christian Church was no exception. The Manichaean heresy, which was worse yet than Marcion's, impelled it to marshal its forces. (Marcion was the most powerful of the heretical thinkers and possibly the most inventive of the Gnostics. In the second century, he had suggested that there had been no real incarnation of Jesus, but only an appearance of incarnation.) The councils were to impose sanctions on errors and to enforce them with the full weight of the imperial and episcopal powers. After having died in Roman circuses, Christians were destined to become intimately acquainted with circuses created by fellow Christians, and all for the crime of assigning God and Satan territories that were different from the ones the Church Fathers assigned them.

In the meantime, no one was yet able to say where the Devil had come from, nor whether he was an effect or a cause. That question was specious, and inspired—was it not?—by the spirit of Evil, since it was dictated by logic when, after the Fathers in general and Tertullian in particular, everyone knew, or believed they knew, that philosophy was the work of the Devil. Night was falling.

CHAPTER 15

The Great Night of the West

From the Middle Ages to the French Revolution

Satan emerged from the first four centuries of Christianity in a strange position: he definitely existed, but no one knew who he was or why he had been born. In philosophical terms, it could be concluded that his existence had preceded his essence. Each authority had his own ideas on the topic, but there was no general agreement and thus no general theory of the Devil.

The ecumenical councils attempted to fill this gap. The first of them, the Nicene, approached the question indirectly—if no one knew who the Devil was, it was at least possible to know who he was not. For Constantine, the Nicene Council's organizer, the goal was to prune all the theories and to make sure that Christianity, whose emperor he claimed to be, didn't wander off in all directions and so eventually disintegrate. More than anything, the council was a disciplinary review, and its principal aim was to eliminate Arianism, a doctrine whose logical consequences threatened to produce a dangerous image of the Devil. When the debate about the consubstantiality of the Father and Son was concluded—if a phrase has to sum it up, it would be "Begotten, not made"—the participants were asked to sign the minutes. Arius, the founder of Arianism, and two other bishops, Second of Ptolemais and Theonas of

Marmarica, refused. They were excommunicated and not invited to the celebratory banquet. The young Church had decided that the Devil was not a creation of Jesus.

However, much more than that was needed to restrain the imaginations that continued to elaborate on the theme of this malevolent entity; eventually, the Devil came to be assigned so much power that it was necessary to intervene once again. In the last quarter of the fourth century, in Spain, Priscillian, a layman of high rank who subsequently became a bishop, began to preach a pious and ascetic doctrine—so ascetic, in fact, that it attracted the attention of local bishops. Priscillian, they alleged, took asceticism much too far, and was terrifying his audiences with descriptions of Satan's horrifying powers. Some of this was due, granted, to a heresy that had originated in the East, Encratism, which held that all of humanity was damned, and which rejected marriage as well as the consumption of meat and wine. Priscillian was duly accused of Encratism, and at the conclusion of the Bordeaux Council in 384 he, Euchrotia (a rich woman who had preached his ideas), and four of their companions were burned at the stake on the charge of having performed magic. The method of their execution was decided upon at the urging of bishops Hydatius of Merida and Ithacius of Ossanuba, who had the ear of Emperor Magnus Maximus.[1] Most important, however, the Church was just beginning to nurse its own diabolical phantasms, and it saw Evil lurking everywhere. The condemnation of these heretics was the first installment in the witch trials that would rage through the Middle Ages (and after), only coming to an end with the abolition of the Inquisition.

Priscillianism, however, did not perish with its founder. The paradox was that there had never really been a "Priscillianism," since the martyr's theology was wholly orthodox—it was the Church itself that invented the canard of his heresy.[2] Priscillian was posthumously declared a martyr by his followers, and his "teachings," which he himself had never professed, subsequently gained converts. The doctrine was still flourishing in fifth-century Spain.

An attempt was made to refute Priscillianism at the Council of Toledo in 400, some fifteen years after the executions, but it turned out that there was nothing to refute; all that could be found in the prosecutors' files was one single error of translation. Priscillian had rendered the Greek *agenitos* into the Latin *innascibilis*—in other words, he translated a word that meant "he who was not born" into "he of impossible birth." Generations of grammar-school classicists could as easily have been sent to the stake.

Priscillianism began to spread. Spain was ripe ground for mystics, as is underscored by Saint John of the Cross and Saint Theresa of Avila (where Priscillian had been bishop), and injunctions to renounce the flesh were readily obeyed. At the Second Council of Braga, which was held in Spanish Galicia in 563, it was decided to put an end, once and for all, to the bogeyman that had been created by the two conniving bishops, Hydatius and Ithacius. The council's Eighth Canon declared that "whoever believes the Demon brought certain things to the earth, that by his own power he makes thunder, lightning, storms, and droughts, such as was taught by Priscillian, he should be made anathema."

Priscillian had taught nothing of the kind. The council's real aim, it seems, was to weaken the image of the Devil, which was beginning to frighten the faithful a little too much. Canon Twelve states: "Whoever says that the formation of the human body and its conception in the womb of woman is the work of the Demon, and who by this reason does not believe in the resurrection of the flesh, as was maintained by Mani and Priscillian, he should be made anathema." Mani had never said anything of the kind, either.

The long hunting season against witches was now open. No theologian had yet explained why the angel Lucifer had become demonized, but legislation against him continued. At the Council of Constantinople in 543, whose purpose was to refute Origen, the bishops introduced a new subtlety into the field of demonology. Canon Six stipulated that

Whoever says, "There are two kinds of demon, one of which includes the souls of men and the other those of the profoundly fallen angels; and that of all reasoning beings there is only one spirit that is totally given over to divine love and divine contemplation, and that this spirit became Christ the king of all reasoning beings, and that he created all the bodies that exist in the heavens and on earth and between the heavens and the earth, and that the world is made of elements that are older than he and that subsist in and of themselves, including the dry and the moist, the hot and the cold . . . ," he should be made anathema.[3]

Translation: There is one and only one kind of demon, and incidentally it was not Jesus who created the world.

Matters rested there for some seven centuries until, at the twelfth ecumenical council, the Fourth Lateran Council of 1215, the assembled bishops declared in their first canon: "The Devil and the demons were also created by God; at the moment of their creation they were not evil; they became so through their own sins, and ever since they have busied themselves with the temptation of men."[4] There was still not a word about why the Devil and the demons had become evil, nor about what one was to make of the many biblical passages in which God doesn't seem to be on anything like bad terms with either evil spirits or the Devil. Nevertheless, it was the Church's first official stance on the issue.

By no means, however, did this council's decision set minds at ease about the Devil, who was blamed for mysterious diseases, for possession, and for the natural sciences as well. When the monk Gerbert d'Aurillac, the inventor of the mechanical clock, ascended to the papacy under the name of Sylvester II, it was whispered that he had struck a pact with the Evil One. Until its dissolution, the Inquisition displayed a pronounced aversion to the sciences; apart from Galileo, it also tormented René Descartes and George-Louis Buffon.

While theologians debated such finer points as whether or not the Devil could be redeemed, the Western world was entering into the period of impenetrable darkness—the descent into a practically pathological belief in the existence of the infernal culprit, a belief that, paradoxically, was a boon to the very people who claimed to want his elimination. Thus began one of the longest waves of murder in the name of God (blasphemously so, though it enjoyed the papal blessing) that humanity has ever witnessed—fifteen centuries of insanity and bestial hatred fueled by love of treasure as much as by fanaticism.

The Devil was everywhere, carved on cathedral doors and pulpit pediments, always with the same Pan-like body (hindquarters of a goat, man's torso, lewd eyes), an image that, in this era torn between ribaldry and Gnostic mysticism, betrayed an obvious obsession with sex. The Devil smelled of sulphur, his tail was forked, and his hoofs were cloven (which, according to Mosaic law, classified him as an eminently edible animal). The seventh-century cleric and statesman Isidore of Seville, a prolific scholar described by some as "the father of the Middle Ages" (a dubious title if there ever was one), believed in a new variety of demons, the incubi—angels that had fallen into lasciviousness, fornicators "whose bodies are subtle and ethereal," and who could bring women to endless orgasm. He accused the Dusians of Bohemia of committing Satanic love with incubi as well as succubi.[5]

In pretending to believe such absurdities Isidore was only following Saint Augustine, a self-confessedly repentant rake who, in *The City of God*, had first mentioned the existence of incubi, which he thought to be forest deities; Augustine had spun both them and the succubi out of such Hellenic holdovers as Pan and his Dryads as well as other nymphs. Some detected the odor of Gnosticism in all of this, since Augustine identified nature with Evil, but still, no one was going to pick a quarrel with him. "The acts of demons, incubi or succubi, have increased to the point that it would be rash to deny their existence," he claimed,[6] and Isidore of Seville was certainly not rash. Some ten centuries later, Thomas Aquinas in turn confirmed the existence of the sexual demons.

Whenever people are presented with a cardinal sin forbidden, there are those who feel compelled to violate it. At this point in time there was no lack of impressionable folk who became convinced that they had had carnal relations with the famous demons. Madeleine de la Croix, the abbess of Cordoue, a woman who for thirty years had been considered saintly, revealed in confession (which goes to show that the only thing violated in this instance was the sacramental seal) that "since the age of twelve she had been coupling with the incubi Balban and Patonio as well as with a shameless and wanton demon who appeared to her 'with goat's legs, a man's torso, and the face of a faun.' "[7] In other words, the abbess was both weak of mind and passionate of body.

All over Christendom, the wildest rumors proliferated—stories of girls raped by the convenient incubi, extravagant descriptions of the demons which in some accounts had no backs and spawned monsters (although not always only monsters); it was said that "Cain, Alexander the Great, Plato, the fairy Melusina, Luther, and the whole Hunnish nation" were children of succubi and incubi.[8] This gibberish went on for centuries, and everyone from popes to peasants spouted it. At the height of the eighteenth century, in his delightful *History of the Devil*, which he didn't dare sign with his own name, Daniel Defoe reports the fable about Cromwell having made a pact with the Devil, who gave him the title of Protector but refused him that of king, which threw Cromwell into such a fury that "he died of a burst spleen."[9]

In addition to the stench of filth and excrement (no large city in Europe had a sewer system), the West lived amid miasmas of sulphur that, unfortunately, could lead anyone to the stake, as it did for more than one madwoman, simpleton, or person whose only crime was to have displeased someone else.

One of the more enigmatic and illustrious victims of the diabolical folly was Joan of Arc, who was accused of devilry by Pierre Cauchon, the bishop of Beauvais and overseer of the black comedy of a court that condemned her: "Jehanne, who calls herself the Maiden, is a liar, a nefarious person, a cheater of the people, a diviner, a sower of superstition, a blasphemer against God, a usurper, a disbeliever in the faith of Jesus Christ, a boaster, an idolater, a cruel and dissolute person, an invoker of devils, an apostate, a schismatic, and a heretic." The false crime with which the tribunal (which was in the pay of the English as well as of the Church) condemned Joan to the stake was that she was an "invoker of devils." "What have you done with your mandrake?" one judge asked her. Mandrake, a root that was thought to grow under gallows where hanged men had ejaculated, was considered Satanic. Though one of the judges claimed that she carried "a mandrake between her breasts," Joan didn't even know what the plant was.[10]

The accusation against Joan is a clear precursor of the greatest tragedy of modern times, the universal identification of the Devil with whatever is different. Anything that goes beyond the norm, as Joan certainly did, is demonic. In an avatar of the Greek *phtonos*, envy, everything that is "too" anything—too beautiful, too good, too intelligent, too courageous, too innocent—is and must essentially be devilish.

The roots of the obsession go deeper than politics. In order to make sure that he acquired the treasure of the Knights Templar, Philip the Fair accused their grand master, Jacques Molay, of witchcraft; Molay was executed on March 18, 1314, after a seven-year trial. Clearly, the Templars had never been Satanists, but the charge was convenient; from 1318 to 1326, Pope John XII handed down no less that three anti-Satanic bulls in order to justify the persecution of the Templars. It should be recalled that that particular pope was by no means moved by the Holy Spirit; called "the banker of Avignon," he was a coward and liar who had been terrified of the royal power since 1302, when Philip had had Boniface VIII, one of his predecessors, kidnapped at Anagni. John XII was also the pope who condemned monks who believed that Jesus and his disciples had been poor, and that the spirit of lucre was a total contradiction of Jesus' teachings. This was an extraordinary moment in Christian history, when the leader of Christendom and his acolytes were the preeminent foes of Christ's philosophy.

The bulls handed down by John XII were merely bribes he paid Philip the Fair in order to ensure his own safety and to maintain the fabulous corruption of the papal see at Avignon—"the Babylon of the West," as Petrarch called it. Indeed, Avignon was a festival of graft. The chancellor Alvaro Prelayo, who was otherwise a staunch defender of the papacy, wrote, "When I entered the clerical chambers, I found money-changers and prelates busy weighing and counting the coins heaped up before them."[11] Prelayo only corroborates what a French priest had told Petrarch: "Our two Clements have destroyed more of the Church than seven of your Gregories could ever restore."[12] The two Clements were the fifth and sixth popes of that name; the first of these, the loathsome John XII's direct predecessor, was a puppet who was instrumental in the papacy's move to Avignon.

The royal power needed the Devil to cow its enemies and to justify its extortions, and so it was to satisfy this requirement that the pope proclaimed his bulls. At the highest levels of decision-making, the Devil was considered a propagandistic fiction that served the princes' shadowy and, frankly, base designs. Had any king or pope actually believed in the Devil at the time, he would in the first place have been terrified by his own actions. Yet the Devil was a tool to be used against the populace; the bitter paradox is that the fiction of the "prince of this world" was in fact exploited to conquer the world. As in Mesopotamia and Iran, religion had become a political instrument, and the papacy, it should be remembered, was simultaneously a temporal power.

Nowhere is the politicization of the Christian faith more evident than in the extravagant declaration made by Saint Rémy, the bishop of Rheims, the defender of the Franks and the founder of the sees of Therouanne, Arras, and Laon, when he was baptizing Clovis: "Understand, my son, that the kingdom of France has been predestined by God to defend the Roman Church, which is the sole Church of Christ. One day this kingdom will tower over all the others. It will encompass all the lands of the Roman Empire, and all the kingdoms in the world will be subject to its rule; and it will last until the end of time."[13] It is not difficult to read these words as an attempt to fire Clovis's ambitions as well as to subject his kingdom to the Church (unfortunately—or fortunately—France has never conquered all the kingdoms of the world, and in 1993 it represented 1.2 percent of the globe's population). Other churchmen took part in this concert of fabrications; two and a half centuries later, Raban Maur (780–856), archbishop of Mayence and founder of the abbey at Fulda, went Saint Rémy one better by announcing that

When the end of time [a theme that obviously preoccupied the minds of the holy] is nigh, a descendant of the Frankish kings will reign over all of what was once the Roman Empire. This man will be the greatest of the kings of France and the last of his line. After the most glorious of reigns, he will go to Jerusalem, where he will place his crown and scepter on the Mount of Olives. This is how the Holy Roman and Christian Empire will come to an end.[14]

The Holy Roman Empire has long since met its end, and yet time rolls on. The list of clerks who followed in their footsteps, inventorying demons, their evil, and the crimes that they abetted (crimes as imaginary as the demons themselves) is endless.

In the fourteenth century, a Dominican named Nicholas Eymerich became Inquisitor-General of Catalonia, Aragon, and Mallorca; he published a tract entitled *Directorium inquisitorum*, or the *Handbook of the Inquisitors*. Eymerich, the predecessor of Tomás de Torquemada, was one of the worst monsters that the infernal machinery of the Holy Office ever produced: as an inquisitor, his cruelty provoked such a storm of criticism that he was repudiated by his superiors and remanded back to work on his palimpsests. In the first section of the *Directorium*, Eymerich describes the three cults of the Devil: *latria*, which consisted of praising the Devil and flagellating oneself in his honor, *dulia*, the strange ritual of combining the names of demons with those of the blessed, as well as "curious practices, including the use of the magic circle and other necromancies such as love potions, magical philters, and talismans."

The worst thing was that all this lunacy had the force of law; the merest hint of an accusation on charges of *latria*, *dulia*, or "curious practices" could ruin a life or even lead to the stake. The Inquisition, which had been in existence since the fourth century at least, was formally constituted in 1184 by the collusion of Pope Lucius III with the emperor Frederic Barbarossa. At the instigation of the Holy Office, after 1197 the secular power began systematically to persecute schismatics and heretics, sending them into exile, confiscating their property, razing their houses, stripping them of their legal rights, and, in "serious" cases, executing them—all thanks to the strenuous condemnation of Pedro II of Aragon and Pope Innocent III. The confiscation of property in particular was much taken advantage of.

Formally separated from the Eastern Church since 1054, Catholic Rome considered itself heir to the mantle of pagan Rome, the inventor of the spirit of law and the universal guarantor of justice. As such, it depended on having political power—especially monetary power.

The underlying reasons for the progressive hardening that led to the Inquisition and the wholesale introduction of the death penalty are obvious: all over Europe, the alliance of Church and crown based on divine right and religious ritual meant that the enemy of one was, ipso facto, the enemy of the other. Since each schism and heresy threatened the papal power, it also threatened Christian kings and princes. The Inquisition's zeal in killing "witches" through the tenth and twelfth centuries was not the product of ecclesiastical condemnation alone but also of the condemnation of princes, who in this sense were catering to the desires of the clergy. Neither faith nor charity featured very highly in the process; in fact, the use of the death penalty against schismatics, heretics, and "witches" blatantly flew in the face of Saint John Chrysostom, who had declared that to put a heretic to death is to commit an inexpiable crime.

Little attention, however, was paid to Saint John Chrysostom. A terrible danger was looming on the horizon, and it sowed in the hearts of princes and prelates the same degree of panic they had once tried to instill in the people, and the only force the established powers could marshal against it was the Inquisition. The danger was Catharism.

Catharism (from the Greek *katharos*, "pure," which the Cathars considered themselves to be) was the resurgence in barely altered form of Gnosticism, the nightmare the Church had tried to exorcise in its first centuries. To the Cathars, Satan was simultaneously a god and the "prince of this world," as Jesus himself had called him. From desire to death, all things temporal were his domain, and Earth is really the purgatory in which humanity atones for its sins before it will be allowed to enter the Kingdom of Jesus (which is not of the earth, as Jesus himself also said). However, man cannot reach the Kingdom if he has not, in his lifetime, recreated himself as a "new Adam," which was what Jesus had been (for, as Jesus said a number of times, he was the Son of man). If one does not recreate oneself in such a way, one is condemned to reincarnation and another cycle of earthly life. Jesus was the breath of life, and the "Good Men," as the Cathars called themselves, were his terrestrial ambassadors.

This was certain to annoy the Church, already familiar as it was with such arguments and their ultimate consequences: theologically, what they came down to was a denial of the Incarnation or, in other words, the rejection of organized Christianity. The Cathars rejected baptism, which the Church considered a redemption from original sin in the name of Christ; they recognized only the baptism of the spirit, or *consolamentum*, which they claimed only Christ could bring about. Worse still, the Cathars had established a parallel Church, since the "Perfect Ones," the Catharist leaders, were duly ordained priests, and believers were called upon to kneel before them. Since they had been visited by the Comforter and thus had attained a state of grace, only the Perfect Ones knew God and could intercede with him. The Cathars, in short, threatened papal power. The sect began with a theological debate but ended up raising major political and economic problems.

Not content with the rejection of baptism, the Cathars also denied the transubstantiation of the Host; they partook of the holy wafer, but only symbolically, since they did not believe that the body of Christ was present in it. The supreme provocation was that during the Catharist ritual of Renunciation (a very distant relative of the Catholic Confirmation), the believer had to renounce not Satan and his cohort (his train of demons) but "the prostituted Church of his persecutors."[15] The Church naturally bristled at being called a whore, but it would have to wait for a long time before exacting revenge: not everyone in Christendom was convinced that the Good Men were all that bad.

Catharism almost certainly originated among the Bogomils of Thrace (that is, Bulgaria), which is why its adherents were referred to as "Bulgars," a name that hinted at homosexuality (for good measure, they were in fact also accused of crimes against nature);

they were also to be found in Bosnia and other parts of the Balkans. The movement began in the second half of the tenth century under the leadership of a priest named Bogomil, who had found that neither the institution of the Church nor its teachings answered the real needs of the people. What Bogomil's own needs were is a difficult and unanswered question, although it is often true that individuals foist themselves on the collective in part to satisfy personal desires. Bogomil was undoubtedly ambitious—but there is also no doubt that the Byzantine Church, weighted down as it was by its wealth and court ceremonial, must have alienated the Bulgarians with its pomp, arrogance, and refined mannerisms.

The Bulgarians hated the Byzantines, whose emperor Basil III, "the slayer of Bulgarians," had brutally reduced their kingdom to near slavery in 1018. The Bogomil rebellion was in reality a political revolt, in that Byzantium incarnated temporal as well as spiritual power. The appearance of Bogomil Catharism was almost simultaneous with the fall of the Bulgarian kingdom. Once again, as we shall see, the Devil took on a political role: as the enemies of Byzantium, the Bulgarians were automatically the enemies of its pope, and thus of God.

As long as the rumblings of Gnosticism were limited to the Balkans, the Western Church paid little attention to them; since it was not really threatened, it was happy to let the representatives of the Byzantine Church deal with them. The measures they took were foreseeable: the Bogomils were accused of being agents of Satan.

In eleventh-century Constantinople, at the height of the Bogomil heresy, the monk Euthymius wrote that "the Bogomils have overrun the Byzantine state, and they preach to any and all Christians, trying to deceive their souls, to wrest them from the hands of God and put them in those of Satan their father." Euthymius disdainfully referred to the heretics as *fundagiagites*, those who carry sacks, *torbasi*, or in other words as beggars.[16] He added, "The *fundagiagites* are impious people who secretly serve the Devil," and he strenuously condemned this "unclean heresy that is unsurpassed in calumny and treason against God." Another Byzantine writer, Cosmas the Priest, was equally vituperative:[17] "Externally, the heretics look like sheep—gentle, humble, quiet. Their faces are pale from their hypocritical fasts. They rarely say a word, dare not raise their voices, display no curiosity, and avoid looking strangers in the eye . . . but internally they are wolves and wild beasts."[18] (Cosmas does not mention how to distinguish hypocritical fasters from genuine ones.)

When the number of Bogomils snowballed, the Byzantine emperor Alexius Comnenus decided to strike a decisive blow against them. In 1111, he invited their leader, a monk called Basil, "the arch-satrap of Satan," to dine with him. A screen separated the dining hall from another room. A voluble man, Basil could not keep from preaching at the imperial table. When he was finished, the screen was removed to reveal "the whole synod of the church, all the military chiefs, and the senate in its entirety."[19] Basil was tried on the spot and condemned to the stake; but the flames only galvanized the heresy.

Byzantium was still engaged in its struggle against the Bogomils when they began to spread through the rest of the Balkans into Croatia, Dalmatia, and Bosnia, then into Western Europe and the kingdom of Kiev. Once again, the conquests of "Satan" were made easier by political factors. While religious instruction in Slavic languages (as introduced by Cyril and Methodius) was still respected —that is, up until the tenth century—relative peace reigned in the area. Then, from 923 to 926, Pope John X decided to put into effect the Church's old dream of having Mass celebrated in Latin or Greek exclusively. The people, attached to their linguistic prerogative, rebelled, but the Church clamped down hard: at the Council of Split (in Croatia) in 1061, it was decided that not only would the offices be celebrated only in those two languages but, in addition, no Slav could be elevated to an ecclesiastical position. The churches with clergy of Slavic origin were closed down. The uproar was immense. The authoritarianism of Rome thus fanned the pyres and the Bogomil heresy at the same time—the more one tries to extinguish the Devil, the brighter he burns.

In the meantime, the Bogomils had reached France, where they rebaptized themselves, so to speak, as the Cathars, and where others called them Albigensians, there being a large concentration of them around the town of Albi. Their movement was internationalized and based on networks of greater and greater complexity. In 1167, they held what could be called the "Council of Saint-Felix-de-Caraman," near Toulouse, whose Cathar Church invited the "pope," Nikita, from Constantinople. Also there were Robert de Spernone, the "bishop" of the French branch of the church, Marco, the "bishop" of Lombardy, Sicard Tselareri, the "bishop" of Albi, Gerard Mertserille, the "bishop" of Carcassonne, Raymond de Casalis, the "bishop" of Ararens, all of them accompanied by their councils.[20]

For the Church of Rome, the matter was of the highest gravity, since the council underscored the power of the Cathar churches (which were organized on the Roman model) of Dragovista, Melnikva, Dalmatia, Bosnia, Herzegovina, Lombardy, and now France. The Cathars were thus offering something wholly different from a partition of the world into two churches, one Roman, the other (or the others, more precisely) Eastern. They were clouding the map and upsetting prior political as well as financial arrangements, and so threatening to weaken Rome.[21] And the danger was increasing with time: the shadow of the "Devil" was lengthening over the very lands that were believed to be firmly under papal control. Christian Rome, the heir of ancient Rome, was growing angry.

When the Cathars appeared in Limousin between 1012 and 1020, the local bishops had attempted to enlist the collaboration of the political power in the fight against the heresy, but in vain: the Cathars already enjoyed the personal protection not only of William IX, duke of Aquitaine, but also of the nobility of southern France in general. Worse, the "Good Men" were very popular among the people, who protected them and turned a deaf ear both to the condemnations of the regular clergy as well as to its charges of devilry. A century later, in 1119, the Council of Toulouse called upon the secular power to help Catholicism in its fight against Catharism. The effort was once again wasted.

Rome's reaction turned bitter when the Roman Catholic bishops of Provence refused to obey the orders of Pope Innocent III's representatives, whose exorbitant powers they challenged—the papal legate was even murdered. It was not until 1209 that Rome could at last be sure of the Cistercians' allegiance in its crusade against

Catharism. Once that happened, no scruples held the leaders of Christendom in check: when Arnaud-Amaury, the abbot of Cîteaux who was named papal legate and put at the head of northern French troops, took Beziers in 1209, he was asked how his troops were meant to tell heretics from Catholics. He replied, "Kill them all— God will recognize his own."[22]

However, Arnaud-Amaury couldn't claim the prodigious talent of Robert le Bougre, a repentant Catharist who became a Dominican and France's first inquisitor—the "Hammer of Heretics," as he was named. Le Bougre flattered himself that he could recognize heretics by their manner of speech and their gestures alone.[23] Le Bougre is generally forgotten today, although he burned down the abbey of Mont-Aimé in Champagne in 1239, whose 180 Cathars were incinerated alive after having received the *consolamentum* from their "archbishop." This deed was apparently held against the sinister Le Bougre, who ended his career as a gardener at his order's Paris monastery.

Nevertheless, war had been declared and it was pitiless, staking the Catholic north of France against the Albigensian south. Despite the Treaty of Paris of 1229, which forged an agreement between the two aristocracies, despite the horrors perpetrated by the Inquisition, despite the torching of the citadel of Montségur (two hundred Cathars burned alive) in 1245, which was effected with the help of royal officials, despite the Council of Narbonne in 1235, and despite the *Ad extirpanda* bull of Innocent IV (it was later renewed by Alexander IV), which officially established torture as a means of obtaining the truth and excommunicated any person even suspected of Catharist sympathies, the "Devil" from Bulgaria persisted, not to be stamped out until the last Cathar bishop was burned alive in Carcassonne in 1326; his last Italian colleague had preceded him into the flames just five years before. Yet the end of Catharism brought Provençal culture down in its wake. It was a cruel tradeoff, but not the final one of its kind: the religions of South America were to undergo the same fate a little less than two centuries later.

Once more, it had been demonstrated that the Devil is a political figure. There was nothing in what the Cathars maintained that couldn't have been talked over at any of the councils, whose role, it would seem, should have been conciliatory. The Catharist idea that the Devil is the prince of this world is supported by the words of Jesus himself. Their very apparition, as well as that of the Devil with which the ecclesiastical powers were so quick to equate them, had come about for purely political reasons—the war between Byzantium and Bulgaria—and it was reinforced by the imposition of Latin and Greek as the Church's sole languages. (This was a position that the Church would abandon in the twentieth century, without stirring up sulfurous vapors anywhere but in the minds of a handful of overexcited priests.)

Such happy results could only help to encourage the Inquisition in its battle against Satan, and it seized the opportunity by the horns. The Cathar threat had clearly shown that any challenge to Roman Catholic teaching imperiled the Church's secular power as well as the pillars upon which it rested, the European monarchies. Louis VII, "the Lion"—who had declared war on the Albigensians, stormed Avignon, Arles, and Tarascon, and come to Languedoc to accept the submission of the rebellious towns—paid subsidies to the inquisitors, who bizarrely enough were made responsible for the upkeep of his prisons (although they tried to slip out of this financial burden at the Council of Toulouse in 1229). For centuries, Europe descended into a quasi theocracy in which the ecclesiastical and royal powers were intimately interlinked.

An even greater encouragement for the Inquisition was the fiduciary windfall it derived from its persecutions: when a defendant was convicted of Catharism, and later of sorcery, his property was seized by the Church whether he were condemned to death or not; the persecution of the Albigensians turned out, in this respect, to be a goldmine. On occasion, though, inquisitorial greed was such that it threatened the national economy. In Spain, for instance, the seizures from consecutive persecutions of the Moors, the Jews, the Waldensians, the Menandrians, Sodomites, Basilidians, Joachimites, adulterers, Carpocratians, alchemists, Adamites, blasphemers, fraticelli, Beguines, and other sorcerer-types were a disaster for local economies: in the space of a single day, a whole family could find itself reduced to beggary, and the seized businesses, obviously, were not to reopen—"by reason of anathema." These abuses reached such a point that the advisers of Charles V and the parliament, the Cortès, protested; in several instances, it asked that the inquisitors be put on fixed salaries. Yet this was evidently not the Church's concern; it preferred to reap its prebends at the expense of the "damned." Thus, the Devil made for a flourishing business, and the Holy Office oversaw one of the vastest systems of corruption in history.

In the Middle Ages, the denial of justice was a permanent condition. When, according to what principles of Roman law remained to them, the lawyers of those accused of witchcraft objected that the defense had a right to see the prosecutor's files, they weren't given the time of day. In Spain, for example, the theoretical supreme court, *la Suprema*, allowed the defendant to choose a lawyer from among the members of the Holy Office or those close to it; in reality, the defendant had no choice at all—he or she was assigned a lawyer. Nor did the defendant have the right to call a single witness, and meetings with the lawyer had to take place in the presence of the Inquisitor and his secretary. However, throughout Europe the power of the Inquisitors, who were named by the pope alone, was discretionary, and not even bishops could do anything about it. For the first time in history, the popes themselves had completely denied due process and authorized torture and execution, and thus the Inquisitors were permitted everything. The modern writers who condemn the Nazi and Stalinist legal systems forget that the Inquisition was their ultimate model. Neither the Gestapo nor the GPU-NKVD-KGB invented anything. (It comes as no great surprise that inquisitors were often murdered.)

Meanwhile, scholars were vying with one another to deliberate, define, calculate, postulate, and speculate about the Devil and his demons. Yves of Chartres argued that demons traveled incomparably faster than birds, and Hildebert of Le Mans, in his *Tractatus theologicus*, claimed that the Devil resided neither in Heaven nor on Earth, but in the air, as had been professed by Saint Bruno, the founder of the Carthusians. This was a strange idea in that it limited Evil to only one of the four then-recognized elements (water, air, earth, and fire), but it was by no means the strangest. In his *Liber duodecim quaestionibus*, Honoré of Autun undertook to estimate the number of angels that had followed Satan—half of them, a third, a tenth? Recognizing that there were nine angelic orders, he concluded that only a few had fallen from each.[24] This idea was later adopted by Saint Anselm, who believed that "before the fall of the evil ones, the number of angels had not been perfect." Ignorant of the yet-to-be-invented science of statistics, Honoré of Autun did not address the question of demographic expansion on Earth; given that the earthly population increases geometrically, if there is a constant number of demons, then they will have more and more work on their hands as the human population grows, and individual humans will be correspondingly less and less tempted—at least if demons lack the capacity to reproduce. (However, if that is *not* the case, then what is their birthrate?)

Rupert, the abbot of Deutz, advanced a novel idea: In order to set an example for the other angels, God had allowed Satan time to repent, but the Devil had not taken advantage of the fact. Rupert also adopted the farfetched idea that Satan had fallen "not into Hell, but into the air, which is the lesser heaven."[25] Abelard went farther: he attributed charity to Satan, which was at best unsettling, and "in the sixteenth of his articles, which were condemned in 1141, he denied the direct intervention of the demon and limited his sphere of activities to the natural forces, the elements and plants."[26] The idea of the Devil residing in cabbages and soup greatly disturbed Abelard's critics.

Echoing the opinion of his predecessors, Peter of Poitiers said that the Devil would not go to Hell until the Last Judgment, and that for the time being he was located in the air. Broadening the ideas on the subject, William of Auvergne, the bishop of Paris, deemed that the demons had, in short, become idiots ("he explains that the leader of the demons was so obsessed because his intellectual faculties had been dimmed"[27]), that they were subject to suffering, and that they were constantly quarreling among themselves. Saint Bonaventure ascribed Lucifer's fall to his consciousness of his own beauty, an idea that seriously contradicted all prior descriptions of the Devil as a hideous, hairy, horned, and evil-smelling beast.

The renowned Dominican Albertus Magnus believed too that de-

mons floated in the air, and that succubi and incubi were real—
an idea shared by his pupil, Saint Thomas Aquinas, who explained
in his *Summa theologica* that though demons would eventually have
to inhabit Hell, they will float in the air until Judgment Day in the
form of incubi and succubi. On the subject of incubi and succubi,
Thomas Aquinas differed with numerous scholars and theologians:
he claimed they could not procreate. With respect to demons in
general, he also expressed a personal sympathy that, though it
wasn't exactly the sort of pity Abelard felt for them, nevertheless
was not far from it: a great number of demons were not as bad as
they could have been, yet, hardened as they were in their evil, nor
could they perform much good. Like his predecessors, Thomas
Aquinas pursued his speculations down to licentious detail—if a
succubus, a female demon, engendered anything after having received sperm from a man, it was a giant. At his most extreme,
Aquinas tended to represent the Devil and demons as spiritual, but
this was only a personal opinion; afterward, in the sixteenth century,
Cardinal Cajeton argued somewhat ineffectually that, on the contrary, they were corporeal.

From the very first centuries it had been impossible to come up
with a viable theory about the Devil and demons. The nature of the
sin—envy, lust, or pride—that had brought about Satan's fall from
Heaven was as unknown as his exterior appearance (beautiful or
ugly), the moment when he had fallen (before or after the creation
of the sun or of humanity), whether he was entirely spiritual or
subtly material (or even wholly corporeal), his place of residence,
whether he was intrinsically evil or capable of charity, whether he
was supremely intelligent, as some had said, or only average (or
even dumb), and whether he was likely to be forgiven at the end
of time. This last point, which was obviously fundamental, was
much debated—some, such as Saint Jerome, believed that the
Devil and his demons were redeemable, while others, such as Honoré of Autun, believed them to be utterly forsaken, their redemption
possible only given the inconceivable death of the Word. The problem of the preexistence of the Evil to which Satan succumbed was
still unresolved.

The only points of cohesion vis-à-vis the Devil were furnished by the heretics and schismatics against whom the Church was warring. All Church doctors rejected the two main ideas that conflicted with the Incarnation of Jesus and the Redemption: the material world was not exclusively the Devil's domain, and Jesus had not created him. Paradoxically, though, the Church never took a position on the Devil; it relegated that responsibility to its doctors.[28]

Despite their rationalist nature, these mental chimeras do not differ from similar ones among the Dogons, the Yorubas, or the Inuits: they are logical phantasms, since no Church Father or theologian has ever seen either the Devil or incubi and succubi. They are as poetic as anything collected by ethnologists. Their shocking nature arises not out of their illogic but out of their consequences.

For centuries the Western mind was polluted not by the emanations of the Evil One but by the blood thirst stirred by demonic superstition.[29] Once unleashed by the Inquisition in the Middle Ages, this obsession reached unheard-of heights. In 1581, a certain Fromenteau alleged in a work entitled *Le Cabinet du Roy de France* that a census confirmed the existence of 72 princes of demons and 7,405,920 subordinates.[30] Much faith was placed in nonsense about the Devil, and the wilder it was the greater its audience. It was thought that a witch could get milk out of an axe handle, that wizards walked on water like Jesus, and that one could make oneself invisible and secretly enter houses by reciting incantations.

Witches were seen everywhere, especially in ugly women. Their spells were described, as well as their Sabbaths and their orgies, because to make love for pleasure left no shadow of a doubt as to the Evil One's presence. Two of the day's murkiest minds, Henry Kraemer, called Institoris,[31] and Jacques Sprenger, both Dominicans, published a best-seller on the subject (thirty-four printings from 1486 to 1669, in Strasbourg, Spire, Nuremberg, Cologne, Paris, Lyon, Venice, Frankfurt, and Friburg-am-Brisgau; the book is still in print), the famous *Malleus maleficorum* or *The Hammer of Witches*. It was certainly not the first inquisitorial handbook—Eymerich had written his already—but it was the most widely read because of its abundance of examples and of its apparent common sense.

Paradoxically, the Prince of Seducers was always described as horrible, and his servants—especially the female ones—as repulsively ugly. Daniel Defoe is ironic on this point: "Perhaps witches need to be so horrifyingly ugly in order not to be horrified by the frightful face of their Master. Mother Shipton, our famous English magician and seeress, is indeed painted unflatteringly in her portrait, unless she had the most horrible aspect one could imagine."[32]

Demonomania certainly clouded the Western mind in the most poisonous way, even well after the Albigensian massacre and as far away as the Americas (where the tragic episode of the Salem witch trials occurred in 1697). Here are some examples among thousands. In 1582, in Coulommiers, Abel de la Rue was hanged because, having made a pact with the Devil, he had changed into a spaniel dog and made his neighbors impotent. In 1591, Léonarde Chastenet was burned at the stake because she had cast a spell over fields, had gone to the sabbat and copulated with the Devil; she was eighty years old. In 1611, in Aix, a priest named Gaufridy was accused of having cast a spell on a nun and was burned at the stake.

Always, the persecutors' self-proclaimed love of God quickly revealed its other side; those most possessed by the Devil seem to have been the inquisitors themselves. They had it in not only for heretics but also for the whole rest of the non-Catholic world, especially the Jews. As early as the twelfth century, Walter Map, the archdeacon of Oxford, reported on how the Cathars invoked the Devil:

> Toward the first hours of the night . . . each family waits silently inside its synagogue; then a cat of stunning proportions comes down a rope hanging in their center. At the sight of it, they put out the lights and do not distinctly sing hymns, but murmur them through clenched teeth, and they approach the place where they saw their master, seeking to touch him, and when they find him they kiss him.[33]

Here then is the crux of the matter: the Cathars were Jewish (since they met in synagogues), and vice versa—a subtle inversion. The accusation also often started with a rumor. In 1480, in La Guardia, a village near Avila, "some Jews supposedly kidnapped a child of three or four, inflicted a simulacrum of the Passion upon him by punching him, whipping him, and placing a crown of thorns upon his head."[34] Then they sacrificed him by removing his heart. From 1485 to 1501, well over seven hundred Jews were burned alive in Toledo; in 1490, two years before the discovery of America, two thousand were burned at the stake and fifteen thousand forcibly converted.[35] Jews, homosexuals, Cathars, all were sorcerers in the Devil's service.

Some of the confessions obtained during the Inquisition's trials were certainly brought about by torture—the metal gag, the water torture, the boot, and other monstrosities.[36] Some confessions, however, seem to have been spontaneous. That they were true, that people really thought they had copulated with the Devil, is not the question. Until the beginning of this century, some Catholic authorities maintained that possession was an unarguable reality,[37] and they implicitly did not question these confessions. Yet the Church's explanations do not seem to take into account such established psychological phenomena as suggestion, which can be collective as well as individual.[38] In times of stress, in the presence of threats real or imagined, people can believe themselves the victims of some nonexistent ailment, or that they have perpetrated some terrible deed—especially if, for some reason, they already have feelings of guilt.

Most often, such psychoses have a starting point. In the case of the Salem witches, a historical investigation three centuries after the fact brought several revealing facts to light. Over the winter of 1691–92, several young girls had met regularly in the kitchen of the town's minister, Reverend Parris, where they listened to the voodoo stories told to them by Tituba, a slave from the Antilles. In the girls' eyes, this was already an infraction. They tried to predict the future—for instance, to find out who their husbands would be —by noting the shape of an egg white dropped in cold water. This violation of familial and religious mandates produced great nervous tension in the girls; some suffered from fits and convulsions, which sometimes assumed colorful forms, for instance in the girl who began barking and walking around on all fours. The families were horrified. When the "possessed" were asked who was tormenting them, they provided three names—Tituba's, of course, but also those of a mean-spirited beggar woman named Sarah Goode and of a woman who had committed the unpardonable sin of living with her second husband before they were married. The three unfortunate women were jailed, and, since it was a question of demonic possession, the infernal machine was set in motion.[39]

The Church and the Inquisition clearly exploited these hysterical outbreaks to prove the existence of the Devil and the vital necessity that the faithful strictly adhere to ecclesiastical dictates. The same held true long after the Inquisition came to an end.

Badly mauled in France after the revolution of 1789, the Inquisition survived for a few more years elsewhere in Europe. Yet the fatal blow to it was dealt when Joseph Bonaparte decreed its abolition upon his entry into Madrid in 1808. In 1813, the Cortès declared it a violation of the Spanish constitution. Rome protested, and it was reestablished by Ferdinand VII when he returned from exile in 1814. However, deprived of its income (a just state of affairs), the Spanish Inquisition, one of the most fearsome of all the Inquisitions in its readiness to send people to the stake, grew very weak. The pope, in an attempt to preserve his favored instrument —which the intellectual elite and the educated middle classes rejected—rescinded torture in 1816, but by then it was too late. Abolished once more in Spain after the liberal revolution of 1820, then reinstated by the duke of Angoulême during the French military intervention (the Bourbons had always been its ardent partisans), the Inquisition was definitively suppressed by Queen Christina in 1820. The name of its most famous leader (1420–28), Tomás de Torquemada, one of the most heinous murderers in history and the precursor of the modern Heydrich and Himmler, was to become synonymous with cruelty (he had also been an enemy of his country, since whole populations had fled under his rule). The Inquisition was discredited once and for all.

One of the darkest chapters in the history of infamy was closed —but, for all that, the Devil was still not beaten.

CHAPTER 16

Islam

The Devil as
State Functionary

Islam was born in Arabia in the seventh century, a time when the Arabian peninsula was far from homogenous, culturally or religiously. Islam thus did not escape being influenced by the world that preceded it.

I was born and spent my youth up until the age of nineteen in the only Muslim country that boasted an Islamic university at the time: the country was Egypt, the university that of El-Azhar. A speaker of Arabic, I listened to the sheikhs teaching the Qur'an to students squatting on acres of red rugs in the mosque, swaying their torsos back and forth. The difference between the *Sunna*, the Way, and *Sh'ia*, or Sect of Ali, the two principal branches of Islam, was explained to me very early on. Close contact with Muslims gave me a rudimentary understanding of the four Sunni schools of Qur'an interpretation: the Hanafite, the Malekite, the Shafeite, and the Hanbalite. Traveling and reading introduced me to the various offshoots of the two great strains of Islam: the picturesque *hashashin*, or smokers of hashish (who have disappeared today after leaving us the word "assassin"), the Druze, the Ismailis, the Twelve or Etnashriyya, the Zeydites, the Carmathians, the Fatimites, all of which derive from Sh'ia. There are also the Khawarij, according to whom any believer can be elected calif, the *murjetes* or "temporizers," who refuse to judge human actions because that privilege is reserved to God, the Kadarites, who have almost vanished, the M'utazilites, who stress human liberty and refuse to ascribe any trait to God, the Wahabites, fundamentalists for whom death in a holy war or *jihad* is a guaranteed entry into Paradise, the Bekstashis, disciples of Djelal el-Din of Mevlana who count among their number the celebrated and marvelous whirling dervishes, the Sufis, Gnostic mystics, the Babists or Baha'i, the disciples of Baha'Allah buried on Mount Carmel in Palestine (representatives of whom I even met in Auckland, New Zealand), the Ahmadiyyehs of the Punjab, guardians of Jesus' tomb at Srinagar, and so on.

For years I heard the cries of the *muezzin*—the inviters—to prayer on Fridays, calls that today are broadcast by loudspeakers, in which the Muslim connoisseur measures the muezzin's talent by the faultless weave of his phrasing, by his ability to maintain vocalization, by the purity of his voice, and by the precision of his diction, all the fruits of long training. I once heard them in Java wafting out at dawn beneath the remnants of Krakatoa, and they were exactly what I had heard before in Istanbul and Beirut. The accents were the same, but not so the attitude of the people. Religions travel, but cultures often do not.

Tradition has it that the Prophet had foreseen Islam having seventy-three sects, but that in the end only one would remain. The diversity of the ones I knew already make me feel surprised, even annoyed, when I encounter some Western ideas about Islam. The religion varies infinitely in the way that it is lived from Algiers to Kuala Lumpur, from Teheran to Acre—only ignorance about it is constant.

While the history of the rest of the world—Europe, India, China—has been well known for centuries, that of Arabia only began to emerge with any clarity thanks to a wave of archaeological excavations undertaken in the thirties, concurrently with oil prospecting, by individuals like Wendell Philips. Huge sections of this little continent, which starts at the Syrian desert, the Hamad, and stretches between the Red Sea and the Persian Gulf to the Indian Ocean, are still known only very incompletely. In 1992, archaeologists in Oman discovered the traces of a legendary city, Ubar, one of the great centers of the incense trade. Other sites still rest under the sands.

The Egyptians, Romans, Greeks, Abyssinians, Phoenicians, and Jews passed through and sometimes remained, each leaving their mark. Asians also came, since the trade in gems, coral, pearls, spices, perfumes, silk, glassware, and even animals between the Mediterranean and Asia, then between the Peninsula and Asia, had created roads since at least the first millennium B.C.—at the beginning of the second millennium, for instance, the kings of Mesopotamia imported elephants and monkeys from India by sea.[1] The Middle East has never been the desert we are so ready to imagine; the area, indeed, abounds in gods, kings, and demons. The genealogy of the Devil in Arabia is very fragmented.

Several cultures almost completely unknown to European scholarship have existed here:[2] the Minean kingdom,[3] whose origins date back to the end of the second millennium B.C.; the Sabaeans, ruled by Solomon's celebrated admirer, the Queen of Sheba, who supposedly visited the king sometime around 950 B.C.; the Himyarites, who succeeded the Sabaeans around 115 B.C.; the Hirites; and the kingdoms of Ghassan and Kinda. From the fact that their languages were Semitic it has been deduced that the peninsula's populations and their religions were as well—although this last point is less certain.

Some hundred gods figured in the Minean pantheon, but we know almost nothing about them. Sams (as in the Arabic *Shams*), the sun, a direct descendant of the Babylonian Shamash, is a goddess, while Attar, a divinity of the planet Venus, is masculine—these might be a Minean version of the Babylonian (feminine) Ishtar and Astaroth, who came in a great number of avatars. On the one hand, she would become the goddess of love Astarte, a worthy descendant of the great prehistoric fertility goddess who presided over sacred prostitution in the temples; Christian tradition of the Middle Ages, however, thought she was the Devil, who is called Astaroth in various demonological texts.

Pagan as Astaroth was, the aging Solomon nevertheless paid her homage, since "his heart was not perfect with the Lord his God," and "he went after Ashtoreth, the goddess of the Sidonians."[4] (Indeed, Astaroth is the plural of Asthar; it seems as though the goddess has many forms.) Another king of Israel, Josiah, built a sanctuary to her on the Mount of Olives, as he had already built one dedicated to Kemosh, the god of the Moabites, and another to Milcom, "the abomination of the children of Ammon,"[5] though otherwise he too remained nominally faithful to Yahweh. Clearly, these two kings of Israel felt it difficult to identify the goddess of love and fertility with a devil of any kind.

Imported to Abyssinia, Attar would become the goddess of the heavens Asthar.[6] She was, however, not just a goddess of love and fertility, since Philo of Byblos says that as a sign of her royalty she was represented with a headdress of bull's horns. Whether she was Semitic is another unclear point, since with her horns she immediately recalls the Egyptian Hathor, herself the goddess of fertility and represented with a similar headdress. Yet Hathor was in existence at least a millennium before the oldest inscription that mentions the Sabaeans, which dates from 715 B.C. It therefore cannot be ruled out that some of the gods in the pre-Islamic peninsula were Egyptian; the area had in fact absorbed many other influences, which would be normal for such a crossroads. In addition, it gave its greatest god the epithet of Rahman, "merciful," which strongly suggests a Jewish influence. There was a Jewish city on the Red Sea in the fourth century A.D., and Judaism in any case had a high profile on the peninsula—there were important Jewish communities, with rabbis and schools, at Medina, in Yemen, and in Syria. The Jewish influence even reached Saba, as attests verse 62 of Sura 2 in the Qur'an: "Believers, Jews, Christians, and Sabaeans. . . ."[7]

The Nazarenes—Nasara—could have been the Mandeans, a para-Christian sect sometimes referred to as Christians of Saint John the Baptist. For reasons we shall see below, though, they are much more likely to have been disciples of Jesus, who were particularly in evidence in the peninsula, for instance in the oasis of Najran between Mecca and Yemen, where a number of Christians were martyred in 525 A.D. It is probably not by chance that the reference to the Sabaeans follows that of the Nazarenes in the verse. Would they be the inhabitants of the kingdom of Saba? The hom-

onym might induce one to believe it. This people, however, practiced several religions, and there is no way to tell which one the
Prophet might be referring to. Because Muhammad, as a rule always
very precise in his allusions, would not cite the same sect under
two different names, it seems likely that they were in fact Mandeans
(who are indeed also referred to as Subba or Sabaeans).[8] In the
seventh century, the region was teeming with marginals, heretics,
and schismatics possessed by the need for a religion tailored to
their own specifications, their own dreams.

Islamicists admit that the Zoroastrians were tolerated in Mecca,
as were no doubt also the adherents of other religions—even the
presence of Nestorian Christians cannot be ruled out. Like every
great commercial crossroad, Mecca and the Arabian peninsula as
a whole seems to have been the gathering ground of ancient and
contemporary religions. The land of mirages housed a formidable
collection of Eastern and Western gods.

In 567 at the earliest and 579 at the latest, though most probably
571, Muhammad, the son of Abdallah and Aminah, was born in
Mecca. His parents were members of the huge Qureyshite tribe, a
grouping of several separate clans that shared power in the city.
He never knew his father, who died just as his mother was giving
birth to him, nor was he to have much time with his mother, who
died when he was six: thus, on top of the difficulty of being the
firstborn son came orphanhood. According to tradition, children
were placed in the care of wet nurses from nomadic clans so that
they would grow strong in the pure desert air. Muhammad, however,
was retrieved from his wet nurse early and adopted by his grandfather, Abd el-Mottalib. The boy would have little time with him,
too—the old man was already eighty-two, and he in turn would die
two years later, when Muhammad was eight.

He was adopted once again, this time by his paternal uncle Abu
Taleb, a prosperous merchant who spent much of his time traveling.
Abu Taleb occasionally went to Syria, where he sometimes brought
Muhammad. Tradition holds that the first foreign city the young boy
saw was Basra. This town, the Bossora mentioned in the Old Tes-
tament,[9] was rebuilt by Trajan in 106. By 222, under Alexander
Severus, it had become a rich Roman center; under the reign of

Philip II the Arab, it became a great metropolis, and under the Constantines it was made a Christian episcopal see. A basilica towered over the city when the young prophet first saw it, although neither that nor the city's opulence was what really caught his attention: a precocious adolescent, he was struck by the immense advantages that derive from a universal worldview. At the time, Byzantium was the seat of a faith, a faith that in turn was the guarantor of Byzantium's might. The boy, who came from a city that was rich, granted, but only a hamlet in comparison to a great Byzantine commercial hub, could not have helped but be dazzled. The Qureyshites had not inherited the Roman art of erecting magnificent temples, and in place of a worldview they had nothing but a body of inchoate beliefs. Faith, Muhammad realized, could reshape the world. In quest of that secret power, he listened and looked at everything.

The ninth- and tenth-century Iraqi historian and theologian Al-Tabarri relates that Abu Taleb and Muhammad stopped, along the way, at the hermitage of a syncretist monk named Bahira. This monk, who noted that the branches of one particular tree bent themselves to provide shade for Muhammad, was according to tradition the first person to call him the Envoy of God, *rassul Allah*. After examining the adolescent closely, Bahira also spotted the "seal of the prophet" between his shoulders—this was perhaps a neuroma, but more probably and more simply a lipoma, a benign fatty tumor. The anecdote undoubtedly contains its share of both truth and embellishment.

One wonders which Devil, if any, Muhammad might have known about. Little information is available about his upbringing and education, but they could not have been anything out of the ordinary for his tribe. We cannot know if he had ever heard of the Persian Ahriman, or if his understanding of demons was limited to those that appear in Babylonian religions, the *afarit* whose evil was spread on the desert winds, or if he knew of a syncretistic form of the Jewish Satan that had retained his role from the Old Testament as God's respectful adversary.

What is certain is that he listened attentively to what he was told. The Qur'an's Sura 16.103, which details the criticisms raised against Muhammad by his opponents, reads: "We know that they say: 'A mortal man taught him [the revealed teachings].' " Sura 25.5, contains more damning criticism in that the implication is made that he received his revelations from "others"—that is, from Christians or Jews:[10] "And they say: 'Fables of the ancients he has written: they are dictated to him morning and evening.' "

Some went so far as to challenge his authorship of the Qur'an, claiming instead that it had been written by a Christian monk named Aish, or by a rabbi.[11] Muhammad, in short, was taken to task for having listened too much. Among the things he was accused of, it should be mentioned, was that he had been bewitched (Sura 25.8). That charge apparently stuck, since it is repeated in a slightly modified form in Sura 17.47: "The man you follow is surely bewitched." Muhammad must certainly have been mocked when he began to preach; the Qureyshite clans that had been rallied by his first rivals, Makhzun and Abd Shams, called him "a hallucinator who has been possessed, like the *kahin* [seers], magicians, and poets, by an inferior spirit."[12] Indeed, his teaching strayed from the faith of his ancestors, and this earned him powerful opposition.

Based on these verses, many writers have suggested that Muhammad was influenced by Judeo-Christianity. If this was the case—and it is plausible, although so far unverifiable—and if it did end up influencing the Islamic concept of the Devil, the source must have been New Testamental, since like the Gospels but unlike the Old Testament the Qur'an defines the Devil not as the servant of God but as his sworn enemy: "When you recite the Qur'an, seek refuge in Allah from accursed Satan."[13]

Satan or Shaitan has become "accursed," or "the Lapidated One," which is a powerful image: the Evil One perpetually stoned with shooting stars cast at him by the angels. Only once in the whole Qur'an does he bear a different name, Malik,[14] which is no doubt a reference to the Canaanite Moloch. He is sometimes one, sometimes multiform, as in the Sura in which Muhammad implores his followers to resist "the agents of the Shaitans."[15] Drawing on Sura 7.30, the M'utazilite school of Islam maintains that Shaitan is the father of all damnation.[16]

The Qur'an does not propose a cosmogony. From the very first, it claims to be direct revelation based on a foundation of established myths, which in essence are the Jewish ones of the garden of Eden, Gan'Eden, which it mentions not less than ten times.[17] The garden is, straightforwardly, located on the other side of the world from Gehenna. The Qur'an also agrees with Genesis in referring to the Flood, the only differences being that Noah's Ark is a felucca, and that the mountain it eventually comes to rest upon is Diyarbakir in the upper Jazirah. The story of Sodom and Gomorrah is recounted as it stands. Names from the Old Testament abound—Noah, Abraham, Moses, Isaac, and Jacob are duly Arabized into Nuh, Ibrahim, Mussa, Ishaq, and Yakub. The Temptation in the garden corresponds to the description in Genesis all but for the fact that Eve is not involved. Satan instead talks directly to Adam: "Shall I show you the Tree of Immortality and an everlasting kingdom?"[18]

In the third Sura, Muhammad explicitly mentions the Torah and confirms that it is the law of God. Yet the concept of a unique God symmetrically leads to the concept of a unique Devil, and in this respect Muhammad followed Zoroaster, who at one stroke demoted the gods that had been associated with Ahura Mazda to the rank of demons. Muhammad's Devil became associated with his tribe's ancient gods, the gods of idolaters.

In the Qur'an, however, Satan and his demons do not feature in any of the extraordinary fables that are to be found throughout the intertestamentary literature—they neither couple with mortals nor produce giants, monsters, or famous men. Muhammad ascribes them no hierarchy, language, or intentions, and they are not described: it is not known if they are beautiful or ugly, animal or vegetable. They are assigned no dwelling but Hell. There is one solitary and fleeting reference to the Christian heretical idea that God had created the demons.[19] Satan and his supposed troops are no more than enemies of God and His angels, and their role is in any case quite small; when it mentions the negative aspect of the world, the Qur'an most often speaks of Gehenna, and it does that far less frequently than it mentions Eden or Paradise. As in the Old Testament's Eden with its four rivers, the garden is irrigated by four rivers, one of fresh water, one of milk, one of wine (which, incidentally, goes to show that the Qur'an is quite tolerant of alcohol), and one of honey. The garden is ingeniously filled with terrestrial delights, with *houris* and "immortal ephebes" bearing "overflowing chalices, goblets, and cups."

The Hell of the Qur'an also seems to correspond to New Testamental descriptions: no longer the Old Testament's vision of a place in which souls languish without having to endure dreadful torments, it is the modern Hell, so to speak, in that it is derived from Mazdaism. It is called "Allah's scourge."[20] In twenty-seven separate passages, the Qur'an stresses that its fires are eternal. As in the New Testament, it is where the damned will go after Allah has separated the good from the bad, with the former going to the garden, the latter into "the dwelling place of the arrogant."[21]

This last detail closely recalls intertestamental interpretations of why Satan fell, namely, because of his pride. The "arrogant" are the proud, those who reject the word of God as it is transmitted by Muhammad and his predecessors. Muhammad adopted, lock, stock, and barrel, the intertestamental idea about the real cause of Evil, an idea Christianity itself had adopted: it is due to the individual's claim to individuality. Muhammad made it the basis, the secret basis, of Islam. The claim to being is fundamentally Satanic.

This is the crucial issue. At no other point in the history of religion does the key to *this* history of the Devil so clearly make itself manifest: belief in Satan is produced by the negation of individuality. What the Hellenist Saul-Paul's Christian heirs never precisely formulated—perhaps, or probably, because it would have horrified the Hellenistic world—Islam proclaimed openly and loudly. One must submit to God. Whoever does not abdicate his individuality to Allah is "arrogant" and thus Satan's tool.

Islam's interpretation of Satan makes it the sister religion of Christianity: apart from superficial differences, both shared, until modern times, a total condemnation of individualism. At the very root of the Christian and Islamic philosophy lies the reduction—or rather, the annihilation—of the individual before the Almighty. Among other things, this explains why Christianity and Islam both were once profoundly averse to science, which could be considered an intolerable defiance of God. In this sense, both religions were foretold in the second century B.C. by the book of Enoch and its vituperations against those who claimed they could decipher the movement of celestial bodies.

If one takes a map of the world and plots out where the great scientific discoveries were made in the period between the Middle Ages and the end of the eighteenth century, one finds that the great majority occurred in Protestant countries. By putting him face to face with God, in an open dialogue between Creator and created, Protestantism exalted the individual and conferred a sense of personal liberty upon him. While in the Catholic world even a pope could be suspected of having made a pact with the Devil, in the Protestant world the making of a scientific discovery was practically taken as a sign of God's goodwill toward the inventor. God manifested his preference for some individuals by revealing an infinitesimal portion of the universe's mysteries to them. In Stockholm, René Descartes was a secular saint; in Paris, meanwhile, the Inquisition was beginning to take a lively interest in him (hence his exile in Sweden); in Rome, he would have been condemned as a dangerous freethinker. It is easy to understand why the Inquisition was so wrathful toward Galileo, as well as the reasons behind measures he took to protect himself. Above and beyond the reaction against the Gothic style, which Rome considered the creation of Jews and Freemasons, came the reaction against technical innovation. This is also why fundamentalist Islam has, like the Catholic world, contributed so little to the history of science.

Muhammad's teachings are remarkably austere; in many ways, they come down to the beliefs held by the peninsular tribes, though of course with the added reference to one unique God. At the head of all virtues comes generosity, along with the obligation to give alms, a new form of sacrificing to the Lord that is very closely related to Christian charity.[22] This virtue was a very ancient one to the peoples of the Arabian peninsula, for the most part nomads consigned to a barren desert, although it is possible that by Muhammad's time the growing wealth of traders had contributed to its decline—hence the urgency of his exhortations. Honesty, moderation, humility, and respect for one's neighbors are other virtues that the Qur'an praises highly.

There was little need for a complicated Devil in seventh-century

Arabia. The temptations that cropped up everywhere in the great formerly Roman and now-Byzantine cities were unknown. In this respect, the Qur'an was originally a deeply humanistic document. In G. E. von Grunebaum's words, Muhammad was asking for "more than the physical and military training to which pagan Arabia had become accustomed. The Muslim world was predicated on knowledge: knowledge about the Revelation, knowledge of what the Law required, and, to some degree, the knowledge to draw orthodox conclusions out of the Koran."[23] Although this scheme had complex consequences, as we shall see, it was apparently simple: the might, splendor, and infinite goodness of Allah reign over all, and those who reject or ignore him are consigned to Gehenna and the Devil.

Yet Muhammad's Devil, like his monotheism, was specifically of Judeo-Christian inspiration. With the exception of Mazdaism, its originator, the myth of a unique Devil was, to the best of our knowledge, absent from any of the religions that had ever appeared in the peninsula. If Muhammad introduced him, it was because he was intimately aware that the Devil is essential to the establishment of a centralized power. And that was his ultimate goal: well before he died, he was the great unifier of peoples within and without the great Sassanid and Byzantine hegemonies, peoples who would later, and erroneously, come to be called "Arabs"—Africans, Philistines, converted Yemenite Jews and Christians (or *Gordjis*), Kabyles, Thracians, Macedonians, Kurds, as well as the Georgians and Cherkesskans of Asia Minor. In time, this list of peoples would come to encompass the Asian continent.

Muhammad therefore enjoyed a stature comparable to that of Moses, and he was well aware of the fact. His parallels with the patriarch of the Old Testament were extended to include his own person, and he implicitly refers to himself as the successor of Moses—he beheld Allah on Mount Sinai, the same place where Moses came face to face with the splendor of the Creatory[24]; his staff was the "staff of Moses"[25]; in almost every one of the Suras, he castigates idolaters, as did Moses. The parallel with Moses, whom Muhammad referred to as a "true prophet," is particularly obvious in the "Believers" Sura; in the "Ornaments of Gold," a similar parallel is cultivated with Jesus, whom Muhammad referred to by name as a prophet as well.

Muhammad's attitudes toward Jesus are, surprisingly, little understood in the West. The Gospels' version of John's birth, of the Annunciation, and of Jesus' birth is transcribed almost verbatim after Sura 3. Anticipating by almost seven centuries the solution to the problem of Mary's original sin as devised by the monk Duns Scotus (a solution that led to the dogma of the Immaculate Conception), Muhammad has Mary's mother, Anne, declare during her pregnancy: "Lord . . . I dedicate to your service that which is in my womb."[26] Since she has been consecrated to Allah, Mary could not be subject to Satan, and she is therefore free of original sin.

The miraculous pregnancy of Zacharias' wife, the mother of the future John the Baptist, is related word for word. When the angels tell him that he is going to have a son, Zacharias cries out, "How shall I have a son when I am now overtaken by old age and my wife is barren?"[27]

Likewise, the angels tell Mary that she will give birth to the Messiah:

> The angels said to Mary: "Allah bids you rejoice in a word from Him. His name is the Messiah, Jesus the son of Mary. He shall be noble in this world and in the next, and shall be favored by Allah. He shall preach to men in his cradle and in the prime of manhood, and shall lead a righteous life.
>
> "Lord," she said, "how can I bear a child when no man has touched me?"
>
> He replied: "Such is the will of Allah. He creates who He will. When He decrees a thing He need only say: 'Be,' and it is."[28]

Muhammad, however, does not claim that he himself is predestined to be what he explicitly recognizes Jesus to be, a messiah. He does not claim that he is either predestined or in any special way remarkable. He too is admittedly subject to the Devil—as the celebrated "Satanic Verses" attest.[29] All told, Muhammad's theology differs from that of Roman Christianity on only two points: the Incarnation and the true Crucifixion of Jesus. As we have seen above, other Christians have stumbled over these two points and found themselves mired in heresy.

One can ask what Muhammad's original contributions were, and why they were accountable for the bitter opposition he initially encountered as well as for the staggering success his teachings later enjoyed (as Napoleon pointed out, "the unusual thing about Mahomet is that he conquered half the globe in ten years, while it took three hundred years for Christianity merely to get off the ground"[30]). Though preaching a revelation that was intimately bound to both Judaism and Christianity, Muhammad nevertheless rejected both, even though they each had a great deal of influence and could have provided him with significant support. His reasons for the double rejection are well known: despite the virtue of their prophets, neither religion had effectively disseminated the revelation that had been handed down to them.

What must be taken into consideration is the state of the world at the time. In the Mediterranean, as well as in the East, which was both so near and so very far away, two religions dominated—the Mazdaism of the Persian Sassanid Empire, which stretched from the Euphrates to the Indus, and the Christianity of the Byzantine Empire, which extended from southern Spain to Armenia, Greater Syria, and Egypt, including a small outpost on the eastern edge of the Black Sea, Lycaonia. The two empires were neighbors: the Byzantine Empire began at the Sassanid frontier kingdoms of Pesarmenia, Lakhmidia, and Ghassanidia. The Arabic peninsula was certainly not ignored by both, since each needed its crossroads. Persia controlled southern Arabia, Yemen, and Hadhramaut, and its influence extended over eastern Arabia. Byzantium held the north—Sinai, Palestine, and the territories corresponding to Jordan, Syria, and Lebanon. Still, the way of life in these outer lands was not what it was inside the imperial borders, for the simple reasons of geography and the outlands' essentially tribal nature. In Byzantium and Persia, urbanization had long since drawn in and absorbed the tribes. This is also one of the reasons why there were so many jostling religions in the peninsula, while in Byzantium, especially,

Christianity had been the state religion since Constantine and all foreign ones were unwelcome.

The most important fact for Muhammad was that the religions of both empires were monotheistic. Thenceforth, the world belonged to monotheism, which had military and commercial powers at its disposal incomparably greater than those available to the few polytheistic cities that were still straggling along. It is certainly no insult to the genius of Muhammad to suggest that over the course of his long hours of reflection while he was traveling on camelback he had come to understand the evolution of civilizations toward monotheism; no doubt, he was helped to realize this in his meetings with hanifs, the mysterious monotheistic monks mentioned in Islamic tradition.

They can easily be imagined: anchorites lost in contemplation, inhabited by an indistinct Word, and sometimes, like the monk Bahira who recognized Muhammad as the envoy of God, enlightened. They can be pictured talking about Mithra, Jesus, Moses, perhaps even the Buddha. They were steeped, or rather overflowing, with the surrounding monotheisms they had absorbed—Mazdaist, Judaic, Christian—but they were also the bearers of legends, traditions, and derivations Gnostic, Nestorian, Kanthean, all of this in addition sprinkled through by their own interpretations identifying Jesus with Mithra or Hercules. Nevertheless, they praised the One God they had cobbled together out of fragments found here and there, like the artists of Ravenna assembling the image of the *Pantocrator* from little squares of differently colored glass. Living on dates and honey, holding the least candle to be a miracle, and sometimes barely literate, they were the heralds of Islam: they lived and breathed the desire for a higher spirituality. This is no more than speculation, I hasten to add; but it seems to be confirmed in various passages in the Qur'an that say the world is filled with signs of Allah. And indeed it was.

Where this new name for God originated is not known. The Mandeans whom Muhammad condemned called the "false god" of foreigners Alaha; their own god was "the Great Mana."[31] In Aramaic, Al Aha simply means "the God." The word's etymology certainly does not explain the rejection of Al Aha, which must have taken place because Al Aha was the god of another sect (though which sect we do not know). All that can be supposed is that Muhammad might have been taken with the simplicity of the name "the God" —again, the One God.

The resistance to Muhammad's antitraditionalist teachings is easy to understand: "The pagan Arab was obliged to conform to a social order that, among other things, regulated his relationship with a series of deities, but the problems of religious ceremony and ritual were really of very little importance," writes von Grunebaum.[32] Muhammad established a higher spirituality whose ethical demands made easygoing laxity impossible. He also required a coming to awareness, the knowledge of new dogmas.

Why then did Islam triumph, as Napoleon observed, so quickly? In less than a century, the first two military victories—the taking of Mecca by Muhammad in 629 and the triumphant entry of the calif Omar into Damascus—were followed by the defeat of the Persians at Ctesiphon in 637, the conquest of Mosul in 639, the taking of Egypt the same year by Amr ibn el-Aas, with the concomitant Byzantine evacuation of Alexandria, the takings of Kabul, Bukhara, and Samarkand from 661 to 675, and the fall of Roderic's Visigoth kingdom in 713. In that time, the Persian Empire, one of the two great empires of the day, collapsed under the assaults of neophytes who a few decades earlier had dreamed of little more than getting their caravans safely across the broiling deserts. Islam had set Asia, the East, and the West alight.

It took as little time for the other great empire, the Byzantine, which still bore the grandiloquent name of the Eastern Roman Empire, to let itself be breached in its turn; the Western Empire, already cut to pieces by barbarian invasions, allowed the Muslims to wrest away territories as huge as Spain. Only at Poitiers in 732, exactly a century after Muhammad's death, did a palace mayor named Charles Martel manage to check the Islamic imperialism by stopping the Arab troops under the command of the valiant Abd el-Rahman. Yet the Islamic epic had reached its apogee; it would maintain itself at that peak for another seven centuries before declining.

Until that time, its success was staggering. The first reason for this, in the opening and decisive decades of the seventh century, was the financial enrichment of the Arabian peninsula's population. As had been the case in imperial Rome, where Mithraism, Judaism, and the cult of Isis were welcomed, higher living standards were followed by a heightening of intellectual aspirations. Lukewarm, sometimes pallid paganisms and tepid heresies were no longer enough for the prosperous Arabian commercial classes, which were tired of local rituals. Already timeworn, these rituals paled in comparison to the magnificent example of the neighboring Byzantine and Sassanid imperial religions. The struggle of the Qureyshites against the surviving disciples of Muhammad was a lost cause from the start.

Undoubtedly, the first Muslims took stock of the two great empires' strengths and weaknesses. The mixture of admiration and contempt in which Islam held Byzantium is eloquently reflected in the passage from the ninth-century Arab writer Jahiz:

> Having become interested in the Byzantines, we found that they were doctors, philosophers, and astronomers. They are familiar with the principles of music, are able to create Roman [weights and measures] and know the world of books. They are excellent painters. . . . They possess an architecture different from any other. . . . It is unarguable that they have beauty, are familiar with arithmetic, astrology, and calligraphy, and that they possess courage and a variety of great talents. The Blacks and similar peoples have less intelligence because they lack these qualities.[33]

Even after Islam was established, then, the Muslims continued to admire Byzantium. Since their respective religions were so close, why then did they not also adopt Byzantium's? Jahiz's next passage explains why.

> Despite all this they believe that there are three gods, two secret and one visible, in the same way that a lamp needs oil, a wick, and a reservoir. The same holds true [in their opinion] for the substance of the gods. They claim that a created being became a

creator, a slave a master, that a newly created being became an originally uncreated one . . . they would then hold that what happens to them is of no importance and they would not be proud of their own deeds, which to them would have no value but with respect to their God. Their apology is worse than their crime!

It was the two dogmas of the Trinity and the Incarnation that most offended Islamic monotheism. Nevertheless, Byzantium continued to fascinate, a fascination shared by the less than ardent heretic Christians and Jews whom Byzantium deemed second-class citizens: many soon converted to Islam. Excluded from Byzantine power and splendor, how could they not be moved by the temptation? With Islam, they could participate in the creation of a power that rivaled Byzantium, and they would thus become the Byzantines' equals. They were not wrong.

This wooing of the enemy looks odd; such apostasy seems incomprehensible today. Yet it can be better understood when it is likened to the taste for exoticism among the bourgeoisies of the late nineteenth and early twentieth centuries: after decades of enjoying the opulence of the industrial age, they were suddenly seized by a passion for the foreign. Thus, after the Japanism popularized by the Goncourt brothers came a predilection for "primitive" cultures. In France, colonial expositions launched African and Oceanian fads. In Germany, the discovery of the arts of Papua New Guinea and the Bismarck Archipelago set off a shockwave that gave birth to the German expressionism of *Die Brücke*, then of *Die Blaue Reiter*. The Parisian vogue of Sergey Diaghilev's *Ballets russes*, then those of African art and jazz, then of far-eastern mysticism (fantastically interpreted by, among others, the mystagogue Gurdjieff) are no more than expressions of this eclecticism in the first half of this century.

The apostates who joined Islam in the first centuries acted no differently. They embraced the religion of the conquerors, who glittered with gold, sand, and the youthful vigor of a new religion.

The evolution of nations into states inevitably involves the centralization of religions around One God. Twelve centuries later, despite their profound aversion to Christianity, which was traditionally associated with royalty, the French revolutionaries of 1789 took the same path, effecting a simple linguistic substitution of the words "Supreme Being" for the name "God," which comes down to exactly the same thing. To reject the notion of an immanent deity that transcends popular ethics and popular morality would have been to compromise the very principle of the state. Too steeped in philosophy to be unaware of this, the leaders of the French Revolution didn't risk it. They certainly needed a Devil, and it became the aristocracy.

It is again no insult to Muhammad to pay homage to his political sense, which the history of his triumphs displays amply. For the historian, that is where the revelation lies: it is dual, and it involves mystical inspiration as much as it does political awareness. For Muhammad, the intuition probably preceded the reasoning, and it was the same intuition that evoked the stirring verses in "The Flight of the Soul" by the Muslim mystic and holy martyr Hussein Mansur el Hallaj:

My glance, with the eye of science, has uncovered the pure secret of my
    meditation;
a Light has shined in my mind, more subtle that any graspable idea, and
    I have
plunged under the waves of the sea of my reflections, gliding through it
    like an arrow.[34]

What is clear is that Muhammad created a nation while he created a religion—and that nation, in turn, created new states. The phenomenon would not have been possible without Islam.

As in Zoroastrianism, the first of the totalitarian theocracies, the Devil became a state functionary. He, too, was a guarantor of the Law of Islam, in that whoever strayed from it fell into his talons.

Religious wars were now inevitable, and they were not avoided. In the beginning, they were called Crusades.

CHAPTER 17

Modern Times and the God of Laziness, Hatred, and Nihilism

Buffeted by the storms of the twentieth century, by nuclear fission and then fusion, by the genetic progress that has allowed us to alter living beings, by the sexual revolution that reduced the headiest of the deadly sins to dust, and by the political and cultural upheaval that has forced him to keep constantly on the move, Satan should long since have given up the ghost.

For some, however, he is still very much alive. In 1989, a police officer in Ohio wrote:

> In the face of criminals led or directed by the supernatural, or in encounters with evil beings, philosophies, or principles, traditional police tools are ineffective. When a police officer finds himself confronting the Prince of Darkness or his legions, he had better have the "scourge of Satan" at his side as well as all the spiritual aids and weapons he can muster. In the war against Satanic crimes, Christian officers are the ones best prepared to be the spearhead.[1]

In the eyes of some police officers, Satanists have been practicing for generations—stealing children from nursery schools, killing, kidnapping, and raping. According to some "experts" on Satanic cults, these international, highly organized underground networks are responsible for fifty thousand deaths a year. Satanist families allegedly steal huge numbers of infants for ritual murder—supposedly to liberate their primal forces and "galvanize" their energies.

"Nothing ever changes," as Chekhov said—at least since the dark days of the Inquisition and the Salem witch trials. Nevertheless, in the minds of the many who believe in the Devil, and perhaps also in the minds of many who don't, one thing that has changed is Satan: he now manifests himself in what could be called the "low-level" Satanism that so preoccupies the police.

In one scenario, as soon as children are dropped off at certain nursery schools, Satanists load them into private airplanes and fly them to cult centers. There, the children are forced into coffins, which are then lowered into graves. The celebrants cover them with earth; afterward the high priest of the Satanic ceremony digs the children up and rapes them. The ordeal over, the children are returned to their nurseries.

This reads like the ravings of a madman, and yet tales like this are regularly voiced at police conferences like the one held in Petersburg, Virginia, on September 13, 1988. The paragraph above is based on material from *In Search of Satan*, a book that a high-ranking officer named Robert D. Hicks wrote about the investigations then being conducted by some of his colleagues.

If there were any reason to believe that the Devil exists, it would lie in the tales reported by such cult "specialists." One is tempted to conclude that a good number of police officers are mentally unstable, and best off in therapy or in a straitjacket—case closed. it requires some gullibility to believe that planeloads and truckloads of children are kidnapped, abused, and brought back without anyone being aware of it. What about the parents, pilots, drivers, and the kids themselves? Yet the matter isn't quite that simple: despite their unsettling imagery, there is something to these stories of Satanism and child molestation. In and of itself, the police view of Satanism is a problem, since it implies that the Devil does exist, a conviction that can only please Satanists everywhere; as a whole, though, the police in the United States are no more deranged than police anywhere.

Paul Jasler, a retired police sergeant from Albuquerque, New Mexico, reports the story of a thirteen-year-old boy who repeatedly listened to a heavy metal song called "Possessed" and became convinced that he was a full-fledged Satanist. He persuaded himself that Satan had told him his mother's boyfriend had to die, and that the boy would have to do the killing. The boy was torn between the horror of committing murder and the clearly delusional Satanic edict. "That's how it is, whether you believe it or not," says Jasler.[2] Such cases have become so frequent that sociologists have begun to write books on them.[3]

The U.S. Department of Health and Human Services has reported that in 1988 about one boy and four girls per thousand—or a total of 155,300 cases, quite a significant number—were victims of sexual abuse. Even more alarming, the number of such cases in 1986 was three times what it was in 1980. Pedophilia is not the subject of close attention in the rest of the world, and we do not know how extensive pedophiliac crimes are in France, Great Britain, Germany, and other European nations. From time to time, some incident occurs and the veil is suddenly but briefly lifted; figures are tentatively advanced, but the subject is so repugnant that it is quickly dropped again, to general relief. What is known is that networks for pedophiliac literature exist, and that there are adults who do things to children. Satan, however, is clearly not to blame.

The element specific to the United States is its willingness to believe that pedophilia and pederasty are actually practiced by Satanic cults.[4] A woman named Marti Johnson has publicly declared that for ten years she was subject to ritual sexual abuse until, having grown too old to interest the celebrants, she was elevated to the rank of priestess, then high priestess, in two separate Satanic groups. To cite her own words, "I participated in the sacrifice of a little girl of eight who had been kidnapped in Harrison County, Texas." She described the crime in detail, reporting that the little girl had been drugged and then, wide-eyed with fear, murdered in front of other children.[5]

It is hard to tell if Marti Johnston thought she witnessed or actually did witness what she described, especially given her claim that there are something like a hundred Satanist groups within a 350-mile radius of Tomball, a small Texan town of 6,225 inhabitants. Sought by the police as the witness to a premeditated murder, she disappeared—her excuse being that she was actually hiding from the Satanists, who would silence her if she said anything more.

Nevertheless, other witnesses of the same sort have appeared. Joan Christianson's story is truly awful, but one wonders how much credence to lend to a woman who claims that she was forced to give birth to four or five children whose hearts were subsequently eaten. She claimed that after telling her story publicly she received 10,700 threatening telephone calls, supposed proof of the existence and number of Satanists. The precision of the number of calls also leaves one somewhat skeptical. And then there is the case of "Cheryl," who appeared on the Geraldo Rivera show in 1988: Cheryl was allegedly raped at the age of twelve for the express purpose of producing a child. The baby was sacrificed by its own father, a Satanist, in the presence of the doctor who delivered it.

We have reached the limits either of atrocity or of credulity, or perhaps both. After all, we are talking about people who work for a living, who every day are surrounded by neighbors, employers, or employees, who cannot help but take part in mundane life, where women feed their children milk instead of sticking inverted crucifixes into their chests, and where little girls and boys are hugged, not raped in grim and macabre ceremonies.

There is little new about this new Satanism. In 1750, riots broke out in Paris because of a belief that the police were kidnapping children. The ensuing violence, which was limited to the slums between the Bastille and the Tuileries, witnessed the savage killing of an *exempt*—a police officer—named Labbé; his body was dumped in front of the residence of the lieutenant general of police, Nicolas-René Berryer. The truth was that Berryer, an arrogant, hard, and brutal person, had in fact ordered the police to clear the streets of vagrants, beggars, and especially of indigent children, who were thrown into poorhouses for periods of months or eveny ears. However, popular opinion attributed the arrests to Louis XV and —this is where the myth begins—held that the children were being sacrificed because the king or someone near him had to take baths in children's blood in order to cure some serious illness.[6] Once again, the myth about redemptive blood. During times of social crisis, it seems, the collective mind revives stories about children being sacrificed on the orders of despots—as has been seen in the much more famous legend of the slaughter of the infants in Palestine, allegedly ordered by Herod the Great but in reality an outright fabrication on the part of the Gospel writers.

What the American Satanist myths reveal most clearly is a collective mental crisis. The police in the United States maintain that they are unaware of all these disappeared children—and fifty thousand of them each year would be hard to miss. One in-depth look at the reports of some self-proclaimed witnesses to Satanic horrors concluded explicitly that they are fabrications created to dupe a public overly ready to believe in Satanic rituals.[7] Yet one truth is clear: we have entered into a perverse realm where the invention of Evil produces phantasms that can lead to actual evil. Pathological imitation is an established psychological fact; the depiction of a mode of behavior has its effects on impressionable minds.

One of the worst criminals in American history, "Son of Sam" David Berkowitz, who committed a series of murders in the borough of Queens that terrorized New York city and made headlines for months, wrote a letter to the New York police in which he declared, "I am the monster Beelzebub, the great Behemuuth [sic]." It obviously cannot be said that had Berkowitz been unaware of "Beelzebub," he would not have committed the crimes he did; yet it is likely that his morbid fixation on the Devil structured his criminal behavior. By chance, he had read that a Satan-Beelzebub-Behemoth existed and he started to believe that he was its agent.

It is at this point that Satanism leaves the realm of criminology and enters that of sociology. The Devil has, in effect, become the hero of the loser. This is what underlies the indescribable horror of the murders of Sharon Tate and her houseguests that night in her villa on Cielo Drive: the loser's hatred of the winner, a resurgence of the *phtonos* so feared by the Greeks. Sharon Tate was young, pretty, celebrated, and married to the successful film director Roman Polanski; the hooligans who took Charles Manson for their guru burst into the mansion and for no reason massacred everyone there, then scrawled hate-filled slogans on the walls with the victims' blood. In prison for life, Manson still plays out his charade of "Satanism."

In these cases, it seems that the myth of Satan serves only as the pretext for pornography, sadism, and depravities of all sorts; indeed, it seems that its only real function is to act as the vehicle for mythomaniacal fantasies. Thus, a Virginia priest who was accused of sexually abusing one of his parishioners invoked the Devil's influence: the parishioner herself related that she had participated in the sacrifice and cannibalistic consumption of a child —a classic fantasy. The police investigation revealed that there had been no sacrifice; rather, the parishioner had made everything up to impress the priest, who in turn had then simply given in to his sexual urges. In short, Satanism had provided a behavioral roadmap for the avoidance of personal responsibility for sexual arousal.

A Satanism does exist, however, whose empire is much more vast and does not seem—at first glance, at least—to be the reflection of perverse sexual obsessions. This cult (or rather these cults, since there are a number of them) assumes the appearance of religions, with hierarchies, officiating priests, churches, altars, tapers (black, of course), symbolism—the works. The cults are based on pseudo-philosophical arguments and are riddled with references, albeit confused or often frankly erroneous, to ancient liturgies. The evidence indicates that the adherents do not know that when Beelzeboth, Astaroth, or Lucifer were worshiped in ancient religions, it was not, as we have seen in the preceding chapters, as gods of Evil but, instead, as gods pure and simple. I have tried to point this out to the adepts of one such sect in California—but as Einstein said, a prejudice is harder to break down than the atom.

One of the most famous Satanists is an American named Anton La Vey. Tall, thin, past middle age, clad in black, his upper lip ornamented by a slight mustache, he unmistakably recalls Mephistopheles. In 1966, La Vey founded the "Church of Satan." In his book, *The Satanic Bible*, which enjoyed considerable sales, he declares that "Devil-worship is an entirely self-centered and self-gratifying perversion of religion"—a definition whose sense, I must admit, escapes me.[8] Nevertheless, I think I can detect a whiff of sexual obsession in its language, which seems to reflect an orgiastic, cathouse mentality elevated into a sublime and "revolutionary" ideology.

La Vey has also published *The Sorcerer's Handbook* and *The Satanic Rituals*, both of which also enjoyed a certain success.[9] Interviewed in the media whenever something Satanist makes headlines, La Vey elaborates mystifying and abstruse thoughts:

> The popularity of my books and of Satanism in general is based on America's need for constant change. The Zeitgeist in this country is producing a new society in which television is actually the dominant religion. And of course, despite what TV can do, there's something missing. Satanism compensates for this lack. I should be credited for bringing about a change in society, whether its effects are positive or negative. Catholics were at one time considered devils by Protestants. Protestants were devils to Catholics. The Jews were considered devils by both. The Chinese believed that the white man was the devil. But who can really say what is evil and what isn't?[10]

La Vey's declarations lack philosophical substance, sociological depth, and historical form: they are a bubble inflated by the winds of banality. Not once does La Vey broach the question of Satan's origins; but he does shed light on some things, such as the wave of irrationality that is sweeping over an entire country (one the Western world once viewed as the "laboratory of the future") and the crippling nihilism that, since the beginning of this century, has dominated everything from art to epistemology. Last, as the success of his books confirms, he sincerely expresses the popular need for Satanism. Other belief systems are too complex for minds incapable of concentration; Satanism is at least "gratifying," as La Vey says, and anyone can practice it in whatever form he or she chooses.

The extraordinary—one is tempted to say "fabulous"—paradox (as well as an indicator of the confusion inevitable in such ambiguous concepts as the Devil) is that Satanism has taken credit for the abolition of original sin. The entity responsible for original sin has come to be considered not just the liberator of the working class but even the champion of sexuality as well. Herbert Marcuse, for instance, wrote that the Orphic Eros lessened the impact of original sin (although, by saying this, Marcuse also displayed his lack of knowledge about the myth of Orpheus, who was in fact an antierotic hero, hence medieval Christianity's quick adoption of him).[11]

The Church of Satan is certainly not the only one of its kind; during a stay in California in the seventies, I came across para-, proto-, and pre-Satanic sects whose pretentiously esoteric gibberish—based on references to the Kabbala, to a patently fabricated text entitled the *Necronomicon*, and to the works of the well-known and comical Gurdjieff—repelled me. (I had collected documents about these sects, but they reflected things so impenetrable, mean-spirited, and hopelessly naive that I tossed the material out with the trash—I was unaware at the time of its potential anthropological interest.) I was particularly repelled by the abundance of references to the "magus" Aleister Crowley, a notorious Satanist.[12]

In the United States, Canada, and Great Britain, there are also groups of individuals who call themselves "witches." Some of these, the "white" witches, are quick to point out that they worship not Satan but the forces of nature venerated by "the Celtic peoples of Europe"; others, the "black" ones, worship Satan at sabbaths modeled upon clearly misunderstood descriptions of medieval sabbaths (which are prudently sanitized to ward off the police). These practices differ little, if at all, from the occultism that is to be found all over the Christian world from Siberia to Italy (although, even though I know it well, I am not aware of comparable Satanic rituals in the Muslim world). In France, one Georges Bourdin, who called himself Hamsah Manarah and ran a sect that was established around a thirty-three-meter-high concrete statue, talked the run-of-the-mill nonsense: he claimed having chained Satan *and* Lucifer, and dissolved the "souls" of five hundred fifty-two million demons!

It is evident that the perfect and entirely substanceless fiction devised by the Zoroastrians in the sixth century B.C. (and adopted first by dissident Jews in the third century B.C., and then by Christianity) is still alive and well in the world's supposedly most developed nations. One could hold Satanism in the same contempt we hold astrology, for example, but the problem is that these pre-logical ideas produce real and dangerous consequences—indeed, there is no way to count the various acts of violence brought about by the pathological obsession with the Devil, an obsession that serves as the focal point for serious psychiatric disturbances and impels those suffering from them toward violence, which later can be pardoned as the product of "possession."

The following are two examples of these consequences among thousands. In Rio de Janeiro in 1992, one Marcelo Costa de Andrade was arrested for the brutal rape and murder of fourteen children aged six to thirteen. His mind unbalanced by the sermons of a priest from the "Universal Church of the Kingdom of God" (a priest apparently as deranged as the psychopath: he attributed all physical handicaps to lack of faith in God), Andrade believed he was sending his victims to Heaven and freeing them from Satan's clutches.

In 1989, the United States was deeply shaken by a series of ritualistic crimes committed in Matamoros, a town near the Mexican border. The Mexican police exhumed thirteen corpses during a routine drug-trafficking investigation. The killers, who were members of a Satanist sect, believed that the sacrifice of the thirteen would earn them the Devil's praise. "They thought," said Jim Mattox, the attorney general of Texas, "that the murders would protect them from the world. It was religious mania."[13] If there was any doubt that the murders were sacrificial, the remains of animals killed at the same time as the human victims sealed it. The incident was all the more disturbing in that it came in the wake both of a flood of child sexual abuse cases and the Satanist murder of a teenager near Joplin, Missouri.

Yet it is extremely difficult to believe that Satanism is an exclusively religious matter. A Gallup poll for *U.S. News and World Report* in 1991 showed that the number of Americans who believe in Heaven and Hell increased between 1950 and 1992, from 72 percent to 78 percent with respect to Heaven, and 58 percent to 60 percent with respect to Hell.[14] The same poll estimated that of those Americans who regularly go to church, only 3 percent believe that they are at risk of going to Hell (compared to 7 percent for the nonchurchgoing, a paradox that will be examined below). Those most ready to believe they were going to Hell were men (5 percent, versus 3 percent for women). Those readiest to believe that they could go to Hell were Catholics (5 percent); those least likely to believe it were born-again Christians (3 percent). In other words, to paraphrase Jean-Paul Sartre, Hell is for others—or, rather, the Devil is the other.

These figures are all the more troubling in that the fires of Hiroshima and the incinerators of German camps should have made those of Hell seem considerably paler by comparison. Martin Marty, a professor of the University of Chicago School of Divinity, has said, "Hell has disappeared, but no one realizes it."[15] As we can see, though, this is a grave misapprehension.

Indeed, if from a purely theological point of view opinions vary from one church to another, there are nevertheless few people who believe that the person who eats meat on Friday and the murderer who rapes and kills a child will share the same fate in the hereafter. Yet it is no less true that the obsession with Satan has gripped a good many minds.

Satanists, and among them the authorities who continue to propagate the belief in Satan, are incapable of seeing the absurdity of a cult that by definition is at once destructive and self-destructive, a god of Evil being philosophically incapable of representing anything but destruction; clearly, they are even less capable of understanding the sociopolitical origins of their proselytism. In all seriousness, they stubbornly continue to pander to the great popular need for a countergod who will avenge the less fortunate against a God who protects only the righteous, the rich, the white, and the powerful.

Max Weber observed in *The Protestant Ethic and the Spirit of Capitalism* that God favors the rich. As early as 1920, Weber had also clearly defined the dilemma confronting the Protestant world: the search for salvation, he wrote, "cannot consist, as in Catholicism, of indiscriminately storing up individual works, but . . . must be the systematic self-examination [*selbskontrolle*] of a conscience that at every moment finds itself facing the alternative: elect or damned?"[16] The tension is unbearable; in the end, the faithful rebels, like Satan, into whose embrace he flees.

Our obsession with the Devil is not only the product of obscurantism, superstition, and ordinary gullibility: it is also a revolt against toil and an unjust social order. As the contemporary Italian philosopher Giovanni Papini points out, the Devil represents bread without sweat (it is not by chance that when he tempted Jesus in the desert, the Devil asked him to turn stones into bread).[17] The Devil has become the god of effortless gain through speculation, drug trafficking, smuggling, prostitution, and theft. At the most fundamental level, he is thus the god of laziness, of sin, of incompetence, of unculturedness, and of indifference. He is the secret god of presidents and ministers who consult their astrologists to see what tomorrow will bring. He is the god of business people who rely on insider trading to earn profit.

Weber also foresaw that "the idea of fulfilling one's duty through work haunts our lives. . . . Once the 'fulfilling' of one's professional duty can no longer be related to the highest spiritual and cultural values . . . the individual ceases, in general, to justify it."[18] In this scenario, Satan has become, at the most elevated level, the inspirer of systematic deconstruction, of derisiveness, of the "Void," of philosophers who say that reason has been abolished and of aesthetes who say that talent is inferior to the lack of talent (and who, wanting to provoke but succeeding only in revealing the truth about themselves, say that a bicycle wheel is equal to an Attic masterpiece, that a series of recorded door squeaks is equal to a Beethoven quartet—even that a blank canvas is as beautiful as a Veronese). He is the god of nihilism and despair.

Satan did not only recently begin to invade culture, he was ushered into our cities by illustrious hosts. One of the most justly celebrated geniuses of poetry, Charles Baudelaire, was one of the first to recite the "Litanies of Satan":

> O you, the wisest and most fair of Angels,
> A god betrayed by fate and never praised,
> O Satan, pity me my long misery!

> O prince of exile, who has been wronged,
> And who, defeated, always comes back stronger
> . . . .
> Adoptive parent of those whom wrathful God
> The Father expelled from earthly paradise,
> O Satan, pity me my long misery!

Since we cannot suppose that even in his rebellion Baudelaire confused God with Colonel Aupick, his stepfather, nor with the bourgeoisie of his day, it must be concluded that this is a pose. Yet
since even this pose wasn't radical enough for Baudelaire, he took
it farther still, in "A Prayer":

> Glory and praise to you, Satan, in the heights
> Of Heaven where you reigned, and in the depths
> Of Hell where, vanquished, you mutely dream!

In Baudelaire's day this must have offended the bourgeoisie,
roused the simple-minded, and made everyone else smile. It was a
time when sensitive souls were, like Emma Bovary, suffocating.
Some thirty years later, Arthur Rimbaud was to spend "A Season
in Hell," and Mallarmé would cry out:

> —Heaven is dead—I run to you! Grant, o matter,
> Forgetfulness of the cruel Ideal, and of Sin,
> To this martyr who has come to share the litter
> Where the happy cattle of humanity sleeps.

The tone was established. While J. K. Huysmans was Satanizing,
Ducasse, the bogus Count of Lautréamont, was filling his *Songs of
Maldoror* with blasphemies garlanded by sado-Satanic horrors:
"While the north wind was whistling through the pines, the Creator
opened his door amid the darkness, and let in a pederast."
    The vogue had begun with a pornographer and most annoying
philosopher, Donatien de Sade, a depraved aristocrat whose de-
bauched life lent his writings the smell of truth. One asks what any

of them, the "popes" of Surrealism or priests of fashion, could and can find worthy in descriptions such as: "He shatters crucifixes, images of the Virgin and the Eternal Father, shits on the debris, and sets the whole lot on fire."[19] After Homer, Aeschylus, Shakespeare, and so on, we come to this. For obscure reasons that some call the "fascination of Evil," Sade continues to keep our thinkers busy.

The sickness was no more exclusively French than the clap was exclusively Neapolitan. The English, who were as bored as the French, invented the "Gothic" novel—castles haunted by the damned, oubliettes from which waft up the groans of lost souls, lecherous monks, chlorotic fiancées delivered into the arms of sulfurous lovers who bay insults at the moon. The whole English nineteenth century is possessed by Satan: Mary Shelley's *Frankenstein* appeared in 1818 and the public did not shy away in disgust; Bram Stoker's *Dracula* came out in 1897. Both of them were runaway successes. From here we move on to Germany, which with its *Faust* did not lag behind, and to Russia, which in the next century was to have its "real" Devil, Grigory Yefimovich Rasputin, a monk immune to arsenic and bullets. Not to mention the other devils: the redeemer Ulyanov or Lenin, the cop of cops Dzerzhinski, inventor of the Cheka, and the defrocked Dzhugashvilii, or Stalin—a veritable college of demons. In the United States, Poe was exploring, not without hamming it up sometimes, the hell of an alcoholic imagination in which the Devil assumed the successive masks of the Red Death, the Imp of the Perverse, and, in the end, in "Silence," of Poe himself (" 'Listen to me,' said the Demon, as he placed his hand upon my head. 'The region of which I speak is a dreary region in Libya, by the borders of the river Zaire. . . .' "). Melville dispatched his legendary Captain Ahab off in pursuit of Evil, the fabulous white whale called Moby Dick. And Conrad's whole work was an endless analysis of the Fall, not to be concluded even in the famous passage from *Heart of Darkness* when the smuggler Kurtz cries out on his deathbed, "The horror! The horror!"

The whole of Western culture—literary, artistic, and musical—has been rocked by this obsession with a liberating Devil. What the culture is being liberated from is a stubborn religion, insipid or despotic political powers, and of course boredom—but, above all, from the mundane, the worst plague that God in his thoughtless cruelty ever inflicted upon humans.

Satan is thus the accomplice of the industrial era's every Faust, from the richest to the most disenfranchised. He now appears, as Papini ironically writes, "under a whole new light: as a liberator . . . of humanity. Far from breaking divine law, he wants to redeem the children of mankind from at least one of the consequences of Sin. Besides the spiritual Redeemer, Satan is also the material Redeemer, the friend of man." This is where true Satanism lies—not in the hypocrisies of Californian sects but in those of the elite.

In a singular inversion of roles, after having been born as the defender of the absolute power dreamed of by Zoroastrian priests, the Devil became the ultimate antisocial agent, the Curser of Work. The pillar of Christian theologies, he became by his very existence the destroyer of democracies and, as Cicero wrote two thousand years ago, about superstition, the precursor of totalitarianism. It is for this reason the he has so many friends.

While monotheisms maintained the belief in the existence of Satan, there was some hope that they could control him. However, the Satanist mythology that is being created at the popular level is beyond the control of any organized religion. The popular imagination is, indeed, infinitely more powerful than any church. After having created the figure of Satan, then having had the mythology assumed by not the least of modern philosophers, the religions now find themselves in the position of apprentice sorcerer. Anti-Marxist by definition because they are antimaterialist and spiritualist, they are maintaining a fundamentally pagan myth, which was once a totalitarian tool and is, today, an essentially nihilistic portent of revolution. What I am saying is that religions upholding the myth of Satan are sawing through the worm-riddled branch they themselves are supported by—the social order.

Should we believe in the reality of Satan, in possession, in the so-called paranormal phenomena that are so abundantly—and smugly—described by Satanists, exorcists, and supernaturalists of every ilk? It must be said that the principal reason for believing in Satan is possession, and that possession all too closely resembles the hysteria cases whose explication was the cause of Jean-Martin Charcot's fame. Hysteria is possession: the premonitory mood swings, the loss of consciousness, the contortions eloquently described by the term "clownism" (and so amenable to on-screen gesticulations), the bouts of passion "during which the subject mimics scenes pleasant or painful, erotic or violent," the catatonia. . . .[20] Demonic possession is no more than the expression of hysterical crisis, and proof lies in the fact that it mainly strikes the frustrated, children, and adolescents. If demonic possession were at all real, one would have to ask why it afflicts not secretaries of state, famous writers, or TV hosts but, instead, only individuals of average intellectual and psychological status. Either that or Satan is a laughable enemy who only consorts with the weak.

Of course, Martin Luther thought he had seen the Devil and threw an inkwell at his head, but that wasn't possession—it was more like a hallucination. Without in the least disparaging either his intelligence or his huge corpus of theological and philosophical work, it is well known that Luther was an exalted and visionary character, and that he was very high-strung.

What remains is the supernatural as such. Can immaterial forces manifest themselves, and if they can, do they include evil powers? The topic has been the subject of many a work, although no one is in a position to settle it conclusively. To this day, there is not a single piece of concrete proof for the intervention of forces, benevolent or malevolent, into history; the most famous historical incidents can be explained without recourse to the supernatural. Indeed, the near totality of testimony in favor of the reality of mysterious phenomena is of interest only to a small number of individuals.

Some—and, as I said at the start of these pages, the best-intentioned among them—have thought it possible to detect the work of Satan in the Nazi camps. Through an obscure and probably shameful process of reasoning, some Christians tell themselves that God turned away from sinful nations, particularly the Jewish nation, and delivered them over to Satan. In 1941, when the United States was largely aware of the persecutions then going on in Germany— persecutions that affected Christians as well as Jews—personalities such as Henry Ford, Charles Lindbergh, and Father Coughlin, the founder of the Christian Front and a notorious anti-Semite, as well as William Ward Ayer, pastor of New York's Calvary Baptist Church, and many others continued to publicly praise the Nazis' anti-Semitic policies—to the point that an editorial in the periodical *The Churchman* condemned them by name, vilifying "Lindbergh's anti-Semitic brutality" and declaring that many Christians' anti-Semitism denied them "the right to the name of Christians."[21]

The West never managed to drive from its memory the fabricated words, hate-filled and forged (and thus truly Satanic), that the evangelist Matthew put into the mouth of the Jews: "His blood be on us and on our children!" To think that the death camps—where we sometimes forget that political prisoners, homosexuals, and Gypsies died, too—represented God's revenge is to express the most outrageous and bestial hatred. It is the worst insult to the millions dead in the gulags, who were not Jewish, to Africa's Ibos and Iks, who weren't either, and to the Cambodians slaughtered in the name of the ideology of Pol Pot, a criminal today protected by the United Nations. Satan has nothing to do with any of this, and God even less: it is human idiocy alone.

As I write this, the shadow of Satan is rising again over Europe. A recent poll showed that one German in three thought that there had been a "good side" to Nazism and 4 percent of Germans believed that what happened to the Jews was their own fault. Another poll revealed that nearly 10 percent of Italians believe that the Shoah was an invention, and that nearly one third of them believe that Italian Jews are not really Italians.[22] Have we learned nothing? Don't the people who talk this way realize that tomorrow *they* might be persecuted? Don't they realize that each of them can instantly be demonized by his enemy?

The human being is responsible for history, and the intrusions of religion into history have all, without a single exception from the Crusades on, been disastrous. "Man can perhaps be fooled only by himself," wrote Emerson. Believing that one defends one's God with the sword, humanity has spilled oceans of blood—it has done Satan's work and offended, as deeply as possible, the God of mercy and life. My deep conviction is that every religious war is essentially Satanic, as is every act of exclusion. My conviction is that it is profoundly Satanic to believe in the Devil.

We live under the sign of a nonexistent deity cobbled together twenty-six centuries ago by power-hungry Iranian priests. We live under the sign of Satan. Is this our destiny—are we to let an imaginary monster devour us forever?

Notes

Introduction

1. "La Contagion du Hijab" in *Jeune Afrique* (Mar. 26–Apr. 1, 1992).

1. The Ambiguous Demons of Oceania

1. H. Breuil and R. Lantier, *Les Hommes de la pierre ancienne* (Paris: Payot, 1959).
2. See Georges Dumézil, *Les Dieux souverains des Indo-Européens* (Paris: Gallimard, 1977).
3. Alfred Métraux, *Easter Island: A Stone Age Civilization of the Pacific*, trans. Michael Bullock (Oxford: Oxford University Press, 1957).
4. Paul Bahn and John Flenley, *Easter Island, Earth Island* (London: Thames and Hudson, 1992). The authors point out that the decline of the island's civilization was caused by the exhaustion of its raw materials, especially its forest wealth—something that should temper romantic ideas about the innate wisdom of primitive peoples.
5. Bronislaw Malinowski, *Argonauts of the Western Pacific* (London: Routledge and Sons, 1922).
6. Vittorio Maconi, *Australie et Melanesie* (Paris: Atlas, 1980).
7. In "Three Essays on the Social Life of Primitives," however, Malinowski writes: "The myth as it exists in a savage community, that is, in its primitive form, is not only a story one tells, but also a lived reality." The sentence being liable to misinterpretation, it seems to me that it should be completed with the addition of "a reality lived in the imagination."

8. Bronislaw Malinowski, *The Sexual Life of Savages in North-Western Melanesia* (New York: Harcourt, Brace & World, 1929).

9. Quoted in Geza Roheim, *The Panic of the Gods* (New York: Harper and Row, 1972).

10. Carl Strehlow, *Die Arandta-und-Loritja Stamme in Zentral-Australien* (Frankfurt, 1907–08).

11. Sir James Frazer, *The Golden Bough* (New York: Macmillan, 1922).

12. Maurice Godelier, *La production des grands hommes* (Paris: Fayard, 1982); Gilbert H. Herdt, *Guardians of the Flute: Idioms of Masculinity* (New York: McGraw-Hill, 1981).

13. Frazer, *The Golden Bough.*

14. Ibid.

15. The information in this section is drawn mainly from a study by Deszo Benedek, the most complete available on the Yamis, *The Yami of Irala: The World and I* (A Publication of the Washington Times Corporation, September 1987), and from Krista Weidner's *The Legends of Irala* (Research—Pennsylvania State University, vol. 6, no. 3, Sept. 1985). One Yami rite should be mentioned in particular, the sacrifice by torment of a lizard, whose unjust sufferings are meant to make it want to avenge itself on the person, thief, or evil spirit the sacrificer thinks has done him harm.

16. The information about the Nagas is drawn mainly from *The Nagas* (Geneva: Olizanne, 1990), by Julian Jacobs with Alan MacFarlane, Sarah Harrison, and Anita Herle. Opinions on the linguistic group of the Nagas differ; for instance, according to the article on the "Naga" in the *Encyclopaedia Britannica* (1980), their languages belong to the Tibeto-Birman group.

2. India: Spared from Evil

1. V. L. Serosevskii, *Yakuty* (Petrograd, 1896), cited by Joseph Campbell in *Primitive Mythology: The Masks of God* (New York: Viking-Penguin, 1959).

2. J. P. Mallory, *In Search of the Indo-Europeans: Language, Archaeology and Myth* (London: Thames & Hudson, 1989); Sir Mortimer Wheeler, *The Indus Civilization* (Cambridge: Cambridge University Press, 1960).

3. Wendy Doniger O'Flaherty, trans., *The Rig-Veda* (Harmondsworth, Eng.: Penguin, 1981).

4. Mircea Eliade, *A History of Beliefs and Religious Ideas*, vol. I: *From the Stone Age to the Eleusinian Mysteries* (Chicago: University of Chicago Press, 1955).

5. In this respect, Mott T. Greene's excellent study on *soma, Natural Knowledge in Preclassical Antiquity* (Baltimore: Johns Hopkins University Press, 1992) should be mentioned. Greene shows that the beverage called *soma* in India and *haoma* in Iran—it was consumed during religious ceremonies, led to mass drunkenness, and occupied a primordial position in Indo-Iranian Vedism—was not extracted from one particular plant but from various plants possessing the same hallucinogenic properties. He notes that the Vedas offer a list of substitute plants in case the original could not be obtained. The research of numerous botanists curious

about this beverage has claimed that it could as easily have been milkweed beer or rhubarb wine, though especially after R. Gordon Wasson's classic study, *Soma: Divine Mushroom of Immortality* (New York: Harcourt Brace Jovanovich, 1973), it seems most likely that it was our fly agaric, whose juice contains a powerful hallucinogen. Greene suggests that it could also have been ergotin extracted from rye ergot, an alkaloid powerful enough to have unleashed the attacks of delirium that beset, accidentally, it seems, the priests and nuns of Loudun in the well-known affair of the Devils of Loudun.

6. *The Rig-Veda* (supra, n. 3).
7. Ibid.
8. Walter A. Faiservis, Jr., *The Origins of Oriental Civilization* (New York: New American Library, 1959).
9. André Bareau, *En Suivant Bouddha* (Paris: Philippe Lebaud, 1985).
10. Etienne Lamotte, "La Légende du Bouddha," *Revue de l'histoire des religions* 134 (1947–48), pp. 37–71.

3. China and Japan: Exorcism through Writing

1. *The Tibetan Book of the Dead*, trans. and commentary Francesca Fremantle and Chogyam Trungpa (Boston: Shambhala Dragon Books, 1987).
2. Ibid.
3. Mircea Eliade, *A History of Beliefs and Religious Ideas, vol. II: From Gautama Buddha to the Triumph of Christianity* (Chicago: University of Chicago Press, 1955).
4. J. G. Anderson, *Children of the Yellow Earth*; Kwang-shi Shang, *The Archaeology of Ancient China*, both cited in Eliade, ibid.
5. J. P. Mallory, *In Search of the Indo-Europeans: Language, Archaeology and Myth* (London: Thames and Hudson, 1989). In this vast overview, Mallory cites all the evidence leading us to believe that Indo-Europeans of so-called Andronovo culture settled in western Siberia during the Bronze Age. He also, however, points out the limits of contemporary knowledge: nothing is known, for instance, about what relationship there might have been between the Indo-Europeans of the Andronovo culture and Iranians and Indo-Iranians from other regions. The fact of cultural contact between these "first" Siberians and Indo-European religions is purely speculative.
6. René Grousset, *Histoire de la Chine* (Paris: Fayard, 1942).
7. Eliade (supra n.3).
8. *Mencius*, cited in ibid.
9. Two noted mycologists, R. Gordon Wasson, author of *Mushrooms, Russia and History*, 2 vols (New York, 1959), and René Heim, author of *Champignons toxiques et hallucinogènes* (Paris: Boubée, 1963; repr. 1978), have reported on the ritual consumption of mushrooms among Siberian and northern Asian peoples. This consumption leads to states of delirium involving trance and orgies.
10. Even in the twentieth century, when communication should allow for extremely tight political control, the "levels of intensity" of Maoism, then communism, vary

significantly from one province to another, tending to become lower the farther one goes from Beijing.

11. *Les Entretiens de Confucius*, trans. and with an intro. and notes by Pierre Ryckmans (Paris: Gallimard, 1987).

12. Wu-chi Liu, *A Short History of Confucian Philosophy* (London, 1955).

13. Asoka was also the first to create a "social security" system in the hopes of establishing a true *dharma*, an ideal rule of Buddhist inspiration, in his realm. Free medical care was extended to everyone in the kingdom—even to animals.

14. The Nestorians were a heretical group whose leader, Nestorius, the bishop of Constantinople, refused to accept Mary's epithet of *Theotokos*, "Mother of God," since she was merely human and it is impossible that God were born of a human. According to Nestorius, her epithet ought to have been *Christotokos*, "Mother of Christ." He also argued that insofar as he was human, Jesus possessed a complete and independent personality; Nestorius' enemies, the Alexandrines, conversely, reduced Jesus to "a pure instrument of the Logos." Nestorius and his followers were excommunicated without a hearing at the Council of Chalcedon in 451; yet this did little to dampen their evangelical ardor; contrary to legend it was they, not Thomas or Bartholomew, who brought the Gospels to Asia. Their missions extended not only to Syria, Armenia, and Persia, but beyond to Sri Lanka and India, whose Malabar coast was to count some four thousand Nestorian Christians, later to be called "Christians of Thomas" (from the fact that at the end of the eighth century their ranks were swelled by the refugees who followed Thomas, the bishop of Kana, to India). They even reached Beijing.

15. It was, in fact, claimed during the Han Dynasty that the Buddha was a reincarnation of Lao-Tzu; several emperors had Buddha and Lao-Tzu cults placed beside each other in temples.

16. Kenneth K. S. Ch'en, *Buddhism in China: A Historical Survey* (New York, 1964).

17. Ibid.

18. René Sieffert, *Les Religions du Japon* (Paris: Presses Universitaires de France, 1968).

19. Ibid.

20. Jean Herbert, *Les Dieux nationaux du Japon* (Paris: Albin Michel, 1965).

21. J. M. Martin, *Le Shintoisme ancien* (Paris: Maisonneuve, 1988).

22. Ibid.

4. Zoroaster, the First Ayatollahs, and the True Birth of the Devil

1. I am relying on the theory that Marija Gimbutas proposed in 1963 ("The Indo-Europeans: Archaeological Problems," *American Anthropologist* 65), which is widely accepted by historians. The enigma of the fusion between India and Europe that came about in the third and second millennia B.C. remains to be cleared up.

2. Nothing would prevent us from supposing—although nothing proves it—that the Indo-European peoples who occupied Iran in the third millennium B.C. were in fact descendants of peoples who had lived there since the eighth millennium but

had since migrated elsewhere. (This double migration pattern holds true for the Celts). Still, the hypothesis could only be proven by archaeological evidence, which has yet to be unearthed.

3. Georges Dumézil believes that the Zoroastrian reorganization of the pantheon was the result of historical pressure: "The gods of the other levels [that is, Indra and the Nasatyas], who protected different behaviors and different ideals, and who thus were a threat to the attempt to reform both the violent, turbulent military aristocracy and the greedy and apathetic peasantry, were rejected, condemned, and pilloried" (*Les Dieux souverains des Indo-Européens* [Paris: Gallimard, 1977]). This closely recalls the conflict of some European monarchies with both rebellious minor nobles and uprising peasants.

4. Plato, *Alcibiades* (Cambridge, Mass.: Loeb Classical Library, 1923).

5. Plutarch, "Numa," 4, in *Lives of Famous Men* (Berkeley: University of California Press, 1974).

6. Pliny, *Natural History*, 7.15.3, trans, H. Rackam (Cambridge, Mass.: Harvard University Press, 1938).

7. Zoroaster's teachings have come down to us through the *Avesta*s, also called the *Zend-Avesta*, the sole remnants of a body of cosmogonic, legislative, and liturgical writing that seems to have originally been much more extensive (it has been claimed that it was largely destroyed in the course of Alexander's conquest of Iran). The available *Avesta*s were reconstituted from fragments between the third and seventh centuries A.D., under the Sassanids. They are made up of five parts and include the *Gatha*s, which belong to the central section, and the *Yasna*, the canon that describes the ritual preparation and consumption of the sacred drink *haoma*. The *Gatha*s are hymns written by Zoroaster and supposedly passed down verbatim. The other four parts are the *Visp-Rat*, a collection of homages to Zoroastrian religious leaders, the *Vendidad* or *Videvdat*, which records Zoroastrian civil and religious law, the *Yasht*s, twenty-one hymns to various heroes, including the angels or *yazata*s, and the *Khurda Avesta*, a collection of lesser texts.

8. Brahmanism, which derives from pre-Zoroastrian Vedism, produced a caste system and society dominated, to their overwhelming benefit, by Brahmans.

9. Especially the *Histories* of Herodotus, the *Persians* of Ctesias of Cnide (as they have come down to us through Photius), the *Anabasis* and *Hellenics* of Xenophon, and, to a lesser extent, Berosius's *History of Babylon*, all of which discuss the history of Iran. See René Henry, *Ctesias, la Perse, l'Inde, et les Sommaires de Photius* (Paris: 1947).

10. Mircea Eliade, "Zarathustra and Iranian Religion," in *A History of Beliefs and Religious Ideas* (Chicago: University of Chicago Press, 1955).

11. No one knows what *haoma* really was. John Allegro's *The Sacred Mushroom and the Cross* (1971) seems to indicate that *haoma* (which appears to be similar to the *soma* of northern Asian tribes) was the juice of *Amanita phalloides*, but the research of V. Pavlovna and R. Gordon Wasson (*Mushrooms, Russia and History* [New York, 1959]) and Roger Heim (*Les Champignons toxiques et hallucinogènes* [Paris: Boubée, 1978]) instead point to *Amanita muscaria*. Mott T. Greene's more in-depth study, *Natural Knowledge in Preclassical Antiquity* (Baltimore: Johns

Hopkins University Press, 1992), considerably enlarges the candidate pool. He concludes that this substance was rye ergot, a powerful hallucinogen familiar in the West first because of the seventeenth-century "Devils of Loudun" affair, and second because of its modern popularity in the purified form of LSD-25.

12. Isaiah refers to this legend in his description of the kingdom of Elom's fall and the world's descent into primal chaos: "And wild beasts shall meet with hyenas, the satyr shall cry to his fellow; yea, there shall the night hag [Lilith] alight, and find for herself a resting place" (Isaiah 34:14). In his study on the Lilith legend Jacques Bril notes that she can be found in Job 18:15 of the Jerusalem Bible (*Lilith ou la mère obscure* [Paris: Payot, 1981]).

13. In the third century A.D., another Iranian, Mani, took Zoroaster's thinking farther: since life is nothing but a trial in which the human being is continually subject to Evil's assaults, it follows that our earthly existence makes us vulnerable to impurity. Evil can only come from matter; demons only have a purchase on us because we are made of flesh and blood. Once in the realm of the spirit, we are liberated. Matter, therefore, is bad, spirit pure. The seeds of Gnosticism were planted.

14. The relationship has troubled more than one commentator; there have even been attempts at claiming that the "convergences" between Mazdaism and Judeo-Christianity are due to a post-Christian influence on Mazdaism dating from as late as the Sassanid era, which lasted from the second to the seventh centuries. "These attempts," writes the *Enclyclopedia Brittanica*, "have been discredited." It is quite clear that the similarities long predate Christianity; it is not Christianity that informed Mazdaism but the reverse.

15. Dumézil, *Les Dieux Souverains des Indo-Européens* (supra n.3).

16. M. Molé, *La Légende de Zoroastre selon les textes Pehlevis* (Paris: Presses Universitaires de France, 1967).

17. Jean de Menasce, "Zoroastre," *Encyclopaedia Univeralis*. Like Mircea Eliade, Menasce advances that Zoroaster's overhaul was not as radical as it seems, and that the reform was not inherently dualistic. Yet this argument only underscores how radical Zoroastrianism really was, since it is only after Zoroaster, never before, that this dualism appears. The Vedic pantheon was simplified and "radicalized," with the Mithra-Varuna duo alone remaining in Heaven while the other gods became their antagonists.

18. The extent of Iranian tolerance was remarkable, even if the kings themselves were all Zoroastrians. Cyrus granted the Jews, then in Babylonian captivity, permission to return home and to rebuild Jerusalem. Darius personally authorized the reconstruction of the Temple there, and Ataxerxes I, the protector of Ezra and Nehemiah, allowed Judaism to flourish (as we know, however, the tolerance was not mutual). Nor were the Jews its only beneficiaries; in one of his edicts, Darius ordered the satrap of the province or *paramainos* of Magnesia-on-Meander, Gadatas, to respect the local sanctuary of Apollo. The Greek oracles in general were inviolable all over the empire.

5. Mesopotamia: The Appearance of Sin

1. *The Babylonian Gilgamesh Epic*, ed. Andrew George (yet unpublished), contains previously unpublished fragments. Two versions of the epic exist, the ancient or "Babylonian" and the Ninevite. On the nature, number, and value of the fragments, see Jean Bottéro, *L'Epopée de Gilgamesh* (Paris: Gallimard, 1992).

2. It is still unclear when the Semites first appeared in the area, but they seem to have been there even before the Sumerians. Given that not even the birthplace of the proto-Semitic languages has been identified, it seems that the question is nowhere near being answered. See Georges Roux, *La Mésopotamie—essai d'histoire politique, économique et culturelle* (Paris: Seuil, 1985).

3. Jean Bottéro, *Mésopotamie—l'écriture, la raison, les dieux* (Paris: Gallimard, 1987). The first known writing was apparently in a language "isolated . . . from all other known languages or families of languages, as different from Akkadian as Tibetan is from French." Bottéro relates that in the folklore of Assyrian scholarship, two venerable academics once came to striking each other with their umbrellas over this point.

4. Ibid.

5. Marduk's promotion at Babylon was not mirrored at other religious centers, such as the Sumerian cities of Erech, Nippur, Larsa, Ur, and Kish.

6. E. Cassim, *La Splendeur divine: introduction à l'étude de la mentalité babylonienne* (Paris, 1968).

7. Manfred Lürker, *Lexikon der Gotter und Dämonen* (Munich: Alfred Kramer, 1984).

8. Cited by Henrietta McCall in *Mesopotamian Myths* (London: British Museum, 1990). The version referred to here is the "Armana" version, after its discovery at Tell el-Armana in Egypt, where no doubt it had been left in the course of Assurbanipal's Egyptian campaign.

9. Adapted from Garelli and Leibovici's translation, in *La Naissance du monde selon Akkad*, which Eliade cites.

10. Despite this striking piece of evidence against the Oedipus complex theory, psychoanalysis has never taken the contributions of anthropology and religious history into account. Thus, Bronislaw Malinowski's demolition of the famous theory remains largely—and studiously—ignored by the partisans of psychoanalysis.

11. Alexander Eliot, Mircea Eliade, Joseph Campbell, and Detlef J. Lauf, *L'Univers fantastique des mythes* (Paris: Presses de la Connaissance, 1976).

12. Bottéro (supra n.3).

13. Lürker (supra n.7).

14. Ibid.

15. John Boardman, et al., "The Assyrian and Babylonian Empires and Other States of the Near East from the Eighth to Sixth Centuries B.C.," *The Cambridge Ancient History*, vol. 3 (Cambridge University Press, 1992).

16. Cécile Michel, "L'Administration du palais et ses archives," *Les Dossiers d'archéologie* 171 (May 1992).

17. Ibid.

6. The Celts: Thirty-five Centuries without the Devil

1. The idea that the Celts fanned out in a set number of "waves," an idea that dominated history from Edward Lhwyd in the seventh century to the beginning of the twentieth, has been discredited. As Colin Renfrew notes in *Archaeology and Language: The Puzzle of Indo-European Languages* (New York: Cambridge University Press, 1987), the term "Celt" can be understood in eight senses: in the Roman sense, in the sense of those who called themselves "Celts," in the sense of a linguistic group, in the sense of an archaeological complex in west-central Europe, in the sense of an artistic style, in the sense of a state of mind, in the sense of medieval Ireland, and in the sense of the whole Celtic heritage. If one were to persist in talking about "waves," one would never know who one was talking about. Renfrew also reminds us that we should also not overlook the Celts from periods much earlier than the Roman. This is the course I have taken here: to accept, based on the best of our knowledge, that the Urn-Field people, the proto-Celts, and the Celts (in the traditional, fluid sense) all share the same origins.

2. Duncan Norton-Taylor, *The Celts* (New York: Time-Life, 1974). The term *Fir Bolg*, which refers to the people who occupied the territory corresponding to present-day Belgium, could thus be the origin of the name "Belgae"; the Fir Bolg who so fiercely fought the second-wave Celtic invasions in the fourth and third centuries B.C. were the invaders' predecessors and "ancestors." The proto-Celts are generally referred to according to the cultures that characterized them: the Battle-Ax People, the Campaniform People (from the bell-like shape of their clay goblets), and the Urn-Field People (from their habit of keeping the ashes of the dead in necropolises of urns).

3. The art of the La Tène period (from the name of a site on the bank of Lake Neuchatel) expresses a remarkably original aesthetic, rich in decorative elements, with sinuous spirals and arabesques that call to mind the arts of Asia and the East.

4. John Sharkey, *Celtic Mysteries* (London: Thames and Hudson, 1985).

5. The Edda poems in the collection of the Royal Copenhagen Library were written in the second half of the eighth century. The last person to have owned them privately, Bishop Brynjolf Sveinson of Iceland, thought they were the work of the twelfth-century Icelandic scholar Saemund Sigfusson, although their style would indicate an earlier writer.

6. Sharkey, *Celtic Mysteries* (supra n.4).

7. Theodor Mommsen, *The History of Rome*, vol. 4: *The Gaulish Provinces*, trans. W. P. Dickson (London: J. M. Dent, 1920).

8. Norton-Taylor, *The Celts* (supra n.2).

9. Ibid.

10. Sharkey, *Celtic Mysteries*.

11. Ibid.

12. Georges Dumézil, *Loki* (Paris: Flammarion, 1986).

13. H. R. Ellis Davidson, *Gods and Myths of Northern Europe* (London: Pelican Books, 1964).

14. Alexander Eliot, Mircea Eliade, Joseph Campbell, and Detlef J. Lauf, *L'Univers fantastique des mythes* (Paris: Presses de la Connaissance, 1976).
15. Since our concern is with a theme basic to the Devil—salvation and the fate of the world, or, in other words, eschatology—it would be useful to examine Ragnarök further. The Celtic Ragnarök is definitely *one* end of the world, but it is not *the* end of the world as it occurs in the three monotheisms. After the titanic struggles, "a new earth emerges, green, beautiful, and fertile as it had never been before. A new sun, more brilliant than its predecessor, will reassume its course in the sky," as Eliade writes. (This idea is identical to the one that gained currency under ancient Egypt's New Empire.)

The Celtic end of the world is only the conclusion of one great cycle, and it is followed by the beginning of another. If Loki plays the major role in it, that of a belligerent troublemaker, Eliade writes, it is because "the Germanic myths maintain the doctrine of heroic gods, by which combat preserves the order of the world but also destroys it before the dawn of a new universe." It is good to fight, since fighting keeps the powers in balance and allows the world to be renewed. One echo of this belief can be found in the Mesoamerican practice of potlatch, when during certain feasts all earthenware is destroyed and new sets acquired.
16. The ancient Arabic horse-god mentioned in inscriptions at Palmyra and elsewhere was called Aesir; meanwhile, Loki of the Aesir was the father of the fabled horse Sleipnir.
17. Dumézil, *Loki* (supra n.12).
18. Dumézil expresses amazement, real or feigned, at the marked similarity among myths Celtic, Germanic, and Ossetian or Scythian, and thus he entices the reader into accepting the theory that these various branches of Indo-Aryanism had, after centuries of differentiation, each retained the ancient myths in an almost unaltered form.
19. Mircea Eliade, *A History of Religious Ideas and Beliefs*, vol. 2: *From Gautama Buddha to the Triumph of Christianity* (Chicago: University of Chicago Press, 1979).
20. Jan de Vries has made an extensive study of Loki's literary sources. In the work, de Vries points out that his abasement is a later phenomenon, and that originally Loki was above all a thief: he stole the Apples of Eternal Youth from the gods (much like Hercules seizing the Golden Apples of the Sun), made off with Thor's belt and gloves, and pilfered Freya's necklace. According to Dumézil, this archetype of the thief comes from very early Indo-European mythology; one offshoot of it produced the Hellenic thief-god Hermes.
21. Delaney, *Legends of the Celts* (London: Grafton Books, 1991).
22. Eliade (supra n.19).
23. Delaney, *Legends of the Celts*.
24. G. Sanayev in Dumézil, *Loki* (supra n.12).
25. "Branwen, the Daughter of Llyr," in Delaney, *Legends of the Celts* (supra n.21).
26. The Greeks and Romans called them *druidai, druides, drysidae,* and *dryadae.* Duncan Norton-Taylor writes in *The Celts*, "Pliny the Elder, who occupied the post of procurator of Gaul in the first century A.D., noted that the Greek word for 'oak'

was *drus*, and suggested that perhaps their name derived from that of the tree." In numerous European languages, Norton-Taylor adds, the root *dru* means "strong" (as in the French *dur*), whereas *wid* and some of its variants generally relate to "knowledge." In that the druids both were erudite and carried out some of their rites under oak trees, it remains difficult to settle the etymology of their name.

27. Caesar, *The Conquest of Gaul*, trans. S. A. Handford (Harmondsworth, Eng.: Penguin Books, 1978).

28. Norton-Taylor, *The Celts* (supra n.2); "Muscla Ulad," *Mediaeval and Modern Irish Series* 13 (Dublin, 1941).

29. *La Saga des Feroiens*, trans. Jean Renaud, preface by Régis Boyer (Paris: Aubier-Montaigne, 1983).

30. One could argue that the individualism introduced by Romanticism in the nineteenth century was a consequence of the rediscovery of Celtic culture and myths long veiled behind the classicist cult of the Greco-Roman civilization.

31. Davidson, *Gods and Myths of Northern Europe* (supra n.13).

32. *Grand Atlas Historique* (Paris: Éditions du Livre de Paris-Stock, 1968).

33. Ibid. Nevertheless, England was partially Christianized in the seventh century, with three churches in existence there—the Breton Church in Wales, the Scotch-Irish Church, and the Saxon Church, the only one of the three with close ties to the Church of Rome, thanks to the first archbishop of Canterbury, Saint Augustine, who was sent there by Pope Gregory the Great.

34. Régis Boyer, *Yggdrasil, la religion des anciens Scandinaves* (Paris: Payot, 1992).

7. Greece: The Devil Driven Out by Democracy

1. This is the thesis, taken to its extreme, of Colin Renfrew (*Archaeology and Language: The Puzzle of Indo-European Origins* [New York: Cambridge University Press, 1987]). Based on linguistic evidence, Renfrew suggests that Indo-Europeans from Anatolia had occupied Greece by the middle of the seventh millennium B.C. J. P. Mallory (*In Search of the Indo-Europeans: Language, Archaeology and Myth* [London: Thames and Hudson, 1989]) modifies this theory by granting that Anatolians had occupied the Greek mainland by the date Renfrew claims, but he cites other studies to suggest that the invasion also took place from the other direction, the Balkans.

2. Herodotus, *Histories* 1.146, trans. David Greene (Chicago: University of Chicago Press, 1987).

3. Georges Roux, *La Mesopotamie: essai d'histoire politique, économique et culturelle* (Paris: Seuil, 1985).

4. Euripides, *The Supplicants* 1.400.

5. Dio Chrysostom, "Ninth Discourse," cited by Léonce Paquet in *Les Cyniques Grecs* (Paris: Livre de Poche, 1992).

6. Paquet, *Les Cyniques*.

7. Euripides, *The Supplicants* 1.215.

8. André Bernand, *Sorciers grecs* (Paris: Fayard, 1991).

9. Plato, *The Laws* 908d.

10. Plato, *Phaedo* 81b.

11. The historian Irving Stone has shown that Socrates participated in two attempts at establishing tyranny through a coup d'état, and that it was his fellow citizens' legitimate suspicion that he was plotting a third that brought him before the judges. What sort of tyranny Socrates hoped for can only be inferred, for example, from the near tyranny of the Four Hundred (a coup d'état in which, significantly enough, his disciple and favorite Alcibiades took part). Power in this tyranny would probably have been in the hands of a co-opted council (Irving Stone, *The Trial of Socrates* [Boston: Little, Brown, 1988]). Plato's ideal city as described in *The Republic* was to be ruled by an authoritarian regime. For the disciple as for the master, obviously, all recourse to forces irrational, individual, or outside collective law—the very forces witchcraft claims to invoke—was an abomination. Socrates and Plato were not inveighing against superstition so much as against the individual practice of religion.

12. Plato, *The Laws* 909a–b.

13. Plato, *Eutyphron* 3b–c.

14. Jacqueline de Romilly, *Pourquoi la Grèce?* (Paris: Fallois, 1992).

15. Bernand, *Sorciers grecs* (supra n.8).

16. Alexandre Kojève, *Essai d'une histoire raisonnée de la philosophie païenne*, vol. 3: *La Philosophie héllenistique et les néo-platoniciens* (Paris: Gallimard, 1973).

17. "[T]he Stoics did not (after Aristotle) accept that there was any true interaction or irreversible opposition [between opposites] either in heaven [the cosmos] or in the Primordial Fire" before the cosmos existed (ibid.).

18. Sir James Frazer, *The Golden Bough* (New York: Macmillan, 1922).

19. Mircea Eliade, *A History of Beliefs and Religious Ideas*, vol. 1: *From the Stone Age to the Eleusinian Mysteries* (Chicago: University of Chicago Press, 1979).

20. Ibid.

8. Rome: The Devil Banned

1. This priceless expression of incredulous indignation by Fowler, a British historian of the early twentieth century, is cited by Pierre Boyancé in *Culte des muses chez les philosophes Grecs* (Paris, 1936).

2. "The character of Nero is far from what it appears to be in traditional history, the source of the hackneyed clichés that are popularized in novels and films. Though depicted as a monster from hell, he was adored by the common people of Rome. Though he was depicted as a hysterical clown, a buffoon with a crown, few have understood the intent that underlay his flamenco behavior or admitted that his administration was, if not always a comfort to the Senate, often quite visionary" (Lucien Jerphagnon, *Vivre et philosopher sous les Césars* [Toulouse: Édouard Privat, 1980]).

3. The Romans did not have a written history until the second century B.C. The Greek legend is that Romulus and Remus were distant descendants of the Alban Dynasty established by Aeneas when he fled to Latium in the twelfth century B.C. and founded the city of Lavinium. The adjective "Alban" comes from the fact that

Aeneas's son Ascanius founded the city of Alba Longa. Archaeological evidence partly confirms this; the oldest remains of primitive Latin habitations were uncovered at Lavinium and in the Alban hills (T. Cornell and J. Matthews, *Atlas du monde romain* (Amsterdam: Editions du Fanal, 1986).

4. In the first century B.C., Dionysus of Halicarnassus, a Greek who lived in Rome, claimed that the Etruscans were indigenous Italic-speaking peoples of Italy. This theory is generally discounted, since there are too many reasons to believe Herodotus' version—for example, the striking resemblance between the hewn-rock Etruscan tombs near Lake Vico and Lydian and Lycian tombs in Turkey, or between the Etruscan and the Lydian religions.

5. This at least is a theory that Colin Renfrew cites—and does not refute—in *Archaeology and Language: The Puzzle of Indo-European Origins* (New York: Cambridge University Press, 1987).

6. On this score I recommend the "La Culte de Ceres à Rome" chapter in Pierre Boyancé, *Études sur la religion romain* (Paris, 1972). On one question alone— whether Ceres, who is clearly an avatar of the Great Goddess, is identifiable with other Greek and Latin goddesses—there are as many opinions as there are writers.

7. Dumézil, *Les Dieux souverains des Indo-Européens* (Paris: Gallimard, 1977).

8. Theodore Mommsen, *Histoire romaine*, vol. 1: *Des Commencements de Rome jusqu'aux guerres civiles* (Paris: Robert Laffont, 1985).

9. Ibid.

10. This very significant aspect of Roman religion is described in the opening part of the section on the subject in "Rome et l'Empire romain," *Encyclopaedia Universalis*.

11. Seneca, *Apprendre a vivre—lettres à Lucilius*, ed. and trans. Alain Golomb (Paris: Andrea, 1990).

12. Mommsen, *Histoire romaine* (supra n.8).

13. Exiled by the conspirators Marc Antony and Brutus after the assassination of Julius Caesar, he was murdered on December 7, 43 B.C., at Formos; his enemies had never forgiven him for the *Philippics*. His head and hands were cut off and sent to Rome, where they were displayed on the Rostral Column.

14. Jerome Carcopino, *Daily Life in Ancient Rome* [1941], trans. E. O. Lorimer (Harmondsworth, Eng.: Penguin, 1941).

15. Especially W. Ward Fowler, Cyril Bailey, Friedrich Pfister, and H. Wagenwoort, who according to Boyancé (in *Études sur la religion romaine* [supra n.6]) "have shown how sketchy the nineteenth-century vision of people like Mommsen really was." I would add the name of Arnold Toynbee, who sees world history as one long preparation for the coming of Christianity.

16. "Jupiter et son entourage," in Dumézil, *Les Dieux souverains des Indo-Européens* (supra n.7).

17. Carcopino, *Daily Life* (supra n.14).

18. Plutarch, *Lives* (New York: Modern Library, n.d.).

19. Boyancé discusses this hypothesis very objectively in "Fulvius Noblior et le Dieu ineffable," in *Études sur la religion romaine* (supra n.6).

20. Ibid.

21. Armand Delatte, "Les Doctrines pythagoriciennes des Livres de Numa," *Bulletin de l'Académie Royale de Belgique* (Brussels, 1936).

22. Plutarch writes that Numa attempted "the formulation of a calendar, not with absolute exactness, yet not without some scientific knowledge," and that what he really did was correct the gross errors in Romulus' calendar and add two more months to it. (Plutarch, *Lives*, supra n.18).

23. The whole story is much more complex, so I refer the reader to Boyancé (*Études sur la religion romaine* [supra n.6]), who analyses it with incisive clarity and scholarship.

24. Tacitus, *The Annals of Imperial Rome*, trans. Michael Grant (Harmondsworth, Eng.: Penguin, 1956), 1.73.

25. Mommsen, *Histoire romain* (supra n.8).

26. Georges Minois, *Histoire des enfers* (Paris: Fayard, 1991).

27. Ibid.

28. Perhaps it would help to mention here that no definitive text of Plato's dialogues was established until Thrasylus of Mende and Dercylides at the beginning of the Christian era, and that a Judaic influence cannot therefore be ruled out (see also chapter 7, note 14).

29. Friedrich Nietzsche, *Posthumous Fragments*, 1888–89 14; *Ecce homo* 8.

30. "Das geht auf das Mark," *Der Spiegel* 26 (1992).

31. Mommsen, *Histoire romain* (supra n.8).

32. "Les Romains, peuples de la fides," Boyancé, *Études sur la religion romaine* (supra n.6). After his secular definition of *pietas*, Boyancé paradoxically asserts that it isn't really "so to speak, secular" as much as it is religious. And this is true— but again, only in the Roman sense of the word "religious."

33. "Le mana dans la religion romaine," Boyancé, *Études sur la religion romaine* (supra n.6).

34. Lucien Jerphagnon, *Vivre et philosopher sous les Césars* (Toulouse: Édouard Privat, 1980).

35. See also ibid.

36. Among them Carcopino, who speaks of the "obvious though unformulated approval [that reveals] Tacitus as a disaffected pagan" ("The Decay of Traditional Religion," in *Daily Life* [supra n.14]).

37. Tacitus, *Annals*.

9. Egypt: Unthinkable Damnation

1. Adolf Erman and Ernst Ranke, *La Civilisation égyptienne* (Paris: Payot, 1963).

2. Ibid.

3. Ibid.

4. Erman and Ranke write: "The ferocity with which Akhenaten persecuted the ancient gods, especially the Theban ones, is unique in the history of fanaticism. The name and image of Amon were destroyed wherever they were found; Akhenaten's sectarians went as far as violating private tombs in order to vent their hatred of this detested god."

5. Claude Traunecker, *Les Dieux de l'Égypte* (Paris: Presses Universitaires de France, 1992).

6. Ibid.

7. Wallis E. A. Budge pointed this out in 1899, in his *Egyptian Religion: Egyptian Ideas of the Future Life* (repr. London: Arkana, 1987).

8. S. Morenz, *La Religion égyptienne* (Paris: Payot, 1962).

9. Traunecker, *Les Dieux de l'Égypte* (supra n.5).

10. Pascal Vernus and Jean Yoyotte, *Les Pharaons* (Paris: M. A. Éditions, 1988).

11. Freud built his theory upon the fact that the name Moses or Mose is Egyptian, which is true; it is a suffix found in many names (for example, Ahmose/Ahmosis, Thutmose/Thutmosis). As confirmed by Otto Harassowitz, *Lexikon der Ägyptologie*, 7 vols. (Wiesbaden, 1972–91), it means "child." Yet there is no doubt that it is incomplete and needs to be preceded by another name, that of a god such as Amon or Ptah; the name of the celestial power responsible for the child's birth would have been placed in the initial position. The important point is that neither Freud nor anyone who has ever argued this thesis provides the least conclusive proof that Amenophis IV was pharaoh during the time of Jewish oppression and the Exodus. All sources agree that the pharaoh in question was probably Ramses II. Yet this fact imposes a minimum of fifty-seven years of discrepancy, since Akhenaten died in 1336 B.C. and Ramses II came to power in 1279 (he would remain there for another ninety-six years). It can be assumed that the time of oppression began in the first year of Ramses' reign, a hypothesis based on the evidence that Pithom, the factory town on the road to the Red Sea in which the children of Israel were forced to manufacture bricks, was founded under Ramses (Vernus and Yoyotte, *Les Pharaons*). Yet by the time of Ramses, the "monotheism" of Akhenaten had been completely erased from every inscription and register. Moses could have had no knowledge of it unless he had been born under Akhenaten's reign, which would mean that by the time of the Exodus he would have reached too venerable an age to perform the deeds he did, or even to lay eyes on the Promised Land. The very last vestiges of the Aten cult had been utterly wiped out by the Amon clergy.

12. Vernus and Yoyotte, *Les Pharaons* (supra n.10).

13. "Egyptian Religion," *Encyclopedia Britannica* (1973). The article proposes that the first linkage of ethics with religion might have been tenuously made during the first intermediate period (around 2160 to 2040 B.C.), a time marked by an interesting paradox. Life was more bearable, since after the death of the last Old Empire pharaoh, Pepi II, the provinces were much more autonomous; contemporary writings lay great emphasis on social justice and individual virtue. This easing of life, however, did not offset the disarray caused by the disappearance of the pharaohs' near-tyranny, and the writing and art of the day are a somber reflection on the state of mind of both the nation and the individual. For the first time in Egyptian history, people took a melancholy view of their fate, as if the prospect of earthly happiness somehow only underscored their finitude. It is also interesting to note that, from this point on, the dead no longer had automatic access to the kingdom of the gods; now they had to plead their case to get in.

14. Traunecker, *Les Dieux de l'Égypte* (supra n.5).
15. Sergé Sauneron and Jean Yoyotte, *La Naissance du monde selon l'Égypte ancienne* (Paris: Seuil, 1958); J. P. Allen, "Genesis in Egypt," *Yale Egyptological Studies* 2 (1988).
16. *The Ancient Egyptian Book of the Dead* (Austin: University of Texas Press, 1988).
17. Ibid., chap. 17. The Lord of All's diktat oddly recalls that of God in Genesis, who decides to drown humanity in the Flood. There is little information about an inundation that might have struck Egypt, but it is certain that the considerable rise of the Mediterranean at the end of the last ice age some ten thousand years ago covered a good part of Lower Egypt, and it could be supposed that some memory of this remained among the local peoples. It could as well be supposed that the Nile overflowed disastrously in more recent times, before climatic changes led to the desertification of the Sahara.
18. Traunecker, *Les Dieux de l'Égypte* (supra n.5).
19. Alexandre Moret, *Le Rituel du culte journalier en Égypte* [1902] (Geneva: Slathkine, 1988).
20. Ibid.
21. Budge, *Egyptian Religion* (supra n.7).
22. Ibid.

10. Africa: The Cradle of Religious Ecology

1. C. F. Rey, *The Real Abyssinia* (London, 1935). The length and importance of the Semitic presence, especially the Judaic presence in eastern Africa and more generally along both banks of the Red Sea, are frequently overlooked factors. They are also, however, the basis for the theory that much of the Bible was written not in Palestine but in Arabia south of Mecca: see Kamal Salibi, *La Bible est née en Arabie* (Paris: Grasset, 1985).
2. Well before the modern Suez Canal, shallow-draft vessels crossed back and forth between the Mediterranean and Red Seas. The first of these canals, dug some four thousand years ago, was made up of two distinct segments. One joined the Pelusium branch of the Nile to Wadi Tumilat and the Bitter Lakes; the other extended to the Red Sea. These canals often silted up, and in the pharaonic era they were occasionally dredged. Darius restored and widened them sometime around 510 B.C., and they remained in use through Ptolemaic and Roman times. They silted over completely once the Silk Road established a monopoly over the Asian trade route.
3. Gert Chesi, *Les Derniers Africains* (Paris: Arthaud, 1978).
4. Marcel Griaule, *Les Dieux de l'eau* (Paris: Fayard, 1976).
5. What is to be feared, however, is that this religiosity might be deteriorating or becoming syncretized. In my house in Upper Egypt, I have witnessed devout Muslims invoking "Mari Ghirghis" (Saint George) and "Mari Antoun" (Saint Anthony).
6. Wole Soyinka, *Myth, Literature and the African World* (New York: Cambridge University Press, 1976).

7. René Bureau, "Les Religions: specificités, rivalités, analogies—L'Afrique noire," *Atlas Universalis des religions* (Paris, 1988).

8. A. Ba Hampaten and Germaine Dieterlen, *Koumen, texte initiatique des pasteurs peuls* (Paris: Mouton, 1961).

9. I. Sow, *Les Structures anthropologiques de la folie en Afrique noire* (Paris: Payot, 1978).

10. Roger Caillois addresses this very cogently in "Le pur et l'impure," in *Histoire générale des religions*, vol. 1: (Paris: Quillet, 1948): "Most of the proscriptions in so-called primitive societies are above all against mixing things together, where mixing is defined as simultaneous presence in the same closed space whether or not the contact is direct or indirect."

11. Jean Cazeneuve, *Sociologie du rite* (Paris: Presses Universitaires de France, 1971).

12. Ibid., citing P. W. Perryman.

13. Joseph Campbell, *Primitive Mythology* (New York: Penguin, 1969).

14. The destruction of African religions has been accelerated not only by Islam and Christianity, but also—and above all—by the introduction of political systems predicated on the need to overturn the world order.

15. Sow, *Les Structures anthropologiques* (supra n.9).

16. Griaule, *Les Dieux de l'eau* (supra n.4).

17. Vladimir Grigorieff, *Mythologies du monde entier* (Paris: Marabout, 1986).

18. Cazeneuve, *Sociologie du rite* (supra n.11).

19. Colin Turnbull, *The Mountain People* (New York: Simon & Schuster, 1972).

20. John A. Barnes, "African Models in the Guinea Highlands," *Man* 62.2 (1969), pp. 5–9.

21. Angelo and Alfredo Castiglioni, *Adams Schwarze Kinder* (Zurich: Schweizer, 1977).

22. Griaule, *Les Dieux de l'eau* (supra n.4).

23. Lucien Lévy-Bruhl (citing Harold Reynolds's *Notes on the Azande Tribe of the Congo*) in *La Mentalité primitive* (Paris: Presses Universitaires de France, 1922).

24. Ibid. How Carl Jung interprets the concept of the Yo leads one to agree with Wole Soyinka that some European readings of ancient religions are both condescending and insulting: "The primitive mentality differs from the civilized one in that its conscious mind is much less developed both in terms of scope and of intensity. Functions such as thinking, willing, and so on are not yet differentiated, and [the primitive] is incapable of any conscious effort of the will. . . . Because of the chronically undefined nature of his will, it is difficult to determine whether he has merely dreamed something or actually experienced it" (Carl Jung and Kerenyi, *Essays on a Science of Mythology* [New York: Pantheon Books, 1949]). It would be nice to have been able to ask Jung if the will and thought were ever distinct in, say, Germany under the Third Reich.

25. Leo Frobenius and Douglas Fox, *African Genesis*, cited in Alexander Eliot, Mircea Eliade, Joseph Campbell, Detlef I. Lauf, and Emil Buhere, *L'Univers fantastique des mythes* (Paris: Presses de la Connaissance, 1976).

26. Grigorieff, *Mythologies du monde entier* (supra n.17).

27. Emmanuel Terray, "Organisations, règles et pouvoirs: l'Afrique noire," in *Atlas Universalis des religions*, (supra n.7).

11. The North American Indians: Land and Fatherland

1. A manitou is a supernatural protective power associated with the universal spirit and who appears in dreams. People who shared the same manitou never fought or waged war against each other; if they were of opposite sexes, they could never marry.

2. H. R. Rieder, "Manona et son petit, mythe des Indiens Renard ou Mekwakihag du Wisconsin," in *Le Folk-lore des peaux rouges* (Paris: Payot, 1976).

3. Scalping was not a Native American invention; it was not practiced until after the arrival of the Europeans.

4. The discovery by a Franco-Brazilian archaeological team of inhabited sites at Piedra Furada, Brazil, dating back some thirty-five thousand years undermined the theory that the continent had not been populated until the Second Ice Age, that is, twelve thousand years ago.

5. Lucien Lévy-Bruhl, *La Mentalité primitive* (Paris: Presses Universitaires de France, 1922).

6. Sir James Frazer, *The Golden Bough* (New York: Macmillan, 1922). Frazer situates the Hidatsa in upper Tennessee, whereas the *Encyclopaedia Britannica* locates them in North Dakota.

7. Claude Lévi-Strauss, "Trois dieux Hopis," in *Paroles données* (Paris: Plon, 1984).

8. Manfred Lürker, *Lexikon der Gotter und Dämonen* (Stuttgart: Alfred Kramer, 1984).

9. Ibid.

10. Ibid.

11. René Thévenin and Paul Coze, *Moeurs et histoire des Indiens d'Amérique du Nord* (Paris: Payot, 1928).

12. Frank Waters, *The Book of the Hopi* (New York: Viking, 1963).

13. Marcel Mauss, *Sociologie et anthropologie* (Paris: Presses Universitaires de France, 1950). From a strictly linguistic point of view, *orenda* means, as Mauss points out, "prayer and chanting"—which makes it markedly similar to the Latin *oratio*, even though the Native American languages are not part of the Indo-European group.

14. Ibid.

15. Frazer, *The Golden Bough* (supra n.6).

16. This myth, which Campbell cites in *The Masks of God: Primitive Mythology* (New York: Viking, 1959), was collected in the 1820s by a U.S. government official named Henry Rave Schoolcraft.

17. Mauss, *Sociologie et anthropologie* (supra n.13).

18. Ibid.

19. Waters, *The Book of the Hopi* (supra n.12). For a more detailed look at the pre-Columbian myth of the white god, see chapter 12.

20. Lürker, *Lexikon* (supra n.8).

21. Rieder, "Manona et son petit" (supra n.2).

22. Campbell, *Primitive Mythology* (supra n.16).

23. Ibid.

24. Ibid.

12. The Enigma of Quetzaleoatl, the Feathered Serpent, and the God-Who-Weeps

1. R. Heine-Geldern, "A Roman Find from Pre-Columbian Mexico," *Anthropology Journal of Canada* 5 (1962), pp. 20–22.

2. C. A. Burland, *Les Peuples du soleil* (Paris: Tallandier, 1978). The theory is based on the stylistic evolution of the pottery at Tlatilco, not far from Mexico City; it seems to bear distinct characteristics of the Olmec style.

3. David C. Grove, "The Olmec Legacy," in *Research & Exploration* (Spring 1992); R. A. Joyce, R. Edging, K. Lorenz, and S. D. Gillespie, *Olmec Bloodletting: An Iconographic Study*, Sixth Palenque Roundtable (Norman: University of Oklahoma Press, 1986).

4. J. B. Porter, "Olmec Colossal Heads As Recarved Thrones," *Anthropology and Aesthetics* (1989), pp. 17–18, 23–29.

5. Ibid.

6. Jacques Soustelle, *Les Mayas* (Paris: Flammarion, 1982).

7. Ibid.

8. Ibid. Modern knowledge of the Maya pantheon is principally based on the Dresden Codex; the Codex Peresianus of Paris, which deals with theology, ought to have provided a wealth of information, but unfortunately it is too incomplete to draw conclusions from.

9. Ibid.

10. There is an extraordinary similarity between the myths of Quetzalcoatl and Heracles. Like Heracles, Quetzalcoatl descended into the underworld (although he did so in the company of his brother, Xolotl), voluntarily climbed onto his own funeral pyre, and ascended into the sky, where his name was given to a celestial body (Venus in the case of Quetzalcoatl, and the eponymous constellation in that of Heracles/Hercules). According to one etymology of the name, "Heracles" means "He of the Large Penis"; the same holds true of Quetzalcoatl. In addition, Quetzalcoatl is bearded, which is almost unheard-of in Toltec and Aztec art. In a number of Mediterranean Christian centers, the attributes and adventures of Heracles were ascribed to Jesus.

11. Burland, *Les Peuples du soleil* (supra n.2).

12. And perhaps also the deity of a number of other Mayan centers, such as Palenque, where among other deities an agrarian god was venerated. This deity was worshiped in the form of a foliated cross, a stylized depiction of the corn plant. The "vegetarian" character of Quetzalcoatl was not, perhaps, accepted by all his Mesoamerican cult centers; more important still is to avoid the conclusion that the agricultural deity cults did not sacrifice human beings. Jensen notes that "bloody sacrifice is a feature of agricultural populations."

13. "Aztec Religion," *Encyclopaedia Britannica* (1980). It should be stressed that despite the efforts of Catholic missionaries to identify Tezcatlipoca with the Christian Devil, the natives of New Spain rejected this "graft." The point is fully addressed in Serge Gruzinski, Antoinette Mollinie-Fioravzuti, Carmen Salazar, and

Jean-Michel Sallmann, *Visions indiennes, visions baroques* (Paris: Presses Universitaires de France, 1992).

14. Victor von Hagen, *The Desert Kingdoms of Peru* (London: Weidenfeld and Nicolson, 1964).

15. The only system the Incas had for recording dates and events was based on little cords tied into knots at specific intervals. This system, called *quipu*, was lost once the last persons who could decipher it, the *quipu-comayocs*, died.

16. von Hagen, *The Desert Kingdoms of Peru* (supra n.14).

17. "The Portal of the Sun," write Roberto Magni and Enrico Guidoni (*Inca* [Paris: Fernand Nathan, 1977]), "is the most celebrated monument in the Andes. It consists of a single block of andesite and looks like a massive door (height 2.73 meters, width 3.84 meters, depth .5 meters). The portal is located inside the *kalasasaya* of Tiahuanaco; it probably had a cult function. The upper section of the facade, corresponding to an architrave, is almost entirely covered with a bas-relief, and it rests solidly on quadrangular pillars." To this day, there is no definitive interpretation of the bas-relief, in which one can recognize the very singular God-Who-Weeps.

18. von Hagen, *The Desert Kingdoms of Peru* (supra n.14).

19. Diego Trujillo, cited in ibid.

20. Felipe Guaman Poma de Ayala, *Nueva crónica y bien gobierno*, ed. Arthur Poznansky (New York, 1944).

21. Garcilaso de la Vega, "The Inca," *Los Commentarios reales de los Incas*, ed. Alain Gheerbrant (1961).

22. Ibid.

23. Pedro Cieza de Leon, *The Incas*, trans. Harriet de Onis, ed. Victor von Hagen (Norman: University of Oklahoma Press, 1959).

24. Ibid.

25. According to Wendell C. Bennett, one of the greatest experts on Peruvian art, "the primary force behind the Tiahuanaco expansion was organized religion" (*Ancient Art of the Andes* [New York: Museum of Modern Art, 1954]).

26. Having come down via Spain, they would have been borne along by the Canaries current and then by the northeast trades (both circle from east to west) toward the Southern Equatorial current, which would then have taken them to Central America. A possible return trip, for example for the monk Brendan, could have followed the Gulf Stream and then the North Atlantic Flow (both circle from west to east).

27. To date, the most in-depth study of intercontinental voyages in general and of Old World–New World contact in particular is *Man across the Sea*, a multiauthor work published under the direction of Carroll L. Riley, J. Charles Kelley, Campbell W. Pennington, and Robert L. Rands (Austin: The University of Texas Press, 1971). In spite of its scientific scrupulousness and the abundance of documents it cites to support the thesis of transoceanic voyages long before Columbus and the Age of Navigation, this book remains known to only a few specialists—as was proved by the welter of publications on the occasion of the sesquicentennial of Columbus's "discovery" of America. Ivan Van Sertima's *Ils y étaient avant Colomb* (Paris: Fiammarion, 1981) should also be mentioned, which in spite of its sometimes

questionable speculation and its regrettable lack of both table of contents and index, is filled with little-known documents and interesting contentions.

28. The exact date of Tiahuanaco's construction is unknown. The archaeologist Arthur Poznansky, who has devoted his life to this truly enigmatic site, was in the grip of mystical fancy when in his monumental work he suggested that Tiahuanaco had been built several thousand years ago; based on his reading of certain friezes in the *kalasasaya* temple, he went so far as to claim that it dates from the fifteenth millennium B.C. Poznansky certainly deserves credit for intuiting that the Americas have been inhabited since much longer than the twelfth millennium B.C., as recent archaeological evidence has shown, but he seems to have overlooked one thing: there is no cause to believe that in the tenth or fifteenth millennium B.C. the people of the Americas had reached a level of development, or at least of architectural know-how, that was at the time unmatched anywhere else in the world. Tiahuanaco has inspired many frankly dubious theories: another archaeologist, H. S. Bellamy, believed that the Portal of the Sun is evidence of the earth's having had two moons millennia ago (a thesis also credited by the German Hoerbinger); Daniel Ruzo believes that the sculptures on the 24,000-foot plateau of Marcahuasi east of Lima are of "extreme antiquity." The panoply of theories about Tiahuanaco has been summarized by Marjorie von Harten in her study "Religion and Culture in the Ancient Americas: Systematics," *The Journal of the Institute for the Comparative Study of History, Philosophy and the Sciences* 1 (June 1963). Notwithstanding the real mysteries that surround Tiahuanaco, until further information is available it seems wisest to date its construction at between the seventh and eleventh centuries.

29. von Hagen, *The Desert Kingdoms of Peru*, vol. 6: *The Conquests: The Presumed Road of the Tiahuanaco Invasion of the Peruvian Valleys.* See also Roberto Magni and Enrico Guidoni, *Inca* (Paris: Fernand Nathan, 1977).

30. B. C. Hedrick, "Quetzalcoatl, European or Indigenous," *Man across the Sea,* (supra n.27).

13. Israel: Demons as the Heavenly Servants of the Modern Devil

1. Gaalyah Cornfel, *Archaeology of the Bible, Book by Book* (New York: Harper and Row, 1976).
2. Ibid.
3. Genesis 3:14–15.
4. Genesis 3:1 (Revised Standard Version).
5. Genesis 6:5–6.
6. Genesis 6:7.
7. Genesis 6:13.
8. To this day, there is no coherent theory about the origins of the Hebrews. If the double list of prisoners that Amenophis II of Egypt's Eighteenth Dynasty drew up during his second Canaan campaign (1443 B.C.) is to be believed, and it being granted that the Hebrews were in fact the "Apiru" mentioned in various ancient

texts, then they had no settled status among the peoples of Canaan. The Shosi on the list were nomads, the Huru or Hurrites an indigenous people, and the Nuhasse were from northern Syria; what the Hebrews were, though, is not explained. According to Gaalyah Cornfel (*Archaeology of the Bible*, supra n.1) they probably were not a fixed ethnic group with a single geographical center; yet the fact that the Apiru number among the foreigners employed for Ramses II's massive construction projects supports the idea that they are identifiable with the Ibrim, the Hebrews of Genesis.

9. The Graf-Wellhausen theory holds that Genesis was written by a group of post-Exilic writers, and that it is based on post-Exilic sources as well as on nonreligious traditions that predate the Jewish captivity. The Creation and Flood stories predate the Old Testament by nearly a millennium.

10. Above and beyond textual similarities, Genesis follows the exact same chronology as the Babylonian creation epic or Enuma Elish, and its pattern is almost identical, as Gaalyah Cornfel points out (*Archaeology of the Bible*, supra n.1).

11. W. G. Lambert and A. R. Millard, *Atrahasis: The Babylonian Story of the Flood* (London, 1970); E. A. Sollberger, *The Babylonian Legend of the Flood* (3d ed., London, 1971). Both are cited by Paul Johnson in *A History of the Jews* (New York: Harper and Row, 1988).

12. Genesis 4:7.

13. Job 1:6–12.

14. 1 Kings 22:19–22.

15. Bresciani, *Der Kampf um den Panzer des Inaros*, cited by Bernard Teyssèdre in *Naissance du Diable* (Paris: Albin Michel, 1985).

16. Isaiah 19:14–15.

17. 1 Chronicles 21:1.

18. Jubilees 50:5, H. F. D. Sparks, ed., *The Apocryphal Old Testament* (Oxford: Clarendon Press, 1985).

19. J. Trachtenberg, *The Devil and the Jews* (Philadelphia, 1943); Paul Johnson, *A History of the Jews* (supra n.11).

20. Robert Martin-Achard, "Le Status des morts en Israel," in *Le Monde de la Bible* 78.

21. Job 30:23.

22. The Book of Enoch was lost until 1770, when the English explorer James Bruce reached Gondar, Ethiopia, in the course of his search for the sources of the Nile; there he found an Ethiopian version of the text, which he brought back in 1773. It was published for the first time in 1838, when Archbishop Lawrence brought out his English translation.

23. *The Apocryphal Old Testament* (supra n.18).

24. Proof of this is the actions of the Hasmoneans or Maccabees, the five sons of the priest Mattathias, who wandered through Jerusalem and the countryside forcibly circumcising those Jewish children who had not been circumcised eight days after they were born, as the rite demands.

25. Flavius Josephus, *The Jewish Antiquities* (Cambridge, Mass.: Loeb Classical Library, 1986), p. 266ff.

26. Little has been added to the claim made in 1959 by Roland de Vaux (see *Archaeology and the Dead Sea Scrolls* [Oxford University Press, 1973]), one of the great authorities on the Dead Sea scrolls and the Essenes, that the archaeological evidence is unable to establish which of the Hasmoneans might have been the "Evil Priest" (the evil high priest, that is) responsible for the Master of Justice's execution: Jonathan (152–143 B.C.), Simon (143–134), John Hyrcanus (134–104), Alexander IV Janneus (103–76), or John Hyrcanus II (76–40). The penultimate Hasmonean, John Hyrcanus II, persecuted the Essenes; he ordered their property to be confiscated, and he seems to answer to the description of the "impious priest" who was the Essenes' enemy. All in all, the Habakkuk Commentary seems to point to him as the one responsible for the apparently cruel death of the Master of Justice (see "Le Commentaire d'Abacuc," in *La Bible: Écrits intertestamentaires*, [Paris: Gallimard, 1987]). It must be kept in mind that: (1) according to the Essenes themselves, the Master of Justice was if not the founder then at least the organizer of the Essene community at Qumran, an event that predated the rule of John Hyrcanus II by at least a century; (2) the Essene community had been formed by the middle of the second century B.C., as is unarguably clear from excavations at Qumran (which is to say that they were established sometime between 152 B.C., the date of the high priest Jonathan's accession, and 134 B.C., the date of his nephew Simon's accession, as Father de Vaux points out); (3) the Essenes could not have come together without a leader, which means that the Master of Justice would have to have been a contemporary of Jonathan or Simon (as is pointed out by the experts Geza Vermes and J. T. Milik). The open hostility of John Hyrcanus II could have been no more than upholding the Hasmonean family tradition of treating with equal vindictiveness all the hermits who excoriated them.

27. The actual formation of the sect is linked to the rise of the Maccabee dynasty, and therefore took place after the beginning of the second century B.C. The accession of Jonathan, the son of the heroic Judas of Maccabee, supplanted the legitimate line of Zadok. The last representative of the Zadok line, Onias IV, withdrew into exile during Simon's reign and went to Egypt, where he established the temple of Leontopolis. The "legitimist" Zadok partisans who remained in Judea took offense at the spurning of Deuteronomy and exiled themselves in the desert; this was the origin of the Qumran community. It should be stressed, however, that the Essene community per se predated the desert exile.

28. "Belial" is a clear reference to the Babylonian deity, although it had fallen out of usage by the late period in which the scrolls were being produced. Its appearance can be attributed to the archaic style the writers adopted; they were striving to express their readings of the Old Testament in a more antique tone in order to make them seem more authentic.

29. A distinction is customarily drawn between the Dead Sea manuscripts (the specifically Essene ones found in caves near Qumran) and the intertestamentary writings (this is the Anglo-American term for them; once called "apocryphal," they are now also referred to as "pseudepigraphical"), which their authors intended to be part of the Old Testament but which do not belong to the canonical Bible. The

intertestamentary writings were inspired by the Essenes even though they contain texts that predate the movement and whose transcriptions were Essene-influenced. On this topic, see Marc Philamenko's preface and André Caquot and Marc Philamenko's general introduction to *La Bible: Écrits intertestamentaires*.

30. For more details, see Bernard Teyssèdre's excellent treatment of the subject in chapter 7 of his *Naissance du Diable* (supra n.15), "Qumran: la ténèbre à triple visage."

31. 1 Enoch 40.

32. Jubilees 10.

33. Damascus Document 7:21–8:1–2.

34. Testament of Levi 3:3.

35. Testament of Ruben 4–5.

36. Testament of Simeon 5:3.

37. This little-known point has only been mentioned once before, in John Allegro's *Dead Sea Scrolls: A Reappraisal* (New York: Penguin, 1964), although it was touched upon in my *Les Sources* (Paris: Robert Laffont, 1989), n.31.

38. The Greek Life of Adam and Eve 10–11.

39. Romain Ghirshman, *L'Iran, des origines à l'Islam* (Paris: Payot, 1951).

40. Johnson, *A History of the Jews* (supra n.11), p. 85.

41. Clarisse Herrenschmidt, "Le Mazdéisme," *Le Grand atlas des religions* (1988). The author notes that the text has yet to be fully studied.

42. Ghirshman, *L'Iran*, p. 199.

43. Ibid., p. 244. Some twenty centuries later and under apparently much different circumstances, Israel's foreign policy toward Iran would remain true to tradition.

44. The first description of these entities appears in the Avesta; they are the "Benevolent Spirits" (or, more accurately, the "Auspicious Spirits"), the *amesha spenta* (see chapter 6) who are ranged around Ahura Mazda in a hierarchy that would come to be adopted in 1 Enoch 20, albeit with variations and changes in nomenclature. Several anthropologists have studied the influence of Eastern religions over Judaism, especially Howard Eilberg-Schwartz, a professor of anthropology at Stanford, a rabbi of conservative leanings, and the author of a controversial book, *The Savage in Judaism* (Bloomington: Indiana University Press, 1990). Eilberg-Schwartz advances, for instance, that the origins of circumcision can be traced to Eastern fertility rites, and that the tradition to which it is usually ascribed is based on a misreading of Genesis.

45. Maurice Meuleau and Luce Pietri, "Le Monde et son histoire," vol 1: *Le Monde antique et les débuts du Moyen Age* (Paris: Robert Laffont, 1987), p. 140.

46. Teyssèdre (*Naissance du Diable*, supra n.15) gives in to this temptation, brilliantly outlining why a reflection of Mazdaist theology can be gleaned from the Qumran writings.

47. They nevertheless later returned to Qumran. See de Vaux, *Archaeology of the Dead Sea Scrolls* (supra n.26).

48. 2 Kings 10:21.

49. The War Scroll, 1QM 13.3–5.

50. This is so obvious that it has gone unnoticed—the sort of paradox wonderfully

illustrated in Edgar Allan Poe's "The Purloined Letter"—except for in André Cherpillod's self-published *Les Dieux d'Israel* (Courgenard E-72570); Cherpillod notes that the form "Elohim" is plural, as anyone conversant with Semitic languages knows, and that the Genesis verse (1:3) *Wayyomer elohim yehi or wahyehior* should be read "The gods said, Let there be light, and there was light." B. Lang ("Yahve seul: origine et figure du monothéisme biblique," *Concilium* 197, pp. 35–64) also enumerates the reasons for believing that Judaic monotheism postdates the Exodus.

51. The one exception is Judith, who only exists in the Old Testament (her story is not intertestamentary, and is thus free of Essene influence) apocrypha of the Book of Judith, a patriotic text that dates from the time of Nebuchadrezzar. The Book of Judith is probably the last celebration of Jewish female heroism as it features in several other books in the Old Testament.

14. The Devil in the Early Church: The Confusion of Cause and Effect

1. Rudolf Bultman, *L'Histoire de la tradition synoptique* (Paris: Seuil, 1973).
2. Why John never mentions exorcisms while Matthew, Luke, and Mark trip over one another to report them is a question that will never be answered.
3. Matthew 7:22.
4. Matthew 8:16; Luke 4:40–41.
5. Luke 4:31–37.
6. Mark 9:14–27.
7. Mark 5:1–13.
8. Luke 5:12–13. This behavior, which typifies guilt feelings, shows to what extent the collective neurosis of an entire people awaiting punishment (that is, Judgment and the Apocalypse) had spread by the time of Jesus.
9. Mark 10:46–52.
10. Luke 5:20.
11. Luke 13:10–13. When describing the miraculous cures effected by Jesus, John never says that they are due to the expulsion of demons, which seems to be a feature of the Synoptic Gospels. Nor does John mention the temptation in the desert; he refers to demons only once, when Jesus presciently says to his apostles, "one of you is a demon."
12. Luke 11:14.
13. Matthew 12:43–45. Noting that this speech is different in form and content from others made by Jesus, Bultman finds it "completely devoid of Christian character" and attributes it to Jewish tradition.
14. Mark 7:24–30.
15. Luke 8:26–33; Mark 5:1–13.
16. Luke 22:31. This is the only mention of Satan in the Synoptic Gospels. John makes only one reference to the "prince of this world," which is very much a Gnostic idea: "I will no longer talk much with you, for the ruler of this world is coming" (14:30).

17. After the meeting in Galilee (Matthew), the meeting in Bethany (Luke), and the lunch in Tiberias (John)—the story of the Ascension in Mark is a notorious later addition—Jesus indeed disappeared from the Gospel narratives, although where he went is unknown.

18. Acts 5:3–12. Luke, the author of the Acts, writes that when Ananias's wife, who was his accomplice in "embezzling" his own money, is reproached in the same way three hours later by Peter, she too immediately falls down dead.

19. 1 Corinthians 5:1–5.

20. 2 Corinthians 2:11.

21. *Dictionnaire encyclopédique du Christianisme ancien* (Paris: Cerf, 1990).

22. François Bonifas, *Histoire des dogmes de l'Église chrétienne* (Fischbacher, 1886).

23. Ibid.

24. Ibid.

25. Ibid.

26. "Lactance," in *Dictionnaire encyclopédique*, vol. 2.

27. Epistle of Barnabas 17:1. In Edgar Hennecke and Wilhelm Schneemelcher, eds., *New Testament Apocrypha* (Philadelphia: Westminster Press, 1963–1966). This text, discovered intact with the Codex Sinaiticus in 1859, enjoyed great popularity in the early Church. Origen and Clement of Alexandria both granted it canonical authority, although it definitely was not written by Saul's companion Barnabas; it seems to have been composed after Hadrian's reconstruction of the Temple.

28. *Dictionnaire encyclopédique*.

29. Epistle of Barnabas.

30. "Démons d'après les Pères," *Dictionnaire de théologie catholique* (Paris: Letouzey et Ane, 1924).

31. Bonifas, *Histoire des dogmes* (supra n.22).

32. Tatian, *Discourse to the Greeks* (Oxford: Clarendon Press, 1982).

33. "Athanase," *Dictionnaire encyclopédique*.

34. The complex story of Constantine's accession was intimately bound to the equally complex convolutions of the empire's partitioning. The illegitimate son of Constance I and a tavern matron, Constantine shared, from 308 on, the title "Son of Augustus"—which is to say, imperial prince—with Maximinus Daia, while Licinius held that of Caesar of the Western Provinces. Upon the death of Maximinus Daia, Constantine laid claim to the title of Augustus, which he was able to assume after his armies defeated those of Maxentius, the titular emperor who had been tacitly deposed at the congress of Carnuntum in 308. Only in 323, after he defeated his rival and coemperor Licinius, did Constantine at last consolidate the two thrones of Rome and Byzantium.

35. Marcel Simon, *La Civilisation de l'antiquité et le christianisme* (Paris: Arthaud, 1972).

36. The early Church held him in such high esteem that it bestowed upon him the titles of "blessed" and "saint"; only in the eighteenth century did Pope Benoit XIV have him struck from the catalogue of saints.

37. Simon, *La Civilisation* (supra n.35).

38. Saint Clement, "Exhortation to the Greeks," in *Clement of Alexandria* (London: W. Heinemann, 1919).

39. Maurice Sartre, *L'Orient romain* (Paris: Seuil, 1990).

40. "Even if the line of descent was direct, the Greco-Roman Mithra was only distantly related to his Iranian ancestor" (Maurice Sartre, ibid).

41. There are many excellent works on Gnosis and Gnosticism, among which the most respected are those by H. Leisegang, *La Gnose* (Paris: Payot, 1951); R. M. Grant, *La Gnose et les origines chrétiennes* (Paris: Payot, 1954), and H. C. Puech, *En Quête de la Gnose*, 2 vols. (Paris: Gallimard, 1978). Each takes a personal approach to Gnosis, which the Church Fathers initially interpreted as Christian thought contaminated by Hellenism. Grant, for example, sees it as the expression of Jewish anxiety produced by the catastrophes of 70 and 135 (the successive destructions of Jerusalem). This interpretation is justified, but it seems that the Jewish anxiety heightened receptivity to Gnosticism rather than creating it, since by all evidence the teachings predated the anxiety. Leisegang goes deeper by shedding light on Gnosticism's Egyptian, Greek, and Middle Eastern (Asia Minor) sources; he even mentions the possibility of Asiatic sources. In context of this last possible source, one is struck by the words of Irenaeus, one of the writers who participated in the second-century refutation of Gnosticism. For him, Gnosis—the direct and intuitive knowledge of God, or, in other words, illumination—"brings about the redemption of the inner man," and, according to Marcel Simon (*La Civilisation*, supra n.35) "frees man from himself, from the prison of the sensual, to bring him to his true goal." These are the same goals as in Buddhism, and it seems to me that up to now we have neglected or at least underestimated the influence of the Buddhist doctrines that reached Greece in the fourth century B.C., in the wake of Alexander's campaigns. It should also be pointed out that Hippolytus was one of the rare early Christian writers who mentions the influence of India.

42. John 14:30.

43. Romans 8:3.

44. 1 Corinthians 15:50.

45. Simon, *La Civilisation* (supra n.35).

46. In the third century, Sabellianism, which derived from Monarchism, also questioned the cosmic structure. Named after Sabellius, a priest of perhaps Libyan origin, this so-called modal Monarchism challenged Origen's theory that there are three hypostases—the Father, the Son, and the Holy Spirit—and that all three are divine. The Sabellians argued that, according to Origen's theory, the divine essence of Christ must have undergone the suffering and indignity of Crucifixion, and that was not acceptable, so there can only be one hypostasis, that of God, which manifests itself now as the Son, now as the Holy Spirit. Father and Son were thus modes of one and the same entity. See *Dictionnaire encyclopédique*, and Simon, *La Civilisation* (supra n.35).

47. Contrary to some claims, the name does not come from a presumed heresiarch named Ebion, but from a Hebrew word meaning "weak of mind." Epiphanus of Salamina attributes the birth of the Ebionite heresy to a group he calls the "Elcesites," which apparently sprang up in Parthia, although this explanation is

doubted today. It might, however, deserve another look, since the Elcesites were an Essene Christic movement that probably originated not in Parthia but in Babylon, which was then under Parthian rule. It is first mentioned in 220, when Alcibiades of Apamea brought the Elcesite manifesto, the Book of Helxai, to Rome. Origen mentions the Elcesites twenty years later, when he reports that one of its leaders had just arrived in Caesarea (Eusebius, *Ecclesiastic History* 6.38 [Cambridge, Mass.: Loeb Classical Library, 1926–1932]).

48. Simon Magus's theology appears in two main sources, Irenaeus (*Adversus haereses* 1.1) and Hippolytus, who cites, probably in its entirety, the *Apophasis megala*, or "Great Pronouncement," a faithfully Simoniac document. Irenaeus's description of Simonism seems secondhand and based on later sources.

49. See note 48, above.

15. The Great Night of the West: From the Middle Ages to the French Revolution

1. The tale of Magnus Maximus typifies the convulsions of the late Empire. A Spanish soldier who had accompanied the coemperor Theodosius I on several campaigns, he was eventually posted to Brittany, where he had the restless troops proclaim him the emperor of the province. From there he marched on Gaul, where he defeated Gracian, the former emperor of the East whom Theodosius had reduced to the rank of provincial governor because of his eccentricities and ambition. Theodosius thereupon found himself forced to confer the imperial title of August on Maximus as well as to cede him sovereignty over Gaul, Spain, and Brittany. Some Catholic zealots claimed not only that he was an impostor but also that he was solely responsible for the execution of Priscillian. The truth, however, is very different. Maximus was emperor by rights, and as such he had an entourage of bishops as clerical advisers. If proof is needed, it lies in the fact that Maximus could not have convened the Council of Bordeaux without the bishops' help. In addition, the council met at the instigation of Hydatius and Ithacius. The Church bears the primary responsibility for Priscillian's martyrdom.

2. Priscillian's alleged Encratism was a fable maintained by various councils, and it would have persisted to our day had G. Schepps's discovery of eleven Priscillian texts not proved the fact of his orthodoxy. Priscillian, therefore, was the victim of the Church's delusions: See E. C. Babut, *Priscillien et le priscillienisme* (Paris, 1909).

3. C. J. Hefele, *Histoire des conciles* (Letouzey et Ane, 1908), pt 2, pp. 1192–93.

4. Ibid., p. 1324.

5. Isidore of Seville, *Etymologies*, VIII, 2, Lindsay, (Oxford: Oxford University Press, 1911).

6. St. Augustine, *The City of God* 15.23 (New York: The Modern Library, 1950).

7. Roland Villeneuve, *Dictionnaire du Diable* (Paris: Pierre Bordas, 1989).

8. Ibid.

9. Daniel Defoe, *History of the Devil*, vol. 2. A witty parody of the day's diabolic beliefs, this work has, oddly enough, never been reprinted.

10. In his *Jeanne d'Arc et la mandragore: Nouveau regard de l'histoire* (Paris: Editions du Rocher, 1982), in which he inventories the legal anomalies in the trial of Joan of Arc, Pierre de Sermoise claims it possible that in the end Joan might have been saved from the pyre and another, "a real witch," was burned in her stead. His proof seems plausible, but the fact remains that the conviction of witchcraft would have been enough to burn the maiden, even if it did not actually happen.

11. Alvaro Prelayo, *De planctu ecclesia*, quoted by Ludwig Pastor in *The History of the Popes from the Close of the Middle Ages*, 6 vols. (London: F. I. Antrobus, 1891–98).

12. Francesco Petrarca, *Lettres sans titre*, trans. V. Develay (Paris, 1885), and quoted by E. R. Chambertin in *The Bad Popes* (New York: Dorset, 1969).

13. Quoted by Pierre Carnac, *Prophéties et prophètes de tous les temps*, ed. Gerard Watelet (Paris: Pygmalion, 1991).

14. Ibid.

15. Borislav Primov, *Les Bougres: Histoire du pope Bogomile et de ses adeptes* (Paris: Payot, 1975).

16. Ibid.

17. Not to be confused with Cosmas the Monk, who predated him by some five centuries.

18. Quoted in Primov, *Les Bougres* (supra n.15).

19. "The Tale of Anna Comnenius" in Primov, *Les Bougres*.

20. Primov, *Les Bougres*. Some "bishops" were confirmed by the consolamentum of "Pope" Nikita, while other "bishops" were ordained. The quotation marks are used not for irony but, rather, to avoid confusion with the pope and bishops of the Roman Church.

21. The Catharist movement was itself threatened by schisms because of the latent conflict between the pure Bogomil arm led by "pope" Nikita and the "heretical" Pauline arm, which professed an even more rigid dualism; the Pauline arm was led by another "pope," Petrak or Petar, whose Lombardy branch had its own "bishop" or "counterbishop" named Garatus. The "orthodox" movement ended up with an "antipope" named Bartholomew (Primov, *Les Bougres*). Even had Rome taken no action against it at all, one could imagine that Catharism would have eventually split into two or even three separate movements.

22. Jeffrey Richards, *Sex, Dissidence, and Damnation: Minority Groups in the Middle Ages* (London: Routledge, 1991).

23. Ibid.

24. Ibid.

25. Ibid.

26. Ibid.

27. Ibid.

28. Devil madness was only really ever a factor in countries that fell under the purview of the Roman Church. From the beginning, the Eastern churches, which tended to set down principles as opposed to dogmas, were much more reserved in their attitudes about the Devil, which explains their acceptance of the idea proposed by the fourth-century Alexandrian writer Didymus the Blind, who said that "it is

not desire, only a certain kind of desire, that is evil" (*Fragmenta in proverbia* 9.7). Given the fact that the wilderness is the traditional abode of devils, as in Luke 21:24 and 7:23, hermits have always enjoyed more prestige than monks, since they, the athletes of asceticism, are more likely to come into conflict with devils. Eastern Monarchism is less prone to mysticism than its Western sibling is, since "Eastern mysticism is antivisionary and holds that all imaginal contemplation . . . is a snare of the Devil" (Paul Evdokimov, *L'Orthodoxie* [Neuchatel: Delachaux and Niestle, 1955]). The *Catechisme pour les familles par un groupe de chrétiens orthodoxes* (Paris: Cerf, 1979) remains faithful to ideas about the Devil that appear in the Old and the New Testament, and it does not provide any original interpretations.

29. Grillot de Givry, *Witchcraft, Magic and Alchemy* (New York: Dover, 1971).

30. Ibid.

31. Kraemer's career was nearly cut short because of his own unscrupulousness. He had "borrowed" money and jewelry from a widow, which in 1482 the inquisitor-general ordered him to return. Launching into a deft diversion, Kraemer passionately rallied to the defense of Pope Sixtus VI, who was engaged in a pointless debate with another Dominican, who was campaigning to reconvene the Council of Basel. The inquisitor finally managed to clear himself. See Amand Danet, introduction to *Le Marteau des sorcières* (Paris: Plon, 1973).

32. Defoe, *History of the Devil*, vol. 2 (supra n.9).

33. Walter Map, *De Nugis curialem* (1181–92), quoted in Richards, *Sex, Dissidence, and Damnation* (supra n.22).

34. Richard Lebeau, "1492: L'Age d'or de l'intolérance," *Impact-médecin* (April 10, 1992).

35. Brigitte Leroy, quoted in ibid.

36. The metal gag was a pear-shaped instrument that was forcibly inserted into the mouth, which often caused the teeth to break; its wings were then opened by means of a screw, and the suspect's jaws were forced apart until he made a sign that he was ready to talk. The water torture consisted of tying a victim down and forcing water into his throat through a funnel. The boot was a vice; one of the suspect's limbs was inserted into it and it was tightened until blood vessels and even bones burst open. All these refinements were due to the Inquisition's "charitable" mandate: the suspect could be tortured but not killed.

37. The *Dictionnaire de théologie catholique* (Paris: Letouzey and Ane, 1924) has this to say: "In our day, attempts have been made, in the name of progress in the medical and related sciences, to deny the existence of demonic possession. In the strange condition [of its victims], the desire has been to recognize only unusual morbid affects, and in particular nervous disorders. . . . The permission God gives a demon to take possession of a human's bodily organs and spiritual faculties is sometimes the punishment for certain grave sins committed by the possessed, and in particular carnal sins."

38. In the case of the celebrated "rumor of Orleans" (in France) in the seventies, it was claimed that a Jewish shoemaker in the city had his female clients try on attractive shoes; embedded in their soles, supposedly, was a pin tipped with a powerful narcotic. The women were then spirited off into the white-slave trade.

Obviously, no evidence for this melodramatic fantasy was ever found. The "rumor of Calais" that exploded dramatically in 1992 involved the alleged disemboweling of at first one and then two young boys; the police were mobilized and the school that had apparently been targeted took strong security precautions. There was no trace of truth in this fabrication, either.

39. Laura Shapiro, "The Lesson of Salem," *Newsweek* (Sept. 7, 1992).

16. Islam: The Devil as State Functionary

1. H. W. F. Saggs, *Civilization Before Greece and Rome* (New Haven: Yale University Press, 1989).

2. It was not until the twentieth century that historians such as Wahb ibn Munnabi and El-Hassan ibn Ahmed began to study the ancient history of southern Arabia, as Niel Asher Silberman points out in his study *Between Past and Present: Archaeology, Ideology, and Nationalism in the Modern Middle East* (New York: Holt, 1989). Though familiar to a small number of specialists thanks to the renewed interest in the Arab world raised in the West by the adventures of T. E. Lawrence (and stimulated by the oil explorations of Aramco and the prospect of finding archaeologically virgin territories), this history was very slow to appear. National pride was a hamper to research until the eighties—for instance, the series of digs conducted in 1951 and 1952 by the American Foundation for the Study of Man at the Sanctuary of Balkis (the legendary Queen of Sheba) in Marib was abruptly terminated by the revolution in North Yemen, both for openly political reasons (the new regime was Marxist) and covert religious ones. It was also a sore point to recall that the pre-Muhammadan peoples of the Arabian peninsula had not all been Arabs (a very fluid term) or monotheistic. Nevertheless, it is amazing to note that the ancient history of the Middle East is entirely ignored by a number of authors who deal with the history of religions.

3. The name is originally Greek; the kingdom is also known as the Ma'in and Ma'an.

4. 1 Kings 6:4–5.

5. 1 Kings 23:13.

6. Manfred Lürker, *Lexikon der Gotter und Dämonen* (Stuttgart: Alfred Kramer, 1984).

7. The version of the Qur'an I rely on is the one by André Chouraqui (Paris: Robert Laffont, 1990), which along with Régis Blachère's is closest to the original text. In the note to this verse, Chouraqui writes that "it seems to proclaim that the four monotheistic religions, including the now-vanished Sabaean one, all lead equally to salvation." The identity of the Sabaean religion, Chouraqui also writes, "is discussed by the commentators, who see it as an astrologically informed religion that grew out of Judaism and Mazdaism in the regions of Mosul and Haram."

8. The name "Christians of John the Baptist" is misleading, since the Mandeans were in fact anti-Christian, especially after the Council of Nicea, and they did not recognize *Eshu msiha*, Jesus the Messiah, who they thought was a false prophet and who they called "the Byzantine." The "real Jesus" was called Anush, and like the other one he came into the world "in the time of Pilate." The Muslim idea of a double of Jesus crucified instead of the real one is seemingly not so far away

from this Mandean idea. Gnostics who remained faithful to their teacher John the Baptist, in whose honor they practiced frequent ritual ablutions in running, never standing, water (the way John had in the Jordan River), the Mandeans were related to the Essenes. They seem to have been for the most part unlearned; they did not seem to have a clear grasp, for instance, of the difference between Jews and Christians.

9. 1 Maccabees. 5:26. It is also the city anathematized by Jeremiah (48:24) in his imprecations against Moab.

10. This according to Chouraqui's note.

11. Chouraqui's comment to verse 10:38 is, "Did he forge it?"

12. Maxime Rodinson, *Mahomet* (Paris: Seuil, 1961).

13. 16:98.

14. 43:77. The name also means "the king."

15. 6:121. According to Chouraqui, these demon agents could have been Zoroastrians in Mecca.

16. 7:30.

17. Notably in Suras 45, 46, and 62.

18. 20:20.

19. 37:158.

20. 6:40.

21. 39:72 and 40:27.

22. Rodinson, *Mahomet* (supra n.12).

23. G. E. von Grunebaum, *L'Identité culturelle de l'islam* (Paris: Gallimard, 1973).

24. Chouraqui's notes to 19:52 and 20:79; see also 7:128. The recognition of Moses is confirmed by verse 132, which calls idolaters "enemies of Moses."

25. 20:18, 2:60; 7:12–107; 26:32–45; 27:28, 31.

26. 3:35.

27. 3:40.

28. 3:45–47.

29. Though intending to denounce the goddesses of pre-Islamic Arabia, al-Lat, al-'Uzza, and Manat, who are no doubt idols, the first in the form of a woman, the second of a tree, and the third of a stone (probably a nerolite), under the influence of the Devil Muhammad instead sang their praises. He began thus: "Have you thought on Al-Lat and Al-Uzzah, and, thirdly, on Manat?" Under diabolical inspiration, he then wrote: "They are the sublime birds, and their intercession is dearly hoped for." Tabarri reports that when the Qureyshites heard this verse they were filled with joy and that everyone, Muslim and non-Muslim, prostrated himself. But then the archangel informed Mohammed that he had been tricked by the Devil, and so he deleted the last two lines and replaced them with, "Is He to have daughters and you sons? This is indeed an unfair distinction!" Disrespectfully extrapolated, this is the error that served as the basis for Salman Rushdie's novel *The Satanic Verses*.

30. General Gourgaud, *Journal*, II.

31. N. Siouffi, *Études sur la religion des Soubbas ou Sabéens, leurs dogmes, leurs moeurs*

(Paris, 1880). Ssiouffi was the French consul at Baghdad, and it is through him that we possess much of the information we have on the Mandeans.

32. Grunebaum, *L'Identité culturelle* (supra n.23).

33. Al Jahiz, "Kitab al Akhbar" ("The Book of the New"), in Frank Rosenthal, *The Classical Heritage in Islam* (London: Routledge and Kegan Paul, 1975). Abu Osman ibn Banr el-Jahiz, known as Al-Jahiz, is the first Arab essayist and one of the most celebrated writers in classical Arabian literature. A m'utazil, or member of the sectarian khawarij group, he ended up founding his own sect.

34. Hussein Mansur Hallaj, *Diwan*, trans. Louis Massignon (Paris: Cahiers du Sud, 1955).

17. Modern Times and the God of Laziness, Hatred, and Nihilism

1. Robert D. Hicks, *In Pursuit of Satan: The Police and the Occult* (Buffalo, N.Y.: Prometheus, 1991).

2. "Satan," *Life* (June 1989).

3. David Finkelhor, Linda M. Williams, and Nancy Burns, *Nursery Crimes: Sexual Abuse in Day Care Centers* (Beverly Hills, Calif.: Sage, 1988).

4. I am using these terms in the following senses: "pedophilia" to mean sexual intercourse with very young children, and thus something very criminal; "pederasty," in its etymological and traditional sense of sexual relations with minors of either sex who have reached sexual maturity but not the age of consent.

5. Bill Disessa, "Tale of Child's Ritual Slaying Vexes Lawmen," *Houston Chronicle* (March 6, 1989), cited in Hicks, *In Pursuit of Satan*.

6. Arlette Farge and Jacques Revel, *The Vanishing Children of Paris: Rumor and Politics Before the French Revolution* (Cambridge, Mass.: Harvard University Press, 1992).

7. In a book called *Satan's Underground*, Lauren Stratford (the pseudonym used by Lauren Wilson) recounts stories as distasteful as the ones cited here, but the people who investigated her concluded that she was taking advantage of some gullible Christian groups. The same also seems to be the case with another writer who allegedly witnessed similar horrors, Michelle Smith (author of *Michelle Remembers*). Cited in Hicks, *In Pursuit of Satan* (supra n.1).

8. *The Satanic Bible* (New York: Avon, 1969).

9. *The Satanic Rituals* (New York: Avon, 1972).

10. "Satan," *Life* (June 1989).

11. Herbert Marcuse, *Eros and Civilization* (New York: Vintage Books, 1961). It might be fitting to recall that in the sixties Marcuse's name was linked to that of Wilhelm Reich, a physiologist, fantasist, and the last word in deranged psychoanalysts—as well as a very confused theorist of the sexual revolution, in large part due to certain devices he had invented called "orgone accumulators." Orgones, he believed, was a type of sexual energy that floats freely in the atmosphere (much like demons in scholastic theology). A Marxist of a previously undescribed brand, Reich believed he could liberate the masses through the use of orgone energy.

Notes 361

12. Born in Leamington, Warwickshire, in 1875, Edward Alexander Crowley died in obese decrepitude in 1947, after having in the course of his colorful and scandalous life been associated with a number of famous people ranging from Somerset Maugham (who modeled the protagonist of his novel *The Magician* after him) to Winston Churchill (to whom Crowley once proposed a "foolproof" way of staving off the impending German invasion through magic—it is not hard to imagine what the Lion's response was). In 1953, I had a long talk with Maugham, who called Crowley "an entertaining and most erudite queen." An aesthete who imitated Byron and especially the eighteenth-century writer William Beckford (with whom he shared a taste for transvestism and pretty boys), Crowley organized sessions of what he called "collective love"—in a word, homosexual orgies—that were loosely based on Hermetic-Egyptian models. He presided over these dressed in a madman's idea of high-priestly garb. His work has had a good deal of influence over amateurs of the occult.

13. "Satan," *Life* (June 1989).
14. "Hell's Sober Comeback," *U.S. News and World Report* (March 25, 1991).
15. Ibid.
16. Max Weber, *The Protestant Ethic and the Spirit of Capitalism* (London: Routledge, 1992).
17. Giovanni Papini, "Il Diavolo e il pane senza sudoro," *Il Diavolo* (repr. Milan: Mondadori, 1985).
18. Weber, *The Protestant Ethic.*
19. A collection of nonsense that a well-known French publisher thought fit to reissue in 1991—on Bible paper!
20. Norbert Sillamy, *Dictionnaire de psychologie* (Paris: Bordas, 1987).
21. Cited by Robert W. Ross in *So It Was True: The American Protestant Press and the Nazi Persecution of the Jews* (Minneapolis: University of Minnesota Press, 1980).
22. "Anti-Semitism in Italy Rings True to Echoes in Europe—1 in 3 Germans See a Nazi Good Side," *International Herald-Tribune* (Nov. 7–8, 1992).

Index